Soul on Soul

Music in American Life

A list of books in the series appears at the end of this book.

Soul on Soul

THE LIFE AND MUSIC
OF MARY LOU WILLIAMS

Tammy L. Kernodle

UNIVERSITY OF
ILLINOIS PRESS
Urbana, Chicago, and Springfield

Manufactured in the United States of America
1 2 3 4 5 C P 5 4 3 2 1
∞ This book is printed on acid-free paper.

Library of Congress Cataloging-in-Publication Data
Names: Kernodle, Tammy L., 1969– author.
Title: Soul on soul : the life and music of Mary Lou Williams /
Tammy L. Kernodle.
Description: Urbana : University of Illinois Press, 2020. | Series: Music
in American life | Includes bibliographical references and index. |
Identifiers: LCCN 2020019223 (print) | LCCN 2020019224 (ebook) |
ISBN 9780252043604 (cloth) | ISBN 9780252085536 (paperback) |
ISBN 9780252052484 (ebook)
Subjects: LCSH: Williams, Mary Lou, 1910–1981. | Pianists—
United States—Biography. | Jazz musicians—United States—
Biography. | Composers—United States—Biography.
Classification: LCC ML417.W515 K47 2020 (print) | LCC ML417.
W515 (ebook) | DDC 786.2/165092 [B]—dc23
LC record available at https://lccn.loc.gov/2020019223
LC ebook record available at https://lccn.loc.gov/2020019224

To
"The Smith Girls,"
Carolyn Smith Kernodle, Patsy Smith Parker, Phyllis Smith Sadler

and
The memory of Elsie Coles Toler, Ester Mae Toler Smith,
Virginia Kernodle

CONTENTS

ILLUSTRATIONS

ACKNOWLEDGMENTS

This book is the culmination of a lot of hard work, prayer, and faith. A number of people have contributed to the reality of this book with their time, advice, prayers, and eyes. I am forever indebted to them for their faith and support, as I have struggled against my own insecurities to bring this book to fruition. First of all, I would like to thank God for His guidance, wisdom, patience, and love throughout this process. The journey I have taken over the sixteen years from Danville, Virginia, to Virginia State University to the Ohio State University to Miami University and promotion to associate professor and tenure has been a struggle through which my wild dreams and aspirations have been realized and I have been blessed beyond measure. I offer this work as a testimony to the role God has played in my life and how He can transform that which the world thinks is unusable and deficient into something of value. Thank you, Father, for your undying love and guidance. Second, I would like to thank my family: my mother, Carolyn, and father, Robert; my brothers, Kevin and Michael, and my sister-in-law, Sharonda. I thank them for their understanding, despite my absence from many family events as I sequestered myself in my office with my computer, and most of all for their unflagging faith in and love for me.

Without Annie Kuebler's and Tad Hershorn's sincere commitment to this work, I would still be trying to fill a number of gaps in the life and music of Mary Lou Williams. Your help and support while I worked with the Mary Lou Williams Collection at the Institute of Jazz Studies at Rutgers University were immeasurable. Thank you a thousand times! Many thanks to the staff at the Institute of Jazz Studies; Vivian Perlis and the staff at the Oral History Archives at Yale University; the staff at the Ellington Collection at the Museum of American History, Smithsonian Institution, and the staff at Smithsonian Folkways Recordings.

The spirit of some of Mary's closest friends and associates pervades this book. I thank first Peter O'Brien for trusting me enough to open his heart and mind that I might get a true sense of the person Mary Lou Williams was and the depth of their relationship. Thank you for your tireless reading and critique of this work. Any mistakes or misrepresentations are solely mine. Mario Hancock, who graciously opened his home and heart to me also, thank you for sharing not only your memories of Mary but your personal letters and stories. Your insights brought so much to my understanding of the faith and personality of Mary. Geraldine Garnett, Bobbie Ferguson, and Karen Rollins, I cannot thank you enough for the fellowship and fun I had visiting in Pittsburgh—that was only the beginning of what I hope will be a lifelong relationship. Thank you for opening your home to me and making me feel like more than a researcher invading your life. My deep appreciation to Carline Ray-Russell, Marian Turner, and Jay Allbright, who imparted to me not only fascinating accounts of their experiences with music and Mary Lou Williams but jewels of wisdom that have enriched my life beyond measure. To the photographers Chuck Stewart, Patrick Hinley, and Mikki Ferrill, thank you for allowing me to use your beautiful images of Mary, which add such depth and dimension to this book.

Support for this project was provided in the form of several grants awarded by the Council of Faculty Research at Miami University. The time that these awards allowed me to work without worry about financial obligations was valuable. Without the support of Judith Delzell and Pamela Fox this project would have languished for many years; thank you for going against convention and allowing me to have the time I needed to bring this book to completion. Other individuals ferreted out valuable information and provided me with both print and oral materials: Helen Lindsay of Smithsonian Folkways Recordings; Jeff Place at Smithsonian Folkways and the Ralph Rinzler Folklife Archives and Collections; the staff of the Amos Music Library at Miami University; the staff of Media Services and Interlibrary Loans at the King Library at Miami University; Charles Atkinson, William McDaniels, Burdette Green, and Daniel Avorbedor, who believed in this project when it was just an illusion and a roughly conceived dissertation.

Thanks to the women who saw the importance of writing the stories of those whom history has ignored. Thanks to the sisters of the Mimosa Book Club; Karen Sherman for an open spirit and available ear; April Greer and Penelope Williams for supporting me through this process and always providing me with opportunities to publicly express the greatness of Mary Lou Williams; Leesa Peters, Ethel Norris-Haughton, Cecilia Moore, Margaret Moore, Hazel Moore, Kelly and Dan Malec-Kosak, Pat and Charles Bullock, Ronald and Denise Anderson, and Deliika Blackwell for being there and serving as my biggest cheerleaders. To the scholars who have greatly influenced me, Guthrie Ramsey Jr., Roxanne Reed, Gayle Murchison, Horace Maxille, Susan Cook, and Josephine Wright, I thank you.

I cannot express sufficiently my appreciation to Dr. Emmett Price III, who served as the "midwife" to this project. Your untiring support in all phases of the work and your knowledgeable editorial work made this book much stronger. Thank you, thank you, thank you. Thank you, Nicole Price, for your advice and patience, as I know you sacrified much time with your husband so that this project could be completed. To Elizabeth Swayze, who took a chance on this project and gave it a home at Northeastern University Press, I express deep appreciation. Thanks also go to Sarah Rowley, who took over the project and worked patiently with me.

Many thanks to all whom I may not have named, but who have in many ways contributed to this work.

PREFACE TO THE NEW EDITION

On the morning of Sunday October 3, 2010, I sat in the congregation of the Mt. Zion Baptist Church in Madison, Wisconsin, waiting for the morning service to begin. This service would be unlike your typical first Sunday, which in most African American churches includes singing, the preaching of the Word and the celebration of the ritual of Communion. That morning Mt. Zion augmented its traditional service to include a musical celebration of *Mary Lou's Mass*, the multi-movement mass for peace and justice written by Mary Lou Williams in 1969 and revised over the course of 1970 to 1971. The service was also part of a year-long celebration of the centennial of Williams's birth being held in Madison.

My personal history with *Mary Lou's Mass* has been far-reaching and deeply personal. When I began my life journey with Williams during the early 1990s, it was one of the first compositions I located during my initial research trip to the Institute of Jazz Studies at Rutgers University in Newark, NJ. Even when I began finding the manuscript scores that were the movements of this ecumenical work amidst all of the uncatalogued letters, newspaper clippings, and scores, I was not aware of its musical significance, personal connection to the history of civil rights within the Catholic Church, or its role in the personal spiritual history of its composer. Over the years my consciousness and knowledge of this piece have evolved significantly. But on that morning in October as pianist Geri Allen struck the first notes of the opening movement, "Old Time Spiritual," I was jettisoned back to that moment when the discovery of this work positioned me on a musicological and spiritual journey that has resulted not only in the creation of various forms of scholarship but also helped me understand the intersection of my faith and my love of jazz music. I had heard this work in recorded form and in live performances many times, but on this occasion I experienced *Mary Lou's Mass* in the true essence of what she had envisioned it to be—worship music. A century after her birth, and forty-one years after it was first performed, *Mary Lou's Mass* had been realized in its initial intent—worship music with a progressive social consciousness. People clapped, they shouted "amen," and stood on their feet as vocalists Carmen Lundy, George Shirley, and a community mass choir weaved through the mass's movements. It was the invocation of the Holy Spirit through song and word and, when it was over, all that were there had been transformed. I was personally moved to moments of tears—not the type of tears that come from a memorable performance, but the type that one experiences when the inner (wo)man is moved by the presence of the Holy Spirit. I've revisited this experience in my mind several times over the past years and in those moments I'm always drawn to ask deeper questions about the legacy of Mary Lou Williams, *Mary Lou's Mass,* and its growing popularity with contemporary musicians and congregations.

Although I lived only an hour away from Mary Lou Williams when she lived in Durham, North Carolina, during the last years of her life (1977–1981), I never met her. I did not have a consciousness about jazz during those early years of my life. Like many young kids of my generation, I heard jazz on *Sesame Street* and knew of Miles Davis only because my parents owned an 8-track tape of *Kind of Blue.* But I never engaged fully with jazz in the way I did funk, soul, country, pop, and gospel. It was not until I reached college that I began to listen deeper, especially to other forms of black music. Coming of age at a historical black college in the late 1980s and early 1990s was complex and often messy. Music served as an important marker of this period for me. The AIDS crisis, crack epidemic, and an emerging awareness about apartheid in South Africa and how American corporations were deeply invested in this system of segregation shaped my consciousness of blackness, sexuality, and social activism and my place in it. Billie Holiday, John Coltrane, Sarah Vaughan, Miles Davis, and Clifford Brown alongside SWV, new jack swing, rap, and classical music filled my ears.

I met Mary Lou Williams sonically in the Music and Dance Library at The Ohio State University. It was my second year of graduate school and I was beginning to experiment with playing jazz. My desire to play jazz was steeped in an interaction with Dr. Billy Taylor (1921–2010) during my undergraduate years at Virginia State University (his alma mater). I never seriously pursued playing jazz during those years largely because Beethoven, Mozart, and Chopin dominated most of my practice time. But at OSU I took a chance and asked pianist/organist Hank Marr if I could study with him. I'm sure I stressed him with all of my awkward chord voicings and lack of knowledge about jazz harmony, but he was gracious and patient. One of the most pertinent things he told me was that jazz is a feeling, not just notes or patterns or recycled riffs. It did not matter how "correct" you might play, if there was no feeling then listeners would know it and tune out. Those words framed my first engagement with Williams's music.

On the afternoon I met Mary Lou Williams, I was listening, searching for ideas and understanding. I remember this moment vividly because it changed the trajectory of my life and work as a future scholar. I was listening to the *Smithsonian Collection of Jazz Piano*. The second cassette tape began with Billy Kyle's "Between Sets," then Mary Lou Williams's infectious blues-tinged "Nicole" filtered through the headphones. Instantly I felt something deeply personal and emotional. I asked the library monitor to rewind the tape. I needed to hear this Mary Lou Williams again. Who was this Mary Lou Williams? Why didn't I know her? Instantly I felt exposed by the inadequacy of my education, my listening, my knowledge. I had only heard strong female piano players within the gospel music or church aesthetic. My paternal grandmother had been one such woman. There was something distinctly different that I heard in Williams's playing. After a second listen, I rushed from the listening booth and to the reference shelf. I found a short encyclopedia article on Williams and was intrigued to know that she had written religious compositions. I instantly wanted to know all that I could about her and my relationship with Mary Lou Williams began.

I begin this preface with these two memories because they represent how layered my personal journey with Mary Lou Williams has been. When I decided to write *Soul on Soul*, my intent was to provide another reading of the complexities that frame the lives of creative black women in America. Often the metanarratives of relationships, insecurities, and personal challenges frame how the general public views the lives of female creatives. These metanarratives overshadow any substantive discussion of their creative work and often result in the pathologizing of their lived experiences without consideration of how race, gender, and class shaped those experiences. My goal with this book was to amplify Williams's music, the process undertaken in producing it, and how it intersected with her developing consciousness as a black woman and as a black jazz musician navigating the changing political and social milieus of twentieth-century America and Europe.

The previous edition of *Soul on Soul: The Life and Music of Mary Lou Williams* concluded with her death. Over the years I've often regretted that I did not include a final chapter outlining the extent of Williams's legacy following her death. I would now, through this preface, like to take the opportunity to survey the work advanced by many different scholars, poets, theorists, musicians, and filmmakers that have heightened awareness of Williams and her music since the 1990s. In 2019 National Public Radio featured Williams as part of its *Turning the Tables* series, which unlike previous years focused only on eight women that they felt had significantly impacted the progression American music.[1] Williams, along with Billie Holiday, Maybelle Carter, Marian Anderson, Celia Cruz, Bessie Smith, Sister Rosetta Tharpe, and Ella Fitzgerald, were celebrated through a series of podcasts, articles, and playlists. It is only one example of how Williams's life and music continue to frame the musical consciousness of a new generation of scholars, educators and listeners.

In the years that have passed since Mary Lou Williams's death in 1981, the curation of her legacy has taken on many forms. The Mary Lou Williams Foundation, which was established during the final year of her life, has been central in this work. Headed by Williams's former manager and religious confidant, Father Peter O'Brien, the foundation's mission extends beyond preserving her musical legacy to also continuing her work in mentoring jazz musicians and promoting jazz education. The foundation manages the licensing and distribution of Williams's music, most notably the works published by the Cecilia Music Company, which she founded in the 1960s. In 2005 the foundation revived Mary Records, the imprint Williams launched in 1964 as the medium to disseminate recordings of her religious works and launched the Mary Lou Williams Collective. The Collective, a performing group led by composer and pianist Geri Allen, focused on new interpretations of Williams's music. In addition to live performances and lectures, the group produced two recordings: *Zodiac Suite Revisited* in 2006 and *The Complete Sacred Works of Mary Lou Williams* in 2010.

In 1983 Duke University, in fulfillment of a promise to build a black cultural center on the campus, established the Mary Lou Williams Center for Black Culture. This center, which remains a central part of the Duke experience for students of color, reflects the enduring legacy of Williams at the elite university. After all, her appointment to the music faculty came only fourteen years after the first black undergraduate students were admitted. Each spring the campus celebrates Mary Lou Williams Day, which honors her contributions to the campus community during her tenure from 1977 to 1981.

A decade later jazz pianist, educator, and activist Dr. Billy Taylor (1921–2010) established the Mary Lou Williams Women in Jazz Festival at the Kennedy Center for the Performing Arts in Washington, D.C. The initial goal of the festival was to spotlight the talents and contributions of jazz women. Taylor, who served as Artistic Advisor for Jazz at the Kennedy Center from 1994 until 2010, recounted in later years the skepticism he initially faced in launching the festival:

> When I first went to the Kennedy Center, I said, "I want to do a women's jazz festival." They said, "Well, can you find enough women?" They had not seen, at that time, enough women in music to think they could sustain a festival. But I was able to identify a hundred women right there.[2]

Since its inception, the Mary Lou Williams Jazz Festival has provided a platform for both established and aspiring jazz women. It epitomized Williams's legacy of assisting and promoting other musicians, sometimes, as you will read, to her own detriment.

CURATING MARY LOU'S LEGACY

There are multiple archival collections that contain ephemera related to Williams's life and music. The Mary Lou Williams "Music on My Mind" Collection, housed at the Schomburg Center for Research in Black Culture in New York, contains materials used by filmmaker Joanne Burke during the production of her documentary *Mary Lou Williams: Music on My Mind* (1990). Duke University's Jazz Archive serves as the home to the Linda Dahl Collection. Established in 2000, the collection contains materials collected by Dahl while writing the monograph *Morning Glory: A Biography of Mary Lou Williams*. These collections are relatively small in size in comparison to the Mary Lou Williams Collection at the Institute of Jazz Studies (IJS) at Rutgers University in Newark, New Jersey, which contains many of the items Williams preserved and collected during her lifetime.

In 1995 Father O'Brien began donating Williams's personal materials and memorabilia to the IJS. Over the next few years, library staff led by archivist Annie Kuebler (1951–2012) worked to catalog the 170 boxes of materials, which included personal correspondence, legal records, manuscripts, photographs, recordings, and other ephemera. Although a number of scholars, myself included, were given access to these materials before the cataloguing was complete, the Mary Lou Williams Collection did not officially open to the public until 2000. The collection's importance has been immeasurable, spawning numerous dissertations, theses, articles, monographs (including this one), performances, recordings, and artistic works.

SEEING MARY LOU: MARY LOU WILLIAMS ON SCREEN

Mary Lou Williams's contributions to jazz have been the subject of a number of different documentaries. One of the earliest documentaries to feature content on Mary Lou Williams is the 1981 three-part series *Women in Jazz*. Directed by Burrill Crohn and narrated by pianist/composer Marian McPartland, the documentary surveys the history of notable female jazz instrumentalists, explores the gendered politics that frame the presence of women performances on stage and in the studio, and discusses the creative process of improvisation. The last five minutes of the final installment, "The Creative Force," surveys Williams's career and features footage of her last live performance. Burke's *Mary Lou Williams: Music on My Mind* in 1990 was the first concentrated treatment of Williams's life and career. One of the important aspects of this film is how it provides a lens into Williams's final years at Duke University and her working relationship with O'Brien. Carol Bash's 2015 film *Mary Lou Williams: The Lady Who Swings the Bands* extends beyond the content of those first documentaries. Bash vividly couples commentary that considers the gender and racial politics Williams navigated throughout her career with narration, performed by actress Alfre Woodard, drawn from Williams's personal writings. Musicians Geri Allen, Terri Lyne Carrington, Esperanza Spalding, and Billy Taylor provide important commentary of Williams's role in progressing the compositional and performative aspects of jazz. Judy Chaikin's documentary *The Girls in the Band* (2011) situates Williams within the larger contextual discussion of the history and contributions of female jazz instrumentalists.

PERFORMING MARY LOU

The restoration of Williams's large catalog of scores has been central to the programming of these works in recent years. While a number of musicians have worked in these efforts, Theodore Buehrer's work in this endeavor is noteworthy. Buehrer has worked closely with Jazz at Lincoln Center to produce performance editions of Williams's works that have been programed by the Jazz at Lincoln Center Orchestra and included in the Essentially Ellington curriculum. In 2013 Buehrer edited a critical edition of selected big band works, which was published by

A-R Editions as part of the Music of the United States of America (MUSA) series. Vibraphonist Cecilia Smith and pianists Penelope Williams and Deanna Witkowski are among a number of musicians who have promoted Williams's music through concerts and lectures. Their interpretations of Williams's vast catalog of music have significantly shaped my own understanding of her aesthetic as a composer and pianist. Cecilia Smith's Mary Lou Williams Resurgence Project (MLWRP) bears particular mention due to its expansive and holistic engagement with Williams's oeuvre. The MLWRP developed out of a concert of Williams's music Smith was asked to give at Our Lady of Victory Church in Brooklyn. Subsequently, the vibraphonist/composer launched a series of programs and collaborative projects that employ the full range of Williams's compositional output: works for big band and small ensemble and the sacred works.

Despite the vastness and diversity reflected in Williams's oeuvre, *Mary Lou's Mass* has proven to be her magnum opus. In recent years it has been performed more than any other work. It was resurrected in 1999 with a performance at Washington National Cathedral that featured Marian McPartland, Carmen Lundy, and the Eastern High School choir. The preparation of a full score for this performance precipitated performances around the world, including the performance in Madison, Wisconsin, that I referenced at the beginning of this preface. In 2010 the Alvin Ailey American Dance Theater programmed the full series of dances its founder choreographed to Williams's music in 1970. It was the first time in more than thirty-five years that *Mary Lou's Mass* was performed in its entirety by the Ailey group.

HEARING MARY LOU

The availability of Williams's music via recordings has increased exponentially during this same period. In the early 2000s, Smithsonian Folkways re-issued remastered versions of the albums *Zoning*, *Mary Lou Williams Presents Black Christ of the Andes*, and *Mary Lou's Mass*. Newly discovered recordings appeared as well, including transatlantic recordings *Mary Lou Williams: I Made You Love Paris* (Gitanes Jazz Productions, 2000) and *Mary Lou Williams: The London Sessions* (BMG France, 1997). A number of bands have also produced new interpretations of Williams's catalog, including the Dutch Jazz Orchestra's *The Lady Who Swings the Band: Rediscovered Music of Mary Lou Williams* (Challenge Records, 2005). In 2011 the United States Army Field Band Jazz Ambassadors released *The Legacy of Mary Lou Williams*, the fifth in a series of recordings commemorating individuals who have made significant contributions to jazz. Purchase of the disc also provided consumers with access to downloadable PDFs of selected scores. Other artists have produced albums that couple Williams's works with their own original compositions. Two notable examples include trumpeter Dave Douglas's recording *Soul on Soul* (2000) and saxophonist Virginia Mayhew's *Mary Lou Williams: The Next 100 Years* (2012).

WRITING MARY LOU

In addition to the documentaries, re-issued recordings, and performances, Mary Lou Williams's legacy has also been promoted through a litany of tributes, conferences, and centennial celebrations. All of these have been central to advancing a more inclusive perspective of jazz's history. More importantly, they have shaped important conversations about politics that govern who is being heard on the performing stage and why. In addition to this book and Dahl's *Morning Glory*, two other monographs examine the life of Mary Lou Williams. Farah Jasmine Griffin's *Harlem Nocturne: Women Artists and Progressive Politics During World War II* (2013) situates Williams along with dancer Pearl Primus and writer Ann Petry within the political and cultural milieu of wartime Harlem, which had become a hotbed for black progressive politics. Randal Maurice Jelk's *Faith and Struggle in the Lives of Four African Americans* (2019) explores narratives of personal struggle and the expanding context of black spirituality in late twentieth-century America through a critical examination of the conversion experiences and spirituality of Williams, singer Ethel Waters, boxer Muhammad Ali, and activist Eldridge Cleaver.

The 1990s and early 2000s marked the emergence of new scholarly perspectives that examine Mary Lou Williams's life and music through an array of theoretical and historical frameworks. I can in no way fully survey all of these works, so I discuss only a few here. Gayle Murchison's article "Mary Lou Williams's Hymn 'Black Christ of the Andes (St. Martin De Porres)': Vatican II, Civil Rights, and Jazz as Sacred Music" examines Williams's first sacred composition written in 1963 within the analytical lens of Vatican II and the intersection of jazz and the black civil rights struggle. In "'Mary Lou Williams Plays Like a Man!' Gender, Genius, and Difference in Black Music Discourse," Nicole T. Rustin challenges the notion that black-centered artistic genius is solely male-centered. By analyzing Williams within the theoretical framework of female masculinity, Rustin provides us with the means to reconcile the conflict that existed between the innovation of Williams's compositional voice, her prowess as a pianist, and her femaleness. Kimberly Hannon Teal's article "Posthumously Live: Canon Formation at Jazz at Lincoln Center through the Case of Mary Lou Williams" focuses specifically on the induction of Mary Lou Williams into the Jazz at Lincoln Center's Ertegun Jazz Hall of Fame in 2008. Teal uses this event, which has become central in J@LC's advancement of the jazz repertory movement, to interrogate the organization's efforts to rescript jazz's history within the discourse of democracy and multiculturalism while simultaneously promoting a musical canon.

CONCLUSION

In closing, I want to recognize that, since the publication of the first edition of this book, a few of the voices that contributed to my understanding of who Mary Lou Williams was and what drove her passion for music and people have transitioned. Father O'Brien worked tirelessly to promote the music of Williams during the last two decades of her life and he continued that work until his death in 2015. When I was writing this book, he took great care in editing and talking me through the intricacies of Williams's concertizing and, most of all, her years at Duke University. He was fiercely protective of Williams and the legacy of her music. I believe that his legacy is defined in the body of work (recordings, performances, scholarship) that I have surveyed here.

I met Brother Mario Hancock (1937–2005) at his home in Newark in 1999 and we maintained a strong friendship until his death. I will never forget that initial visit as he sized me up, wondering if I was legit. After several hours of talking and laughing about many things, including Mary Lou Williams, I got ready to head back to Manhattan. Before I walked out of the door, Hancock said "I want to give you something." He told me "I've been saving these for the right person and I believe you're that person." He then handed me a bag filled with pieces of worn paper. They were the letters Mary Lou Williams wrote to him over the years. I was touched that he trusted me with his most intimate memories of Williams. In time I returned the letters, many of which had been damaged due to water in his basement. I worked with a librarian at Miami University to restore as many as I could. Although he had given me the letters, I returned them out of respect for his almost two decade–long friendship with Williams. I learned so much about Williams's humor, passion for life, and her personal struggles from those letters and the time I spent with Brother Mario. Many of those words and memories are captured in this book.

I was having a late-night snack in the basement of the Hilton in Manhattan when I first met pianist Geri Allen (1957–2017). It was during the national conference of the now defunct International Association of Jazz Educators. The conference was noteworthy for bringing together scholars, professional and amateur musicians, clinicians, and musical companies. On that night, Allen walked over and asked if she could join me. The conversation that transpired was the beginning of a friendship that was based on our mutual love of music, our pursuit of a deeper understanding of the relationship between music and culture and of course Mary Lou Williams. For decades Allen curated the legacy of Williams through her performances, lectures, and a cyber symposium (2014). She portrayed Williams in Robert Altman's 1996 film *Kansas City* and worked closely with Father O'Brien to promote Williams's music. In 2004 she began her tenure as the leader of The Mary Lou Williams Collective that recorded new interpretations of the *Zodiac Suite*, the set of symphonic poems Williams composed in the mid-1940s. Allen and vocalist Carmen Lundy worked closely with the Mary Lou Williams Foundation throughout the 2000s curating performances of *Mary Lou's Mass*, including a noteworthy performance in 2003 at the Duke University Chapel, the hallmark of the historic campus that served as Williams's intellectual home the last four years of her life. Allen's collaborations with scholar Farah Jasmine Griffin resulted in the musical theater production *A Conversation with Mary Lou* in 2014. Singer and bassist Carline Ray (1925–2013) was a wonderful person and extraordinary musician. She provided so much insight about Williams, Melba Liston, and the nature of their collaborations. Even after my book was done, we maintained contact through letters (which I hold dear).

In 2001 a friend from graduate school joined me on a road trip to Pittsburgh. I had recently connected with Mary Lou's sister Geraldine Garnett (1923–2016) and she invited me to her home. I went to her home in East Liberty seeking information and insight into who Mary Lou Williams was; I left with new extended members of my family. My friend and I ended up spending the night and we met many members of Mary Lou's family, including her baby sister Margaret "Margie" Burley (d. 2017) and niece Bobbie Ferguson. For years Margie, Geraldine, and Bobbie made the journey to Washington, D.C., to attend the Mary Lou Williams Women in Jazz Festival.

Over the years a number of scholars and reviewers have compared my *Soul on Soul* to Dahl's *Morning Glory*. I never envisioned the two as competing narratives, but more as dialogues emblematic of each author's readings of Williams's life and music through the lens of ephemera, oral histories, interviews, and their own experiences. I still believe this to be the case and I'm happy that the works I have surveyed in this preface, as well as many other works, have expanded that conversation. Although my scholarship has shifted into other areas since 2004, Mary Lou Williams is never far away from me. She still speaks to me, visits me in my dreams, points me to things about her, and at times inspires me to revisit some portion of her story through new scholarship. Every time I revisit these narratives, I find that Duke Ellington's reading of Mary Lou Williams is still very relevant today. No matter how much time passes, Mary Lou Williams remains beyond categorization—she is perpetually contemporary!

Tammy L. Kernodle
April 2020

NOTES

1. "Turning the Tables: 8 Women who Invented American Popular Music," https://www.npr.org/2019/07/31/743415843/turning-the-tables-8-women-who-invented-american-popular-music.
2. "The Mary Lou Williams Women in Jazz Festival," https://jazztimes.com/reviews/live/the-mary-lou-williams-women-in-jazz-festival/. Up until 2014, all of the headliners were female musicians. The name of the festival was changed that year to the Mary Lou Williams Jazz Festival.

BIBLIOGRAPHY

Griffin, Farah Jasmine. *Harlem Nocturne: Women Artists and Progressive Politics During World War II.* New York: Civitas Books, 2013.

Jelks, Randal Maurice. *Faith and Struggle in the Lives of Four African Americans: Ethel Waters, Mary Lou Williams, Eldridge Cleaver, and Muhammad Ali.* London and New York: Bloomsbury Academic, 2019.

Murchison, Gayle. "Mary Lou Williams's Hymn 'Black Christ of the Andes (St. Martin De Porres)': Vatican II, Civil Rights and Jazz as Sacred Music." *The Musical Quarterly* 86, no. 4 (Winter 2002): 591-629

Rustin, Nicole T. "Mary Lou Williams Plays Like a Man!" Gender, Genius, and Difference in Black Music Discourse." *The South Atlantic Quarterly* 104, no. 3 (Summer 2005): 445-62.

Teal, Kimberly Hannon. "Posthumously Live: Canon Formation at Jazz at Lincoln Center through the Case of Mary Lou Williams." *American Music* 32, no. 4 (Winter 2014): 400-422.

INTRODUCTION

Who was the real Mary Lou Williams? Was she the elegant woman who graced the pages of magazines and newspapers for over sixty years? Was she the demanding artist who often drove managers crazy and made unreasonable requests? Was she the embodiment of the jazzwoman's desire to move from a place of marginality to a place of equality? Or was she simply the young girl who had escaped the poverty and monotony of domestic life and lived out a modern-day fairy tale?

More than twenty years after her death, scholars, historians, family, and fans are still trying to understand the complexities that drove Mary Lou Williams to become one of the most celebrated women in jazz. Most important, we are still trying to decide definitively what her legacy will be. After researching the life and work of Mary Lou Williams for a number of years, I am continually amazed at the spirit of survival and persistence Mary exhibited during the seventy-one years she lived. Most notable for me was her ability, especially in her later years, to rise above the negative circumstances of her life to still give openly and lovingly to friends, family, and fans.

Defining Mary Lou Williams is an arduous and consuming task. After all, she is the only jazz performer to date to have played in every stylistic period of jazz, spanning the years from the 1920s to the 1970s. At the time of her death in 1981, Mary Lou Williams had written more than one hundred compositions or arrangements, recorded over a hundred records (in 78, 45, and LP versions), and performed on stages from California to New York, Florida to Canada, London to Copenhagen, and many points in between. So why is it that someone who was so active within the mainstream jazz scene, so prolific in her musical output, has been excluded from major discussions on jazz?

The answer is twofold. First, Mary Lou Williams, unlike many of her male and female colleagues, could not be easily categorized. At a time when most jazz performers perfected a particular style and maintained it, Mary experimented with emerging styles. She not only perfected the techniques utilized by most arrangers in the 1930s and 1940s, she also experimented with unusual instrumental combinations and rhythmic patterns that reshaped the manner in which bandleaders, musicians, and listeners interpreted "swing." In the 1940s, she openly embraced bebop to the disdain of many of her musician friends and experimented with other styles and approaches throughout the 1950s.

Second, Mary Lou Williams, by virtue of her gender, dispelled notions that questioned the musicianship of women jazz musicians. Because she took her craft seriously and refused to adopt theatrics and novelties into her stage performances, many found it difficult to reconcile her noticeable genius with her gender. Thus her talent was often explained or justified by the suggestion that she "played like a man." At times, Mary was pushed into the center of discussions regarding women's place in jazz and criticized heavily for her claims that she had not experienced prejudice or discrimination because of her gender.

What most critics failed to understand about Mary was that she honestly viewed herself as a musician, not as a female musician. Her interaction with men during her early years and the example of strong women within her family encouraged Mary to succeed despite her gender. She viewed her hardships as products of bad business decisions she had made, unscrupulous managers who exploited talented individuals, and the marginal status of jazz musicians in America. While Mary Lou Williams was hardly naïve about the racist and sexist politics that governed the mainstream popular music scene, she refused to be labeled or pigeonholed by individuals who she felt knew very little about the historic evolution of jazz and the fraternity that governed it. Despite many efforts to discredit her contributions, she fought to become a symbol of the resilience and historic significance of jazz.

In the early 1940s she declared her musical and personal independence from the one man who had both heralded and misused her musical talents—Andy Kirk. The next forty years of her life consisted of a continuing battle for recognition, equality, and acceptance. More important, the last years of her life saw the flowering of Mary's faith and her desire to use her music in ways that would raise social consciousness and bring emotional healing to her listeners. In the end, the story of Mary Lou Williams's life is not only filled with sexual escapades, bad business decisions, lukewarm reviews, and lackluster recordings. It is an epic tale of the experiences of a woman who had no concept of limitations. It is a story of triumphs and tragedies.

The tragedy of Mary Lou Williams lies not in her broken marriages, her relentless bouts with poverty, and her extreme loneliness; instead, it lies in the inability of critics, musicians, scholars, historians, and listeners to look beyond the narrow stereotypes that question the intellectual abilities of women. Thus we now witness her legacy in jazz being relegated to a few quotes by other musicians or token four-sentence paragraphs that tell nothing of the genius that went into every piano solo, sax or brass riff, or line of text.

Mary Lou Williams's sixty-year career was enhanced by her constant need to innovate and experiment. She integrated black vernacular forms unashamedly into mainstream forms, thus introducing white and black listeners to musical genres that they had never before heard or that they found difficult to decipher. She furthered the efforts of Duke Ellington in expanding the compositional language of jazz through large-scale extended compositions that integrated compositional elements of classical music with jazz. The 1944 and 1945 performances of her twelve-movement *Zodiac Suite* reflected not only her interest in the composers Stravinsky, Schoenberg, and Hindemith, but her desire to expand beyond the big band arranging style that had made her popular. During the same period, Mary Lou became a midwife to the modern jazz age when she acted as friend, mentor, and teacher to Thelonious Monk, Charlie Parker, Kenny "Klook" Clarke, Bud Powell, and Dizzy Gillespie.

In the 1960s, after a six-year hiatus from the jazz scene, Mary Lou Williams began, once again, reconceptualizing jazz and creating religious compositions that adapted elements of jazz. These compositions, both hymns and masses, not only reflected her evolution as a composer but served as evidence of the liturgical changes that were taking place within the Catholic Church at that time. Mary was adamant about using her music to "heal disturbed souls" and devoted her life to helping others. Even when lines were drawn between the avant-gardists and the musically and philosophically opposed rest of the jazz community in the seventies, Mary tried to mediate between both groups. Once, she tried to use a concert with the pianist Cecil Taylor as a means of bringing the disputing schools together, but the two factions turned the concert into a heavyweight fight rather than a peaceful resolution.

There can be no one reading of Mary Lou Williams's life, as she was an individual full of contradictions and complexities. Though she was very self-effacing, she also desired the attention and fame that her fellow performers and composers received. Strong and independent, she nevertheless had a propensity to make bad choices about men and poor business decisions that sometimes left her totally dependent on others. She was a woman of strong, enduring faith, yet she still indulged in horoscopes and astrological readings. Most consistently, she was a woman who loved soul food dinners of yams, collard greens, and ham hocks, playing cards, laughing out loud, telling jokes, and creating good music.

Chapter 1

I DREAM A WORLD

How can we sing the songs of the Lord while in a foreign land?
—Psalm 137:4

In 1977, at the age of sixty-seven, Mary Lou Williams—a noted pianist, composer, and activist—left her New York apartment and headed for the rural academic environment of Duke University in Durham, North Carolina. It was the culminating event of a career that had spanned more than fifty years and had yielded a myriad of compositions, performances, and historic firsts. The "little piano girl" of East Liberty had come a long way from the poverty that defined her early years in Atlanta, Georgia, and still haunted her during the 1960s while jazz struggled to stabilize its place in American popular culture. As artist-in-residence, a first for Duke, Williams witnessed the fruition of her childhood dreams of bridging cultural gaps through music and the victory of her crusade of the past decade to educate others about the cultural roots of jazz.

Unfortunately, in less than four years, Mary Lou Williams would pass from this world to the next. She would succumb to the cancer that ravaged her body, just as Americans were rediscovering her as an innovative pianist and composer. Her legacy, however, was not lost in the numerous obituaries that chronicled her life of pain and triumph. In the years since her death, Mary Lou Williams's legacy has been sustained by recordings, festivals, buildings, and private collections that bear her name.

From the very beginning, it was obvious that Mary was an exceptional child. The second of two children, Mary Elfrieda Scruggs was born in Atlanta, Georgia, on May 8, 1910, to Virginia Riser and Joseph Scruggs.[1] Twenty-three years old and unmarried at the time of the birth, Virginia assumed sole responsibility for raising her children after Scruggs, who was already married with children of his own, abandoned her.

Joseph Scruggs was never mentioned in family discussions and was not identified as Mary's father until the late 1930s. It was then that twenty-eight-year-old Mary met her half brother Willis Scruggs, while traveling through Georgia with Andy Kirk and the Twelve Clouds of Joy. Willis introduced Mary to her father, but the meeting proved to be less than congenial. For many years, Mary and other sources had identified Mose Winn as her father. Shortly after Virginia had conceived Mary, she married Winn, though she divorced him soon afterwards. Virginia's retention of Winn's last name and the public knowledge of this marriage may have contributed to this speculative paternity. For the first ten or eleven years of her life, Mary assumed that Mose Winn was her father, which also accounts for the several surnames attributed to her in the early literature.[2]

The unique nature of Mary's spirit was heralded immediately after her delivery, when the midwife announced to Virginia and the other women of the family that the child had been born with a "veil" over her eyes, caused by a portion of the membrane becoming attached to the face of the infant while she passed through the birth canal. Within southern black folklore, this veil was an omen that the child would have extrasensory perception or second sight—the ability to see spirits or ghosts. Mary would spend most of her childhood and adolescent years terrified by her visions; but in later years she learned to channel this energy into her music. She said it enabled her to compose some of her greatest arrangements spontaneously, without notation. Later, Virginia recounted many of the visions Mary saw as a child and shared with family members.

Mary's visions continued into adulthood. While traveling with the Andy Kirk band, her husband, John Williams, tied her to the bed because of the visions she had. Mary recounted one of those instances:

> When I was with the Andy Kirk band my husband used to have to tie me in bed because in a hotel, a very bad hotel, I remember walking up the steps going into the hotel and I saw a man standing at the top with his head hanging off. I'd run or something, you know what I mean, and they'd say, there she goes again. It's like a nightmare. Whatever happened in that room, maybe a suicide or I don't know what it is, I'd see strange things from it, you know.[3]

* * *

The early years in Atlanta were particularly difficult for Virginia, Mary, and her older sister, Mamie. Only four years older than Mary, Mamie assumed responsibility for the young girl while their mother worked. Without financial support from Scruggs, Virginia was forced to work long hours and was often away from her children.

Virginia had been the oldest child born to former slaves, Anna Jane Riser and Andrew Riser. In defiance of her servitude during slavery, Anna Jane refused to retain the name of her slave master after her emancipation, instead marrying Andrew Riser. She gave birth to three children: Virginia in 1887, Anna Mae in 1904, and Andrew Jr. in 1912.[4] Described by family members as a strong woman who ran her household with unrelenting discipline, Anna Jane reminded her children and subsequent grandchildren of the trials black people had endured during slavery and pushed them to become good citizens who contributed something to their community.

Not much is known of the older Andrew Riser except that he was quiet, worked hard, liked to build things, and often kept the women in line when their weekend celebrations got out of hand. He talked and played with Mary, thus providing her with a strong male presence. The two of them would occasionally take walks and watch the trains pass over the nearby trestle. According to Mary, Andrew often passed out candy to the neighborhood children and once built a train that had a real boiler.[5] His life aspirations extended beyond his work as a laborer, but Jim Crow laws and discrimination never allowed him to achieve them. Nevertheless, he diligently saved his money in hopes of one day owning real estate. In many ways, he provided Mary with the attention that she needed as a young child and that Virginia's work schedule wouldn't allow her to give.

Work and church became the backbone of the Riser household and all family members contributed to the stability of the home through their labor and to their community through participation in their church. Described as being of a deep and beautiful hue of chocolate brown with a petite frame, Virginia was a free spirit and enjoyed life to its fullest. She loved music and is remembered playing the organ, singing, or dancing. Working in the homes of whites during the week, Virginia spent most of her Sundays at the local Baptist church. Though her talent might have inspired a musical career, Virginia's race, gender, and geographic location dictated a different course.

Though black minstrel troupes and the stage performances of black prima donnas such as Emma Louise, Marie Selika Williams, and Sissieretta Jones (also known as "Black Patti"—a reference to the diva Adelina Patti) had brought the music and musical talents of blacks to America's mainstream stages, few black musicians or singers pursued the life of the stage as an occupation during the late nineteenth and early twentieth centuries. Women were often cautioned against pursuing these aspirations, since the lifestyle exposed them to harsher realities than domestic work. Black women, in particular, were restricted in their means of public expression and often limited their music making to the home or church. Virginia was no exception. By 1906, the year of the birth of her first child, Mamie, Virginia found herself constrained by both her gender and her race in turn-of-the-century Atlanta.

Even decades after the dismantling of slavery—the institution that had fueled the southern economy for centuries—the opportunities for blacks in the southern United States were limited. Within self-contained black communities, little had changed since the end of the Civil War. Poverty and the enactment of segregation laws served as daily reminders of the resistance to their integration into American society. Promises of a "new start" for Anna Jane, Andrew, and other freed slaves were tainted by the social and economic chaos of the Reconstruction years and the political activities of southern politicians and northern carpetbaggers. Reconstruction governments and agencies, supposedly designed to help blacks become a part of society, failed primarily because northern industrialists joined with southern farmers and enacted new ways to disenfranchise blacks. LeRoi Jones (also known as Amiri Baraka) has asserted that this alliance grew out of the fear "that a coalition of the poor and disenfranchised southern whites, the disillusioned agrarian interests, and newly freed Negroes, might prove too strong a threat" to the northerners' aspirations to exercise "absolute political and economic control of the South."[6]

The devastation of the southern economy during the Civil War and the enactment of "Jim Crow" laws after the Reconstruction years left the Risers and other black families with few options other than agricultural labor or northern migration. Men found it easier to move throughout the South and North in search of employment and new lives, but women did not have such opportunities. Most remained in areas where they could receive community and familial support. Thus agricultural work, domestic service, and taking in the laundry of whites and blacks became the main forms of employment for southern black women.

With almost 2.7 million black women and girls over the age of ten in the southern black population, there was a need for jobs that could provide substantial income. By 1890, 38.7 percent of southern women worked in agriculture, 30.8 percent in household domestic service, 15.6 percent in laundry work, and a negligible 2.8 percent in manufacturing.[7] Sharecropping, a system of peonage that drew in those individuals who succumbed to financial need, became one of the major forms of employment for both men and women.

Anna Jane, Virginia, and Anna Mae chose laundry and domestic work over the backbreaking work and low wages of sharecropping, but even these jobs had their drawbacks. Domestic work was as time-consuming as agricultural work and often separated families for long periods of time. Although an improvement over agricultural work, domestic service was demanding and left little time for family life. With the birth of one child in 1906 and another in 1910 and the lack of any support by the fathers, Virginia faced a dismal economic situation. The limited financial support the Risers offered and the scarce employment opportunities for black women in the South placed Virginia at a disadvantage. At a time when Mary and Mamie needed their mother the most, she was forced to leave her children with Anna Jane and her grandmother Matilda Parker (Mary's great-grandmother, who was believed to have been a full-blooded Native American). Virginia hired herself out as a domestic and was often required to stay at the home of her employer.

Like most domestics, Virginia lived in the households where she was employed and worked as many as fourteen hours a day. She was allowed to visit her own family once every two weeks, but her main focus was expected to be the welfare of her employer's family. Like all domestics, she was vulnerable to the sexual advances of her male employers, who knew they could easily exploit their domestics without repercussions; after all, no one would believe the allegations of a black woman against a white man. It is not known if Virginia suffered from this type of sexual exploitation, as this would not have been discussed in the presence of children, but most domestics did. Virginia and other domestic women workers were further exploited when unscrupulous employers occasionally decided not to pay employees their wages or paid them at a lower rate than was initially agreed upon. In time, Virginia opted to leave domestic servitude for laundry work. Taking in the laundry of white Atlantans and some blacks afforded Virginia the opportunity to spend more time with her children, although the two girls were still mostly left to their own devices. Despite Virginia's hard work, the family still lived in near-poverty conditions, which was not uncommon for most working-class blacks in Atlanta and other areas of the South.

Most black Atlantans in the early 1900s lived in underdeveloped neighborhoods. Houses were made of cheap materials set on shaky brick piles, located on crudely constructed roads and in the dark hollows of alleys. As the black population of Atlanta began to increase, the areas in which they resided expanded and in most cases the living conditions worsened. Mary and her family lived in a "shotgun" house, so called because "a bullet fired in the front would go straight out the back." [8] The shotgun house, a common sight in the South, was actually African in origin. The structure was designed to act as a breezeway: the air entering the front gallery would circulate and cool the bedrooms, usually two, and any additional rooms beyond. This architecture made these homes bearable in the extreme temperatures of southern summers and was common for working-class and poor neighborhoods where multiple families shared outhouses and public wells.

Virginia, like most black Atlantans, found relief in the parties she, Anna Jane, and other family members hosted on weekends. They would drink, sing, and dance, escaping the pressures of life through laughter and intoxication. But the weekends in the Riser home were not just about liquor, parties, or Decatur Street, the entertainment district of black Atlanta and an alternative to the house parties. Sunday was dedicated to religious activities, which included Sunday school, morning worship, and sometimes an afternoon service at a different church. These activities continued into the week as the family attended prayer meetings or organizational meetings. During the summer, revivals provided Virginia and other congregants with services of spiritual rejuvenation, surely needed in the tense racial, social, and economic environment of the South. The black church of the early twentieth century continued in its role as the cultural and social nucleus of the black community. Most of these early churches, including the nameless Baptist church Virginia and her family attended, grew from very humble beginnings, such as abandoned buildings or railroad cars. These churches often became the center of black communal life. By 1870 eight black churches existed in Atlanta, and less than a decade later, the number had increased by fourteen. These churches served a multitude of spiritual, social, and political functions. Virginia, Anna Jane, and their families were very active within their respective congregations. Virginia, through her participation within her church, provided a strong spiritual foundation for her children, which Mary later built upon following her conversion to Catholicism in the 1950s.

Women constituted the majority in these congregations, but none held positions of leadership, nor could they make decisions regarding the church. This no doubt bothered vocal women like Virginia, her mother, Anna Jane, and her grandmother Matilda, who were accustomed to expressing their opinions very strongly. Many churches went as far as to institute rules that forbade women to vote or participate in official debates. Despite these initiatives, Virginia, Anna Jane, and other women parishioners worked diligently in their churches, many times sustaining the congregations financially. Virginia served as the church pianist and organist, often performing liturgical dances to raise money for the church. On the Sundays when Virginia would dance, the men of the church pulled a curtain down across the pulpit. She danced in a style that later became associated more with Holiness and Apostolic churches than with the Baptists. Virginia's role as a pianist or organist would not have been unique at that time, as the church was a permissible place for public music making for women.

Virginia's participation in the church as a dancer indicates something significant about the theological perspective of the congregation and the pastor of her Atlanta church. The Baptist, Methodist, and African Methodist Episcopal churches often looked down on dancing, declaring it sinful, profane, and secular. But the Apostolic and Holiness denominations embraced dancing and incorporated it into the free spirit of their worship services. These denominations, commonly known as the Sanctified Church, adapted practices that were more akin to African religious traditions than were their predecessors. Over the years, the use of dance within the Sanctified Church presented itself in various forms, ranging from holy dancing, also known as shouting, to liturgical dance, a tradition that combined sacred worship with dance often used to "usher in the spirit," and featured choreographed dance performances. It was these practices, along with the belief that the spirit manifested itself by the speaking of "tongues," that led to the expulsion of the Holiness movement from the Baptist denominations during the early twentieth century.[9] This theological and musical approach to worship in Virginia's Atlanta church may have been connected with the expulsion of some churches from the Baptist denomination and may account for Mary's assertions that this church was Baptist despite these practices.

Nevertheless, it is not the denomination of the church that is of great importance, but the residual effects these early experiences had on Mary's spiritual and musical development. This early exposure to religious worship and reverence for God served as the spiritual foundation for Mary's conversion to Catholicism in the 1950s. Musically, these experiences provided Mary with a strong knowledge of the spirituals, hymns, and sacred songs of blacks. Mary often sat on her mother's lap while Virginia played an old pump organ at their local church. One day, after listening intently to her mother play, Mary sat down and played, note for note, a tune that her mother had played minutes earlier. Later, Mary would recount that her mother, startled by her daughter's sudden display of talent, dropped her and ran from the church to summon the neighbors.[10] In the 1960s and 1970s Mary would often draw connections between the spirituals, blues, and rag compositions she had heard during her early years and the jazz styles that developed during the subsequent years of the twentieth century.

In the black aesthetic, it was often believed that altering one's ability to play "by ear" or to improvise was a distortion of natural talent. Virginia recognized the raw nature of Mary's talent and did not allow the young girl to receive formal musical training for fear that it would "corrupt" this naturalness. Virginia, like many black musicians, had begun playing by ear, but after taking lessons for a short period had "ended up not playing at all, just reading music."[11] Music and church brought some comfort to what was an increasingly difficult life for Mary and her family. Virginia, like other southern black women, found herself more disenfranchised as time went on.

In the South, Jim Crow, racial intimidation, and increasing vigilante violence made life for blacks very harsh. The country's economic shift from an agrarian to an industrial society further disenfranchised black southern workers with no relief in sight. Black farmers and field hands faced greater poverty, as boll weevil infestations, inclement weather, and terrorism enacted by white southerners became staples of life. Mary's childhood in Atlanta was filled with visions of lynchings and other acts of hatred against blacks. She once saw a man's head "split open with an ax" in an act of terrorism and intimidation; in her innocence she went over to comfort him.[12]

Thus, many southern blacks looked to the urban North as the "promised land" of their hopes for a better life. Virginia Scruggs was no exception. After meeting and marrying a young laborer named Fletcher Burley, she and her family moved north.[13] Described by the relatives as tall and light-skinned, Burley had two brothers, Julius and Tom, who died when he was only five years old. Virginia's marriage to Burley brought stability to the household and, in time, it was decided that the family would be better off leaving Georgia. In 1915 Virginia, Fletcher, five-year-old Mary, nine-year-old Mamie, and other members of the family left for Pittsburgh, Pennsylvania, to start a new life.

* * *

Pittsburgh was one of the many destinations to which southern blacks headed during the first peak of the Great Migration. The city offered many advantages to blacks settling there, especially with the promise of consistent employment in the steel and coal industries. From 1916 until

1919 Pittsburgh's shops, mines, hotels, and private homes sought new workers to replace the diminishing numbers of emigrant workers during World War I and white women who had left for better-paying jobs. Pittsburgh faced a major shift in the racial makeup of its workforce, which had consisted largely of European immigrants. Since World War I had disrupted the flow of immigrant workers settling in the city, employers looked to southern blacks as an alternative.

News of job openings and housing opportunities was dispatched to areas of the rural South in hopes of inspiring blacks to migrate. Peter Gottlieb wrote, "Newspapers and magazines swelled the flow of information between Pittsburgh and prospective migrants in the South. Pittsburgh's major black newspaper, the *Pittsburgh Courier,* printed 'society' and 'local events' columns. Southern blacks that first learned about Pittsburgh by word of mouth could soon read reports from the *Courier* and other sources." [14] Good news and talk of "money hanging from the trees" from relatives who had resettled in the North also spurred southerners to pack up and leave southern life behind. Black men relayed stories of jobs in the steel mills such as Carnegie Steel, American Wire and Steel, the A. M. Byers Company iron mill, and other foundries that paid double or even triple the amount they had made in the fields of the South. Most women found temporary positions at department stores and factories, as well as domestic work.

Work opportunities were greater for men than for women, and living conditions proved more accommodating to single traveling men than to families. But women made the trip as well. [15] Despite the miles that separated most of these blacks from their southern roots, many were able to maintain their family and community connections. Many made a ritual of returning "home" at least once during the course of a year, while others, unable to cope with living conditions and the mores of urban life, returned home for good.

Migrants to Pittsburgh generally lived in the Hill District inside the city boundaries or the rooming house districts of the mill towns in the surrounding area. The several evolving black neighborhoods in the city included the Strip District, Second Avenue downtown, East Liberty, North Side, and Lawrenceville. Beginning in 1916, the racial segregation of blacks increased and many blacks were pushed out of certain districts. Within some of the racially segregated areas created for blacks, migrants

often formed their own enclaves, by default occupying the most dilapi-
dated, poorly equipped, and unsanitary structures.[16]

Work became increasingly sporadic as the 1920s brought stagnation
to the steel industry. Male workers suffered periods of layoffs and unem-
ployment, while female workers relied on domestic work to offset these
periods. What was perhaps more significant for southerners was the racial discrimination they still encountered. White northerners' resistance
to black progress diminished the black southerners' hopes for equality
and prosperity. The most obvious forms of racism were the herding of
blacks into deteriorating housing districts and the refusal to rent to
blacks in more attractive areas. This discrimination was known to esca-
late even further when the "black areas" were raided by the police, who
suspected the resettled blacks of the increasing crime in the city. More
disheartening was the resistance and resentment most southern blacks
experienced from northern middle-class blacks. Southerners were seen
as inferior "outsiders," who disrupted the progress of the black middle
class's efforts to elevate the race. Newspapers carried articles that spoke
of the "backward" behavior and ignorance of southern migrants and
thereby created an unbreachable divide between the two groups.

Though Virginia and her family had similarly unpleasant experiences
in Pittsburgh, the family managed to escape the unsanitary housing offered to migrants. Despite various setbacks, the family made a smooth
transition into their new northern life. This was accomplished primarily
because of the family connections that Virginia had in the city. Several of
her relatives had migrated north in the preceding years and had established themselves. The sisters of Mary's grandmother Anna Jane lived in
Philadelphia, and Mary's great-grandparents had settled in Pittsburgh
with their other children.[17] This provided Virginia with two things that
would make the difference in her life in the North: a ready-made support
system and stable housing. For some time, the family lived with Virginia's aunt on Broadway. That house was located between two white
families, and it seems from family accounts that they had lived comfort-
ably before the arrival of their migrating relatives. Upon their arrival,
however, the neighbors greeted the newcomers with flying bricks and
racial epithets. Perhaps the white neighbors had mistakenly believed the
family to be white or immigrants; descriptions of family members indicate that, with the exception of Mary, most were very fair in complexion,

with blond or light-colored hair. "My great-grandparents were born, I guess, about a year after slaves were freed," Mary recalled. "They were both very fair, my grandmother especially. My grandfather had blond hair. She used to tell how they used to put them out in the sun and try to parch them black because they were very, very fair." The family, like many lighter-skinned blacks at the time, may have unintentionally "passed" for white, only because they were not asked about their racial background.

The hate-filled neighbors soon realized that their threats and acts of violence were not going to turn the family away and the harassment stopped. Music and a child's innocence would eventually resolve the racial tensions between Mary's family and her neighbors. Without her mother's knowledge, Mary began visiting and playing piano for her neighbors. It was not until the young girl broke her arm and could not continue her visits that her mother discovered her secret. "I was never in the house," explained Mary. "Once when I broke my arm, the neighbors came to the house asking for the 'little piano girl.' And my mother said, 'What have you been doing?' I said, 'Playing the piano at their house.'" [18] The visits soon resumed and Mary's talent blossomed.

Mary's stepfather, Fletcher Burley, became one of the leading supporters of her musical talent. The family settled on Euclid Avenue in an area called East Liberty, an all-white neighborhood located approximately six miles from downtown Pittsburgh. During their early days in East Liberty, the Burley family learned firsthand how to overcome racial prejudice and intolerance. The family continued, like many blacks in the city, to struggle financially and moved two more times before settling in a home on Hamilton Avenue on the perimeter of Homewood and East Liberty. [19] Two years later, in 1917, Virginia had her third child, a girl named Grace, and the family moved to a house on Larimer Avenue.

It was on Larimer Avenue that Virginia and Anna Jane launched their laundry business. The two earned such a reputation for their work that during their peak years they employed six other women. Geraldine, another of Mary's younger sisters, recalled that her mother and grandmother ran the business out of their kitchen. They had all the supplies they needed, including a big press, which enabled them to handle larger items from area businesses. She also remembered being taught how to press and fold shirts so that they maintained that crisp look and how much pride her mother and grandmother took in their work. The business, however, was short-lived and eventually both went back to residential laundry and working as domestics. Little is known of the dissolution of the business. The venture may have been a victim of the Depression or perhaps it did not produce enough revenue in its later years to sustain itself. Nevertheless, the family continued to support itself despite the loss in income.

In time, the family moved to Shakespeare Street. During this period, it is believed, Mary was enrolled in the Shakespeare School, a small preparatory school that most children in the neighborhood attended before going to the Lincoln Elementary School. Meanwhile, Virginia gave birth in 1919 to another child, the second of six with Burley, a son named Howard, who would later fight in the Buffalo Division during World War II.

Howard's birth came days after Mary was enrolled at the Lincoln School, an environment in which her musical ability grew rapidly. Mary's teachers identified her unusual talent from the very beginning and did all they could to provide her with extracurricular experiences that would encourage her development. This was the guidance Mary needed but hardly received from Virginia, who was still struggling to sustain her household. By the time of the move to Pittsburgh, Virginia had become less musically involved in the church, and she is not known to have played or sung during these years.[20] Nevertheless, Mary's talent continued to grow and she was soon drawn into the city's musical scene.

Chapter 2

TAKE ME TO FROGGY BOTTOM: THE EARLY MUSICAL YEARS

"Froggy Bottom was where nobody ever worried and they just sank down to the bottom of things, like frogs in a pool, lounging around and leading a carefree life."
—Mary Lou Williams

The Burley family's move to Pittsburgh held the possibility of a new life and financial stability. By 1920 the city had become one of eight major destinations for migrating African Americans. World War I, which contributed to the influx of migrants to Pittsburgh, had created a greater need for labor, offering a chance for blacks seeking a better future. However, many migrants, including Mary's family, discovered that the North was not the "promised land" that so many had claimed it to be. Life in the North was defined by forced segregation, exclusion from labor unions and skilled work, and a higher cost of living. Many African Americans sought comfort on the street corners and in the saloons that peppered their neighborhoods, and it was here that the vernacular music and folk traditions of the South continued to develop. These forms, although dismissed initially, would eventually influence emerging black and white traditions in the North.[1]

Mary and Mamie seemed to adjust to life in the North. No doubt the two thought that the move would mean that their mother, Virginia, would not have to work as hard as before or be separated from them as often. But this would prove not to be true. The family scrambled more than ever to maintain the household income, and Virginia became less involved in their everyday lives. Mary took to the streets of East Liberty and the Hill District, discovering the active and diverse musical culture of the neighborhood. It was the music of street corner musicians, of the Victrolas that spilled their musical sounds out the windows of the houses that lined the streets, and of the theater musicians that influenced Mary's early musical style. She continued to practice the piano and often took to the streets to learn more and earn much-needed money through her performances. A very small and thin child, Mary was often eclipsed by other children, but her musical talent garnered her attention she would not normally have received. She and a cousin would often dance on street corners for money. The duo became so well known that many times Mary earned more than her stepfather's weekly pay.

Laborers such as Fletcher Burley were drawn to northern cities by prospects of well-paying jobs, better living conditions, and job security. But the reality of the situation was the complete opposite. Most migrants found themselves excluded from labor unions, which might have protected their rights to better wages, working conditions, and jobs that were categorized as skilled labor. The latter paid on average more than double the rate of other jobs. White workers often refused to work beside black workers, threatening strikes and work shutdowns if black workers were hired or trained for jobs that offered any type of advancement. Instead, blacks had become resigned to the dirtiest and most dangerous work. Their wages barely covered the most basic household expenses, so many searched for ways to supplement their incomes. Fletcher Burley attended gambling parties where he generally earned enough money to sustain the household. Others rented out beds in shifts. Night workers slept during the day in the beds that were vacated by day workers, and vice versa. No amenities were offered to these renters and most rooms were crowded with as many beds as the space could accommodate.[2] But the most common form of supplemental income came in the form of rent parties. Fletcher, Virginia, and many of their friends and family who had also migrated from Atlanta often found comfort in these weekend activities, which included their own house parties, similar to those given in Georgia. Rent parties were usually thrown in an effort to pay bills; they also offered a means of escape from the pressures of the workweek.

Over time the Saturday-night or rent parties became a staple in the economic and cultural lives of migrants. The food and music provided contributed strongly to the popularity of such gatherings, which generally started after midnight and went "well into dawn in a miasma of smoke, booze, collard greens, and hot music."

Unlike the management of many of the nightclubs and theaters, sponsors of rent parties did not discriminate among guests and anyone with the admission price was welcomed. Invitations to these parties were "handed out in the streets, in bars, in barbershops and in beauty parlors, or were left in mailboxes or in apartment house elevators." [3] The invitations were sometimes printed on little cards with promises of a joyful time, but mostly they were printed on flyers and displayed throughout the neighborhoods or passed by word of mouth. Either way, partyers were assured that they would be provided with good entertainment and the best food.

> Hey! Hey!
> Come on boys and girls let's shake that thing
> Where?
> Hot Poppa Sam's
> West 134th Street, three flights up
> Jelly Roll Smith at the piano
> Saturday night. . .
> Hey! Hey!
> Fall in line, and watch your step,
> For there'll be lots of Browns with
> Plenty of Pep at
> A *Social Whist Party*
> Refreshments just it. Music won't quit.
> Shake it in the morning. Shake it at night
> At a Social Matinee Party . . .
> Music too tight. Refreshments just right. [4]

Musically, these parties became the crucible for the development of black vernacular forms, especially piano styles such as stride, boogie-woogie, and a blues-oriented, improvised tradition of ragtime that differed from the classic rag compositions of Scott Joplin. The rent party phenomenon was not a creation of the urban environment, as is commonly believed, but a retention of the customs and practices of many southern blacks. Those living in the larger southern cities often hosted parties to supplement the family's income. These parties were the lifeblood of families of low economic status who "sought to combine their troubles with a little joy.[5]

The same could be said of the parties that Mary's parents often hosted on Friday and Saturday nights. Their East Liberty home would be filled with dancing, drinking, and laughing. As a young child, Mary often watched these nocturnal activities from the stairs or a dark corner. She learned quickly the role music played in expressing the experiences of working-class blacks. But over time, Mary and her other siblings saw less and less of her mother singing, dancing, or playing the piano. Virginia's musical activities had seemingly been replaced by her need to work and provide a stable environment for her expanding family. It was during these early years that Mary discovered the truth regarding her paternity. The overzealous comments of a relative revealed that Mose Winn, who Mary had always believed was her father, was not her biological father but a man her mother had married and divorced shortly before Mary's birth. Despite the revelation, Virginia and Fletcher never treated Mary any differently from their other children and never spoke of the incident again. Geraldine Garnett, a younger sister, asserted that the illegitimacy of Mary's birth was never discussed because no one was ever judgmental about such matters. "Family was family, and it was not a matter of who was a biological or half brother or sister."[6] Geraldine maintained that Virginia loved all her children equally. She was a tough, strong-willed woman who wanted to provide her children with survival skills. The emotional pain that Mary could have suffered was eclipsed by Fletcher Burley's unconditional love for her. Mary in later years would recount that Fletcher "almost put his own kids aside for me, if I needed anything. Well, he was very charitable. Sometimes I'd bring kids in that didn't have shoes and he'd give them money to buy shoes or to buy clothing."[7] In time, he would prove to be just as influential to her musically as the theater shows she attended and the records to which she listened.

He was considered a very good, bad man, not overbearing, but he was treacherous if you made him angry. Everybody in Pittsburgh knew about this and nobody even tried to harm me. He worked everyday; he would not gamble with that money. He'd take the money home and give it to my mother for her bills and whatnot and he'd go up the street and have a friend throw him in the game. That's what they called it—that is, give him a stake in the game.[8]

Fletcher purchased Mary a player piano with the piano rolls of Jelly Roll Morton and James P. Johnson and often requested that the young girl play the blues and boogie-woogie for him. This would account for the strong influence of these two forms on her later approach to improvisation and arranging for big band ensembles. Most important to Mary's relationship with Fletcher and her musical development was the hands-on experience she received through her interaction with him. He often took her out with him, arranging for her to play the piano after sneaking her into nightclubs and poker parties under his "huge scratchy overcoats." Before the card games began, she would play a couple of tunes, and he would put a dollar in a hat and persuade others to add to the pot as she played. Minus his initial contribution, the kitty went entirely to Mary. Fletcher also took her to Saturday hops or rent parties, where she had her first encounters with boogie pianists who played to dancing couples and partygoers. She was sometimes hired at a dollar an hour for three hours at these functions, and her mixture of the blues, boogie-woogie, and other styles often added to the excitement of the environment. Together with the daily visits to her neighbor's house, these sessions were helping Mary become a seasoned performer, and she soon earned the appellation the "little piano girl." Mary's mother did not know about the "outings" with Fletcher until years later. She then accepted them as part of Mary's evolution as a musician.

After school and on weekends Mary would often spend hours at the piano trying to play the Fats Waller and Jelly Roll Morton tunes she heard on the records she owned. These music studies included not only the music of these jazz greats but also the spirituals her mother had played in their Atlanta church and the blues and boogie-woogie tunes that Fletcher liked so much. It is not surprising that later in Mary's career her statements about the evolution and history of jazz would be centered on the spiritual and the blues. She was often quoted as saying that these two genres were the foundation of jazz.

Mary rejected the efforts of friends and family members to get her to entertain herself in other ways, and day after day she would sit and work out her musical ideas. "Kids would come to call for me—my half brother would come over, he was about two years younger, he'd come over to play with me—but I'd be busy at the piano. Sometimes I'd stop and go and play with him a little while, and then come back in to the piano, getting my own sounds, and I've been doing that all my life." [9] This level of dedication and her daily performance for neighbors provided Mary with extra income in addition to the weekly allowance she received from her uncle, stepfather, and grandfather in exchange for playing their favorite tunes. "My uncle liked Irish songs. My grandfather liked the classics and my stepfather liked boogie-woogie. So he'd give me more money than my uncle or grandfather." [10] Many times, her neighborhood performances netted her $20 or $30, and the additional money from family increased those earnings considerably. Mary's teachers and other members of the community also acknowledged her natural talent. Miss Milholland, principal of the Lincoln School, which Mary attended, took the young girl to afternoon teas at Carnegie Tech, where Mary played her improvisations of light classical pieces. A mortician in the neighborhood periodically invited Mary to play for the afternoon teas he hosted. Mary was so small at the time that she had to play while sitting on someone's lap. She would play her standard repertoire first, which consisted of classical works and popular songs, then take requests. She earned a dollar an hour for her services and often amassed additional money from tips. [11] Hugh Floyd, who married Mary's older sister, Mamie, took her to theaters to see the vaudeville shows, which featured Earl Hines and other pianists appearing in Pittsburgh. These musicians often invited Mary to join them in jam sessions and her talent astounded them.

At one of the many vaudeville shows that came through Pittsburgh, Mary met two pianists who would influence her stylistic development, Jack Howard and Lovie Austin. Howard, a Pittsburgh piano player and local phenomenon known for his left-hand-dominated ragtime compositions, influenced Mary's left-hand styling. His tremendous left-hand stretch (he played a lot of tenths) and his penchant for playing so hard that many thought the piano would break were noted in Pittsburgh-area jazz circles and would show up in Mary's solos.[12] He told Mary always to play the left hand louder than the right because that's where the beat and the feeling is. "It's just like a drum keeping a steady beat," he said, and he provided her with professional advice that would "have taken me years and years to learn."[13] From Lovie Austin she learned stage presence. Lovie made a big impression on Mary with her ability to maintain her glamorous persona while scribbling the music for subsequent performances, conducting with her head, and playing with her left hand. This fascinated Mary, who knew she wanted one day to be doing the same.

Mary's rapid development as a musician was matched only by her development as a young woman. Although she remained quite thin, Mary grew inch by inch. Her Mayan features grew more defined, and her wavy black hair grew longer. But Mary seemed less concerned with her physical development and more interested in her musical development. By age ten, music had become the one consistent aspect of her life. The Burley house continued to expand as Virginia gave birth to two more children, the twins Geraldine and Jerry, who were born on Mary's birthday, May 8, in 1920. For years the joint celebration of their birthdays was Mary's reason for returning to Pittsburgh each year. Less than three years later, two other children, Margaret and Josephine, had been born into the already crowded house, and Mary began living with her sister Mamie and her husband.

Meanwhile, her talent brought her to the attention of several union bands that worked Pittsburgh's theaters. Occasionally Mary would perform with these aggregations, training her ears to the nuances of dance band music. At the time, Mary could not read music and often relied on perfect pitch and a natural ear for musical form as a means of masquerading her shortcomings. She often listened to the first chorus and duplicated exactly what she heard. She never told the bandleaders that she could not read music and her secret was never detected. In fact, her ability to copy the arrangements proficiently made her the top choice of most regional bands as a replacement pianist. Eventually Mary graduated from Pittsburgh-based performances with these groups to tours that sometimes took her to other parts of Pennsylvania and even into Ohio. During these travels, prepubescent Mary was accompanied by a chaperone selected by her mother. The frequency of such trips increased in the mid-1920s, and Virginia often allowed the young girl to travel alone with the bands. Mary did not recognize the uniqueness of her experiences or the danger she was in as a young black girl alone among all those men. A guardian angel came in the form of Roland Mayfield, who owned a nightclub in East Liberty and was reportedly one of the wealthiest black men in the city. He was called the "Black Prince of East Liberty," and from their initial meeting when she was twelve until the late 1970s, Mary and Mayfield would remain close friends. He often came to her rescue, providing money when bookings were canceled, the promoter skipped out with the band's pay, or she was stranded outside Pittsburgh.

The support and encouragement that Mary received from her family and friends were unusual at that time, as Americans still had very strong views about the presence of women in public entertainment. It was commonly thought that entertainment was not a suitable career for women and that no self-respecting woman would pursue such interests, especially outside the realm of classical music.[14] Mary's family was a study in contradiction of those views. The men of her family in particular took great care to help her grow musically, and this may well account for her later ability to infiltrate the ranks of the male jazz fraternity, unlike most women at the time. Most women, with the exception of Lovie Austin, Julia Lee, or Lil Hardin Armstrong, made their presence known in jazz and blues as vocalists, the more acceptable role for women. But the strength of Mary's playing, her self-esteem, and the depth of her talent brought open admiration from older, more seasoned musicians. As a preteen, she participated in practice sessions with bands such as Earl Hines's orchestra. The Mellons, one of the wealthiest families in Pittsburgh, also invited Mary to play for their parties, and she was paid substantial amounts of money for her services. Mary continued to evolve into a consummate professional musician, and in 1925, she began working with local union bands regularly. She was spotted by a member of a band called McKinney's Cotton Pickers during one of these gigs and asked to join the band.

McKinney's Cotton Pickers was a dance orchestra formed in Springfield, Ohio, shortly after World War I. The band was known for its musical versatility and showmanship, which blended comedy routines and light music with jazz compositions.[15] Mary's stint with the Cotton Pickers and other regional bands provided her with the credibility she needed to enter the mainstream jazz scene. At a time when most girls were playing dressup, Mary was doing one-nighters in Memphis, Kansas City, and other parts of the Midwest. This constant traveling frequently interrupted her education and robbed Mary of what most would consider a normal childhood. But these experiences demonstrated to Mary that there was more to life than backbreaking work and poverty. By virtue of her talent, Mary was being saved from the life of domestic service and industrial work that had robbed her mother and so many black women of their youth. Like Alberta Hunter, Bessie Smith, Lovie Austin, and other notable black women performers who preceded her, Mary realized that her music was one, if not the only, way to escape the hard life that awaited most black women.

* * *

Mary's musical education was furthered through Pittsburgh's popularity with traveling troupes and vaudeville shows. Unlike most young women who sought careers in entertainment as a means of escaping poverty and hard labor, Mary performed primarily out of love for music. Socially more adept than many of the young girls on the tent show circuit, Mary still had much to learn about life outside the Pittsburgh area.

Vaudeville, by the early 1920s, had taken America by storm, appealing not only to white audiences but also to black ones. It had replaced the minstrel show as the dominant form of American entertainment and provided its audiences with more sophisticated performances than its predecessors. Although blacks were not at first an important part of the vaudeville tradition, over time many performers moved on from the minstrel-like venues of the black theater and created new forms of vaudeville that appealed to black audiences.

Unlike the tent and medicine shows of the early twentieth century, in which many African Americans, including "Ma" Rainey and Bessie Smith, found fame, vaudeville had its own chain of theaters. B. F. Keith, who opened the prototype for respectable vaudeville theaters in Boston in 1882, developed a network of theaters from the East Coast to Chicago. The Keith circuit worked in association with Martin Beck's Orpheum Circuit, which controlled major vaudeville houses west and south of Chicago. These circuits dominated vaudeville. On the Keith-Orpheum circuits, vaudeville flourished from the late 1890s through the early 1930s.

Only the most celebrated and talented black performers initially had access to these big-time vaudeville circuits. Black performers who were fortunate enough to integrate into mainstream vaudeville were generally employed in stock companies or cast in specific vaudeville shows that perpetuated racial stereotypes.[16] However, these performers faced difficulties that their white counterparts often escaped. Financial sponsorship for black shows was lacking, and many were subject to second-class bookings. There was also racism among some of the owners and managers, leaving performers at their mercy. But in 1912 a former minstrel and vaudeville performer named Sherman Dudley became a booking agent for black vaudeville talent on a circuit known as the Theater Owners Booking Association, or TOBA. It was started by the Memphis-based businessman F. A. Barrasso in 1907 in an attempt to improve conditions.[17]

The TOBA, also known as "Tough on Black Actors or Asses," became the main vehicle through which vaudeville bookings for African American performers could be handled efficiently. The circuit stretched from Cleveland to Galveston and from Kansas City to Jacksonville. Pittsburgh, having increased its black population considerably since the early teens, became one of the major stops on the circuit. It was through these shows that Mary saw the possibilities of life beyond industrial or domestic work and poverty. Her stepfather, Fletcher Burley, and her brother-in-law, Hugh Floyd, often took Mary to the TOBA shows, where the young girl watched and listened in amazement to the action that took place both on the stage and in the pit. These shows were tabloid editions of musical comedies with three shows given nightly, each about forty-five minutes long. TOBA audiences were outspoken and inhospitable to acts that either were lackluster or strayed too far from the preferred black performance style. There was no hook to drag inept performers off the stage when the boos reached a crescendo, but the audience would greet unpopular acts with derisive catcalls and an occasional flying object. That was usually enough to tighten up a performer's act. The TOBA, with its all-black audiences and often shabby, ill-kept theaters, was the perfect incubator for the developing forms of black music, dance, and comedy.[18]

Unknown to its audiences, the TOBA was plagued with persistent problems. One was that many of the performers were unreliable, especially in shows that were inconsistent in their popularity. Drunkenness and temporary incarceration often took musicians and performers away from their responsibilities, which left promoters or bandleaders looking for replacements. One such episode, in 1922, provided Mary with the opportunity to join the vaudeville show *Hits and Bits*. At first the proprietor of the show, Buzzin' Harris, scoffed at the notion that a young girl could play the piano well enough to be considered for his show, but Mary's talent won him over. She played such a rousing version of "Who Stole the Lock Off the Henhouse Door?," a ragtime composition she had learned from her mother, that Harris was struck dumb. He was amazed at Mary's strength and sense of rhythm. He hummed the score to the show and Mary picked it up immediately. He offered her the job.[19] After much debate, Mary's mother allowed her to leave school months before summer vacation to travel with the band, noting that the opportunity would provide the family with much-needed income. Mary recalled the incident as follows:

> The "Hits and Bits" show came to Pittsburgh, and their pianist was quite the drunkard; this particular time, he didn't show up at all. Someone told the manager of the show: "There's a little girl out East City that can do the job." Well they brought him the six miles from downtown out to East Liberty—and there I was outside on the sidewalk, playing hopscotch with the kids. He was disgusted: "You're recommending *her* for my show— that's ridiculous." However, he went in the house, and he had me sit down and play for him. Immediately, he wanted to sign me up. My mother had to arrange for me to have two-and-a-half months away from school to play with this show.[20]

The booking was for two months, with Mary's salary set at $30 a week, which in the 1920s was a lot of money, considering that male workers averaged a salary of $11 a week and women earned $8 or $9 a week. Initially, Mary was chaperoned by a friend of her mother, but at some point during the extended stint, the chaperone returned to Pittsburgh. Mary was left alone and clearly was not aware of the danger she was exposed to. Despite years of performing in Pittsburgh's nightclubs, gambling houses, and rent parties, Mary was remarkably naïve. She did not understand that her reputation as Fletcher Burley's daughter, and the protection that provided, did not extend outside the city. In one instance, an older man lured Mary and other young girls traveling with the troupe into a room. He began giving them whiskey and Coca-Cola to get them drunk; more than likely, he hoped to sexually assault them. Just as Mary began feeling the alcohol, an older girl named Margaret Warren came into the room and took the girls out. "He was just about to do his act, with us," recounted Mary. "And she came into the room. I was so sick. He put it in Coca-Cola and we thought we were drinking Coca-Cola. None of us knew the taste of whiskey. She came in and she took a stick and she was beating all over his head." [21] Margaret and Mary established a long-lasting friendship that consisted of the older girl protecting the younger from the vices of life on the road.

This early tour took Mary west to Detroit, Chicago, Cincinnati, and St. Louis. Along the way she made the acquaintance of many notable musicians, including Louis Armstrong, to whom Mary was introduced by Earl Hines. Hines and Armstrong were working at the Vendome Theatre in Chicago with Erskine Tate's orchestra. After the show, members of the *Hits and Bits* band took Mary over to the Sunset cabaret to hear King Oliver's band. There she met Louis Armstrong. She also had an opportunity to meet the woman who had inspired her—Lovie Austin, who had settled in Chicago and was making a name for herself with her band. In St. Louis she encountered Charlie Creath, then known as the "Riverboat King." Creath, known for his "growling" trumpet style, an approach that the Ellington horn section would adopt later, spent the majority of his career in St. Louis performing on the Streckfus fleet of riverboats. [22] These early meetings with jazz greats were the beginning of long relationships Mary would have with notable jazz men and women.

Although Mary gained the respect of audiences and other musicians with her musical talent, she said years later that she did not take her music seriously. On many occasions, antics to please the crowds dominated her playing. While such novelties entertained audiences, among musicians they brought into question the integrity of a performer. Mary began to take music and her playing seriously only when a fellow musician warned her about diluting her talent with cheap tricks. "I had invented a specialty where I played 'Milenburg Joys' by spreading a sheet over the keys and playing mostly with my elbows," said Mary. "Then I played a wild break while spinning around on the stool and brought the house down. I thought I was terrific until an older musician came up to me and told me he detected one special chord in my playing, and that because of that one chord, how ridiculous it was to clown. From then on, I settled down to play seriously." [23] This admonition would remain with

Mary throughout her career and sometimes led her to resist entertaining audiences.

Mary's stint with *Hits and Bits* was short-lived; after eight weeks she returned to Pittsburgh and resumed school at Westinghouse Junior High. Westinghouse was one of several public schools in the city that provided students with a musical education. Each student had the opportunity to study a variety of instruments. During her short tenure there, Mary experimented with many instruments, including the violin. After Mary played "The Sheik of Araby" on one string, her teacher advised her to "forget it and stick to piano." Later Billy Strayhorn and Erroll Garner attended the same school and developed their musical skills under the same tutelage.

Pittsburgh in the mid-1920s was an exciting city musically and Mary, because of her talent and reputation among musicians, was at the nexus of that scene. She often jammed with the bands and musicians who passed through the city. Many became her mentors. Todd Rhodes, a pianist with McKinney's Cotton Pickers, often took young Mary out jamming. According to Mary, "Some nights we jammed all the way from East Liberty down to Wylie Avenue, then a notorious section of town which was held in dread by so-called decent people. We always wound up in the Subway on Wylie, a hole in the ground to which the cream of the crop came to enjoy the finest in the way of entertainment. For me it was a paradise. Visiting musicians made straight for the place to listen to artists like Louise Mann and Baby Hines, Earl's first wife."[24] When not jamming on Wylie Avenue with other musicians, Mary sometimes traveled with home talent shows that toured the region. These shows were booked into small theaters, and the same program was performed each night.

Mary's fun times in Pittsburgh and the surrounding region were soon ended when she needed once again to support the family. Fletcher Burley became ill in 1924, and at the end of the school year Mary returned to the *Hits and Bits* show. She would unfortunately never complete her education, but she would gain valuable experience through these early years of performing. During this return engagement with the group, Mary met a man who would make a considerable contribution to her musical and personal development, John Williams. Williams, known as "Bearcat" among musicians, was a young saxophonist born in Memphis, Tennessee, in 1905. He had traveled with several bands on the TOBA circuit and met Mary when he joined *Hits and Bits*.

The TOBA had proven to be a godsend for struggling black performers, as it offered bookings for extended periods and eliminated the desperate search for the next engagement that plagued all but the top acts. Since the association could effectively determine which artists were playing specific theaters, it partially offset the sometimes unethical dealings of small-time theater owners who were known to withhold payment or cancel bookings on a whim. One of the many drawbacks of the circuits was that theater owners did not pay traveling expenses, so many artists avoided schedules involving long-distance travel. Most performers received minimal pay, with minor acts barely breaking even on those tours. The worst aspect of working the circuit was its extensive travel in the South, where blacks, and particularly northern black entertainers, were not welcome. According to John Williams, the troupe "would play [Columbus, Ohio] the first week. Then, whoever booked us would [send us to] maybe Louisville the next week. Then we'd get a telegram telling us [where our next gig was]. They sent us telegrams, saying, 'Well you open next week at such and such [and] your salary is [whatever the booking agent negotiated].' That was the real TOBA and we didn't make no money." [25]

The TOBA circuit provided performers not only with an escape from the monotony of black life, which included mainly agricultural or domestic work, but also with a view of how other blacks lived in various parts of the United States. While traveling on the circuit, John played plantations and towns where the social code was dictated by Jim Crow laws. The things he witnessed were foreign to him, as he had been born and raised in Memphis, which boasted a strong working-class and middle-class black community. Many of these experiences introduced John to a level of discrimination he had never known. In particular, he was shocked by extreme poverty and sharecropping. While traveling through Arkansas and Mississippi, he encountered blacks who were living under a system of servitude comparable to slavery. In his own words:

> Every year they would have picnics down in Arkansas, down there where they were picking cotton and stuff like that. And they would send to Memphis for music. We would play in Arkansas and Mississippi, around in there. I would play plantations and those picnics. We

would start out about twelve o'clock in the day, play a few numbers and all like that. You would see people coming from miles [around]. Some would come on mule backs. Some was walking and all. Coming to Masta So-and-So's picnic, he was giving for his help. They would play baseball. Not on a baseball diamond, but on the ground where corn and stuff would be. They'd go bare-foot. Guys and girlfriends both coming in on a mule. Both riding a mule.[26]

Despite John's complaint that he and other musicians made no money on the TOBA, such episodes reminded him that financially and emotionally he was much better off than most of his southern counterparts.

Meanwhile, Mary continued to blossom into womanhood and became more aware of her emerging femininity. She remained very thin, weighing for a number of years less than a hundred pounds, but her dark eyes, high cheekbones, and bright smile combined into a type of beauty that escaped some of the lighter-skinned women featured as chorus girls. Although John found her very attractive, it would be a while before he would pursue a relationship with Mary. Together they would have some exciting experiences with the TOBA, but there were also very disheartening times, as they encountered the many hazards of working the circuit for black performers.

With increasing racial hostility in the North and West and Jim Crow at its peak in the South, accommodations and restaurants serving black travelers became ever harder to locate. The theaters that many of these performers played often proved not to be safe either. Some were owned or managed by crooked and outspoken racists who, while profiting from African American performers and patrons, displayed outright contempt for them. Many towns also had curfews for blacks, which meant that overnight travel was a violation of local laws. Working in those towns often required obtaining a pass in order to leave the theater after a performance. Atlanta, a major stop on the TOBA circuit, was one of the cities that banned blacks from the streets after certain hours.[27] In Indiana, the band was not allowed to stay within a town's limits or purchase supplies from the area merchants. John recalled:

There were some bad days like when we played Tipton, Indiana, at a carnival for three days. They didn't sell nothing to black people. No black people were in that county. The white guy that booked us, we'd write out a list and he'd go downtown and bring a bushel basket of sandwiches and things, so we'd have food for three days. For sleeping they had this big barn. We had to sleep in this barn on hay. We had about two bales of hay brought out there and you'd see each guy trying to get a whole lot of hay so he and his girlfriend could sleep soft. So we slept up there in Tipton, Indiana, in a barn for three days. We could come down to do the show and at night that's where we would sleep.[28]

Although John and Mary knew each other professionally, survival during these days on the TOBA circuit helped foster a personal relationship. They met when nineteen-year-old John Williams received an invitation to join *Hits and Bits* in Cincinnati, where Mary had already earned distinction with her piano playing. John recalled, "I first met Mary in 1924. The guy who was leader of the band then put in his notice to quit, because he saw how scarce the money was. His name was Shirley Clay [and he] was out of Chicago. But I didn't know that, I was just meeting everybody. So after the first week we played in Cincinnati, his notice was out. They liked my playing, so Harris, the owner of the show, made me the leader of the band. It was called John Williams's Syncopated Players. Mary was already there at fourteen."[29]

Mary was attracted to John's playing and nothing else at first. But he soon won her over with his charismatic ways. Williams was dark in complexion with smooth skin, a tall, well-built frame, and short, wavy hair. The combination of musical talent and good looks made him popular among the women who frequented the theater and tent shows. But Williams was interested in the thin, brown-skinned girl from Pittsburgh, who pounded the piano like a two-hundred-pound man. After spending some time talking about life and music, the two became a couple. The rough nature of the road and the dwindling salaries of the tour made it necessary for members of the troupe to partner up. When there were romantic sparks, performers often paired off in common-law marriages. The TOBA favored its headliners with good salaries, but those below top billing were subjected to low salaries, inadequate or no housing, cramped and makeshift dressing rooms, and poor lighting and staging.

In addition, in a life on the road where black performers were often subject to the whims of whites, coupling up ensured that female performers had someone to protect them from physical and sexual violence. In John's words:

> You had a girlfriend or your wife. Two would live as cheap as one. That was the thing you had to do. Well, [there was] Mary and a girlfriend, who was a little older than her. She was looking out for Mary, because she was so young. Well, they lived together but after Mary got all enthused about my playing—my saxophone playing and all that—we teamed [up]. This was my girlfriend. Well, we lived together and the other girl, she started living with the straight man, and everybody, all the girls on there, they had a man to protect her. We weren't married, we just lived [together]. That was happening at shows throughout all the big cities: Kansas City, Louisville, Chicago.[30]

One of the major problems performers faced on the circuit was the cancellation of bookings without notice. Shows would sometimes be stranded far from their home base without any notion of when their bookings would resume. In 1925, this happened to Mary and John when the *Hits and Bits* show disbanded in Kansas City. Mary maintained contact with her family by letter and whenever possible would send money to help her mother cover the household expenses, especially as her stepfather's health continued to decline.

The Kansas City stop came after a year of consistent bookings that sometimes alternated between the TOBA and other circuits. Mary and John caught a big break, however, when they heard that the dancers Seymour James and Jeanette Taylor were auditioning bands to add to their show. Jeanette Taylor (dates unknown) and Seymour James (1899–1926) formed one of the few black acts featured on the all-white Keith-Orpheum circuit; Bill "Bojangles" Robinson was another. Taylor, a singer and dancer, was married to the entertainer Perry Bradford and toured with him from 1908 to 1911. She was known for doing an eccentric dance with her eyes crossed. Around 1917, the two dissolved their marriage, and Taylor became the wife and dance partner of Seymour James.[31]

The act, called Seymour and Jeanette, had been working with pit bands, but James became ill and the show had to be revamped. According to Mary, James "could no longer dance flat out. He was famed for a wild strut, which he performed with cane, and it was said that the dance had stretched his heart to the size of a saucer, which seemed likely to anyone who had seen him strutting. He needed a supporting attraction, and it was our job to accompany and provide a couple of specialty numbers." [32] John's band, consisting of Mary and various musicians from around Kansas City, auditioned and was hired. James was skeptical of Mary's talent when he arrived at the first rehearsal with the band. Mary's diminutive size and young-looking face alarmed both him and Taylor. "What's that kid doing here?" James exclaimed. When John explained that she was the pianist, Taylor said a child could not be a part of the act. John assured them the band would work, and once they played "one or two of [their] showiest things, the band was booked." [33] For John and Mary, this was a step up from the TOBA shows. "It was practically the rags-to-riches routine. We were on our way to the top theatre circuits direct from TOBA, one of the toughest." [34]

At first James and Taylor debated with John how Mary should dress during the performances. The duo wanted Mary to dress like a man, which was customary at that time. But John refused, saying that a female musician would draw the audience in. The performers traveled to Chicago, where they rehearsed the act. They were booked to perform in New York, Minneapolis, Omaha, and Kansas City. The band worked for a total of thirty-four minutes a day, with John making $60 and Mary and the other band members receiving $50 a week. According to John, "that was terrific money. You couldn't spend $25 a week doing nothing as fast as food, transportation, and rooming. 'Cause all your rooms were $3 to $5 a week. So we were just flush with money. [Mary] and I together was a hundred and ten dollars. Oh, man, that was just all the money in the world." [35]

The band arrived in New York on Easter Sunday 1926 and the excitement, nightlife, and people of Harlem awaited them. Seymour and Jeanette were booked at the famous Lincoln Theater. The Lincoln, along with the Crescent Theater on 135th Street between Lenox and Fifth Avenue, had come to be known as Harlem's "Off-Broadway" district. These theaters opened their doors to black patrons when the Lafayette and the Alhambra, the other prominent theaters in Harlem, catered only to white customers. The band's tenure at the Lincoln was successful and caused some tension with James, the headliner. According to Mary, the band "thought at any moment we might lose the job because of the way the public was going for our 'Tiger Rag.' This featured Sylvester Briscoe's crazy act of playing trombone with both hands behind his back, the instrument somehow wedged between his mouth and the foot. This may sound impossible, but it is the truth. I never knew how he did it, and never saw anyone who could imitate him." [36] Some nights the audience's reaction to the band was so overwhelming that the movie that generally followed their performance was not shown, to allow the band to play an encore.

Mary and John were booked for forty-two straight weeks with Seymour and Jeanette. Typically, vaudeville acts were booked for that length of time with the summer months off. The show played Minneapolis for a week, Omaha for a week, and Kansas City for a week. James's health began to worsen in Kansas City, and Taylor considered canceling the tour, but she set it back for a month, hoping that his health would get better. Mary, in the meantime, returned home to Pittsburgh and visited with family while awaiting news. Mary's visits home were not ceremonious and she often fell back into her role of daughter, sister, and aunt. Because of the crowded conditions of the Burley home, Mary stayed with her sister Mamie. If she sent money home or purchased particular things for the family, it was not highlighted or discussed with other family members. During these times Mary dissociated herself from her persona as performer and often wanted nothing more than to consume Virginia's dinners of collard greens, yams, and her other favorite dishes. But within a week or two of Mary's return to Pittsburgh, Seymour James died. Taylor, pressured by the need to try to fulfill committed dates and wanting to take her mind off her grief, called the band together and they went back to New York.

*　　*　　*

To seventeen-year-old Mary, Harlem was both exciting and frightening. In 1927 it was a bustling haven for migrant blacks from the eastern seaboard seeking new lives, and the cradle of the new black cultural renaissance. Since 1900 blacks had been migrating to the borough, abandoning the West Side, where they had previously been concentrated. This migration to Harlem was due in part to the overcrowded conditions and increased eruptions of anti-black feelings. Up until 1900 Harlem had been largely a white neighborhood, but by 1930 most of this population was replaced by blacks who inhabited every part of the district.

Harlem was bordered on the north by 155th Street, on the south by 110th Street, on the west by Morningside Drive and St. Nicolas Avenue, and on the east by the East River. Until 1914 the theaters that lined Seventh Avenue and 125th Street catered only to whites. The black theaters were the Lincoln and the Crescent, in Harlem's "Off-Broadway" on 135th Street. Harlem's "Broadway" encompassed Seventh Avenue and beyond and south toward 125th Street. The cultural and geographical line of demarcation, 110th Street, which had separated black Harlem from white New York, was slowly shifting as whites began coming uptown for black entertainment.[37]

The Harlem Mary came to in the late 1920s had a split personality. The Harlem Renaissance had peaked as black intellectuals, writers, painters, and composers attempted to provide America with a different representation of black life. This renaissance, also known as the New Negro Movement, separated black highbrow and lowbrow cultures. On one side was the Harlem of W. E. B. Du Bois, Langston Hughes, Paul Robeson, and other members of the black elite. But the Harlem of the working class was much different. Average Harlemites struggled daily to make ends meet and released their stress through the music and dance of the rent parties, churches, nightclubs, and ballrooms scattered around the borough. Mary's experiences in New York would place her at the heart of a developing New York jazz scene.

Harlem's nightlife was defined by four institutions that served as the crucible for the new form of jazz that would flourish in the next decades. They were the rent parties, which not only provided Harlemites with a way to meet their monthly expenses but cultivated a style of piano music known as stride, which would bridge the divide between the ragtime tradition of the early 1900s and the emerging modern jazz piano approach; the Cotton Club, known as the "aristocrat of Harlem," offering upscale entertainment to white customers only; Connie's Inn, the swankiest of Harlem nightclubs; and the Savoy Ballroom, where the swing movement was conceived and birthed. Harlem was at its musical and cultural peak.

Mary, Jeanette Taylor, and a smaller set of the band were once again booked at the Lincoln Theater off Lenox Avenue. This engagement gave

Mary the opportunity to work with some of New York's hottest musicians, including Sonny Greer, Bubber Miley, and Tricky Sam Nanton, who were members of Duke Ellington's Washingtonians. Ellington had recently returned to New York with a revised version of his band. This early collaboration between Mary and Ellington began their lifelong relationship. But it was Mary's interaction with the pianist Fats Waller that made the biggest impact on her in the early years. Waller had become the darling of New York and one of many pianists who defined the stride style of piano. Like many of the musicians at that time, he did not limit himself to one instrument or one style, and he earned a reputation for his stage presence, his use of the organ in jazz settings, and his compositional abilities. Mary met Waller at Connie's Inn, the famed nightclub on Seventh Avenue, while he was preparing for a new show. Fats Waller (born Thomas Wright, 1904–43) had already established his reputation in the city while serving as an organist at the Lincoln and Lafayette theaters. According to Mary, "When they'd [the technicians of the Lincoln and Lafayette theaters] turn the light on, people would scream, when he sat down people would scream. I never saw such a thing. When he finished, that was the end; they had to let it cool off." [38]

Connie's Inn opened in 1923 under the ownership of Connie and George Immerman. It proved to be a strong rival of the Cotton Club and was said to be the home of Waller's best-known shows and compositions (*Hot Chocolates*, 1929; *Keep Shufflin'*, 1928). [39] Young Mary watched as Waller improvised at the piano all the numbers for the production. When the rehearsal was over, one of Mary's friends bet Waller that Mary could replay all the numbers he had just written. Although nervous, Mary managed to "play nearly everything I had heard Fats play. He was knocked out, picking me up and throwing me in the air and roaring like a crazy man." [40]

Taylor, hoping to recapture the success she had had with her husband, hired a dancer to replace James, but the new arrangement did not sit well with the promoters and the audiences, so the group disbanded. Mary, however, had made a reputation among musicians and was hired at Connie's Inn to play intermission piano while the Ellington band doubled at the Lafayette Theater. This gig exposed her to many musicians, including the pianists Clarence Williams (1893–1965) and Jelly Roll Morton (1890–1941), who criticized her playing of his composition "The Pearls." [41] Unable to fully support themselves with the sparse opportunities that the city presented, Mary and John decided to return to Pittsburgh, where John joined Mamie Smith's band.

Smith, who had ignited the blues craze in 1920 with her recording "Crazy Blues," was attempting a comeback. But John's stint with the blueswoman was short-lived. He and Mary lived with her parents for a month before leaving for Memphis to stay with John's family.

Chapter 3

FROM EAST LIBERTY (PITTSBURGH) TO BEALE STREET (MEMPHIS) TO EIGHTEENTH AND VINE (KANSAS CITY)

The Memphis that Mary and John arrived in was a vibrant city that had become a hotbed of activity with the migration of blacks to the North and West. The city, once a Chickasaw Indian enclave, and the first major riverboat port north of New Orleans, cultivated both black and white folk traditions. It had become the center of the black vaudeville circuit, and traveling variety shows were popular at the Palace Theater. The site of the South's first major race riot, in 1866, Memphis was a city segregated by economics and race but drawn together by music. The only other southern city with such diverse musical and cultural traditions at this time was New Orleans.

Memphis in the 1920s had been shaped by two phenomena: the

enactment of Jim Crow laws following the Civil War, and the yellow fever epidemic of 1873. During the years after the Civil War, racial tensions grew in Memphis and throughout Tennessee. Following the race riot in 1866, a secret society, initially founded as an outlet for former soldiers and known as the Ku Klux Klan, was formed in Pulaski, Tennessee. Focused on retaining the power of southern whites, the Klan took as its purpose the policing of blacks and their Unionist supporters. Its terror campaign, coupled with the enactment of laws that attempted to define the "Negro's place in southern society," led to the disenfranchisement of blacks throughout the South.[1]

The ethnic diversity that had once defined Memphis disappeared during the yellow fever outbreak, when the German population fled to St. Louis and the Irish poor, who were unable to leave the city, died in the slums. White flight and a significant number of deaths in the white sections of the city left Memphis primarily to the blacks, whose death totals were minuscule in relation to those of other populations. By 1890 African Americans constituted 50 percent of the population. In the reconstruction of Memphis, a black center of commerce emerged. Beale Street was the principal avenue that separated black and white Memphis. Known as the "Main Street of Negro America," Beale Street offered patrons various forms of entertainment. Musically, the city boasted diversity that most southern cities its size, with the exception of New Orleans, lacked. The fiddling and banjo playing of country folks were exploited, as were the traditions of black laborers and showmen such as W. C. Handy.

Vaudeville and the blues had roused the music scene in Memphis as early as 1907. Both had grown in popularity in part because of the efforts of two men: F. A. Barrasso, owner of the Palace Theater and conceiver of the TOBA, and E. H. "Boss" Crump, the mayor of the city. Barrasso, noting the popularity of black vaudeville and blues performers, thought that organizing theater owners around the South into a circuit that mirrored what northern theaters had done with white vaudeville would ensure consistent bookings and audiences. Although Barrasso conceptualized the TOBA, it was his brother Anselmo who organized it. The circuit, as discussed in chapter 2, provided performers with consistent employment but was viewed as something of a "plantation system for black performers."[2] Nevertheless, the popularity of TOBA artists and their music among white Memphians brought more and more black talent to the city.

The center of the Memphis music scene was Beale Street and the Palace Theater. As the major theater in the city, the Palace maintained a consistent offering of white and black performers. Black troupes became so popular among white Memphians that the theater instituted a special policy for them. The "Midnight Ramble" policy established special shows for whites on Thursday evenings at 11:30 P.M. The success of these shows, coupled with the ever-growing popularity of the blues and other forms of vernacular music, catapulted Beale Street to the status of the first nationally famed black entertainment district.[3] Notable clubs and establishments that lined Beale Street included the Hole-In-The-Wall, where crap games ran both day and night but patrons never won because of the establishment's rules, which fined players for anything deemed inappropriate during the games. Spitting on the dice or dropping them on the floor resulted in a fine, so money won during the course of a game was taken in payment for violations.[4] The Monarch Club, a favorite of country people, who could get "any kind of moonshine, or dope like reefers and cocaine" at the establishment, was one of the many establishments owned by Jim Kinnane, the "Czar of the Memphis Underworld."[5] But the favorite hangout for musicians was Pee Wee's. W. C. Handy frequented the establishment during his early days in Memphis, and the club was known for featuring rolling blues piano. The cloakroom was said to have been stacked with "horns, guitars, violins, bull-fiddles and banjos and anyone could just pick an instrument and play."[6] Bandleaders or singers seeking musicians would often go to Pee Wee's or to Howard Yancy's office on Beale. Yancy managed most of the jug bands in the city, and his office served as a meeting place where musicians, black and white, came seeking engagements.[7]

Politically, two institutions governed Memphis: E. H. Crump and Jim Crow. Crump, known affectionately as "Boss," made his name in 1908 by trying to stomp out vice on Beale Street. During his first year in office he not only ran the city but also came to control the entire state of Tennessee. His reign would span some forty years, during which time he would enact poll tax laws to control the black vote and to stifle the city from growing politically. But like other city "bosses" at that time, Crump capitalized on the important assets of the city, and for him this meant supporting the music scene. He often sponsored engagements that featured blues and jug band musicians, but he was also a staunch supporter of the segregation laws that governed Memphis and the majority of the South. These laws established a dualistic southern society: one that embraced certain aspects of black culture but also oppressed blacks under legislation that established "separate" existences that gave blacks limited power. For Mary this was a new experience, and she soon discovered that the mores of the South were not compatible with her northern upbringing.

Mary's visit to Memphis was less than happy, as she soon discovered that John's parents had saved for him to go to college and study law. He, however, had chosen to pursue a career in music, of which they did not approve.[8] Seventeen-year-old Mary was undaunted by the family's behavior and after a quiet wedding, in 1926, decided to spend some time getting to know them. Mary knew nothing of what was expected of her as a wife and lover. John recalled that she was an adequate cook and kept their living space clean, but she had little desire for sex. In any other situation this would have led to disaster, but their desire to pursue music careers eclipsed the need to maintain what many would deem normal domestic lives.

Soon after arriving, John formed the Syncopators with freelance musicians in the city. At first the band settled for whatever work was available, but later the aggregation, well steered by John's business acumen, secured not only a regular date at the famous Pink Rose Ballroom but also the best wages offered to a black band in the city at that time. In 1954, in a series of articles documenting her experiences, Mary stated that John was "a smooth talker and a shrewd character," and he soon maneuvered his new combo into clubs and hotels that "ordinarily never employed a coloured outfit."[9] John also started the musicians' union in the city, which standardized working conditions for musicians. Before the establishment of the union, musicians worked "from eight o'clock till three or four in the morning and they'd get paid two dollars," but by the time John left in 1928, city musicians were making $20 to $25 and the leader $30.[10]

Shortly after the band's personnel was stable and working steadily, John received a telegram from the Oklahoma-based bandleader Terence T. Holder, asking John to join his band. The Dark Clouds of Joy, under the leadership of Holder, were one of the more popular bands in the southwestern jazz scene, which had come to be defined by numerous ter-ritorial bands.[11] The Clouds were one of the top two bands in Dallas and consisted of many of the best musicians that the region had to offer, in-cluding the trumpeter Carl Tatti Smith, the pianist Lloyd Glen, and a tuba player from Denver named Andy Kirk. The band initially was a ten-piece unit consisting of three brass, three saxes, and a rhythm section of four. When Andy Kirk joined the Dark Clouds of Joy in 1925 there was no arranger associated with the group, and the band's sound was built primarily around the improvisations of Holder and the alto saxophonist Alvin "Fats" Wall. Kirk, in an effort to standardize the group's repertory, wrote down exceptional choruses played by the two and later added har-mony for the other saxophones. This provided the band with composi-tions that could be used for multiple purposes. The band, according to Andy Kirk, usually played an introduction and two choruses of a tune, then an encore. The encore was the same tune with a slightly different sound. "We used a modulation for the introduction, then went into a special chorus, or featured a solo, then out." [12] Playing such sets in ball-rooms from Dallas to Tulsa to Kansas City helped establish the reputa-tion of the band, which worked consistently between Tulsa and Okla-homa City. Claude Williams, a violinist and one of the original Clouds of Joy, remembered that the bands worked the Louvre Ballroom in Tulsa for three months and then went to Oklahoma City and played three months. They played mainly what were called "jitney" dances: "That's where you buy a bunch of tickets and there'd be a gang of girls standing around and you just go and ask a girl for a dance and if she accepts . . . you give them one of the tickets. The girl was just there to dance, and the man had to pay for the dance." [13] In these instances, the band's selections were guided by the dance master, who called selections according to their tempo.

As the group's popularity grew, Holder added new members, expand-ing the personnel to twelve musicians. As one of the first notable bari-tone saxophonists, John Williams was sought by many bands. When he received the telegram in 1927 inviting him to join Holder's band, John initially declined the offer. Only after Holder promised a salary of $60 per week, more than he had ever made in Memphis, did John seriously consider the offer. The invitation was the opportunity of a lifetime and held the possibility of greater things. As John planned his departure, he and Mary decided that she should remain in Memphis and complete the

Syncopators' bookings. With no saxophonist in the band, Mary enlisted the help of Jimmie Lunceford, who had recently come to the city. Although the Williamses had befriended Lunceford from the time he arrived in Memphis, he was not considered a possible member of the Syncopators until after John's departure. With John as a consummate saxophonist and with the type of repertoire the band played, there was no need to have two saxes in the band. When asked about the decision to add the future bandleader to the band, Mary simply replied, "I had no alto player, so I asked Jimmy." [14]

The group played consistently around Memphis in 1927, and its success was based primarily on its rhythmic approaches and interpretations of popular tunes. The band's approach to jazz mirrored the new trend, which favored combos that played with a beat and called themselves jazz bands. As was true in her early years with the TOBA, Mary's stint as leader of the Syncopators was not without its own set of adventures. Some club owners refused to pay the musicians, and Mary often found herself the only member of the band willing to stand up to these "hustlers." On one occasion, the gangster who had hired them at a nightclub outside Memphis refused to pay, claiming, "I can get all the musicians I want. $2 a dozen." Lunceford and the other band members refused to argue with the man and went back to Memphis, leaving Mary behind screaming, "I WANT MY MONEY!" Although the man's wife and his mother both warned her about his violent temper, Mary continued to protest until she was paid. [15]

In addition to playing with the Syncopators, Mary took several solo dates, which proved to be just as dangerous as many of the gigs with the Syncopators. Being a young, talented, and attractive black woman on the wrong side of the Mason-Dixon line was quite an experience for the pianist. Knowing that she was unfamiliar with the ways of the South, many of Mary's employers threatened her with beating or lynching when she didn't conform to southern customs. Having spent the majority of her life in the North, Mary often forgot how blacks were expected to act in the segregated South, and she found herself in precarious situations. In one instance, she fell asleep on the streetcar and did not move to the back when white patrons boarded. When she awoke, the streetcar was empty and the driver was threatening to harm her. Mary recounted the incident: "One night I went to sleep on the streetcar. Usually when you sat in the front and it began to get crowded with whites you had to move to the back. I was sleeping so when we got to the end of the streetcar line the conductor said, 'You're going to be hurt, little girl, because you're supposed to move in the back.' I said, 'I went to sleep.' When the car made the last stop I started screaming on him and scratching him. I didn't understand this, you know." [16]

In another incident, while working at an establishment on the outskirts of the city, Mary faced a more dangerous situation. These roadhouses, where Mary often played, were popular after-hours hangouts that provided food, drink, and music (whether recorded or live) for those wishing to dance and hear music after the closing time of regular ballrooms. Although Mrs. Singleton, the owner of the roadhouse, was kind, many of the patrons who frequented the establishment were not. "These people were ringing a bell and saying, 'I want this,' and telling me, 'You're from the North and if you don't do as we want you to do, yeah, we'll lynch you,'" recalled Mary.[17] Once she was almost kidnapped by a "fan," who came night after night to listen attentively to the petite, almond-eyed pianist. One evening, the cook tipped Mary off that the man was interested in more than just her piano playing. He had offered the cook $50 to help him take her to his place in Mississippi. When she learned of the kidnapping plot, a terrified Mary ran to the washroom, locked the door, and climbed out the window. She was too frightened ever to return for her pay and later learned that the man had stayed in Memphis for two weeks, trying to take Mary to Mississippi. That night she learned a lesson that would remain with her until death—that her talent did not shield her from the reality of being a black woman living in a hostile environment.

* * *

In 1928 Mary finished her engagements in Memphis and left for Oklahoma City to join her husband. The trip of more than seven hundred miles was quite taxing for the young woman, as most of the major roadways in the South were not paved or in good condition. The pianist had to be concerned not only with being a black woman traveling across the country without male companionship but also with the hazards that lay on the roadway. Mary headed off in the couple's Chevrolet with John's mother and a friend in tow. "I hit the highway. The Chev wasn't much of a 'short' to look at. It looked like a red bathtub in fact, but ran like one of those streamlined trains on the Pennsylvania Railroad, and was the craziest for wear and tear. Unfortunately, we had miles of dirt and turtleback roads to travel, and these excuses for highways were studded with sharp stones. To top it all, it was August and hot as a doodle. Every 40 or 50 miles we stopped to change tyres or clean out the carburetor."[18]

When Mary arrived in Oklahoma in August of 1928, she was surprised at how successful Holder's band had become. The Dark Clouds of Joy had gained status as one of the leading territorial bands in the Southwest, playing mainly dance music. Although jazz was becoming quite popular throughout the region, the Clouds' repertoire emphasized romantic ballads, pop tunes, and both Viennese and popular waltzes.

John, quite anxious to have his wife's talents displayed, immediately invited Mary to the band's next rehearsal, hoping to garner her an audition with Holder. The musicianship and showmanship of the band impressed Mary. "John was anxious to show me off musically, for he was proud of my ability. Though out of my mind from the journey, I went without sleep to make rehearsal the next morning. Holder's boys rehearsed two days a week, beginning 11 A.M.; and I was in the hall by nine. I don't know what Holder's band made of me, but I thought them the handsomest bunch of intellectuals I had seen so far. . . . They played jazz numbers and better commercial things. They were all reading like mad, and I had to admit it was a good and different orchestra: smooth showmanship (minus the 'Tom-ing' or comedic antics that bands often used to draw in white audiences) coupled with musical ability."[19]

The musicians' showmanship defied all the stereotypes of the vaudeville bands and entertained their audiences without compromising their respectability. There was no blackface and none of the comic antics that had diminished the talents and respectability of many of the musicians who played on the TOBA.[20] One of the Clouds' novelty acts was the composition "Casey Jones," during which the group dressed up in engineers' black caps and tied red bandannas around their necks. Kirk would borrow a cigarette from one of the band members and blow smoke into the tubing of his horn. At the point when the entire band entered, Kirk would appear with smoke billowing out of his tuba. "The crowds loved it, especially white audiences," recalled Kirk.[21]

At that time the Clouds had managed to secure all the best engagements in Oklahoma, but financially the record was inconsistent. By 1928 the financial problems that plagued the group intensified. Holder, who was an excellent musician and soloist, often mismanaged the group's money. According to John Williams and Claude Williams (no relation), Holder consistently took the band's money for his personal use. John said of these early years:

> T. Holder had a habit of using the band's money. He just kept it. 'Cause he and his wife were having trouble. He went to Dallas [where she was]. We went to Oklahoma City, and so I learned later that he had done that two or three times. You know, just didn't show up on payday. We'd work and be waiting for the money. They [the band members] decided they didn't want T-Hol to run the band anymore. Andy was the oldest in age, didn't smoke or drink or nothing like that. So we voted into taking his name and [him] leading the band.[22]

Under new leadership the band was transformed from the Dark Clouds of Joy, a name that Kirk found degrading, to Andy Kirk and the Twelve Clouds of Joy. Andy Kirk, a Colorado native, had studied with the father of the orchestra leader Paul Whiteman. By age twenty, the young man was working with the George Morrison Orchestra as a tuba player.[23] His stint with the Denver-based orchestra proved to be the training he needed when he joined the Holder band in 1925.

With Holder gone, several of the original Clouds, including "Fats" Wall, left. Kirk immediately began searching for musicians to fill the vacant spots. The band competed with both the black regional bands and the white union bands, which were jealous of the Clouds' success. Rivalry with the white bands proved to be quite costly. The Clouds worked six days a week, from Tuesday through Sunday, all year. Mondays were usually the off days and their opportunity to play for black audiences. During one of their Monday gigs, the union officials, apparently at the prompting of white union members, changed the pay scale without notifying Kirk. The band was unknowingly paid according to the original scale, placing it in violation of union rules. The band was fined as much as $1,000: $100 per man and $500 for Andy. At this time Mary's stepfather died, forcing her to return to Pittsburgh while John and the other band members worked out their problems.

The Clouds did not remain unemployed for long. The manager for the Pla-Mor, the main ballroom in Kansas City, came to audition the band. He was impressed and moved the band to Kansas City, where they headlined at the Pla-Mor. After attending to her personal and family business, Mary joined her husband in Kansas City in 1929 and found the city to be musically "a heavenly city." "Music everywhere in the Negro section of town and fifty or more cabarets rocking on Twelfth and Eighteenth Streets. Kirk's band was drawing them into the handsome Pla-Mor Ballroom when my husband, John Williams, had me return to him in Kaycee. This was my first visit to Missouri's jazz metropolis, a city that was to have a big influence on my career." [24]

*　*　*

Major cities in the Southwest, especially Kansas City, Missouri, had opened their doors to jazz musicians and their craft since the turn of the century. The closing of the red light district of New Orleans, starting in 1917, led to a decline in employment opportunities for many jazz musicians. While many turned to part-time, blue-collar jobs, others joined minstrel shows and traveled throughout the South. There were, however, many who migrated northward and westward to urban cities such as Chicago and Kansas City. With artists such as Joe "King" Oliver, Johnny Dodds, Sidney Bechet, and Louis Armstrong relocating to the North, new centers of jazz began developing.

Many of these musicians continued advancing New Orleans–style jazz, and it became the foundation for a Chicago style of jazz. However, this style did not directly influence the southwestern jazz scene. By the 1920s, Kansas City had become the crossroads for many musicians and bands leaving New Orleans heading north and those from Texas and Oklahoma seeking consistent work. Because many of the best-paying jobs were in Chicago, very few of the premier players remained in Kansas City. From 1920 to 1940 the Southwest fostered a new style that grew out of a grassroots movement among territorial bands. In this region, music and creativity could be fostered without the politics and other woes that faced musicians in New York or Chicago.

The Kansas City, Missouri, that Mary Williams came to in the late 1920s was a simple provincial town controlled by Tom Pendergast, who served as the boss of the Democratic Party from 1927 to 1938 and carved the city into segregated neighborhoods. Despite the segregation, blacks managed to create their own separate but fulfilled lives. Social clubs were a way of life and blacks owned their own theaters, nightclubs, ballrooms, bars and grills, as well as homes in residential areas. Saturday nights were full of card games, cabarets, and dances given by social clubs, lodges, and Greek-letter organizations. Sunday mornings were dedicated to worship, while afternoons were spent cheering the Kansas City Monarchs and other teams of the Negro Baseball League, and the community was kept informed of the happenings in the city and beyond by the independent black newspaper the *Kansas City Call*.[25]

For many, social life in Kaycee was centered on jazz and the establishments that cultivated the music. The club district extended from the southern boundary of Eighteenth Street to the northern boundary of Twelfth Street. In this area, six blocks square, fifty cabarets with live music existed during the peak years of Pendergast's regime. The two main clubs for jazz were the Sunset Club at Eighteenth and Highland and the Subway Club at Eighteenth and Vine. The Sunset Club was white-owned but the black manager, Piney Brown, became a mentor for jazz musicians, and the establishment became one of the earliest and most popular places to jam. The Subway Club was "the" place for jam sessions. Participants in the all-night events were supplied with all the food and liquor they could ingest, and out-of-town jazz musicians would not miss an opportunity to play in the many "cutting contests," which pitted the city's best pianists against each other to find the most musically and technically creative. Beyond the Eighteenth and Vine district, Kansas City was peppered with a wide array of nightclubs, which included the Boulevard Lounge, the Cherry Blossom, the Vanity Fair, the Lone Star, the Panama, the Elk's Rest, and the Old Kentucky Bar-B-Que. In addition to these clubs, jazz was also being played and refined in the white dance halls where black bands frequently played. The most notable were the Fairyland Park, which was on the edge of town, the Pla-Mor on Main Street, and the Roseland, which catered to white and black patrons.

The music emanating from these establishments reflected a reinterpretation of the jazz styles that were being cultivated elsewhere. Kansas City was attracting musicians migrating from New Orleans en route to the North (Chicago) and the West (Los Angeles and San Francisco). Because Kaycee was considered "off the beaten track," the jazz style developed there was exempt from the extramusical agents that had shaped music in Chicago and New York. Kansas City was geographically far enough from the two cities that the recording industry, which dictated their traditions, had no effect. Kansas City jazz expanded the instrumentation and musicality of New Orleans jazz. New Orleans jazz used the cornet, clarinet, trombone, tuba, snare and bass drums, banjo, and piano as the basis of its instrumentation. Kansas City musicians added to these the saxophone and a new musical approach built around the improvisations of individual jazz musicians and an urbanized form of the country blues. The three-part improvised polyphonic melodic style that defined New Orleans jazz was reduced to simple repeated phrases in Kansas City jazz. These repeated phrases, also known as riffs, became the foundation for the melody, harmonies, and rhythmic pattern of a composition. Once this foundation was established, solos were added. Most sections of improvisation were based on popular songs or the twelve-bar blues. The blues was the primary musical foundation for both fast and slow numbers, and riffs were usually played between and behind solos.

It was the inherent characteristics of Kansas City's style, however, that increased its popularity. Three major musical features distinguished Kansas City jazz from other geographic jazz styles. First, it provided a flexible framework for big band jazz with the combination of ensemble and solo passages that called for improvisation and unwritten solos, allowing players to push the musical boundaries of their arrangements. Second, the Kansas City style was the only style that used unspoiled blues singers such as Jimmy Rushing and Big Joe Turner as band vocalists and integral parts of an orchestra. Lastly, it allowed and encouraged the utmost technical inventiveness and adventurousness among the players. For this reason, Kansas City jazz, more than any other style, became the incubator of the musical revolution in jazz, even while its most radical innovators remained rooted in the blues.[26]

Kansas City, at the time when the Clouds were at the Pla-Mor, was under the control of Tom Pendergast, his political friends, and gangsters, who managed most of the clubs. Missourians had easy access to drinking, gambling, and other vices. Pendergast and his passive encouragement of corruption and gang rule in Kansas City provided the necessary backing for the growing musical culture of the city. Most Kansas City natives enjoyed the blues, boogie-woogie, ragtime, and jazz bands that were an integral part of the nightlife. The many cabarets, show bars, and taverns of the city served as the agents that melted these styles together into Kansas City jazz. More important, the support of the jazz scene by gangsters and politicians only provided a more stable environment for the employment of musicians, and many musicians and gangsters maintained close relationships.

Eddie Banfield, who played with many bands, including Bennie Moten's, Count Basie's, and Duke Ellington's, described Piney Brown, manager of the Sunset Club, as follows:

> Piney was like a patron saint to all musicians. He used to take care of them. Most all the playing and jamming happened at Piney's place. Piney was a man, he didn't care how much it cost; if you needed money to pay your rent he would give it to you and take you out to buy booze. He was a man you could always depend on for something if you needed it, as a musician.[27]

Ellis Burton, gangster and owner of the Yellow Front Café in the mid-1920s and early 1930s, also took care of Kansas City musicians. He "was the kind of guy that just liked musicians, and he had music around the clock." Sam Price, vocalist and dancer with Alphonso Trent's band, recounted Burton's contribution to the Kansas City jazz scene:

> He had a gambling joint, and he'd have music from eight o'clock in the morning until like about two o'clock in the afternoon. And then from two till eight, and around eight o'clock at night he'd have two bands alternating until the next morning. Just like Monte Carlo or Las Vegas. Continuous music, and he was good to musicians. If you went up to him and told him that you didn't have a job, that was right up his alley, 'cause he'd help you get a room, give you some food, give you some money, and really help you.[28]

Andy Kirk and the Clouds benefited from the stability of the Kaycee scene and in time acquired enough money with their steady engagement at the Pla-Mor and alternating gigs in other cities to pay off the fine they had been assessed in Oklahoma. According to John Williams, the band would play the Pla-Mor for four days, then go to Topeka and play three days. Then they'd play one day in St. Louis. These engagements supplied the band with enough revenue not only to cover their fines but also to maintain their households. But the time of happiness and prosperity would soon end.

On the last Tuesday of October 1929, Wall Street crashed, bringing major economic repercussions to working-class Americans and enter-

tainers. The effects of the crash were felt immediately in the black community, which was largely blue collar and directly hit by the sweeping
layoffs. The effects of "Black Tuesday" eventually trickled down not only
to the white community, which was forced to alter its lifestyle, but also
to the entertainment community.[29] Big-time vaudeville troupes, already
severely strained by network radio and the introduction of sound
movies, dissolved; diminishing patronage compelled theater owners to
close or eliminate more expensive live entertainment and turn to motion
pictures. The TOBA managed to outlast white vaudeville and was viable
into the early 1930s, but many of its theaters closed. In 1929 there were
eighty theaters in the circuit, but by 1932 most of them were showing
films only. Sherman Dudley, who had almost single-handedly galvanized
the circuit, was forced to sell his theaters and booking agency in 1929,
and within the next three years the TOBA network fell into ruin. The enthusiasm for jazz among whites, which had been spurred by the success
of white bandleaders such as Paul Whiteman, ended, and live entertainment fell into decline. Broadway theaters closed or became movie
houses, and orchestra jobs vanished as ballrooms closed. From 1929 to
1930 in New York alone, 105 dance halls closed, with the majority of
clubs in Minneapolis, Los Angeles, and Chicago following. Salaries for
dance hall work were now dependent on the number of people in the
house, and desperate managers "turned to the marathons and walka-
thons that created spectacles of endurance and pain in the dog-eat-dog
world of the Depression."[30] But the larger national scenario had little if
no effect on the Kansas City jazz scene, which sustained itself through
the activities of the city's nightlife.

*   *   *

During the late 1920s, Mary, not an official member of the Kirk band,
would sit in occasionally, stirring audiences with her boogie-woogie renditions. She spent the majority of her time in Kansas City going to the
many cabarets of the Eighteenth and Vine district. Accompanied by two
young women known now only as Lucille and Louise, Mary explored the
nightclubs of Kansas City and gained a reputation among both native
and out-of-town musicians for playing "boss piano." Mary seemingly
soaked up the blues, boogie-woogie, ragtime, and jazz that were heard
nightly in the cutting contests and on several occasions participated in

some of these jam sessions. In 1954 Mary recalled a famous jam session that included the saxophonists Coleman Hawkins, Lester Young, Ben Webster, and Herschel Evans.

> The Cherry Blossom was a new night club richly deco-rated in Japanese style even to the beautiful little brown-skinned waitress. The word went around that Hawkins was in the Cherry Blossom and within about half an hour there were Lester Young, Ben Webster, Herschel Evans, Herman Walder and one or two unknown tenors piling in the club to blow. Coleman didn't know the Kaycee tenor men were so terrific and he couldn't get himself together though he played all morning. I hap-pened to be nodding that night, and around 4 A.M. I awoke to hear someone pecking on my screen. I opened the window on Ben Webster. He was saying, "Get up pussycat. We're jamming and all the pianists are tired out now. Hawkins has got his shirt off and is still blow-ing. You got to come down." Sure enough when we got there Hawkins was in his singlet taking turns with the Kaycee men. It seems he had run into something he didn't expect. . . . When at last he gave up, he got straight in his car and drove to St. Louis.[31]

As a pianist Mary would be greatly influenced by the "happenings" of Kansas City's nightlife, but the Kirk band shaped her evolution into a composer and arranger. Through trial and error and instructional ses-sions with Kirk, Mary learned the basics of jazz arranging. For an hour each day, Kirk came to Mary's house and she watched how he voiced his arrangements. "Andy knew that I had ideas—I was writing all along but I couldn't write it down. I'd give them ideas during the rehearsals. Maybe they wanted to play a song like 'Singing in the Rain' and I'd say, 'Well, lis-ten to this.' Andy would take it down real fast but sometimes they didn't at all." After several weeks, Mary decided to write her own arrangement. Although problematic, the composition showed much promise. Kirk cor-rected the voicings of several of the instruments and Mary began writing at a feverish pace. But the two often heard the music differently and Mary struggled to re-create the sounds she heard in her head.

I discovered chords and Andy used to say to me, "You can't do that. It's against the rules of writing music." I said, "But I hear a sixth in this chord." He said, "But you can't do it." I said, "I'm going to do it." I did the arrangement of, before I did "Walkin'," trumpet and three saxophones. We only had three saxophones and one trumpet and trombone, something like that. So what I did, I put a trumpet in and I had three saxophones to play four-part harmony. He kept telling me it was against the rules of the chord. In that year I guess it was, but I was hearing—I found these things on the piano and I said, this will sound good—it sounds good here. After a while I started arranging it.[32]

These early attempts to convert notes from her head to paper were often awkward, but the band continued to aid Mary in her development. In the case of "Little Joe from Chicago," which will be discussed at greater length in a later chapter, the initial arrangement consisted of passages that "sounded so funny [that] everyone went into hysterics." Although upset by the reaction of the band, Mary continued to experiment with new ideas, and eventually her arrangements would become the essence of Kirk's mature swing sound.[33]

*　　*　　*

In the 1920s many of the white-owned record companies took an interest in blues and jazz. Their marketing strategy was geared primarily toward blacks, with the intent to create a recording industry based on recordings of blues singers like Ma Rainey and Bessie Smith and bands such as Joe Oliver's and Bennie Moten's. "Race records" was the term used to describe phonographic recordings of black performers that were marketed to black audiences from 1921 to 1959. Over time, these series came to include recordings of sermons, classic and rural blues, jug bands, and gospel music.[34] Okeh Records was the first company to produce several series of these recordings, and their success inspired competing companies to release their own series of race records, including Paramount's 1200s, Columbia's 14000s, and Vocalion's 100s. These series focused initially on artists in Chicago, New York, and the smaller markets of Cincinnati, Ohio, and Richmond, Indiana. Kansas City was largely ignored until Bennie Moten's band gained recognition outside the city and launched a successful but short-lived recording career. In 1929 Jack Kapp and Dick Voynow, recording executives for the Brunswick label and its subsidiary Vocalion, went to Kansas City in hopes of signing black dance bands that could contribute to their growing catalogue of race records. Both labels had started in the race record game much later than Okeh, with Vocalion beginning its race record series in 1926 and Brunswick the preceding year.[35] But the launches were successful and in 1929 the labels were actively looking for another Kansas City band that could rival the success of Bennie Moten's Orchestra, which was recording with a competitive label. Kapp and Voynow heard about the Clouds' popularity and approached the band about the possibility of recording. A private audition was quickly arranged. On the day of the audition, all band members assembled at the Pla-Mor, except the pianist, Marion Jackson. He and Claude Williams had gone to Topeka, Kansas, and drank and partied. On their way back to Kansas City, they crashed the car and Jackson was injured badly. Concerned that this would be their one and only opportunity, Kirk asked John Williams to call in Mary to fill in on piano. Mary's ability to play anything at any time not only helped the band gain a recording contract with Brunswick/Vocalion but also impressed the bandleader. Kirk would later state that "no one had the wildest idea she'd be a big factor in our landing an excellent two-year recording contract, or wilder yet, that she would make jazz history."[36] Yet he retained Jackson as the band's pianist, explaining that he believed the hard life of "one-nighters" would be difficult for a woman. Kirk's justification for retaining Jackson is fraught with contradiction, because by this time he was fully aware of Mary's touring schedule on the TOBA circuit. It is more likely that Kirk felt a certain amount of loyalty to Jackson and thought that he needed the income more than Mary, who was married to John Williams. Whatever the reason, Kirk was adamant about keeping Jackson and went forward with the recording dates.

The first recording session with Vocalion was planned for November 7, 1929, at radio station KMBV in Kansas City. Jackson did show up for the session but was replaced by Mary when Jack Kapp insisted that she play. Kirk would later state that "because Mary Lou made the audition I felt it only fair that she make the record date too," but sources indicated that his initial intentions were the complete opposite.[37] Nevertheless, Jackson was replaced and the band recorded "Blues Clarinet Stomp" and Mary's first arrangement, "Mess-A-Stomp." The next session, for Brunswick on November 11, 1929, yielded another Mary original, "Froggy Bottom" (Brunswick 01211), which had already proven to be quite popular with audiences, and a collaborative effort between Kirk and Mary called "Corky Stomp" (Brunswick 01211).[38] Although released separately, the tunes "Froggy Bottom" and "Mess-A-Stomp" proved to be quite successful in the retail market.

The recordings reveal some important aspects of Mary's early compositional style. Both compositions are rooted in the Kansas City approach of constructing performances on short, tuneful riffs with an emphasis on laid-back swing rhythms. "Mess-A-Stomp," although written as an up-tempo piece, is rhythmically bogged down by the band's inability to swing in a relaxed manner. Following a short introduction by the horns and a noticeable rhythmic break, the clarinet enters with the main melody, accompanied by the horns and a rhythm section comprising banjo, piano, and tuba. Although the drums are included in the ensemble they are hardly audible on the extant recordings. Another rhythmic break shifts the song into a banjo solo accompanied by Kirk's very noticeable tuba. The saxes enter with a short riff that leads into a trumpet solo, accompanied by clarinet, saxes, and rhythm section. Mary enters with an unaccompanied piano solo that is a synthesis of the boogie-woogie and stride piano styles. Mary's mastery of the stride style is prominent and she often punctuates the syncopated melodies played by the right hand with heavy left-hand motives. This interaction between a strong swinging left hand and a melodically syncopated right hand is characteristic of Mary's style.

The ensemble returns with a new melodic motive, and the drummer, for the first time, is audible in the form of rhythmic cymbal punctuations. Following a short banjo solo, the horns and the saxes exchange melodic material in a short section of call and response before the performance ends with the ensemble playing a final sustained chord and cymbal crash. There are two unifying sections of this composition: the soulful trumpet and piano solos. These solos alter the mood of the arrangement by changing it from the static rhythm of the opening section—with the clarinet soloist and the ensemble—to the last chorus, consisting of the call-and-response passages between the brass and reed sections.

It is in this early arrangement that one hears Mary—whose style had been groomed in the blues she heard as a young child, the vaudeville shows of the TOBA, and the jam sessions and nightlife of Kansas City—attempting to fuse these idioms into the "sweet" band rhythms and harmonies that had defined Kirk's sound until this point. This was the beginning of the "loosening" of the Kirk sound. The difficulty the band had in swinging the written rhythm is evidence that Mary's arrangement set rhythmic requirements that the band had not encountered in previous arrangements.

On "Froggy Bottom," the necessary rhythmic adjustments were made, primarily because of the dominance of Mary's piano. The performance offers early insight into the formulation of Mary's piano style, which displayed remnants of Earl Hines's approach as she consistently broke up the "stride time" in the left hand with displaced chords and disjunct harmonies, "walking" tenths, right-hand octaves, and tremolos; also heard is her trademark style of stomping rhythmic accents in the left hand (à la Jack Howard). But what is most evident in these early recordings is Mary's desire to transfer the soul and emotion of the blues, boogie-woogie, and other black vernacular forms to big band arrangements. These approaches and others discussed later would position the Kirk band in the continuum between the New Orleans style of jazz, the Kansas City approaches of Bennie Moten and later Count Basie, and the emerging East Coast style of swing. They would earn Mary the distinction of being one of the most innovative arrangers of the swing era, but they would also cause disagreements between Mary and Kirk.

Following this recording session, Kirk set out to improve the overall sound of the band. With the popularity of "Froggy Bottom" and "Mess-A-Stomp," Kirk noted that the band's appeal rested mainly in its crisp brass section, the ability of the rhythm section to swing consistently, and its overall appeal to dancers. In previous arrangements Kirk had managed to combine the jazz approaches of southwestern bands with an easy and appealing beat, but Mary's arrangements had offered a slightly different musical perspective. These differences in approaches would widen the gap between Kirk and Mary as he worked to become one of the leading "sweet" bandleaders and she wanted to remain true to her roots of blues and jazz.

Kirk's musical intentions were fueled by the anxieties and emotional despondency that the Depression years created. The result was a cultural crisis that altered musical preferences. Jazz, which provided the soundtrack to the decadence and spirited living of the 1920s, became the cultural scapegoat of the 1930s and 1940s. One writer declared, "The public, suffering from retribution for material overindulgence and neglect of spiritual values, was in no mood for the reckless promptings of jazz." Most bands, including Kirk's, responded by turning to "personality leaders" and "successful formulas" that "soothed audiences with romantic ballads set to muted trumpets, sweet saxophones and subdued drums."[39] Kirk knew that it was sweet bands and not the rhythmically driven hot bands that were working during the worst of the Depression. It was the subdued dinner music and the dancing at plush hotels that was sustaining them, not the "jaunty extroverted" approach of 1920s jazz. This conflict would continue until Mary's departure from the band in 1941, but neither could deny that the Clouds' popularity was increasing. In 1930 Fletcher Henderson happened by the Pla-Mor during a visit to Kansas City and was impressed with the Clouds' sound. He thought the Clouds would be perfect to replace him at the Roseland ballroom in New York while his orchestra toured the Midwest. Henderson immediately wired Lou Brecker, owner of the Roseland, and recommended that he hire the band. Brecker took Henderson's recommendation, and the band was booked for a six-week engagement.

With the closing of many Deep South theaters on the TOBA circuit, urban theaters in the North assumed a more important role in the careers of black performers. Harlem, already considered the mecca of the black northward migration, became even more important to aspiring entertainers. Before the Depression the New York jazz scene had held much promise. In the 1920s the jazz capital had shifted from Chicago to Harlem and later Broadway, because of Chicago's enforcement of Prohibition in nightclubs. Jazz musicians headed to New York, but the excitement of the scene in the late 1920s was soon eclipsed by the uncertainty of life in Depression America. East Side speakeasies closed, but Harlem nightlife continued. Although the "black and tan clubs" of 1920s Harlem lost much of their clientele, theaters and ballrooms continued to offer the best in black entertainment.

The Roseland, Arcadia, and Savoy ballrooms were the more prominent of the spots in New York where dancers and audiences could cut their teeth on swing. Located on West 51st Street in New York, the Roseland ballroom, following its opening in 1919, quickly became the center for dancing and hot music in the city. Although its clientele was mainly white during the early years, black bands were booked consistently.

Fletcher Henderson, whose orchestra served as the house band from 1924 to 1942, made the club famous with his battles with the Sam Lanin band, which played on the opposite bandstand. The bands that played the New York ballrooms catered to the dancing tastes of the audiences, so during their early years not much jazz was actually played. This, however, did not prevent rivalries between the bands from forming. Weekly battles between the bands inhabiting the bandstands provided dancers with their swing "fix" and greatly influenced the evolution of the genre. The Kirk band was soon initiated into the East Coast school of swing, in which bands had to be capable of providing dancers with swinging rhythms. Arriving in New York in January 1930, the band settled into a six-week stint that pitted it against Milt Shaw's band for two weeks, the Casa Loma Orchestra for two weeks, and Freddy Bergen's band for two weeks. New York audiences embraced the band, which was largely unknown outside the southwestern region. The Clouds had cleared a considerable professional hurdle with their successful engagement at the Roseland.

With their newfound fame, Kirk and the Clouds were called in for three more recording sessions in Chicago with Brunswick in 1930. On their way to Chicago, they played a series of one-nighters in places such as Columbia and Hannibal, Missouri, and LaSalle, Illinois. When the band arrived in Chicago, in April 1930, Mary was not with them, as she had returned to Kansas City. Both Kapp and Voynow wanted to know immediately where Mary was, claiming that they "liked her style." Mary was sent for. Although tired when she arrived in Chicago, Mary went straight to the studio and recorded the tracks with the band. Once again, the band recorded one of Mary's original compositions, as well as pieces made famous by other bands. The session consisted of Mary's arrangement "Mary's Idea" (Brunswick 4863), King Oliver's "Snag It" (Brunswick 4878), and Henderson's "Sweet and Hot" (Brunswick 4878). The sessions for Brunswick would go into late 1930 and yield several recordings under the appellations Andy Kirk and His Twelve Clouds of Joy and Seven Little Clouds of Joy, a septet made up of Cloud members.

These sessions also yielded two solo performances by Mary. Mary recorded two original compositions, "Drag 'Em," which she described as a blues, and "Night Life," an up-tempo piece that highlighted her ability to improvise in the Harlem stride style during break periods from the Clouds sessions. These two compositions would later be marketed as solo recordings and marked Mary's first appearance on wax as a solo artist. At the time she had no sense of how popular these tracks would be and never raised the question of royalties. (These recordings were redistributed and included in an album of "barrelhouse piano" during the 1940s, but Mary was never paid. Shortly after their release, Mary threatened legal action in order to stop the redistribution.) As a marketing ploy, Kapp, figuring that "Mary" was too plain a name to put on the label, added "Lou" to her name. From that point until her death in 1981, Mary would be known professionally as Mary Lou Williams.

Despite the interest these early recordings drew, the Clouds would not record again until 1936. They set out on a tour of one-nighters and college dates across Pennsylvania, Ohio, and upstate New York before once again reaching New York City late in 1930.

Chapter 4

UNTIL THE REAL THING
COMES ALONG:
THE ANDY KIRK YEARS (1931–42)

Though she had been used as a novelty in the Kirk band before 1930, Mary continued to gain recognition as a pianist. Her swinging right hand and strong left hand captured the attention of waning audiences whose senses were often dulled by the sweet compositions of the band. More than anything, Kirk wanted the Clouds to step out of the category of regional band to become a dance orchestra of national prominence, especially as the music began moving out of cultural marginality to mainstream acceptability. The swing or big band movement is considered to have hit its peak in the middle to late 1930s. However, as early as the late 1920s, the seeds of the movement were already being planted in the arrangements played by the orchestras of Fletcher Henderson, Don

Redman, Bennie Moten, and Duke Ellington. New York and the south-western dance bands and "society" orchestras were already experiment-ing with new forms of dance music that borrowed from the pre-jazz tra-ditions of blues and ragtime and the early jazz traditions of New Orleans and Chicago in the early 1930s. The music would come to reflect a new sense of purpose and identity in the younger generation of musicians, and its rhythmic, harmonic, and melodic elements gradually bridged the musical and philosophical perspectives of black and white America.

In New York the separate and unequal worlds of Harlem and other boroughs of New York met in a type of musical copulation on the dance floors and bandstands of the Cotton Club, Connie's Inn, and the Rose-land, Arcadia, and Savoy ballrooms. Young Americans, black and white, found an escape from the anxieties of early post-Depression America in the emerging dance culture and the music of black Americans. White in-terest in black culture, especially dance and theater, was signaled by the success of the Broadway production *Shuffle Along* (1927) and the popu-larity of the Charleston, the shimmy, and the Black Bottom, all dances created in the black community. Harlem in the late 1920s was "a hot-house of fervent dance activity that would foreshadow the swing era and the popularity of big bands," and whites easily legitimized their interest in black music and culture by deeming it a part of the larger New York experience. As Ted Gioia explained, "The procurement of black enter-tainment for white audiences soon became, inevitably and fortuitously, a mini-industry, a burgeoning microcosm of New York nightlife as a whole. Their appetites whetted by these dances and shows, white audi-ences began seeking even greater verisimilitude in their samples of Afri-can American culture." [1] Unfortunately, by the time the swing movement was in full bloom, these cultural and musical links with black America would be suppressed or completely ignored.

By the early 1930s, two varying traditions of big band music were de-veloping: the New York tradition and the southwestern tradition. The New York tradition evolved out of the dance band and society orchestra traditions of the early 1900s. The architects of this style, which focused on brilliant technique, a clean sound, and emotional lightness, were James Reese Europe, who began to synthesize "society" music and jazz shortly before his death in 1919; Don Redman; and later Fletcher Henderson. Arrangers and bandleaders looked to popular songs of the day as the basis for their arrangements and often sacrificed the creative efforts of musicians by almost totally eliminating improvisation. The music of the southwestern bands, as discussed in chapter 3, operated out of a different philosophical approach, with its marriage of ragtime, blues, and dance music, a loose structure, and its emphasis on the swing rhythm and improvisation. However, both traditions would contribute to the new jazz aesthetic, commonly known as swing, that was taking America by storm by the mid-1930s.

By 1931 it was apparent that America was entering a new economic and social period, and so was Mary. Incapable of ignoring the contribution Mary was making to the band any longer, Kirk officially made Mary a member of the Twelve Clouds of Joy that year. In time, it would prove to be the best business decision the bandleader ever made. Mary began playing full-time with the band while the group was serving as the pit orchestra for the Pearl Theater in Philadelphia. Kirk decided to use two pianos during the performance—Mary on a small upright and the regular pianist on the grand. Over these two pianos Kirk built an enclosure, which held the drums, then played by Ben Thigpen. Kirk chose to build his performances around this novelty, thinking that the audiences would take to the spectacle, but for Mary the idea and its effect were somewhat disconcerting. "It was tough going; I was used to a large piano but our regular man, Jack, had the Steinway and I was doing my best with what seemed like a two-octaves 'Tom Thumb.' And I could hear practically nothing but the thunder of drums overhead. This routine had lasted about a week when Jack failed to make the show one night. I graduated to the grand—and solo honours—and it seems my playing surprised everyone in the theatre including Sam Stiefle, who owned the place." Mary's talent was unquestionable, but her reliability and consistency made the decision to replace Jack easy. Following an argument with Stiefle, which yielded no change in Kirk's position, Jack was nonetheless given two weeks' pay and a ticket home.[2] Mary officially became the band's arranger and pianist, marking the first time since Lil Hardin Armstrong joined Joe King Oliver's Creole Jazz Band and later Louis Armstrong's Hot Five and Seven during the 1920s that a woman instrumentalist held a central position in a mainstream jazz band. Mary would become one of the few female jazz instrumentalists to escape the "ghetto" of all-female orchestras and novelty groups in the 1930s and 1940s, and her presence on the bandstand countered widely held assumptions about women's abilities to participate in jazz as instrumentalists. Although the stint at the Pearl Theater provided steady work for the Clouds, Kirk worried that it would diminish the band's popularity with audiences outside Philadelphia. When he got an offer to perform at the Winwood Beach Park Ballroom near Kansas City, the band returned to that city.

When the Clouds got back in late 1930, they found the music scene to be more active than before and more receptive to the jazz sounds that so many cities in the Midwest were rejecting. Kansas City was not beset by many of the racial problems experienced in other cities, and musicians from all over the South and Southwest found their way there, where they and their talents were accepted. The interest of record companies such as Decca, Vocalion, and Brunswick in the burgeoning Kansas City jazz scene only intensified Kirk's desire to achieve the level of national recognition that Bennie Moten, another prominent Kansas Citian, Fletcher Henderson, and Don Redman had received. But Kirk's approach to swing was much different from the style introduced by Moten and later perfected by Count Basie. Kirk had managed to combine the jazz ideas of the southwestern bands with the easy beat and fluid articulation of the George Morrison Orchestra, of which he had been a member. Morrison, as described by Gunther Schuller, was one of many black musicians at the turn of the century who did not make the full transition into jazz. His early musical aspirations had been in classical music, but the racism of the concert tradition had put an end to his dreams. He formed in Denver one of the premier dance orchestras, whose repertory consisted of waltzes and sentimental popular ballads. Kirk was just one of the notable jazz musicians to serve in the band, which at one time boasted of having Jelly Roll Morton, Jimmie Lunceford, and Alphonso Trent as members. Because the orchestra played primarily for white society dances, it never abandoned the "sweet" approach that defined most white bands in favor of the "hot" rhythms of jazz. Instead, it mostly played in a two-beat style and with little if any improvisation. It was this rhythmic approach, which rejected the faster four-beat style, that influenced Kirk's approach to jazz.[3] In time it became apparent that, unlike the East Coast bands of Henderson and Ellington and later Count Basie, the Clouds aimed not "to win battles of music but to please dancers."[4]

* * *

When the Winwood Beach Park Ballroom closed for the winter season, Kirk accepted a sixteen-week run at the famous Savoy Ballroom in

New York. The ballroom was a landmark in Harlem, encompassing an entire city block from 140th Street to 141st Street. The opening of the Savoy had considerably changed New York's social patterns. It was the first fully integrated ballroom in the city, bringing black and white bands and dancers together. There was constant music offered, as the ballroom featured two or three bands a night. It consisted of a two-hundred-by-fifty-foot dance floor, two bandstands, and a retractable stage, but its popularity was established by the jazz dance craze that was started there. In a short time, the Savoy had become the most popular ballroom in Harlem and had earned the distinction of being the "Home of Happy Feet" and the "birthplace of the Lindy Hop." Mary, who knew of the importance of playing at the ballroom, was overwhelmed but musically invigorated by the experience. Mary played the tunes Kirk called, but occasionally when the action was waning and the crowds wanted more, Kirk would call on Mary to play tunes such as "Froggy Bottom" or "Mary's Idea," which were guaranteed to ignite the dancers. Mary knew from the moment the Clouds arrived in New York that the band was on its way, because success at the Savoy generally meant national recognition. Indeed, the success at the Savoy led to a tour of other eastern states. But the wide-stretching arm of racism and the economic fallout from the Depression would halt Kirk's pursuit of recognition and fame, just as it hit other black bands.

The experience of most black swing bands during the 1930s was much different from that of their white counterparts. The popularity of swing beyond the speakeasies, nightclubs, and jazz sessions of Kansas City and Harlem reinforced racial divisions within the jazz scene. Black bands were almost never offered jobs at prominent hotels or on commercial radio programs, and in the few instances when they were, they were often the victims of professional jealousy, as noted in chapter 3. Black bands were frequently excluded from advertising spots because hotel owners and radio sponsors feared southern backlash against the promotion of prominent Negroes. Thus, black bands had to rely on hit records and touring to make their names and fortunes. But touring did not ensure the level of success that jukebox play could bring. The jukebox, which propelled record sales in the 1930s and 1940s, became the measure of achievement, but race records and the mechanisms of their marketing made it almost impossible for black bands to crack the jukebox market, because white business owners, the major proprietors of the machines, refused to buy recordings by black bands. The race record initiative, which had seemed like the agent that would elevate black talent, had unfortunately created a segregated market that excluded the music of black bands from the mainstream. Although some, such as Ella Fitzgerald and Chick Webb ("A Tisket a Tasket"), scored crossover hits, the majority of black bands were confined to a musical "ghetto" that denied them professional opportunities. Hollywood and the popularity of movies in the 1930s and 1940s brought exposure to many white bandleaders, but black bands were not given the same opportunities. Those who managed to break the color barrier in early Hollywood, such as Ellington and Armstrong, simply played their instruments or accompanied white stars and in some disturbing cases were cast in roles that only perpetuated the stereotyped images of blacks.[5] The "whitewashing" of swing by the media in the 1930s dictated that most of the black bands stayed on the road doing endless one-nighters in order to sustain themselves financially. The Kirk band was no exception.

Mary described those early years with the Kirk band as her "starvation days." The band spent the majority of its time traveling and playing one-nighters and at times was denied pay by unscrupulous promoters and club owners. The band would often "play long strings of one-nighters, traveling perhaps 300 miles between cities after playing. You know those 20's cars didn't have heaters or windshield wipers. In winter, the roads were sheets of ice. There were some terrible accidents and delays. We'd arrive in town too late to play and we'd be stranded there without the money to buy gasoline to get to our next gig. Sometimes after we played, Kirk would come back with his head down and we'd know we hadn't been paid."[6] Years later Mary would recount the band's attempts to survive during these times, which included relying on local musicians for meals or occasionally raiding a cornfield. Conditions grew so bad during the early 1930s that on one occasion Mary had to make a dress out of a hotel's curtains, because her clothes had worn out. "It was pretty horrible now that I look back on it," she said. "But then we'd have fun, we were like a family."[7] It was the camaraderie, the family-like support system of the jazz scene, and the Pendergast political "machine" in Kansas City that enabled the Kirk band to remain intact even through the Depression. Refuge was found once again in Kansas City.

Following a short-lived and financially unsuccessful tour of several eastern states in late 1930, the band was featured at the El Torrean and

Fairyland Park ballrooms and managed to pull in a good amount of money. The bustling scene in Kansas City created an illusion that all was well in the Midwest and Southwest, and in 1932 the band left the city on a tour of theaters in those regions. But life outside Kansas City proved to be quite difficult, and despite their best efforts, the band members faced financial hardship as theaters began closing. When theaters on the Malco Theatre tour closed in 1933, the Clouds found themselves stranded without future bookings or income. The band managed to secure a few small bookings and raise enough money to make it to Memphis, John Williams's hometown. They hoped to find employment at the Fair Park Ballroom, where only a few years earlier John and Mary had worked. The band eventually replaced Joe Sander's ensemble and earned enough money to return to Kansas City.

The Kansas City they returned to was still unaffected by the Depression, and it seemed as if the liquor poured more freely and patrons danced more than ever. Pendergast had managed the impossible by creating a financial windfall that sustained the city. Kirk insinuated himself back into the club scene, and before long the band was booked into many of the top dance halls of the city, including the Vanity Fair, the Pla-Mor, and the Fairyland Park. During this period Kirk began adding to the band's personnel and reshaping its overall sound. Kansas City had some of the best musicians to offer, and in 1932 Kirk added Irving Rudolph and Paul and Ben Webster to the group. In 1933 he heard the singer-dancer Pha Terrell singing at a nightclub and hired him on for a short road tour through Denver and Oklahoma. The new sound brought some welcome attention, and in 1934 the band was offered an opportunity for a nightly broadcast on the CBS radio network. The program was well received by audiences throughout Texas and neighboring states and greatly increased the popularity of the band.

Despite the Clouds' success with both black and white audiences, Kirk was still unable to convince Brunswick/Vocalion to let the band record music other than that marketed under their race records series. Since its music was popular with all types of audiences, Kirk thought that the band's recordings should reflect its diverse musical style. The addition of the new members to the band since the previous recording sessions had brought significant changes to the band's sound: Mary's piano had become the core of the Kirk rhythm section and her innovative arrangements provided an interesting link between black folk traditions, in the form of blues and boogie-woogie, and the sophisticated orchestra style pioneered by Redman, Henderson, and Ellington; the addition of Terrell had expanded the band's repertoire beyond dance music and opened up the possibility for the performance of romantic ballads; and Ben Webster's presence in the sax section brought completeness to the sound. But the executives would not budge; the race record market was too profitable to take a chance on recording a black band playing "sweet" music.

In 1934 the American branch of the British-owned Decca Record Company purchased the Brunswick and Vocalion pre-1932 catalogues. With Jack Kapp at the helm, the company continued to issue its "race series." Decca had acquired with the labels Fletcher Henderson, the Dorsey Brothers, and Count Basie, and it was interested in adding the Clouds to the roster as well. Although at the time the opportunity seemed ideal for Kirk and the Clouds, it would eventually prove to be a costly mistake for him and for Basie, who signed exploitive recording contracts that denied them royalty payments. The band continued touring throughout 1933 and 1934 and went through considerable personnel changes. Kirk traded Ben Webster to Fletcher Henderson for Lester Young, who was soon replaced by Dick Wilson, whom Kirk had met during a stint in Cincinnati. Kirk, wanting to ensure the band's future, signed up the agent Joe Glaser, who headed the Associated Booking Corporation and managed Louis Armstrong, as manager of the band. In no time, Glaser managed to book the Clouds at the Astoria Nightclub in Baltimore for two weeks, which provided Kirk with an open door to the New York scene. After the two-week engagement, Kirk and the Clouds traveled on to New York to meet with Kapp about recording for Decca.

* * *

The East Coast swing scene had grown profoundly in its influence since the Clouds' last performance there in the early 1930s. Black swing bands had come to represent the flowering of black culture in the North. With New York as the newly established capital of jazz, bands based there acted as traveling representatives of modernity as they toured the nation, performed on radio and recordings, and played for dancers at countless ballrooms and clubs. When the Cotton Club and Connie's Inn, the two major establishments supporting jazz in the early 1930s, moved downtown and as upper-class "slumming" in Harlem declined, the black youth of New York turned to the music of the Apollo Theatre, which had by the mid-1930s emerged as the pinnacle of black variety entertainment onstage, and to the Savoy Ballroom for solidarity. The migration of Kansas City bands to the city marked a regeneration of black dance music, as these aggregations created an atmosphere that allowed black patrons to "stomp" away their personal and social troubles. Bands such as the Clouds and Count Basie's orchestra became models of hope in the black community and provided audiences with a link to their cultural roots. According to Lewis Erenberg:

> Rather than losing their "blackness" to sophisticated arrangements and precision playing, the big bands continued to play ceremonial roles in the black community. They presided as ministers of the Saturday night function in dancehalls, theaters, and clubs nationwide. When Ellington, for example, built a band style on the "growling" or speaking nature of the instruments, he was including blacks in the tradition of "speaking" instrumentation that went back to Africa, whether blacks knew it or not. Count Basie's heavy use of call and response in powerhouse fashion resonated with the deepest elements of the black religious experience. Whatever their outward appearances, both Ellington and Basie represented a tradition of reveling—rooted in the blues tradition— that glorified the experience of blacks apart from the work-driven white world that often excluded them.[8]

This was never more evident than in the audiences Kirk played to during this stint. Mary's incorporation of the blues, boogie-woogie, and the call-and-response tradition into the popular song format and her use of memorable chord progressions and ensemble passages in arrangements brought her to the attention of other bandleaders, who were eager to draw the young woman away from the Kirk band.

In 1936, more than six years after their first recording session, Andy Kirk and His Twelve Clouds of Joy finally recorded their first series of race records for Decca. The lull in Kirk's recording career may well be accounted for by the economic fallout of the Depression. In the years following the crash, record companies suffered considerably. With the decline of phonograph sales, companies were inundated with a growing surplus of records. There were many attempts to boost record purchases, including lowering the price from 75 to 35 cents, but the industry still could not compete with free and accessible radio. Columbia Records, which had dominated the industry in the 1920s, went bankrupt, and Paramount folded. The smaller labels consolidated into three major firms: Decca, RCA Victor, and Columbia. By the end of 1930, a year after the Clouds' first recording sessions, most of these companies had eliminated their race record series. The 1936 sessions with Decca would prove to be pivotal in securing the Clouds' place in jazz history and Mary's place as one of the swing era's greatest arrangers. Since 1930, the band had undergone several major personnel changes, but the group had maintained its musical integrity. The aggregation now included Pha Terrell, on vocals; Paul King, Earl Thomson, and Harry Lawson on trumpets; the trombonist Ted Donnelly; John Williams, John Harrington, and Dick Wilson on reeds; the violinist Claude Williams; Andy Kirk on baritone saxophone; and a rhythm section that consisted of Mary Lou, the guitarist Ted Robinson, the bassist Booker Collins, and Ben Thigpen on drums. Mary wrote arrangements for the sessions at a furious pace. She claimed that she "must have done twenty in one week," including "Cloudy," featuring Terrell on vocals (Decca 1208), "Corky" (Decca 772), "Froggy Bottom" (Columbia DB-5000)—the first two were new arrangements and the last a completely different tune with the same title as the 1929 recording—and "Steppin' Pretty" (Decca 931) and "Walkin' and Swingin'" (Columbia DB/MC-5023). In the weeks before the recording session, Mary would not leave her room and had her meals brought to her.

"Walkin' and Swingin'," which featured the tenor saxophonist Dick Wilson, employed an innovative combination of a trumpet with four saxes to create the sound of five reeds. "Corky," a reworking of the band's 1929 recording "Corky Stomp," reflects how the band's sound was beginning to yield to the new form of swing that black bands were developing during this period. For this version, Mary replaced the static, clumsy rhythm of the previous version, which was better suited to the tuba-banjo combination of early bands, with a more laid-back swing rhythm that is established by the guitar, the bass, and the drummer's use of the brushes. The melody, presented by the clarinet initially in the lower range, is often offset by brass call and response with the unusual combination of three saxes and trumpet in harmony. Following an ensemble passage, the clarinet returns with a solo in the higher register and a duplication of the call and response from the previous chorus. Mary enters with the piano solo that directly borrows from the melody. Her left hand, which dominated so many of her solos up to this point, is more tempered, and her right hand takes the lead with rapidly moving scalular motives. The entire performance is an indication of how Mary reconceptualized existing material and created a seemingly new composition. "Froggy Bottom," also recorded by the Kirk band in 1929, became a solo composition newly titled "Overhand (The New Froggy Bottom)." The first session with Decca on March 2, 1936, yielded "Walkin' and Swingin'," "Moten's Swing," and "Lotta Sax Appeal" (Decca 1946). The next day, March 3, the band recorded another Williams arrangement, entitled "Git" (Decca 931), and "All the Jive Is Gone" (Decca 744). The session on March 4, 1936, produced three of Mary Lou's arrangements: "Froggy Bottom," "Bearcat Shuffle" (Decca 1046), and "Steppin' Pretty."

Despite Kapp's excitement over the recorded sessions, Kirk was still unhappy with being limited to "hot" jazz selections. He wanted to record material other than race music. Decca, more than the other majors, still recruited black bands for the sole purpose of recording uninhibited swing. Because of the restrictive nature of the race record market, record companies felt it best to record "hot" arrangements that would be received better by black consumers.[9] Kirk, who wanted more than ever to maintain his connection with the band's "sweet" sound, pushed the subject of recording new material that the band had been working on. Kapp listened to the bandleader's suggestion, but he wanted the band to record "Christopher Columbus," a tune that Fletcher Henderson had made famous months earlier.

When Kirk pushed the issue, Kapp responded, "What's the matter with you? You've got something good going for you. Why do you want to do what the white boys are doing?" Kirk recalled, "Right then I saw his commercial motives, saw why he had originally wanted to record us in Kansas City. It was for the race market only. He specifically wanted us to make things like 'Froggy Bottom,' 'Blues Clarinet Stomp,' and numbers like that."[10] The band agreed to record "Christopher Columbus" (Decca 729), but only if Kapp agreed to hear the other material. After the playback of the song, Kirk reminded Kapp of their agreement. Kapp relented and the band played a ballad that was based on a tune called "A

Slave Song," taken from the unsuccessful musical *Blackbirds*. Kirk described the genesis of the song: "Three kids with ukuleles hustled from one club to another singing and playing it and all the Kansas City bands picked it up. Harriet Calloway [no relation to Cab] put words to it." [11] Kapp agreed to record the piece, but not without some alterations. Sammy Chan and Saul Chapman were called in to write new lyrics and on April 2, 1936, the tune, renamed "Until the Real Thing Comes Along," was recorded. [12] The record opened the door for other tunes in a similar vein to be recorded by the band, including "What'll I Tell My Heart" and a tribute to Mary Lou featuring Harry Mills on vocals called "The Lady Who Swings the Band." Both were recorded on December 9, 1936.

The 1936 recording of these tunes increased Kirk's record sales substantially. In fact, sales increased from ten thousand to one hundred thousand units. "Real Thing" widened the Clouds' audience and was the band's "real breakthrough from race records." The success of the recording drew much-desired attention, and later that year the band was contracted for a stint at the famed Apollo Theatre in Harlem. Advertisements for the event exclaimed that "no orchestra has received such acclaim during the current season as this one. They established attendance records in theaters in other parts of the country and are certain to repeat at the Apollo." [13] It was clear that the group was rising to a new level of popularity—one that required a new perspective outside the standard representation of blacks.

During the early 1930s, band agencies had changed their role in the careers of jazz bands. These organizations, which acted as impersonal mediators between bandleaders and the industry, had grown in size and power. Larger agencies such as the William Morris Agency and General Artists concentrated primarily on white commercial bands, but smaller firms like those headed by Moe Gale, Irving Mills, and Joe Glaser specialized in black artists and bands. The success of "Until the Real Thing Comes Along" had brought the Clouds the type of attention that would ensure the lucrative bookings. Glaser and Kirk worked out an agreement that provided the bandleader with steady bookings while assigning 20 to 40 percent of the band's earnings to the agent. Glaser immediately signed the group to a contract for an off-and-on stint at the Grand Terrace in Chicago. The group's performances there were broadcast throughout the Midwest and the South and expanded their listening public.

From 1936 until 1939, the Twelve Clouds of Joy, alternating with the

Henderson, Armstrong, and Earl Hines bands at the Grand Terrace, continued to score major hits with Mary's arrangements and playing. They once again returned to New York, where they played the Savoy Ballroom for a second time. Dempsey Travis, a Savoy regular, recounted one performance:

> On the Sunday night that Kirk appeared at the Savoy, you could hardly get near the place. People must have been turned away by the thousands, because I got there around five that evening and there was a long line four abreast, waiting to get in. The dance was set to start at seven o'clock. It was held inside and it was hot as all get-out because there was no room for any air to stir any-place. People were jammed in that ballroom like boat people. The thrill of the evening for everyone occurred when Kirk's band began to play "Until the Real Thing Comes Along" and Pha Terrell opened his mouth and everyone went wild. . . . I've never had an experience like that in my life. When they played tunes like this, the Kirk band could be as smooth and soft as Guy Lombardo and his Royal Canadians. And when they played Mary Lou Williams' arrangements of "Froggy Bottom," and "Little Joe from Chicago," "Moten's Swing," and "Walkin' and Swingin'," they made Count Basie stand back and look. Mary Lou's arrangements gave the band a real Kansas City beat.[14]

During this tour Mary had the opportunity to meet the vocalist Billie Holiday, who was later featured with her at Café Society. It was evident by this time that Mary's arrangements, coupled with the popularity of the vocalist Pha Terrell and the tenor saxophonist Dick Wilson, were propelling the Clouds, not Andy Kirk, but the bandleader was still not willing to pay Mary more than the nominal fee of $3 per arrangement or half a cent net per record made.[15] His exploitation of her talent did not go unquestioned and other bandleaders took note. Earl Hines purchased "Walkin' and Swingin'" for $10, and "Casa Lomas" for $50. The Casa-lomas Orchestra purchased the same for $50. Kirk was not concerned about the popularity of Mary as an arranger as much as he was focused on promoting the band.

Kirk's broadcasts from Chicago sparked a tour of the South from 1937 until 1940. The Clouds averaged some fifty thousand miles a year, which consisted mainly of one-nighters in Georgia, Mississippi, Alabama, the Carolinas, Tennessee, Louisiana, Oklahoma, and Texas. It was during a stopover in Atlanta that Mary was reunited with her half brother Willis Scruggs. They had not seen each other for over twenty years, but Willis was well aware of his sister's accomplishments. Willis recalled: "When I learned the Kirk band was coming to Atlanta, I bought tickets to see Mary Lou. After the engagement I took her around town, showing her our old neighborhood and the home place." [16] Willis also took Mary to the home of her father, Joseph, who had abandoned her family at her birth. The meeting resulted in a confrontation between Joseph Scruggs and Mary, and she never saw him again.

Life was hard for black bands in the Jim Crow South, as they were not allotted the same luxuries as white bands. They faced opposition from white southerners who saw them as being "agitators and troublemakers" and who were more than happy to end a night's performance in violence. As Lewis Erenberg pointed out in *Swingin' the Dream,* well-dressed, professional black northern bands touring the South did not fit the racially subordinate image demanded by the system of segregation. So every means was taken to remind them of their inferiority. "Freedom of movement, decent shelter and the opportunity to eat and go to the bathroom in privacy and with dignity were denied at every turn." [17] Kirk would recount years later that "as long as we [blacks] were there as servants, we were treated well. On every job the message got to us in one way or another: Keep your place. You're here as servants. Please the customers and everything will be fine." [18]

Although the Clouds were denied lodging and basic amenities in many of the white establishments, these instances provided them with opportunities to interact with southern blacks. Kirk said that had it not been for segregation, "we'd have missed out on a whole country full of folks who put us up in their homes, cooked dinners and breakfasts for us, told us how to get along in Alabama and Mississippi, helped us out in trouble and became our friends for life." [19] These years were exceedingly hard for Mary; life on the road in Jim Crow America brought even more hardships to women than to men. Mary's ongoing battles with Kirk over the band's sound and her arrangements only worsened, and the band's wages were extremely low. Sidemen in the band were making only $8.50 a night and were paying $2 or $3 for a decent room, when it could be found. Mary thought the band members deserved at least $15 since they had managed, despite considerable hardships, to stay together. Despite all that she was contributing to the band, Mary was receiving only $75 a week, and Terrell received even less.[20] This discouraged Mary, and she began to lose interest in the band. She recalled that she "sometimes sat on the stand working crossword puzzles only playing with my left hand. Every place we played had to turn people away, and my fans must have been disappointed with my conduct. If they were, I wasn't bothering at the time."[21]

While Mary grew more disenchanted with the Kirk band, other bandleaders began calling on her services as an arranger. In 1937 she produced "In the Groove" (Brunswick 02441), a collaboration with Dick Wilson, and Benny Goodman asked Mary to write a blues for his band. The result was "Roll 'Em," which followed her successful "Camel Hop," Goodman's theme song for his radio show sponsored by Camel cigarettes. "Roll 'Em" is a boogie-woogie piece based on a very simple blues motive. It employs four-bar breaks by the soloist and full band during the first chorus. This approach is not unusual for boogie-woogie compositions: Pine Top Smith first employed it in his famous "Pine Top's Boogie Woogie." The composition is structured into four choruses. Following the first chorus, the second chorus enters with the trumpets offering motivic punctuations, then joining the whole band in the eight-measure melody, which has no repeating phrases. The third chorus begins with a four-bar break followed by an ensemble passage with saxes and trumpets. Only in the final chorus are the traditional call-and-response sequences between the saxes and the brass heard. Goodman's success with this composition rested on the boogie-woogie bass line. Although boogie-woogie was somewhat new to most big band listeners, John Hammond had popularized it by 1938 through his *From Spirituals to Swing* concert. For years, Goodman would include the piece in his repertory, and before long he returned to Mary for other arrangements.[22]

In addition to Goodman, Louis Armstrong, Earl Hines, Gus Arnheim, Glen Gray, and Tommy Dorsey called upon Mary for compositions. But tensions between Kirk, who took the band back into the studio in 1938, and Mary had not diminished. The band recorded Mary's "Twinklin'" (Decca 2483) and the unforgettable "Little Joe from Chicago" (Decca 1710), which Mary dedicated to Joe Glaser and Joe Louis during the August 2 session.[23] "Little Joe" is a composition based on a boogie-woogie riff introduced by Mary in the first chorus. It is the first widely known big band arrangement to successfully transfer the rhythm and emotion of the boogie-woogie tradition to the big band format. Although Mary had used the rhythmic structure of boogie-woogie in her solos during previous recordings and in "Roll 'Em," "Little Joe" is the first arrangement that transfers the rhythm to the entire ensemble, not to a single instrument. The riff becomes the ostinato bass line that is sustained throughout the performance. After the rhythm is established, the clarinet presents the main melody. This melody, in traditional fashion, is accented by countermelodies played by the reed and brass instruments. The third and fourth choruses of the composition, which is written in the AABA popular song form, feature the band members singing Mary's spirited lyrics in unison. A transition played by the trumpets leads into a sax solo, followed by the sixth chorus, featuring call-and-response passages executed by the saxes and the brass. With the boogie-woogie rhythm intact, the final chorus enters with the original melody, played by the clarinet.

The popularity of "Little Joe" further increased Mary's fame as an arranger and she received numerous offers to leave the Clouds. She turned them all down, explaining later that she felt a sense of loyalty to the band, but she was still unhappy. There are many accounts of Mary's tenure with the Andy Kirk band and of what ultimately led to her departure, but as early as 1939 Mary had begun working outside the Kirk organization. She and Pha Terrell continued to express their disappointment over the band's wages. Kirk's response, according to Mary, was to bring in new members who could enhance their popularity. Harold "Shorty" Baker was added on trumpet, Henry Wells on trombone and vocals, Floyd Smith on guitar, and the vocalist June Richmond. During the same year Mary and other Kirk band members played on a recording for Mildred Bailey orchestrated by John Hammond, and Mary recorded with other groups comprising assorted members of the Kirk band under various names. But as her popularity as a pianist and arranger increased, her personal life seemed to unravel.

*   *   *

As early as 1938, Mary and John had begun growing apart. The attention that John had once received was now eclipsed by Mary's stardom. Although they still lived together and often slept in the same bed, they rarely spent their free time together or talked to each other. According to John, Mary began to smoke pot, and "I didn't so I was considered a square." "We separated because I didn't want to get on that kick. She ran with her kick, I ran with my kick. We slept together all through 1938. It was no sex between the two of us. Girls were hitting on me. Guys were hitting on her. She told me when we were kids, if I ever see anybody that I think I love better, then give her a chance."[24] Although John and Mary had maintained a loving relationship, there were indications early in their marriage that each was engaging in affairs. In Tulsa, John had a relationship with a young woman who believed that he was going to leave Mary and marry her. At the time Mary knew nothing about the affair because the wives of band members were protecting her. Three women in particular, Bessie Lawson, Othie Harrington, and Mabel Durham often ran interference so that Mary wouldn't encounter John's lovers. In Mary's words:

> They lived across the street from me, and when I got out
> to go to the store or anything, I noticed they'd come out
> of the house and go to the store with me. [John] had met
> one of the natives down there and she was very, very jeal-
> ous of him. He was kidding around with her and she was
> trying to kill me. She was more in love with him than he
> was with her.[25]

Mary's affairs generally ended once the mystique wore off. Once, Mary told John she was in love with Ben Webster and wanted to marry him. Having grown up with Webster, John knew that he "was the worse guy in the world. Ben don't care nothing about no woman to marry. 'He loves me,' she said. You know how some young people are when you say I love you. They believe what the man says. So I said, 'Okay, I'll pay for the divorce if Ben will marry you.'"[26] When John confronted Ben, the saxophonist admitted that he was not ready to be married. Nevertheless, John and Mary separated in the late 1930s, and John, unable to adjust to the changes in the Kirk band, left. For a short time, he and Kirk's wife, Mary, owned a restaurant, but in 1942 he joined Earl Hines's band.

Life in the Kirk band worsened for Mary when John left. In 1941 Dick Wilson, who had collaborated with Mary on several compositions and had shared her passion for pushing the boundaries of the music, died of tuberculosis at the age of thirty. Death, sickness, and better opportunities had taken many of the original Clouds, and though they were replaced, the camaraderie that had defined the band dissolved. And the jazz scene of the early 1940s was governed by a new generation of musicians who believed that there was no place for women in jazz, except for the occasional vocalist.

Swing had offered a feeling of freedom for the younger generation. This freedom was, from an audience standpoint, not restricted to men. But in onstage representation, it was clear that this freedom was overwhelmingly a male preserve. Although female swing fans and even all-female bands had been accepted by certain segments of the public, men received the majority of the publicity, and it became accepted wisdom that swing was a representation of young white American male angst. In 1936, the debate over the role of women in jazz began in the pages of *Down Beat* magazine. By 1938 the discussion had escalated to scathing editorials belittling the talent of women instrumentalists and demeaning cartoons emphasizing sexuality over musicianship. The controversy reflected a transition in the aesthetic of jazz, which had openly accepted women musicians into its ranks during the years following the Depression.

In the Kirk band, money issues and personality clashes caused more problems than the gender of its members. Mary opted to remain in the band despite her growing cynicism.[27] She recalled how things gradually got worse: "Looking back, I can smile at our life on the road. Towards the end, though, there was no more brotherly love. I had lost so much through thefts that for a solid year I had to sleep with everything I owned. When someone broke in my trunk and took earrings, Indian head pennies and silver dollars, which I cherished, I decided to leave."[28] Mary later explained in broader terms her decision to leave: "Fame broke down the Kirk band. People wanted to hear our hits exactly as we recorded them. There were the predictable arguments over money and jealousies that splintered the band into cliques."[29]

In 1942, after twelve years with the Twelve Clouds of Joy, Mary arrived in Washington, D.C., and found ten dead keys on the piano. She took her bags off the bus and left the band to make her own way. She returned to her hometown of Pittsburgh.[30]

Chapter 5

HOW DO YOU KEEP
THE MUSIC PLAYING?

For over a decade, Mary Lou Williams had operated within the collegial but male-dominated boundaries of the Andy Kirk band. Although the experience had been less than perfect, it had earned her a level of fame that was comparable to that of many of her well-known counterparts. No woman other than the vocalists Billie Holiday and Ella Fitzgerald had so dominated the swing scene or earned the genuine respect of bandleaders and musicians alike. Mary had seemingly broken through the "glass ceiling" that had prevented many talented jazzwomen from pursuing their professional goals. Mary herself had been the victim of professional jealousy but would often dismiss it because she saw herself not merely as a woman musician but as a musician. Her attitude often elicited criticism from others who felt that Mary's position as the "leading lady" of jazz obligated her to speak to the discrimination that women musicians experienced. Mary had no intention of being an activist or spokesperson for what could safely be termed feminist causes. Instead, she wanted to write music, expand her knowledge of the art form by studying the compositions of European composers, and find happiness in her personal life. Although she would not readily admit it, Mary's life had taken a negative turn since John Williams left the Clouds and their marriage dissolved. John had served as a professional adviser and protector during those years, and now Mary found herself faced with difficult personal and professional issues.

In what was perceived by many as a split-second decision, Mary had walked away from the stability of the Andy Kirk band and possibly from music altogether. In the days between Mary's disappearance and the discovery that she had returned to Pittsburgh, rumors and innuendos suggested that Mary's actions were indicative of women's inability to deal rationally with professional and personal challenges. Few, including Andy Kirk, took into consideration the long and tumultuous road Mary had traveled to get to this place of prominence. Now thirty-two, Mary had spent the last twenty years performing regularly, first on the TOBA circuit and later with the Kirk band. That life had deprived her of various childhood and adolescent experiences. She had felt extreme economic poverty, which no doubt had caused some physical challenges, and she had opted to deny any maternal aspirations and forgo a stable domestic life for a life of performing and writing music. While Mary had few regrets about these choices, they nevertheless had affected her life in both positive and negative ways. Life on the road had afforded her opportunities that escaped most black women, but her marriage had suffered. She had maintained her musical integrity despite the marginalization of the race record industry, but she saw her femininity sacrificed as a consequence.

By the time Mary reached the Steel City, as Pittsburgh was often called, she had decided to take a break from life on the road and her music career in order to pursue other avenues. Working steadily since the 1920s had left her more exhausted than wealthy, and disillusioned about the diminishing level of creativity in jazz. At Mamie's home, Mary settled back into her role of sister, daughter, and aunt. Daily she would go to her mother's home—which by this time housed not only Virginia and her but Mary's younger sister Geraldine's family and Margaret, the youngest of Virginia's children—to visit and play cards. Although the house was crowded, it was filled with love and stability, something Mary had longed for and missed. Mary loved the time she spent laughing and reminiscing about her early years, and then there were soul food dinners of collard greens, sweet potatoes, and corn bread. It seemed that Mary's departure from life on the road was final until two weeks after she'd walked away from the Kirk band, when the trumpeter Harold "Shorty" Baker showed up in Pittsburgh. He had joined the Clouds in 1940, and during the next two years a strong friendship with Mary had blossomed. Before 1942 the two had never been more than friends, but a more intimate relationship developed during the months Harold spent in Pittsburgh. Inspired by his growing love for Mary, Harold decided not to return to the Kirk band. The departure of Harold and Mary was not met with enthusiasm, and Kirk, convinced that both would return when faced with penalties from the union, filed a grievance with the musicians' union in Kansas City. Harold and Mary received letters informing them that they had violated union policies and faced stiff penalties, but neither was persuaded to return. They negotiated with the union and Harold paid a small fine. Both were free from Kirk, but the implications of the escape would be far-reaching. In his 1989 memoir Kirk would speak of Mary affectionately but exclude Harold Baker from any discussion, despite his two-year stint with the band and his subsequent fame with the Duke Ellington band.

Meanwhile, Harold worked harder than ever trying to convince Mary to return to jazz. She would soon relent, unable to withstand the constant barrage of pleas from some of Pittsburgh's most promising musicians. According to Mary, every day the young drummer Art Blakey would come to her house in East Liberty and beg her to start a band with him. Mary declined the offer only to be faced with Blakey again the next day. Although she was deeply flattered by Blakey's desire to play with her, Mary was not sure if she was ready to let go of the peace and tranquillity she had for another career in music. Mary knew that the jazz scene was becoming more and more competitive, especially for black bands that still were marginalized by the mainstream media. Since returning to Pittsburgh, Mary had yet to sit down at a piano to play or arrange any tunes. She had divorced herself from the trappings of popularity and fame and seemed happy. Blakey continued to pursue her, and for two months he was a regular part of Mary's day until she finally said she would play with him.

Pittsburgh, which had long been one of the major stops on the touring schedule of jazz bands and vaudeville shows, was birthing some soon-to-be-influential musicians. The force of this new generation of musicians, which included Billy Strayhorn, Erroll Garner, Billy Eckstine, and Kenny Clarke, would soon be felt beyond the regional scene of Pittsburgh and contribute to the development of the modern postwar jazz scene. Mary, who at thirty-two constituted—with Earl "Fatha" Hines— the "old guard" of the Pittsburgh jazz scene, formed a group with Harold Baker, Art Blakey, and the tenor saxophonist Orlando Wright (who later converted to Islam and changed his name to Musa Kalim). Mary worked up some arrangements of popular tunes, including some combo settings of her Kirk hits, and the band began rehearsing. Mary worked hard to balance Blakey's loud and at the time unmanageable style with her swinging piano and Wright's and Baker's lyricism. The group rehearsed every day and eventually was booked in Cleveland at Mason's Farm.

Mason's Farm was a fairly large establishment that provided not only live music but a floor show similar to those of the old vaudeville days, with chorus girls and a comedian.[1] The group, which doesn't seem to have had an official name, was initially contracted to play until September, the end of the summer season. However, the popularity of the band forced the proprietors to extend the contract until November. The experience provided Mary with what she had desired during her years with the Kirk band—an opportunity to play pure, unadulterated music that was not governed by record playlists, major bookings, or the hassles of stardom. The band drew in huge crowds, and other musicians, such as the blues singer Joe Williams, would often stop by to sit in. The band even came to the attention of Duke Ellington, who was booked to perform in the city. One evening Ellington, accompanied by Ben Webster and several other members of his group, came by to hear the band and talk with Mary. It had been a number of years since Mary and his band the Washingtonians had played together in the pit orchestra at the Lincoln in Harlem, but the two had remained friends and deeply admired each other's work. Mary would later say that she wasn't aware of how great the band's reputation was until Ellington showed up.[2]

The night turned into a jam session in the style of 1930s Kansas City. The musicians spent hours battling one another to see who could produce the most intricate and innovative improvisations. It was a high point for Mary and the band. But the emotional high of the experience could not eclipse the feelings of animosity that were developing between Harold Baker and the other members of the band. Despite the cohesive sound of the band and the acclaim the group had received, Blakey, Wright, and the other members did not want Baker in the band. The group had wanted to create an aggregation consisting mainly of Pittsburghers, and since Baker was not from there, they felt he should leave. Tensions in the group had risen so high at one point that Baker and the others had almost come to blows.[3] Mary was unaware of these feelings and thought that the attention they had received from Ellington and others who had come through Cleveland would strengthen their upcoming bookings in New York.

The morning after the jam session, Mary was still buzzing and excitedly thinking of new arrangements for the band. But the other members of the group were secretly meeting with Baker to discuss his future. Harold never told Mary about the meeting and resolved the mounting conflicts by accepting an offer from Ellington to join his band. Although musically and emotionally attached to Mary, he was more than happy to go. Mary, bewildered by Harold's sudden departure but happy for him nevertheless, soon discovered the motives of the other band members. Mary was angry, but she turned to figuring out how the band could make up for Baker's absence. Not only had he provided the group with a strong, balanced sound, he had provided Mary with the type of emotional support that she had had with John Williams. Blakey, who had responded to Baker's acceptance of Ellington's offer with "It's good he's gone," promised Mary that he knew a much better trumpeter who was a native Pittsburgher. "He's the greatest," Blakey insisted, and he and Mary set off to talk with the candidate. The band had already been booked into a club in New York and would have to regroup musically as soon as possible. The trumpeter was brought in, but the session was a disaster. He could not play the parts and proved inept as a musician.[4] It soon became evident that Blakey and the others had underestimated the talent of Baker, who could play ten nonstop solo choruses and still maintain all the ensemble passages.

In the weeks before the New York booking, Mary worked feverishly to find a suitable replacement. She auditioned numerous trumpet players but could not find one who could provide the sound she desired. Despite her reservations, Mary decided to attempt to fulfill the arrangement in New York, but when the group arrived in the city they learned that the booking had fallen through. Mary took the news very badly and feared that she had made a big mistake in taking such chances. The other musicians, although somewhat upset, relished the fact that they were in New York. But for Mary, this was too close to her experiences during her early years with the Kirk band. It was one thing to struggle as a wide-eyed twenty-something, but she had no intentions of struggling now.

The band continued to rehearse, but for Mary the sound worsened with each meeting. With no bookings, and very little chance of any, considering their output, Mary grew depressed and retreated to the room she had rented at the Dewey Square Hotel. For two weeks she secluded herself and thought about how the band could either find bookings in New York or raise enough money to return to Pittsburgh. When her own efforts generated nothing, she called on John Hammond, who put her in contact with Louise Crane, heiress to the Crane paper fortune, who had recently begun representing entertainers. Crane, excited to be working with the famous Mary Lou Williams, secured for the band a booking at Kelly's Stable for four weeks.

The club was located on West 52nd Street, in the heart of New York's evolving jazz district, and had featured many top name musicians, including Hot Lips Page, Bud Freeman, and Coleman Hawkins, who had debuted his famous rendition of "Body and Soul" there in 1939. The stars were seemingly lining up again for Mary, but her optimism about the band would be short-lived. Despite the warm reception the band received during the gig, Mary grew more depressed over the sound. What she heard and what others heard were vastly different. Without a strong trumpeter, the band's sound was uneven and inconsistent. Further auditions yielded no one capable of meeting Mary's expectations, and she secretly decided to disband the group when the opportunity presented itself. The opportunity came sooner than expected when Harold Baker, touring with the Ellington band, wrote to Mary and invited her to join him in Chicago. Mary, sensing that this was the answer to her problems, did not hesitate. She immediately began preparing to meet Harold in Chicago. She never took time to consider the ramifications of her actions. She was still contractually obligated to Louise Crane and the other band members, but she simply packed her bags and left her troubles behind her. These types of emotional, somewhat irrational decisions would mark Mary's life and career throughout the next ten to fifteen years and would often make initially manageable situations worse.

Mary arrived in Chicago to find Harold waiting for her. Their initial weeks together were blissful, but things began to change quickly. Mary had come to the Windy City without any money or any thought of how she would support herself. She had assumed from Harold's invitation that he wanted her to come and be with him and that he would support her. Ideally that would have been the case, but Mary had not thought of the ramifications of totally relying on Harold for everything. Mary had no doubt concluded that going to Chicago would be much like her experience with John Williams in the late 1920s, when she joined him in Kansas City. She would join Harold, spend most of her days around their house, then spend her nights going from nightclub to nightclub, waiting for an opportunity to sit in with the band or start her own group. But Mary never took into consideration the difference between her relationship with John Williams and her relationship with Harold Baker. Mary had been married to John, which obligated him to support her financially. She was simply a lover of Harold, who loved her but felt less responsible for her. History did not repeat itself for Mary, and soon the relationship was strained by her lack of money. She began planning ways to make money and support the makeshift household she was building with Harold. Unable to find, according to her high standards, suitable musicians to start a group with, Mary wrote to her friend and former manager, Joe Glaser, for a loan. It had been a while since the two had spoken, but Mary felt sure that he would help her. In a letter dated November 10, 1942, Glaser wrote to Mary that he did not understand how she, as "one of the greatest pianists and composers in the country," had gotten herself into that situation. Glaser did not understand how she had become financially obligated to Harold Baker, a man who was not her husband. "You know deep down in your heart that you are not doing the right thing and I assure you that it is time for you to come to your senses," he insisted, and he offered to help her get bookings in Chicago.[5]

In the weeks that followed Glaser's response, Mary appeared more uncertain about her career and her relationship with Harold Baker. More important, she was bored with life on the road with the band. By Mary's standards, the band lacked the type of camaraderie and family environment that she had experienced with the Kirk band. Mary thought there were "too many stars" and "half of them didn't speak to each other." When the band members were speaking and "felt like playing they'd arrange some of the band's oldies spontaneously right on the stand."[6] But in Mary's recollection these instances were few. Unable to decide what she needed to do, she confided to the alto saxophonist Johnny Hodges that the touring was monotonous and that she wanted to go back to Pittsburgh or New York. He convinced Mary not to leave, and she accompanied the band to the next gig in Johnstown, Ohio, near Cleveland. Mary saw the band transform itself during this performance. In one night the band seemed to have worked through personality difficulties and musical deficiencies to produce what Mary deemed a memorable performance. The band was swinging and Mary led the audience in wild applause.

Despite the turnaround of the band, Mary knew she still had to make some decisions about her life. After leaving the Kirk band she had vowed never to work with a big band again, but now an offer from Woody Herman to join his band seemed momentarily a solution to her problems. But Mary opted instead to accept Joe Glaser's offer to help her establish her own band. Claiming that he was unable to work effectively to promote her as long as she was with Baker and obligated to Crane, Glaser urged Mary to make a couple of choices. First, he asked her to choose between her unstable relationship with Harold Baker and her music. Second, he informed her that she would have to consider some type of settlement with Louise Crane, who claimed to have lost a considerable amount of money because of Mary's sudden departure. Glaser assured Mary that if she addressed these issues, it would be only a few months before she could once again be making her own money and reestablishing her career.

Mary remained indecisive about his first request. After all, some years earlier it had been Glaser who had urged her to leave John Williams, stating that John would never tolerate her being a bigger star than he. Although it is not clear if Mary believed Glaser's assertions about her husband, it is known that the agent negotiated a larger salary for Mary within the Kirk aggregation. Now once again he was urging her to put love aside and believe in promises of making her a star. Glaser's motivations were clear: if he was to manage Mary, he would have to be the only man in her life. That is not to suggest that he desired a sexual or intimate relationship with Mary, but he wanted complete control over her image and what she would or would not do. This, of course, would not be possible with another man, especially a husband or lover, in her life. Mary thought long and hard about Glaser's proposal. She decided to accompany Harold to Philadelphia for Thanksgiving and go into New York the following day to meet with Glaser face-to-face. The meeting was productive, and Mary decided to sever her contract with Louise Crane, on the understanding that she would repay the money she owed to the agent in installments of $25 a month, starting in January.

However, she did not agree with Glaser about Harold Baker, and she left New York immediately for Washington, D.C., with him. Ellington's band had been booked for a series of gigs in the D.C./Maryland/ Virginia area. The first date was slated for the Howard Theater in Ellington's hometown of Washington, D.C., followed by a stint at the Royal Theater in Baltimore. Mary and Harold decided to marry and planned the ceremony around the Baltimore date. On December 10, 1942, Mary Lou Williams married Harold Baker. It was a marriage that could not have been scripted better if conceived in a jazz fairy tale: the "Queen of the Ivories" marries the "Man with the Golden Trumpet." The splendor would soon tarnish during the harsh life on the road, and allegations of physical abuse would surface. Practically speaking the marriage survived only six months, but the two never officially divorced, a fact that came to light at the time of Baker's death in 1966; Mary then discovered that she was still Mary Lou Baker and heir to his estate.

For the six months of this marriage, Mary traveled with Harold and the Ellington band. The experience was déjà vu at its best, as it mirrored Mary's early years with John Williams traveling on the road with the Kirk band. Mary once again endured the hectic schedule of one-nighters, the harsh traveling conditions, and the pains of domestic instability. She found little solace in her role as Harold's wife but found her own creative juices being stirred by Ellington's. The bandleader worked feverishly and often employed other arrangers to provide him with suitable arrangements. Mary was no exception. He asked her on several occasions to write some compositions for the band, but Mary refused, saying she didn't think she could contribute anything to the Ellington repertoire. When she finally acceded to his requests, Mary produced fifteen arrangements for the band.[7] It is not clear whether Mary wrote any later works for Ellington, but in the late 1960s she did send the bandleader some arrangements for consideration. There is no indication that he responded.

The arrangements produced in 1943 did find a place in the band's repertoire. Mary is credited with arranging several works played during Ellington's famous 1943 Carnegie Hall concert, including "Variations on Stardust," which according to critics featured "two choruses of beautiful trumpeting by Harold Baker."[8] Her most memorable contribution to the Ellington catalogue, however, was her interpretation of Irving Berlin's "Blue Skies." It was initially not a composition that solely featured the trumpet section; it drew on solos from various members of the band. There was one chorus of solo clarinet by Jimmy Hamilton, followed by a solo by the tenor saxophonist Al Sears. Following a release played by Claude Jones, Rex Stewart ended the piece with an exciting trumpet cadenza. In 1946, when it was recorded by Ellington, the work became a showcase for the trumpet section and got a new title, "Trumpets No End."[9] It was a suitable addition to Ellington's repertoire, which consistently included new compositions that featured the extraordinary abilities of his players, and was a hit with audiences.

The touring, however, was tedious, and Mary's relationship with Harold deteriorated. More devastating to the relationship was the domestic violence some say Mary suffered at the hands of her husband. Mary never substantiated most of the accusations of abuse publicly, but both often bore physical scars from the couple's violent encounters. It was obvious by this time that Mary's personal and professional life was at a standstill. She had to make some changes and soon. By the time the band reached Canada for a series of concert dates, Mary was convinced that returning to New York was the key to repairing her marriage and reigniting her career. She settled into a small apartment on Hamilton Terrace in the heart of Harlem's Sugar Hill district and awaited Harold's return. It is not clear if Baker ever visited the Hamilton Terrace apartment, but it would be years before Mary would see him again. Two years after joining Ellington's band, Baker was charged with draft dodging and immediately sent to basic training. From 1944 to 1946, Harold Baker served in the U.S. Army, and although he initially wrote to Mary expressing his love and desire for reconciliation, in time the two discarded their relationship and found love in the arms of other people. Later, steeped in the wisdom of past years, Mary justified the ending of her marriages by stating that she "didn't marry men. I married horns. After about two weeks of marriage, I was ready to get up and write some music. I was in love with Ben Webster longer than anybody, and that was about a month." [10]

*   *   *

The New York jazz scene Mary returned to in 1943 was no longer centered on the nightlife of Harlem but had moved to the nightclubs that lined 52nd Street. Musicians continued to create new musical narratives in the brownstones and cabarets that lined Harlem's streets, but it was clear that the area was no longer at the center of the evolution of jazz. In addition to the geographical changes that defined this embryonic stage of the modern jazz movement, the forward momentum of the swing style was halted by the war and the American Federation of Musicians' strike against the recording industry. The escalation of America's role in World War II meant that supplies of shellac, a material needed for the manufacture of records, were being rationed. Together with rationing, the recording strike inevitably brought the industry to a standstill from 1942 to 1944.

The strike had been conceived by the president of the American Federation of Musicians, James Petrillo, who announced in the early summer of 1942 that there would be a ban on the recording of all union musicians unless an arrangement could be made that paid royalties for performances played on radio stations and jukeboxes. The problem lay in the fact that musicians were not being adequately rewarded for these performances; moreover, jukeboxes in bars and nightclubs deprived musicians of work in "live" settings. At first Petrillo focused his efforts on radio stations and jukebox owners, but with no way of ensuring that recordings would be sold exclusively for home use, he turned his attention to the recording industry as well.

The ban applied to all the recordings of union musicians, regardless of use. Companies worked feverishly to make as many records as possible before the August 1 deadline, and when the date arrived, most of the major labels had stockpiled enough new recordings to sustain themselves through the next few months. The halting of recording may have stopped the documentation of evolving jazz styles but it did not stop the progression. The underground jazz scene was busy experimenting with new harmonic and rhythmic approaches that would radically alter the jazz discourse, so that new ideas seemed to have come out of nowhere when the ban was lifted in 1944.

This newest movement was headed by a small group of young musicians who had cut their teeth on swing but believed that the popularity and commercialization of the style had led to the dilution of the music. The rejection of improvisation, blue tonality, polyrhythms, and all the traits that connected big band music with its African heritage had brought about the integration of jazz into the mainstream but had pushed black musicians and bandleaders into obscurity. Bebop would be these musicians' response to the "whitening" of jazz and the commercialization of the music. In its infancy, defined by midnight jam sessions in small, obscure locations, this new style of jazz evolved out of the need to create something that couldn't be co-opted by less-than-talented musicians.

Mary, always drawn to musical innovation and expansion beyond the prescribed boundaries, soon became a willing participant in this movement. But she had been absent from the New York scene for some time and needed to reestablish her credentials with the musicians' union. It was a lengthy process that could take from three to six months, but Mary knew that only with membership in Local 802 could she legally perform in New York. Mary almost endangered her chances of getting a union card in mid-1943, when she took a nonunion job with the tenor saxophonist Illinois Jacquet, the drummer Kenny "Klook" Clarke, and the bassist Oscar Pettiford at a Bronx dance hall. Dizzy Gillespie, who knew of Mary's need to work, offered the gig to her despite her lack of union credentials. The job was on 149th Street, and Dizzy left Mary in charge of the group, which featured some of the most innovative young musicians the New York scene had to offer. The band had a solid, well-balanced sound that managed to swing to the approval of audiences and dancers. On the day of the gig, the dance hall prominently advertised Mary, who still had a reputation with New York audiences who remembered her years with the Kirk band. The dance hall was packed and it became evident to Mary that the proprietors were making too much money to be paying the group only $5 or $6 per musician. Mary decided to stage a walkout until the fee was raised. "I told the guys," she recounted, "we're not gonna play any more. Let's take an intermission." She told the manager, "We can't play for this kinda money; you'll have to give us more money." [11] Fearing that Mary would follow through with her threats to pull the band, the manager relented and paid Mary $20 and the other band members slightly less. All was going well until union delegates, who rarely attended such events, showed up. They were drawn by the large crowds that had gathered at the dance hall and wanted to see who was attracting such attention. Mary and the other band members weren't aware of the delegates' presence until a week later, when they received summonses to appear before the union board. Mary was cited for playing a non-union gig, and the other members were cited for playing with a non-union player. The offenses could have meant the revoking of Clarke's, Jacquet's, and Pettiford's union credentials and the rejection of Mary's application. However, when the board learned of Mary's efforts in getting higher wages for the band, they were all let off with a warning, and soon afterward Mary received her union card.[12] Her reentry into the New York scene was secured when she called on her friend the impresario John Hammond.

Seven years earlier, Hammond had staged the highly acclaimed *From Spirituals to Swing* concert in Carnegie Hall that launched the careers of the Kansas City musicians Big Joe Turner and Pete Johnson. His influence in the New York jazz scene was further cemented in 1939 when he became a partner in a new nightclub on 52nd Street. This nightclub not only would change the way in which jazz was showcased in New York, it would draw jazz into left-wing culture. Café Society, opened in 1938 by Barney Josephson, a former New Jersey shoe salesman, featured quality entertainment in an environment where black and white patrons mixed freely. Josephson thought that New York was ready for a different kind of nightclub and named his establishment with a satirical gibe at the wealthy café society crowd. The L-shaped basement room held just over two hundred people and was decorated by progressive artists who adorned the walls with murals parodying society's swells. From the beginning Josephson's target audience was artists, college students, progressive thinkers, and jazz fans. Hammond not only provided much-needed financial support but often convinced Josephson to book musicians he represented. By 1940 the Café Society venture was so successful that Josephson had opened a second and larger branch on 58th Street. The 52nd Street location became known as Café Society Downtown and the newer one as Café Society Uptown. In 1943 Mary joined the impressive roster of musicians and vocalists that at various times included Billie Holiday, Imogene Coca, Lena Horne, Hazel Scott, and Josh White. The club offered three shows a night, at nine, twelve, and two in the morning, and attracted an eclectic clientele that ranged from Ernest Hemingway and Eleanor Roosevelt to Joe Louis and Paul Robeson.[13]

The supportive nature of Café Society did not quell Mary's fears of performing as a solo artist, and her anxiety grew as the date of her inaugural performance drew near. After twelve years with the Kirk band and a brief stint as the leader of a short-lived sextet, Mary found it increasingly difficult to conceive of herself as a solo musician. Like many musicians who were products of the swing era, she had grown accustomed to the support of other musicians. Solo piano or even working in a smaller combo setting required more effort on the part of the musician, and Mary feared that she "might be shaky on solo piano."[14]

On the night of her opening, people packed Café Society Downtown to witness Mary's return to the New York jazz scene. The large crowd boosted Mary's confidence, but during the first couple of months she revisited her fears nightly and often arrived late. No matter what time Mary arrived, audiences waited patiently, wanting to hear and see the beautiful woman who could create the most innovative interpretations of their favorite standards. Josephson, although pleased with the crowds that Mary attracted, felt that the pianist could be more affectionate with the audience. He had had much success in crafting the stage etiquette of many of his black female performers. He drew out of Lena Horne his conception of "blackness" and convinced her to exchange the stock popular songs, done by most female vocalists at the time, for the blues. He manufactured her into a "Negro" talent and taught her to capitalize on her exotic beauty. He had done much the same with the pianist Hazel Scott, by making the most of her beauty and spotlighting her talent for "jazzing" the classics. Scott became the darling of Café Society Uptown and eventually expanded her career to Hollywood.

Josephson tried to mold Mary in a similar fashion, but remembering the lessons of her youth and the admonition against "clowning" she had received from veteran musicians, Mary resisted these attempts. "Mary was very self-effacing," Josephson recalled. "She was more shy then. If she'd had the bounce of Hazel Scott, she'd have been *bigger* than Hazel and gotten all the publicity, because she was a better pianist. *Nobody* could touch her, man or woman. I put people down when they call her the greatest female pianist. She's the *greatest,* and that includes the Garners and all, because she can compose, too. That she didn't emphasize showmanship was the only thing that held Mary back."[15] Mary, in an effort to distinguish herself as a "serious" jazz musician, never smiled while playing and rarely interacted with the audience. She knew that the stakes were higher for women musicians, because critics and others would find any excuse to discredit a woman's talent. Discussion of the role of women in jazz was already heating up, and as one of the few women musicians on the mainstream scene, Mary often found her name invoked as the model for other women musicians. That she was a standard-bearer for women despite herself was evident in the commentaries written about Mary during this period. The July 26, 1943, issue of *Time* reported not only that Mary was "no kitten on the keys" but that she "was not selling a pretty face or a low *décolletage,* or tricky swinging of Bach or Chopin. She was playing the blues, stomps, and boogie-woogie in the native Afro-American way—an art in which, at 33, she is already a veteran." [16] The writer's comments reflected the type of critical discussion concerning women jazz musicians that often set the musical abilities of Mary and Hazel Scott against each other, although the latter is not referred to by name. Mary seemingly ignored these discussions and focused her energies not on these pointless analyses but on her musical development. She viewed herself simply as a musician, not as an activist for racial or gender causes in jazz. Josephson nevertheless persisted, trying everything possible to get Mary to smile and interact with the audience, but Mary was steadfast in her rejection of what she thought was Josephson's way of getting her to act "like Hazel Scott." [17] This is not to say that Mary thought less of Scott's musical ability or stage etiquette, but simply that Mary did not desire to become the type of performer Josephson had shaped Scott into. More important, Mary, after all these years, seemed to fear the stigma critics attached to female musicians who resorted to novelties to draw in audiences.

*   *   *

As much as Mary tried to remain at a distance from discussions of gender and jazz or the talents of her female counterparts, she always seemed drawn into them. The first public dialogue about the place of women instrumentalists in jazz began in 1938. In the February issue of *Down Beat,* a writer, cloaked in anonymity, declared, "Outside of a few sepia females, the woman musician never was born capable of sending anyone further than the nearest exit. As a whole [women are] emotionally unstable [and] could never be consistent performers on musical instruments."[18] These statements were met with an immediate response, and over the next few years *Down Beat* would revisit the subject. The discourse that arose stigmatized even further the efforts of jazzwomen, most notably instrumentalists, although vocalists were satirized in demeaning cartoons.

The critical debates of the 1940s often presented Mary, at least in many mainstream white publications, as the antithesis of commercially motivated, novel musicians like Hazel Scott. The conflict that pitted these two women against each other was born not out of personal or professional interactions between the two but out of the sexual politics of jazz. Each woman had unwittingly given validity to the notions of "gendered spaces" that critics were advocating. In other words, each consciously or unconsciously had subscribed to the enactment of acceptable roles for women.

Hazel Scott and Mary Williams had similar backgrounds. Both had been identified as child prodigies, based on their extraordinary musical talents at an early age, and both had been influenced musically by their mothers' music making. Hazel's mother was the famed reed player Alma Long Scott, and Mary's mother had been a church musician who also had an affinity for the blues. Yet each pianist had been guided into her music career differently, and there were differences in their musical development. Mary was shielded from formal musical training for fear it would corrupt her natural ability, and she developed her talents while working the vaudeville circuit. Hazel, however, enrolled at Juilliard at an early age with hopes of becoming a concert pianist and played in her mother's all-female orchestra, the American Creolians, during her teen years. Both displayed a mastery of the boogie-woogie piano style, but Scott, after discovering that her chances of becoming a concert pianist were slim, adopted as her trademark the practice of "jazzing the classics." It was this kind of performance that brought into question, for some critics, the depth of her talent as a jazz musician and improviser. Mary, on the other hand, because of the innovation of her arrangements and her emphasis on improvisation, represented the personification of the "serious" female jazz musician.

Further complicating this analysis is the physical image that each woman projected. There is no question as to the gender of either, but by working within different roles as musicians, each created a gendered space in which she was forced to operate. Scott, who was considerably lighter in complexion than Mary, adapted to instrumental performance the "sex kitten" identity that had been reserved primarily for vocalists. She was often referred to as the "instrumental Lena Horne," which implies that physical beauty is overemphasized to distract the audience from lack of musical ability. Scott's beauty and sophistication did draw her out of the nightclub scene and to Hollywood, but that move underscored the fact that she was a talented musician. She alternated between the roles of exotic sex kitten and sophisticated race woman as artist, as signaled by her desertion of jazz and the persona of the jazz musician following her marriage to the famed preacher Adam Clayton Powell Jr. She was one of the few black artists who refused to appear before segregated audiences and often harshly criticized the industry for its ill-treatment of blacks. Her first film appearance came in 1943, the same year critics began comparing her with Mary, in Columbia Pictures' *Something to Shout About*. Her popularity with movie audiences only intensified her efforts to present realistic images of blacks, and she often appeared in movies as herself, seated at the piano.

Mary, on the other hand, although beautiful, was often described as being able to play as well as or better than most men. Writers often centered their discussions on the masculine qualities of her abilities, largely ignoring the feminine qualities of her physical beauty. Paradoxically, the woman musician could not, through her adoption of a serious and cerebral musical approach, maintain her femininity. Ironically, after their respective stints at Café Society, both women would use their public personas to bring attention to the plight of the black community: Scott through her refusal to perform in segregated venues, the images she presented on the Hollywood screen throughout the 1940s, and her marriage to Powell; Mary through the rehabilitation of addicted musicians, and her efforts to educate others about the evolution of jazz and its connections to the experiences of blacks in America.

Chapter 6

LOVE ON A TWO-WAY STREET: BARNEY JOSEPHSON AND MOE ASCH

Mary's experience at Café Society exposed her to new audiences and provided her with an environment that encouraged new levels of experimentation. After leaving the Kirk band, Mary had stopped writing arrangements, with the exception of those she produced for Duke Ellington in the early 1940s. But the lively scene of Café Society reignited her musical passions. She found inspiration in simple things, from the sound of the subway to the everyday activities outside her Hamilton Terrace apartment. Sometimes a melody or tune would come to her while she was riding the subway to Café Society, and by the time she arrived at the club, she would have a complete arrangement worked out. She would then consult with the drummer, J. C. Heard, who would listen to what

Mary played and follow along. Heard and Mary produced some memorable performances at Café Society that were simple arrangements of such standard tunes as "Limehouse Blues" or her originals, such as "Roll 'Em." Mary thrived on these moments and often lost herself in the emotion of the performance. She would string together numerous choruses of innovative and unrelenting improvisations, to the approval of club regulars and other musicians who stopped by to hear what Mary was "brewing" up.

Café Society quickly became known around the city as a place to hear good music, but it also garnered a reputation for its political leanings. It is not clear if Barney Josephson was directly involved with the American Communist Party, but Café Society became a meeting place for many supporters of leftist causes. His personal beliefs suggest he agreed with the notions espoused by the left, and his advocacy of Café Society performers' involvement in political events would later expose him to allegations of treachery.

Despite Josephson's best efforts to create a nightclub in which black and white patrons were treated equally, the establishment occasionally attracted patrons who did not adjust well to the open environment. These "biased people," as Mary described them, would often provoke the anger of Josephson, who would have them escorted out; or they would start fights with other patrons and sometimes performers. The blues singer Josh White, whose evocative performances drew white women to the club, was often the spark for such fights. However, on one occasion Mary became the center of a melee after a fan requested that she play "Roll 'Em" again. According to Mary, the man screamed, "Play it again," then ran up on the stage and grabbed her. Eddie Heywood, whose band regularly played the club, came to Mary's aid. When the patron would not let her go, Heywood punched the man and a fight ensued. Mary escaped without being injured, but she was more guarded during her sets after that.

Mary's stint at Café Society not only influenced her musical development, but also led to a brief involvement in leftist activities. Unlike many who found their way to the political left through unionization, most jazz musicians were drawn into the movement through the popularity of their music among the young constituents of the Congress of Industrial Organizations, the CIO. Black musicians, especially those in New York, were attracted to the rhetoric of the Harlem Popular Front, which headed campaigns to free the Scottsboro Nine and end lynching and discrimination throughout the South. Ironically, most of the musicians, like Mary, rarely considered themselves "political" artists and became associated with left-wing politics only through their participation in benefit concerts that supported political initiatives. Mary's participation in such events began in October 1943, when she was asked to perform at a political rally for a city council candidate, Benjamin J. Davis Jr.

Davis, an open and acknowledged Communist who had been endorsed by Adam Clayton Powell Jr., had ignited the passions of Harlemites, and they worked feverishly to elect him. As enthusiasm for Davis grew, the Non-Partisan Committee to Elect Benjamin Davis to the City Council planned a rally at the Golden Gate Ballroom on 140th Street at Lenox Avenue in Harlem. The massive auditorium, which held five thousand people, was contracted for October 24, and the admission charge was set at $2.75 for reserved seats and 50 cents for general admission. The pianist Teddy Wilson, the chairman of the stage, screen, and radio artists' division of the Non-Partisan Committee, coordinated the entertainment, which featured a who's who of black performers. Wilson's Café Society colleagues, including Mary, Josh White, Art Tatum, Billie Holiday, Coleman Hawkins, and Hazel Scott, performed during the rally. Although Paul Robeson was the advertised featured performer of the night, the committee knew that the caliber of all the talent Wilson had collected would draw more Harlemites to the unprecedented event. According to Davis, who recounted the incident in the memoir he wrote during a prison term in the 1950s, "There was scarcely a name band or popular entertainer who did not volunteer their services. The Golden Gate was sold out ten days before the rally."[1] *New Masses,* one of the prominent Harlem Popular Front publications, advertised the event as "Harlem's Event of the Year," and the *New York Age,* one of two Harlem-based newspapers, heralded the event as "The All Star Victory Show."

On the day of the rally, the auditorium was filled to capacity, with thousands of other hopefuls waiting outside. The fire department closed off the ballroom two hours before the performance, and the committee rented an additional hall six blocks away, where the artists gave a second performance. With the votes of black, whites, and Jews, Davis became the first black Communist candidate elected to the city council. Mary's involvement in the benefit marked the beginning of her personal involvement in these leftist political affairs.

The rhetoric of the Harlem Popular Front appealed to Mary as well as to famous Harlemites, including Langston Hughes, who asked Mary to write music for lyrics he had penned for the radical Southern Negro Youth Congress. Although most publications regarding Communism list Mary among participants in their activities, her activities were mainly limited to benefits held for Davis's campaigns. It was rumored that Mary once held Communist meetings in her Hamilton Terrace apartment, but neither Mary nor any of her friends have referred to these activities. However, Father Peter O'Brien, Mary's manager in the 1960s and 1970s, stated that Mary did host such meetings. Regardless of these speculations, documentary evidence shows only that she performed at benefits such as an April 1944 celebration of Paul Robeson's birthday, another rally the same year at the Golden Gate Ballroom, and a concert for Davis's reelection bid in 1945.

It is not clear whether Mary volunteered for these and dozens of other events that she referred to vaguely in interviews; Barney Josephson and John Hammond often offered her talents and those of other Café Society performers without their knowledge for the advancement of some political or social cause. Mary's involvement with the Popular Front and its causes was also governed by her recording contract with Moe Asch and Asch Records, to be discussed in more detail later in this chapter. In testimony before the House Committee on Un-American Activities in 1950, Hazel Scott said that Josephson often lent her name and the names of other performers to "affairs" without consulting the artists. She explained, "It is standard procedure in the entertainment business for an employer to sign up his artists for various causes."[2] Mary, in later years, said that these commitments, which sometimes numbered as many as four a night, actually discouraged her from becoming involved in political activities.

Moe Asch's involvement in left-wing politics has not been clearly substantiated, but in November 1944 he planned a nationwide tour of his artists in support of President Franklin D. Roosevelt's reelection bid. The tour, known as the FDR Bandwagon, was sponsored by the Communist Party, then called the Communist Political Association, and was one of the first open political endeavors of the organization. Mary Lou joined Woody Guthrie, Cisco Houston, and an assortment of dancers, including Helen Tamiris, and performers in what would prove to be an unsuccessful venture. The first official performance of the Bandwagon, in Boston, was interrupted by stink bombs, and not much is known about other performances with the exception of the New York dates. In his November 18 column in the *New York Age,* Ted Yates wrote, "One of the best jobs performed during the campaign was the one by the FDR 'Bandwagon' group. A handshake to Rollin Smith, Mary Lou Williams, Jack DeMerchant, and Laura Duncan." [3]

Surprisingly, Mary was not a victim of the anti-Communist witch-hunts of the late 1940s and 1950s. Like many other musicians, she had simply been taken in by the propaganda of individuals who claimed to want to help the artistic community and the black race. Mary would later say, "There's not one musician I think would be in any kind of political anything if they weren't disturbed about the race, as being abused and whatnot of the race, trying to help the poor." [4] Many had had no notions of overthrowing the government or erecting a new Communist regime, but the Red-baiters were not easily persuaded. Mary's decision to end her affiliation with Harlem Popular Front causes early on may well account for her exclusion from the harassment of the House Un-American Activities Committee. By 1948 the anti-Communist zealots had begun their assault on jazz people of the left, and before the 1950s were over, Josephson would be forced to sell Café Society Downtown and Duke Ellington, Josh White, Hazel Scott, and Lena Horne would be publicly humiliated and forced to distance themselves from organizations and individuals, most notably Paul Robeson, that they had supported during the 1940s.

Despite Mary's interpretation of the political agenda of Café Society, she found success at the establishment. Her popularity with supper club audiences brought her to the attention of Moe Asch, founder of Asch Records, an up-and-coming independent label. Asch had formed the company in the early 1940s and had so far focused his attention on Jewish music, folk music, and the blues. The WEVD building where Asch produced his recordings had by 1944 become a part of a progressive musical and political triangle. This triangle consisted of WEVD, the Café Society, and the Village Vanguard, two of the prominent avant-garde nightclubs. Mary, through her affiliation with Café Society, sat at the center of this developing cultural, musical, and political milieu. At the urging of the jazz writer Charles Edward Smith, Asch began signing up jazz musicians and became significant in recording pioneer jazz musicians in the 1940s.

It is commonly believed that Mary waxed her first sessions for Asch in

March 1944, but actually Mary had recorded in February three sides of solo piano, which were only recently released. Mary's first combo session with the label, on March 12, 1944, featured the bassist Al Lucas and the drummer Jack "the Bear" Parker, who often accompanied her at Café Society and had only a week earlier recorded a session with her for Milt Gabler and the World Broadcasting Systems.[5] The Gabler session, which was produced for radio broadcast and not commercial purchase, produced eight sides: "8th Avenue Express," "Taurus Mood" (which later became a part of the *Zodiac Suite*), "People Will Say We're in Love," "Froggy Bottom," "Roll 'Em," "Limehouse Blues," "Marcheta," and a medley of "Cloudy," "What's Your Story, Morning Glory?" and "Ghost of Love." The combination of Williams, Lucas, and Parker was expanded for the Asch session to include more Café Society players, the trumpeter Frankie Newton, the clarinetist Edmund Hall, and the trombonist Vic Dickenson. The session yielded five sides: "Lullaby of the Leaves," "Roll 'Em," "Yesterday's Kisses," "Satchel Mouth Baby," and "Little Joe from Chicago." "Lullaby of the Leaves" (Asch 1004) is a composition by Edgar Sampson, who also wrote "Stompin' at the Savoy"; it was the only arrangement recorded during this session that was not by Mary Lou. "Roll 'Em" and "Little Joe from Chicago" were her reworkings of earlier compositions. "Little Joe," in particular, provides a clear example of Mary's ability to reinterpret material in new and innovative ways. In its original form, the performance was based on a boogie-woogie ostinato and melody established by Mary's piano in the opening bars. But the 1944 version begins with a slow bluesy introduction that is dominated by the trumpet, which engages in a loosely based sequence of call-and-response passages with the trombone, the clarinet, and the rhythm section. The motivic material presented in this section has no obvious connections with the main melody presented in the original version of "Little Joe," and it establishes a melancholy mood that is almost reminiscent of the introduction of Jelly Roll Morton's "Dead Man Blues." But Mary's introduction is not as structured or contextualized as Morton's, which is based on New Orleans funeral processions.

The introduction is interrupted by a sudden stop in the rhythm and Mary's introduction of the boogie-woogie bass line. The entrance of this motive marks a considerable change in the tempo and mood of the piece. However, the performance never reaches the speed of the original recording by Andy Kirk or the subsequent one by Benny Goodman and maintains a moderate, laid-back tempo. Following the first chorus of boogie-woogie, the trombone enters, accompanied by the rhythm section, which maintains the eight-beat ostinato that defines the melody. The ensemble playing a blues cadenza figure interrupts the last bars of the solo, which segues into the third and fourth choruses, featuring primarily clarinet and rhythm section in the first half of the chorus, but embellished with chordal punctuations by the remaining horns in the second half of the chorus. The fifth chorus begins with the group singing "Little Joe" followed by block chords played by Mary. Unlike the previous version, which featured the band singing two choruses of text, this group sustains the words "Little Joe" while Mary plays underneath. A glissando played by Mary segues into another chorus of boogie-woogie that is interrupted by chordal punctuations in the higher register that introduce a second clarinet solo. The composition takes on a completely different persona in this setting and—but for the enunciation of "Little Joe" and the original boogie-woogie figure—could be mistaken for a new work.

"Yesterday's Kisses" (Asch 1003) was a new Mary Lou composition that featured her, Edmund Hall on clarinet, and Al Lucas on bass, and foreshadowed her transition into modern jazz. The piece is centered on a swing rhythm that employs call and response between the musicians in the A passages, and ensemble passages in the bridge (B). The combination of instruments and their ability to swing fluidly defines the short performance. Unfortunately, American audiences would not hear the track until it was issued in the 1970s with a reissue of the remainder of Mary's Asch catalogue. Timme Rosenkrantz later released it on the Danish label Baronet (Baronet 3).[6] "Satchel Mouth Baby" (Asch 502) was a swinging yet relaxed tune reminiscent of the material Mary wrote during the 1930s. It has a simple melody that the band sings and some noteworthy solos by the performers. These recordings, while somewhat simplistic in their overall approach, present enjoyable performances without the novelty of some comparable smaller group recordings and document Mary's evolution as a composer and pianist since her last recordings with the Andy Kirk band and smaller aggregations in the late 1930s. Although Mary was the obvious leader on these recordings, it is evident that, as in previous recordings, she never overshadowed the performances of her sidemen; rather, she used her piano to cement the swinging rhythmic groove of the band.

On April 19 Mary returned to the studio and recorded several sides of solo piano. They included "Drag 'Em," "Mary's Boogie," and "St. Louis Blues." Although Mary's work is often excluded from discussions of boogie-woogie or stride piano, both "Drag 'Em" and "Mary's Boogie" are indications of her excellent adaptation of these styles. Stanley Dance expressed this best in 1978 when, in his review of the reissues of these recordings, he wrote, "As accompanist or soloist, she always exudes authority. She plays favorites like 'Drag 'Em' and 'Blue Skies' and there is the marvelous 'Mary's Boogie' on which she shows she belongs with Pete Johnson and Jay McShann right in the top class of Kansas City specialists."[7] In the late spring, Asch released three sides from each of the first two sessions on ten-inch single records: "Little Joe from Chicago" (Asch 1002), "Roll 'Em" (Asch 1003), and "St. Louis Blues" (Asch 1004). Each disc contained one side with the sextet, backed by a side of solo piano. Later, six of the sextet sides were packaged as *Mary Lou Williams and Her Chosen Five* and released as a set. Charles Edward Smith, who wrote the album's liner notes, asserted that the recordings were a superior example of ensemble piano work. In his words, "Ensemble piano talent is rare in jazz and Mary Lou Williams has it to an unusual degree. Her acceptance of other musicians is not—here are thirty-two bars and I'll be back later—but a really collaborative effort."[8] The recording was received favorably and marked the beginning of a very personal and unique relationship between Asch and Mary.

By the summer of 1944, Mary had become Asch's first exclusive artist, which delighted them both. To Mary, Asch was generous and accepting, making his studio always available to her. He never interfered in or gave direction for her recordings. Only on one occasion, when she brought Coleman Hawkins along on a recording date that had been scheduled for solo piano, did Asch demur. Mary remembered, "He never told a performer how to record or what to do. If you only burped, Moe recorded it. It was different because Moe Asch had more love and he had more respect for jazz artists. Often he would take us to dinner, the nicest dinners, steak dinners, the nicest places and it was his idea that an artist should be heard if they're talented. He'd turn the tape on and go away, let you record anything you wanted to record, and it always worked out great."[9] Asch not only gave Mary freedom to be as creative as she could, but also brought her more royalties than she was to receive from any other recording company. Asch's treatment of Mary was unusual and reflected his respect for her talent, but it also reflected his knowledge of her position as one of the few notable female jazz instrumentalists on the scene. Although there were other respected female players, it was clear that Mary was considered the Grande Dame of Jazz, and with the announcement of Hazel Scott's potential retirement from public performing, Mary's position was set.

In early June Mary returned to the studio and recorded four sides with the tenor saxophonist Don Byas. This June 5 session once again employed Lucas, Parker, and Dickenson on bass, drums, and trombone, respectively, and added Dick Vance on trumpet and Claude Greene on clarinet. These sides included Hoagy Carmichael's composition "Stardust" (Asch 552-1), Mary's composition "Gjon Mili Jam Session" (Asch 552-2), written in honor of the photographer Gjon Mili, and a collaboration between Byas and Mary called "Man o' Mine" (Asch 552-2). Mili was one of New York's artistic elite who befriended Mary in the 1940s and photographed her for months, seeking the right photo that captured her essence. He finally captured the image he wanted and included the portrait in an exhibition at the Museum of Modern Art. The portrait featured Mary glamorously coiffed and seated at a piano with her image reflecting off the piano lid. The image was a testament to both her beauty and her strength, as her hands were prominently featured spread on the keyboard. Mary and Mili developed a deep appreciation for each other's art and sought ways in which to immortalize their friendship. For Mili it would be the now famous photo of Mary, and for Mary it was the composition "Gjon Mili Jam Session." The work was a tribute to a party held at the famed photographer's home. For this event Mili had managed to gather every jazz musician of prominence in New York. Duke Ellington, Billie Holiday, James P. Johnson, Cozy Cole, and Mary were just some of the musicians who attended the party. From this potpourri of musicians sprang a jam session that was unparalleled. In 1945 Mary would perform a larger arrangement of the composition during her Town Hall concert. With the exception of these two performances, the piece was never played again, becoming one of many of Mary's compositions that fell into obscurity.

On August 10 Mary recorded with Bill Coleman on trumpet and Al Hall on bass before heading out of town on what she referred to as an "ill-fated" tour. The tour was the FDR Bandwagon, one of Asch's many political endeavors involving artists on his label. The August 10 session produced seven sides, including "Russian Lullaby" (Asch 351-1), "Blue

Skies" (Asch 351-1), "Persian Rug" (Asch 351-2), "Night and Day" (Asch 351-2), "I Found a New Baby" (Asch 351-3), and Mary's "You Know Baby" (Asch 351-3) and "Carcinoma" (Asch 552-3).

Before the end of 1944, Mary would return to Asch's studios and record another set of ensemble sides, including a December 11 session with Josh White on vocals. The four-year-plus relationship between Mary and Asch would greatly alter her perspective of her role as an artist and musician, as she realized the benefits of having exclusive control over the production of her music. Mary's artistic control during her Asch years was not limited to musical performance; she also selected the images featured on the covers of her recordings. In typical Mary fashion, she enlisted the aid of her friend (and alleged lover) David Stone Martin and assisted him in launching another career. Martin had served as a graphic designer with the Office of Strategic Services and later as art director of the Office of War Information. But in 1944 he started drawing album covers for Asch, and they became the label's trademark.

In October 1945 Josephson moved Mary from Café Society Downtown to the uptown branch of the establishment as a replacement for Hazel Scott, who had decided to marry Adam Clayton Powell Jr. and give up performing. Mary, contracted for three shows, six nights a week, at $300, was being groomed "as the queen of the ivories now that Hazel Scott has filed intentions of divorcing herself from the theatrical profession." [10] But Mary favored the small, intimate setting of the downtown establishment and did not welcome the move. Café Society Uptown catered to a more upscale crowd, and Mary worried that her serious demeanor would not go over well with the audience, but the move engendered what would be her most experimental creations.

It was during her nightly performances at Café Society Uptown that Mary began working on a new set of compositions based on the signs of the zodiac. She had conceived the idea of writing and debuting a movement each week at Café Society, but she wrote only three movements while at the nightclub; still, she intended to complete the cycle. Josephson, eager to provide his performers with every opportunity for advancement, secured an opportunity for Mary to have her own thirty-minute radio show on WNEW in New York. The two agreed that the best strategy for the show would be to introduce one of the zodiac compositions each week. This would ensure that audiences would tune in each time. Because she had completed the first three movements while at Café

Society, the first three weeks of the show went off without a hitch, but Mary soon encountered problems, as she could not conceive any more ideas to write the remaining movements. "I couldn't write anymore," she recalled, "like my inspiration had left me. So what I did to finish them, I went on WNEW every Sunday and I had Nola Studios to record the program as I played it. So I wrote the rest—I just played them off like that." Although Mary had no deep interest in astrology, she thought that the characteristics presumed to attach to these signs would be a way of sketching musical portraits of specific persons born under those signs. When asked about the genesis of these works, she said: "I read a book about astrology, and though I didn't know too much about it I decided to do this suite as based on musicians I knew born under the various signs." [11]

In June 1945 Mary, along with Al Lucas and Jack Parker, returned to the Asch studios and recorded seven of the twelve movements: one as a trio, one, "Aries," as a duo with bass, and the remaining five as piano solos (there are several alternate takes). These sides would be the only recordings Mary made for Asch in 1945. Unlike her previous arrangements, these were individual compositions that displayed no motivic relationship, although they are often referred to as one complete musical idea. Each sign was conceived musically as a separate and individual idea. "Aries" was written for Ben Webster and Billie Holiday, who had both supported Mary musically during the most experimental periods of her life—Webster during her Kansas City and Andy Kirk years, and Holiday during Mary's early months at Café Society. Mary created two different versions of the movement, which she said represented musical freedom, because both Webster and Holiday had through their musical approaches expanded the boundaries of jazz. "Taurus," recorded previously under the title "Taurus Mood" in 1944, was dedicated to Duke Ellington, Ellis Larkins, and herself. Of the movements recorded during this session, "Taurus" is the one composition that lacks a strict musical direction. In the liner notes to the recording, Mary stated, "Taurians are stubborn, they procrastinate, but they also know in what direction they're going. Dig the rhythm section. These guys didn't know what I was going to play and they're following. That's real jazz. I'd arrange this today with a lot going on." [12]

"Gemini," written for Benny Goodman, Mary's former husband, Harold Baker, and Miles Davis and added later, is the only movement to contain two different melodies, each representing the varying nature of the Gemini. "Cancer" was written for Lem Davis, an alto saxophonist with the Eddie Heywood band. The trombonist Vic Dickenson, who had contributed some exciting solos and ensemble work on Mary's first Asch recordings, was commemorated in "Leo." Dizzy Gillespie, Mary's closest friend, was honored with "Libra," along with Art Tatum, Thelonious Monk, and Bud Powell. "Scorpio," which was written for Imogene Coca, Ethel Waters, Al Lucas, and Katherine Dunham, was later adapted into a ballet by Dunham. "Sagittarius," written for Eddie Heywood and Bob Cranshaw, was one of the five solo compositions (the others are "Libra," "Capricorn," "Aquarius," and "Pisces"). "Aquarius" was dedicated to President Franklin D. Roosevelt, for whom Mary wrote "Ballot Box Boogie" during his 1944 reelection campaign, and to her Café Society colleague Josh White and the dancer Eartha Kitt, whom she'd met during her many travels. "Pisces" was written in the form of a jazz waltz and dedicated to Barney Josephson and the bassist Al Hall. "Capricorn" and "Virgo" were written for the trumpeter Frankie Newton and the impresario Leonard Feather, respectively.

The *Zodiac Suite,* although continually in a state of recomposition as Mary rescored and reconceived the movements, reflected Mary's expanding perspectives on jazz. Her subsequent versions would place the composition in the category of Duke Ellington's extended works, which also combined elements of the classical tradition with jazz. Mary viewed the completion of the work as the beginning of a new phase in her development as a composer. She stated in the liner notes to the 1945 recording, "As a composer and musician, I have worked all my life to write and develop serious music that is both original and creative. 'The Zodiac Suite' is the beginning of a real fulfillment of one of my ambitions." [13]

In the meantime, Mary continued her nightly stints at Café Society, her weekly radio program on WNEW, and occasional stage performances. In May she substituted for Hazel Scott, who was ill, during two performances at the Roxy Theatre. Her performance was so well received that Sam Rauch, the main promoter for the establishment, announced plans to feature her in future productions.[14] Only a week later, the *New York Age* reported Mary's successful stint at the Roxy. The newspaper also sent get-well messages to the pianist, reporting that she had been hit by a car and had received a broken nose.[15] Mary's short hospitalization for the injury generated rumors that included allegations of drug abuse. But publicly it was announced only that Mary had been injured in a car accident.

The source of these press reports was more than likely Josephson, who was not completely sure of the circumstances behind the injury. The biographer Linda Dahl wrote that Mary's own varying explanations fueled the misconceptions. Mary first told friends that she had undergone cosmetic surgery. The few people who actually knew the truth did not disclose the information at the time. Johnnie Gary, the stage manager for the floorshows at Café Society, picked Mary up upon her release from the hospital. When he arrived, "she was all bandaged up like a mummy. I brought her to her apartment, I said, 'Who mugged you?' 'You better never tell this 'til the day I die,' Mary replied. 'I had a nose job. But you tell Barney I was in a car accident.'" [16] The results proved to be less than pleasing, and Mary had to return to the hospital weeks later to have her nose rebroken. Josephson, continuing in his role as protector and father figure, showed up at Mary's apartment offering legal advice, but Mary's lack of interest indicated to him that an accident was not the real reason for the injury. Dahl concluded that what set off the episode was not a desire to become more glamorous but violence at the hands of Eddie Heywood's bass player. If this is true, it would be one of many instances of physical violence Mary endured at the hands of the men in her life. She never discussed the matter publicly, but she often bore the scars from these encounters.[17] Her friends simply ignored them or spoke of them privately.

Regardless of the true nature of the incident, the injury and temporary disfiguration did not prevent Mary from accepting an offer to star in an all-black variety show starring Ethel Waters and Josh White. *Blue Holiday,* which was originally called *The Wishing Tree,* was slated to be Ethel Waters's much-anticipated return to Broadway and called on the contributions of many notable performers, including Katherine Dunham, the dancer Josephine Premice, and Josh White. It featured three new songs penned by Duke Ellington. *Blue Holiday* was slated to play seven days a week at the Belasco Theater, but the pathetic opening shortened the run of the production. The critic for the *New York Age* wrote of the reaction of the opening-night audience: "a conglomeration of million-dollar talent was misused and misdirected. There was absolutely no continuity to the revue along with the fact that the program itself was not carried through as printed. Several performers did not put in appearances." After praising the performances of Waters and Josh White, the critic asserted that Mary "fell below par," and that as a whole the performance left much to be desired.[18] Despite all attempts by producers and performers to reformat the show, *Blue Holiday* failed to live up to its potential in subsequent performances and closed after one week.

*   *   *

As Mary continued to navigate through the New York scene, a new underground jazz movement grabbed her attention. This movement was headed by a group of young musicians who believed that swing had diluted jazz and had pushed black musicians and bandleaders into obscurity. This newly conceived sound, called bebop or rebop because of the rapid-fire phrases musicians played, would become these musicians' response to swing and to the commercialization of jazz. Their ultimate goal was to create something that could not be stolen by less-than-talented musicians. Eventually the new genre would come to signify the growing sense of militancy in the black community and the evolving image of the black male musician.

After her nightly performances at Café Society, Mary would head uptown to a club called Minton's Playhouse, on West 118th Street. It was there that this new jazz was being conceived, through the experimentations of the pianist Thelonious Monk, the trumpeter Dizzy Gillespie, the drummers Kenny Clarke and Max Roach, the trombonist J. J. Johnson, and others. Minton's was not a large place, but the intimate environment was excellent for the type of exploration taking place there. The cabaret and the bandstand were at the rear of the back room, where the wall was covered with strange paintings depicting weird characters sitting on a brass bed, jamming, or chatting. The bar was in the front and featured a jukebox to which the daytime people danced. Thelonious Monk was one of the first beboppers to be associated with Minton's, while the other musicians, Charlie Parker, Dizzy Gillespie, and Max Roach, supported themselves with work for swing bands. Monk set the stage for bebop harmonies with his complex chord changes, which few could play with him. But those who could follow Monk, such as the guitarist Charlie Christian, fed this experimentation. Mary, who had befriended Christian in the late 1930s and had introduced him to John Hammond, who in turn convinced Benny Goodman to add him to his roster, would spend countless nights with the guitarist working on compositions that explored these new approaches to jazz.

These musicians and Mary Lou Williams had much in common. Despite the seven- to ten-year age difference between Mary and the boppers, they had shared similar experiences in their rise to prominence in the jazz scene. Most had risen through the ranks of local and territorial bands, and by 1942 they had reached the level of the national or acclaimed dance bands. They returned to New York long enough to establish a reputation with the musicians there, and they fell into the company of others who shared similar interests and attitudes in the after-hours clubs and jam sessions. Just as Mary had become disillusioned with jazz and disengaged herself from the world of swing when she quit the Kirk band in 1942, most of the beboppers had these feelings and began imagining an alternative to the usual career path in jazz. The harmonies and rhythms these musicians were experimenting with were nothing new for Mary. During her years in Kansas City, she would often play what she called "zombie music." This style, according to her, consisted of "mainly 'outré' chords, new 'out' harmonies based on 'off' sounds."[19] Mary's interaction with the boppers extended beyond the clubs. Her apartment at 63 Hamilton Terrace in Harlem became the setting for a modern-day "salon" that paralleled nineteenth-century French musical circles. Each night she hosted musicians as they sat around discussing music, listening to recordings, and writing new tunes. "It was like the thirties," she said. "Musicians helped each other and didn't just think of themselves. Monk, Tadd Dameron, Kenny Dorham, Bud Powell, Aaron Bridgers, Billy Strayhorn, plus various disc jockeys and newspapermen, would be in and out of my place at all hours and we'd really ball."[20]

> I had a white rug on the floor and we'd sit on the floor and each one would take turns playing—because most of them needed inspiration and they wrote the music up here at the house. If they wrote at home they'd bring it here for me to hear it and see how I liked it. Mel Tormé used to come here, Sarah Vaughan, even Leonard Feather, Benny Goodman. Seemed like it was more in-

spiration for them than I had out of the house. I had to
go down to Nola's and get my inspiration. Dizzy,
Miles—just all the musicians came here. Seemed like I
was inspiration or something for them.[21]

Monk in particular was drawn to Mary. She had first met him as a
teenager in 1934, when he was touring with a tent show. Inspired by the
harmonic ideas Monk played, Mary adopted them into her own work
and began improvising on them with Kirk's tenor saxophonist, Dick
Wilson. Monk in turn valued her opinion greatly and often camped at
her house.

> I remember once one morning I got sleepy so I said, "I'm
> going to bed." When the guys left, the door was open
> and Monk rang the doorbell and he came inside. He dis-
> covered that I was asleep—it was around eight o'clock
> in the morning. I had a big, big twin bed, so when I woke
> up I saw something on the other bed and I screamed. He
> yelled too and ran out the door and ran into the closet
> and the clothes fell on him. I said, "What are you doing
> here?" He said, "Well, I wanted to write something or
> play something and you were sleeping and I didn't want
> to bother you," and he was lying on his back with this
> tam on. That was the funniest thing.[22]

Of the beboppers, Mary was the closest to Monk, Powell, and Gillespie. But Monk, more than the others, frequently asked Mary for her
musical opinion. "Monk would write a tune and he'd come here and
play it for two or three months. I'd say, 'Why do you keep playing the
same thing over and over?' He'd say, 'I'm trying to see if it's a hit. It'll
stay with you if it's a hit.'"[23] Later in the 1950s, when they both were in
Paris, Mary would introduce Monk to Baroness Pannonica de Koenigswarter, commonly referred to as Nica, who would become the patron
saint of jazz musicians.[24]

Mary became the matriarch of the modern jazz movement when she
opened her apartment and ears to the musical and personal concerns of
bebop musicians. She would eventually become a victim of the schism
that developed from the advent of bop. It was assumed that Mary, as a
proponent of early jazz styles, would denounce the genre, as did many of

her early jazz colleagues, but Mary wouldn't and thereby lost the friend-ship of many older musicians. Mary's relationship with the boppers "cre-ated a jealousy." "When bop came along," she said, "they felt that it was so strange that it wasn't right, that it wasn't good. You know, you always have that dissension. They didn't understand it and it was so far out. I understand that a lot of musicians were in the army. When they came out and heard that, they put their instruments down and got a job working. They thought maybe the music was too tough to play." [25] Mary em-braced the experimental sounds largely because she was well aware of how the industry could be stifling to one's creativity, since she had faced similar challenges during her tenure with the Clouds of Joy. Mary simply accepted the musicians and their music and provided inspiration for their ideas.

She also aided many of these musicians in finding employment when swing bands began disappearing. "The older musicians put them down and they couldn't find work because of the crazy music they were play-ing. I put them to work with me." [26] One such musician was her Cleve-land bandmate and fellow Pittsburgher Art Blakey, whom Mary took on as the drummer for her combo. Her relationship with the boppers often led to her personally "saving" the musicians from ruining their lives and careers. During one period, the Birdland nightclub offered Mary $75 a week to take care of Bud Powell, but she declined the offer. Powell suf-fered from psychotic episodes during which he would not show up for gigs or would refuse to play. Once when the pianist was playing the nightclub, Mary decided to drop in and judge his behavior for herself. She recalled:

> I went down there and I slipped in on Bud Powell. . . .
> Bud Powell was really gone; he was out of his mind.
> Something happened—it wasn't his drinking or smok-ing or anything else. I think from my feelings and Bud being around me I think he was over-sensitive, you know.
> He felt everybody, felt everything because he was so ter-rific in his music. Usually when he'd get into these things I'd take him home and make him take a hot bath and just put him in my front room and make him sleep.
> When he got up he'd play like mad and he'd go like mad.
> But if he had an engagement at Birdland or places like

that, for about three days he was all right and the fourth day he was gone, he was out of sight, and nobody could do anything with him.[27]

She shared a similar relationship with Charlie Parker, who "would always call and ask me if I liked some of the things he had written and when he did the strings he asked me to come down to Birdland."[28] Mary's influence with the younger generation of musicians even extended to Miles Davis, who she claimed got the idea for the "Birth of Cool" sessions from her. "Miles happened to be with me one day and Milton Orent. Milton and I were just saying a combination of things and I mentioned about a tuba and I think that that thing, that sound that Miles got on a record, was an idea of me just thinking of instruments, and he called me back and thanked me. We were all just sitting here naming instruments that we'd like to do things with, you know. He thanked me."[29]

When asked about her relationship with these younger musicians, Mary remarked,

> I considered myself lucky having men like Monk and Bud playing me the things they had composed. And I have always upheld and had faith in the boppers, for they originated something but looked like losing credit for it. Too often have I seen people being so chummy with creative musicians, then—when the people have dug what is happening—put down the creators and proclaim themselves king of jazz, swing or whatever. So the boppers worked out a music that was hard to steal. I'll say this for the "leeches," though: they tried. I've seen them in Minton's busily writing on their shirt cuffs or scribbling on the tablecloth. And even our own guys, I'm afraid, did not give Monk the credit he had coming. Why they even stole his idea of the beret and bop glasses.[30]

Although Mary maintained a very close relationship with the beboppers and was one of a few of the "older" musicians to publicly acknowledge their contributions, it was not until the late 1940s that she would produce her first compositions that reflected the bebop style. But Mary, despite her influence on the beboppers, would never be viewed as an innovator in the style.

Throughout the summer of 1945, Mary remained busy, balancing her schedule at Café Society with performances at various events, including a jam session at Lincoln Square Center, where she shared the bill with Dizzy Gillespie, Ben Webster, Slam Stewart, and others, and a short solo stint at the McKinley Theater in the Bronx. By the fall Mary had become a well-established fixture of the New York scene, with live audiences, record buyers, and the press acclaiming her talent with every opportunity. Jimmy Butts and Pitt Smith, writers for the *New York Age,* wrote in their September 1 "Places and Personalities" column that Mary had lived up to her reputation as the "Queen of the Ivories," earning the distinction because of her successes at Café Society and WNEW. The writers explained that while WNEW had originally planned to feature Mary's radio program for only twelve weeks, its popularity had caused the network to extend her show indefinitely. In closing, the writers advised that if readers hadn't "seen her at Café Society or heard her over the networks," they should be sure to hear her at the McKinley Theater.[31]

Mary's popularity increased as Asch released more of the material Mary had recorded. From March until the early fall, Asch Records released several Mary Lou Williams recordings, including her renditions of Irving Berlin's "Blue Skies," "Russian Lullaby," "Night and Day," and "I Found a New Baby." One review of the recording, Asch 351, which also included the tunes "Persian Rug" and "You Know Baby," stated, "Mary Lou's work is consistently pleasant, bassist Hall is a mighty man, and trumpeter Coleman has some exceedingly fine moments." [32] Three months later, Asch released the two tracks Mary had recorded with Josh White, "Froggy Bottom" and "The Minute Man," the proceeds of which were slated to be donated in part to the National Service Fund of the Disabled American Veterans.

Mary's already busy schedule tightened when in late 1945 she accepted additional recording opportunities with other labels. Believing that the opportunities would allow her to expand her audience and experiment with new formats and material, Mary would soon learn that the creative freedom Asch had given her would not extend to other labels. Her first session teamed her with Leonard Feather, then working for Continental Records, who had approached Mary with an offer to record with an all-female group. Mary was reluctant at first, knowing that most of these recordings were viewed as novelties and rarely taken seriously by record companies or critics. Feather persisted and Mary finally agreed to

participate in the session, but only with the assurance that the best female musicians available would be contracted. Mary knew that there
were but a few women who were capable of playing at the level she required. Mary also knew that the only way that these recordings would
surpass the novelty status would be with the right combination of musicians and material. She was skeptical that Feather could come up with
notable musicians; after all, most talented women musicians either were
attempting to maintain their careers in the remaining all-female swing
bands or had exited the scene to raise families or pursue other employment opportunities, as jobs vacated by enlisted male musicians were now
being reclaimed.

Having previously worked with several female musicians during recording sessions, Feather was sure he knew the right ones to complement
Mary's playing. He put together the vibraphonist Marjorie Hyams, who
had worked with Woody Herman, the guitarist Mary Osborne, the
bassist June Rotenberg, and the drummer Bridget O'Flynn. The combination of instruments mirrored a group Feather had successfully employed during a series of sessions with the bassist Slam Stewart earlier
that year. Feather was sure he could duplicate the success of those sessions with this group. Mary agreed with Feather's selection, but shortly
before the group was slated to go into the studio, Rotenberg backed out,
citing a previous commitment. Unable to locate another competent female bassist in New York on such short notice, Mary and Feather decided to hire the bassist Billy Taylor for the sessions. To disguise Taylor's
gender, Feather dubbed him "Bea Taylor" and restricted the media's access to the recording sessions. "No photographers and, needless to say,
no potential reviewers were invited to the date, which was for Continental. The secret was so well kept that thirty-five years later, when the
records were reissued on Onyx, Dan Morgenstern observed in his liner
notes: 'The Misses Taylor or O'Flynn, on whom I have no biographical
data, do nicely.'" [33] This first session resulted in the recording of two of
Feather's original compositions, "Blues at Mary Lou's" (Continental
6032), and "D.D.T." (Continental 6021), in addition to "Rumba Rebop" (Continental 6032), "(She's) He's Funny That Way" (Continental
6021), and Mary's composition "Timme Time." The last was never released commercially, and "He's Funny That Way" was released on *Mary
Osborne with Mary Lou Williams Girl Stars*. The recordings were well

received, and the formula would be revisited in 1946, when Feather recorded a series of women in jazz.

In November 1945 Mary returned to Café Society Uptown in what was described as "an indefinite engagement." [34] Although the nightly crowds at the Uptown provided concrete evidence of Mary's talent and popularity with New York audiences, she felt that the format limited her musically. She was desperately seeking other ways to write and perform jazz. Resolution would come soon, at the end of 1945, when she interrupted her stint at the Uptown long enough to premiere her *Zodiac Suite* in an extended format at Town Hall.

Chapter 7

UNDER THE SIGNS OF THE ZODIAC

Mary was grateful for the opportunities Barney Josephson had provided over the years, but she was not very happy with the musical rut she found herself in. She had produced some notable arrangements during her performances at the nightclub, but the majority of the patrons that filled Café Society came to hear Mary play "Roll 'Em," "Walkin' and Swingin'," and the other compositions she had made famous with the Kirk band. This format was stifling for Mary and left her with little room to spread her compositional wings. Mary found some release in her weekly radio program, but again there were certain expectations that dictated how she would use her time.

Mary seemed happy with the recording she made of her *Zodiac Suite* in 1945, but as always she was thinking of new ways of playing the twelve pieces. Her studies of the scores of Hindemith, Stravinsky, and other classical composers, along with the nightly experiments with the beboppers, had inspired Mary to look beyond composing for combo and solo piano. These factors, in concert with Mary's experiences with Duke Ellington and the business savvy of Josephson, would set the stage for Mary's orchestral debut of the *Zodiac Suite*.

In 1943, Duke Ellington, then considered one of the top jazz band-leaders of the swing era, had premiered at Carnegie Hall an epic orchestral work chronicling the experiences of blacks in America. It was a historic event in that no other black band had ever been the only act on the program at the concert venue. There, waiting in the shadows, was Mary Lou Williams, who realized that the premiere of *Black, Brown, and Beige* was monumental not simply because it was performed at Carnegie Hall but because it expanded the compositional possibilities of jazz. Ellington, who had written notable dance tunes and popular songs since the 1920s, had managed in three movements to fuse classical form and jazz sensibilities and forever change the manner in which jazz was perceived. The reaction was mixed, with some charging Ellington with betraying his musical roots, but Mary's reaction was much different. As an arranger she had violated every practical "rule" of composition in order to re-create the musical sounds she heard in her head, and this maverick approach had set her apart from her colleagues. Ellington's exploration of new and different musical sounds and approaches was a confirmation for Mary that jazz did not have to be one thing or sound one way. It excited her, and two years later it would inspire her to pursue similar avenues.

Mary aspired to have the *Zodiac Suite* performed in an orchestral setting, just like Ellington's *Black, Brown, and Beige*. Theoretically, her work was distantly related to many of Ellington's, in that it sought to portray real-life personalities through music. Ellington had mastered this form with his compositions "Willie 'the Lion' Smith," "Bojangles," "Bert Williams," and "Jack the Bear." But unlike these pieces, which were individual compositions, the twelve movements of the *Zodiac Suite* would be blended into one epic work. Mary took her idea for an orchestral version to Barney Josephson, who agreed to sponsor the concert financially and secured Town Hall as the venue. Mary began rescoring the movements, expanding the instrumentation to twelve instruments:

oboe, flute, French horn, tenor sax (appears only in "Cancer"), five strings, piano, bass, and drums. Motivically, the revised suite drew from previous ideas, but more attention was given to areas that could be improvised on in combo or solo settings. Mary explored new compositional approaches that allowed the extended ensemble to maintain the jazz feeling of the piece.

The work was rehearsed and on December 31, 1945, it was presented by Edmund Hall's chamber orchestra, conducted by Milton Orent. The chamber orchestra was aided by Mary Lou's own big band, which consisted of Ben Webster on tenor, Eddie Banfield on clarinet, the trombonist Henderson Chambers, the trumpeter Irving Randolph, the bassist Al Hall, and the drummer J. C. Heard. Much like Ellington's 1943 Carnegie Hall concert, the program combined the premiere of the *Zodiac Suite* with performances of some of Mary Lou's most popular compositions. The concert was divided into two halves, the first devoted primarily to the suite and the second a presentation of jazz and boogie-woogie. It was a musical marriage of Mary's past and present. During the second half, Mary performed, in both solo and trio formats, a medley of "What's Your Story, Morning Glory?," "Cloudy," "Ghost of Love," and "Froggy Bottom." The entire medley was instrumental, with the exception of the "Froggy Bottom" portion, which featured a small group singing the simple lyrics that Josh White had only months earlier recorded. The small jazz band also played "Lonely Moments," a composition Mary had written years earlier, and an expanded version of "Gjon Mili Jam Session."

The concert drew a who's who of the New York scene. In Mary's estimation, the evening was progressing well until the orchestra got to the special arrangement of "Roll 'Em," which was the only "traditional" jazz number performed by the group. "The long drawn-out string threw some of the other musicians," recalled Mary. "I think the conductor lost the place, and for a moment I thought we had it. Everyone seemed to be playing a different page, and I'll never forget Ben Webster's big eyes fixed on me. I thought I would blow a blood vessel any second. I remember yelling: 'Count eight and play letter "J."' Somehow we got them out of "Roll 'Em.'"[1]

Despite what Mary perceived as a disastrous performance of "Roll 'Em," the audience and critics received the concert warmly. The *New York Times* reported that the *Zodiac Suite* was a "rather ambitious work, consisting of numbers named after the various constellations, [which] was performed by the Ed Hall combination, with Miss Williams at the piano. The piano's part was largely that of the old 'continuo' in early music, and individual instruments, such as the drums and the double bass, the tenor saxophone, the trumpet, and a singer (Hope Foye) spotlighted particular constellations. The composition was scarcely a jazz piece at all, making its appeal as more serious work—how success-ful time will tell."[2] Barry Ulanov, writing for *Metronome*, credited Mary with "a brave try, a partial success and the courage of her musical convictions."

> Her concert at Town Hall, on Sunday afternoon 31 De-cember, was in spite of many lapses, a handsome demon-stration of the music she believes in and I believe in, the music of the future, I think. In spite of under rehearsing, some very sloppy ensemble work and an occasional spot of poor conception and construction, the *Zodiac Suite* offered some very touching moments. Most impressive was the use of jazz horns against string and woodwind backing. With Ben Webster and Mouse Randolph to blow the jazz, Mary Lou to supply the material and Milt to give it scoring depth, these sections really came on.[3]

Mary, exhausted from the experience, was ill for a week following the concert. When she regained her health, she returned to Town Hall to gather the acetates that Josephson had paid to have made. The staff at Town Hall could not locate the recordings, and it was assumed that they had been stolen. Some years later, Mary would deduce that Timme Rosenkrantz had stolen them and planned to release them. Mary fig-ured that no one else would have had the type of backstage access that Rosenkrantz had, except Josephson. He may well have approached the engineer and told him that he would deliver the acetates to Mary, who was surrounded by reporters, well-wishers, and fans. Rosenkrantz, who was known for his dubious dealings, never gave the recordings to Mary, thinking he would release them on his Danish-based label. In 1991, the recordings were issued in their entirety. Mary never heard what the or-chestral debut of the suite sounded like. She would, however, have the opportunity to perform a portion of the work again in less than six months.

The year 1946 marked the beginning of the transition of the mainstream New York scene from its emphasis on swing and big band music to the "new" sounds of bebop. For Mary the year began with her regular gig at Café Society, but she also accepted a commission to write the score for the director Herman Schumlin's new play, *Jeb*. In February she returned to the Asch studios to record several sides of solo piano for the producer's new label, the Disc Company of America. Moe Asch had dissolved his partnership with Herbert Harris and Stinson Records in 1945. Three years of solid business had not enabled Asch to accumulate enough capital to pay his artists and press the amount of records needed to sustain the company's catalogue. Between January 1943 and November 1945, the two sides reached a settlement, with Asch agreeing to sell to Harris and his partner Irving Prosky all the master recordings. The agreement also gave Harris and Prosky the right to use the Asch Records name but forbade Asch to do so. Prosky and Harris forfeited any rights to the Asch studios, and the producer was hired at a weekly salary of $125 to instruct the pair in the completion of the records. Asch remained obligated to Stinson through the production of Mary's *Zodiac Suite,* an album of folk songs by Josh White, and an album of French poetry. The agreement also stipulated that Asch would never make or sell records with the same title by the same artist as those sold under the Asch-Stinson label. A second contract signed on December 22 allowed the sale of all the musicians' contracts with Asch and Harris and Prosky for a dollar.[4] None of the artists who had recorded with Asch ever made new recordings for Stinson after the dissolution of the partnership. By January 1946 Asch had regrouped, signed with Clark Phonograph Company for the pressing of his albums, and launched the Disc Company of America.[5]

The February 16, 1946, session included "How High the Moon" (Disc 5025), "The Man I Love" (Disc 5026), "Cloudy" (Disc 5025), "Blue Skies" (Disc 5026), "These Foolish Things Remind Me of You" (Disc 5027), and "Lonely Moments" (Disc 5027). They would be Mary's last recordings as an "exclusive" artist of Moe Asch. The public and the critics greeted them enthusiastically. In the July 15, 1946, edition of *Down Beat,* the record critic wrote, "If nothing else, this album would be noteworthy for a good left hand beat, and rarest of all, a tone that sings even while jumping. Then too there is an engaging simplicity to Mary Lou's playing which is welcome relief amidst all the frantic scale players. Seems to me she did 'Cloudy' while with Andy Kirk, while 'Moments' is an original done first for orchestra. I recommend most sincerely that Hazel Scott listen to this side and compare it with her own playing. The comparison honestly made should be fruitful for her future pianistic progress."[6] A review for *Billboard* asserted, "There is sheer melodic beauty in the piano improvisations developed by Mary Lou Williams for six solo sides that make up this album. Her piano moods, running the gamut from classical to barrelhouse, make them a desired set of disks. It is pure piano jazz throughout."[7]

Happy with the critical response her recent releases were receiving, Mary received additional good news when the impresario Norman Granz approached her with an opportunity to perform the *Zodiac Suite* with the Carnegie Pops Orchestra, as part of its concerts celebrating jazz. Mary, aware of her popularity with New York audiences, accepted Granz's offer but asked for what the promoter thought was an exorbitant payment. Granz, in his usual fashion, lost his temper and told Mary that she wasn't worth anything to him and that he "knew a town where none of [her] records ever sold."[8] Mary was angry at first but soon discovered from others and through interaction with Granz that this was just his way. Although she did not receive her requested price, Mary negotiated a deal with Granz that allowed her to perform three movements of the suite with the orchestra. Mary was determined "to hear [her] work played by 100 paper men,"[9] a colloquial term for classical musicians, and wouldn't let money stop her dream from coming true. (In actuality Mary produced seventy parts, not a hundred.) The concert was booked at Carnegie Hall, and Mary was left with little over a week to produce the orchestral scores. Having never written for a symphonic orchestra before, Mary enlisted the help of Milton Orent.

Orent, a bassist and staff arranger with NBC Radio, had befriended Mary when he prepared some arrangements for the Clouds in the 1930s. Over the years their relationship grew and it was rumored that the two were lovers. Regardless of their personal relationship, there developed a strong musical bond. In the years following the performance of the *Zodiac Suite* at Carnegie Hall, the two would collaborate on several projects, including what has been deemed the first bop song, "In the Land of Oo Bla Dee," and a pop song called "Pittsburgh." Dizzy Gillespie, Benny Goodman, and Mary recorded the latter during the late 1940s and early 1950s. Orent inspired Mary to expand her musical perspective and talked with her extensively about the technical aspects of music. They would often visit the library on East Fifty-eighth Street, listen to music, and read scores of the works of Hindemith, Schoenberg, Berg, and other German composers. Orent even "made a present of a few scores and records. The reason I was so ahead in modern harmony was that I absorbed it from Milt. He knew so much about chords and things. He knew a great deal about Schoenberg, Hindemith, and others before it became the thing. After being around him a while I decided to dig intellectual music." [10]

It is not clear how many movements were actually scored by Mary and how many by Orent, but some sources have reported that he scored two of the three movements, "Aquarius" and "Sagittarius." Orent had other obligations that prevented him from aiding Mary in the completion of the scores, so she worked on "Scorpio" alone. According to Mary, "He had a gig coming up Saturday that he had forgotten about. It was an important gig, like he was the leader, and he had to go up in the country to play bass. So he said, 'Pussycat'—that was my nickname then—'I can't finish the arrangements.' I said, 'Oh, goodness, I'll finish them myself.' I did 'Scorpio.' He was so surprised. I had never written for a symphony in my life." [11] Under the encouragement of Moe Asch, Norman Granz, and David Stone Martin, Mary began arranging the remaining movements. Using a method similar to her way of arranging and writing during her days with Andy Kirk, Mary "laid out the paper on the floor and arranged 'Scorpio.' It was 7:00 in the evening when I started and the writing didn't take that long, but then I had to copy all the parts—for [seventy] pieces." When she finished the parts of the suite, Mary decided to compose a blues for the orchestra.

> The day before the big night Milton had to leave town for his summer job, I stayed up the best part of the night working on a blues for the orchestra. I had already arranged "Libra," "Scorpio" and "Aquarius," dedicating the last to President Roosevelt. The blues was an idea that came on that last minute. I called Milt, a hundred miles away, and asked "what about having the symphony play a jazz piece?" His reply was: "Don't do that, Pussycat." I took no notice. It was 6:30 P.M. when I began this piece of craziness. Before I knew it, it was seven

in the morning and I had just finished copying for the five basses. After grabbing a few hours' sleep, I made the 2 P.M. rehearsal.[12]

The rehearsal the next day proved to be quite rewarding. At first Mary was a little hesitant in presenting her new compositions, but finally she decided to "go with it." Mary recalled:

> I took all my arrangements in, Mr. Rybb was there, the manager of the Carnegie, and I was afraid to pass the blues out. So I had the girl [Ann Kullmer, the conductor] to rehearse just the "Zodiac Suite." When someone called Mr. Rybb to the phone I said, "Wait a minute, wait a minute. I gave you the wrong arrangement. Here, this one." So I passed it out fast while he was away and they played it and the musicians went wild. They never played anything like that before. . . . I had them doing a boogie thing and they'd play a blues on it. I had no difficulty in teaching them how to phrase it or do it. Yeah, 36 violins, they stood up and played this kind of a boppish chorus.[13]

The June 22, 1946, concert was performed by a seventy-member orchestra with Herman Neumann as conductor. The musicians earnestly practiced the music and the night of the concert managed to pull it off. Both the conductor and Mary were very nervous the afternoon of the concert, but after the music started both settled down. "After the intro., I had four choruses of fast boogie, then oboe and trumpet playing, written solos; last, but not least I gave the 36 violins two bop choruses, and I must say they tackled them bravely. At the concert that night the performance was quite sensational. The boys in the symphony applauded louder than the audiences and, to prove they meant it, carried on like mad backstage."[14] Mary left the concert more assured of her abilities. In contrast to the previous concert, Mary eventually received copies of the recordings made from the performance.

Despite the musical high that the Carnegie Hall concert gave her, Mary was physically exhausted. Working consistently since the early 1920s and juggling regular performances at the Café Society with specialty concerts was taking its toll. In the summer of 1946, Mary Lou decided to take a vacation from the music scene. What she would en-counter on the streets of Harlem, where she lived, would forever change her perspective of black life in America.

* * *

The Harlem Mary stepped out into in 1946 was a far cry from the mythical and real-life Harlem of the renaissance years. The "Negro Heaven," as so many writers, poets, musicians, and painters had por-trayed the area, was now only a memory. Much had happened to Harlem since Mary had first visited there in the 1920s with the TOBA, in the 1930s with the Andy Kirk orchestra, or even in the early 1940s, when she became an active participant in the evolving modern jazz movement. Most members of the black elite, who had defined upper-class black life on Sugar Hill and Strivers Row, had died or were no longer the players in Harlem society. The new generation of middle-class and elite blacks had dispersed to the suburban neighborhoods of Westchester County, Long Island, Connecticut, and the new "suburban Sugar Hill" enclave of St. Albans, in Queens. There Louis Armstrong, Count Basie, Mercer Ellington, Ella Fitzgerald, and other notable blacks established a new sense of black society with their expensive homes. Mary, however, was determined to stay in Harlem and would do so until her move to Durham, North Carolina, in 1977. Even then she would keep her apart-ment on Hamilton Terrace.

Harlem's nightlife, which had drawn so many uptown in the 1920s and 1930s, was practically nonexistent by the mid-1940s. The end of Prohibition in 1933 had drawn many patrons to downtown establish-ments, which served up legal liquor and suitable entertainment, and the riots of 1935 and 1943 had frightened away even the most devoted fans. The deathblow to Harlem's nightlife was dealt when several of the pop-ular nightclubs, including the Cotton Club, closed or moved to down-town locations. By the late 1940s the Apollo Theatre was the only place uptown that offered stage shows as lively and entertaining as those of the old Harlem, and jazz could hardly be heard. For the first time since the 1920s, Harlem was not the center of the jazz movement in New York. Most of the leaders of the new school of jazz ignored Harlem and its min-imal wages. They headed for the jazz clubs that lined West Fifty-second Street in search of fame, recognition, and wealth. Mary was not so will-ing to give up on Harlem or its people. She walked the streets looking for ways to combat the ever-growing cloud of poverty and hopelessness that enveloped Harlemites. "From Lenox to 125th Street and 8th Avenue I cruised all over Harlem. Never had I been in such a terrible but fascinating environment among people who roamed the streets lamping [*sic*] for someone to devour. Truthfully, it was fascinating to watch one race of people live off each other. I wondered why the shrewd brains never ventured downtown where the real gold was." [15] Despite the conditions in Harlem, Mary felt a connection with the people. After all, she knew first-hand the type of desperation that poverty bred. Despite her awareness of the criminal inclinations of many Harlemites, Mary was often lured into a financial bind by the hard-luck stories of neighbors. "I got mixed up with the wrong characters. When someone gave me a line I swallowed it hook and sinker. The next thing, someone I considered a friend had got me in a swindle. I was having fun like a babe in the woods; lost so much money, which I regularly drew from my postal savings, that the authorities thought some goon was blackmailing me." [16] Mary's generosity offered temporary relief to her neighbors, but true economic empowerment would not come for Harlemites without substantial social changes in New York. Mary, on the other hand, found herself in financial straits and after six months was forced to return to full-time performing. But going back would prove more difficult than Mary ever imagined.

*　*　*

The jazz scene, which Mary had vacated only six months earlier, had been transformed by the evolving modern jazz movement. As dance halls began closing because of the "death of swing," club owners scrambled to recapture the dwindling crowds, who thought that bebop was too complicated, noisy, and even unpatriotic in its approach. The proliferation of nightclubs on Fifty-second Street meant that club owners battled one another for top-shelf performers, and musicians could bargain over their salaries. Mary's "vacation" from jazz came at a time when her popularity should have ensured her audiences and bookings, but club owners were uninterested in hiring her and she found herself trying to reestablish her presence in the clubs. She once again turned to Joe Glaser. Glaser worked consistently to secure bookings for Mary and tried to expand her audience by sending pictures of her to "practically every European country in the world." He was convinced, primarily by the use of the photo on the cover of *Jazz Magazine,* that he could soon book her on a European tour. Mary's focus, however, was on the New York jazz scene. Unable to garner what she thought were suitable bookings there, Mary opted for dates that took her to Chicago, Boston, Philadelphia, and her hometown, Pittsburgh. When Mary returned to New York, club owners and record companies were once again interested in her. She was offered several opportunities to record with different companies, but none was willing to offer her a recording contract comparable to her agreement with Asch Records, which was barely operating because of its financial problems. Disappointed by her inability to break through the "glass ceiling" developing in jazz, Mary accepted these sporadic opportunities to record, believing that they would allow her to expand her audience and experiment with new formats and material.

Inspired by the all-female recordings he had produced in 1945, Leonard Feather contracted Mary to record with her all-female trio for a series featuring various groups of women musicians. Steve Sholes, an executive with RCA Victor, had signed on to the project. It would be called the *Girls in Jazz* album. Feather would later dismiss the sexist title by stating that the musicians never objected. "Women might have been uneasy about being called girls, but nobody was sensitive enough (or brave enough) to voice any objection." [17] The six sessions for the album included two with Mary, one with Beryl Booker and Her Trio, one with the International Sweethearts of Rhythm, and one with the Vivien Garry Quintet. Mary's first session on July 24 brought together Marjorie Hyams and Mary Osborne, but June Rotenberg replaced Billy Taylor on bass and the drummer Rose Gottesman replaced Bridget O'Flynn. It yielded five sides: three Mary originals, "Fifth Dimension," "Harmony Grits," and "Boogie Misterioso," one of Feather's compositions, "Conversation (Jump Caprice)," and the standard "It Must Be True." A second session on October 7 featured a trio consisting of Mary, Rotenberg, and O'Flynn. For the session Mary wrote "Waltz Boogie," which was set in a swinging ¾ meter. The combination proved successful and in late 1946 RCA Victor released *Girls in Jazz*. Mary and the multiple combinations of sidemen who had worked with her during the sessions were featured on six sides. Reviews of the recordings were mixed. *Metronome* reported in its January 1947 edition, "'Waltz Boogie' is, in the strictest sense of the word, unique. Mary Lou dreamed up a charming melody in ¾ time set to boogie patterns which are, of course, done here in six-to-the-bar style. This not only gets a great mood, but proves that you really can get a good jazz beat in waltz time." In May the same journal asserted that "It Must Be True" and "Harmony Grits" were bad recordings that featured the "worst Mary Lou Williams piano."

Through late 1946 and early 1947, Mary continued to play solo and combo stints at various locations. However, in April 1947 Mary's trio with June Rotenberg and Marjorie Hyams was contracted to perform at Carnegie Hall as a part of the Concerts in Jazz series. The group was well received and the press exclaimed that the "thing about the femmes' playing which sold the crowd was their obvious and infectious enjoyment in what they were doing." [18] Michael Levin, who reviewed the concert for *Down Beat* wrote:

> New York concert audiences are so accustomed to indifferent playing by gathered stars, that they got a tremendous boost from the three girls playing for their own enjoyment rather than to cut each other. Also, all three musicians used ideas, not devices. There are undoubtedly soloists their equal in each instrument, but very few who in a public performance would stick so closely to playing good jazz rather than displaying dazzling techniques and learned tricks. [19]

Despite the trio's success, the group disbanded, and Mary returned to Asch's studios for what would be her last sessions for Disc. The first session was released under the title *The Mary Lou Williams Ensemble*. The band was in fact Milton Orent and Frank Roth's Orchestra. The group recorded "Lonely Moments," which she had featured during the 1945 Town Hall concert, and "Whistle Blues." On April 5 she was recorded with Charlie Ventura's sextet during a performance at Carnegie Hall. That session yielded one track released on the Verve label, called "Just You, Just Me." Later that year, along with Kenny Dorham, Johnny Smith, and Grachan Moncur, Mary recorded two originals: "Kool" and "Mary Lou." One critic, proclaiming the merits of the recordings upon their release, asserted, "There is no femme musician in the country within miles of her." *Down Beat* wrote:

> "Mary Lou" includes some verbal extolling of piano playing by members of the band, but leaves some room for her sparkling tone and excursions into chordal col-

oring. "Kool" has some inexcusably sloppy guitar and muted trumpet at the outset, all made up for by her playing. Mary Lou, like Coleman Hawkins, is one of the few and amazing musicians who have been top-notchers for over 15 years, yet are staying up with everything that any young jazzman today is playing.[20]

In late 1946 and early 1947 Mary had continued to play sporadically at Café Society, but the club's popularity was diminishing as accusations of Communist affiliations were leveled against Barney Josephson and some of his most notable performers. Mary, like most of the performers at Café Society, greatly respected Josephson for his business sense and his drive for equity for black performers, but his political leanings and liberal, left-wing attitude presented serious problems. Josh White, who often shared the bill with Mary during the early 1940s, testified voluntarily before the House Committee on Un-American Activities after the FBI questioned and intimidated him. Hazel Scott, whose political beliefs would lessen her mainstream popularity during the 1950s, also testified before the committee and is believed to have implied that Josephson initiated involvement in questionable activities. Mary escaped scrutiny and turned her attention to her career. After more than twenty years of performing, she assumed that by now she would have earned a level of distinction within the jazz scene that would garner her top billing and larger salaries. But Mary and other musicians could not have imagined what would happen to their careers in 1948.

In June 1947 James Petrillo and the American Federation of Musicians voted to impose another strike against the recording industry, after Congress brought in the Taft-Hartley Act, under which the original agreement between the union and the record companies was deemed illegal. To counteract the threat to union funds, the group decided that the contract between the union and the industry would not be renewed, and a ban would begin on January 1, 1948. As they had before the first strike, record companies scrambled to stockpile records and transcriptions. The ban would last almost eleven months, and it meant that Mary, along with other members of the union, made no records from January to December. The only exceptions would be a few government-issue V-discs ("Victory-discs") made with Benny Goodman in the fall of 1948.

More crippling to the jazz scene was the demise of Fifty-second Street.

The famous street that had been the center of the swing movement and the cradle of the modern jazz movement could no longer sustain itself, and many of the venues that lined the street closed. In April 1948 *Metronome* announced, "The street is dead!" The seven nightclubs that regularly featured jazz were either closed or barely existing. Kelly's Stable, where Mary's inaugural New York performance had happened in the early 1940s, was now a Chinese restaurant. Dixon's Club 18 (also called the Troubadour) suffered the same fate. The Downbeat folded and reopened under a new name, featuring girlie shows, and the Onyx, no longer able to make money with live music, now featured Symphony Sid playing records for his WHOM audience and conducting celebrity interviews.[21]

The collapse of Fifty-second Street and the recording ban made it increasingly difficult for musicians to sustain themselves financially. Mary was no exception. Instead of succumbing to financial pressures, which had led many musicians to look for more stable employment in Europe and others to give up their careers for day jobs, Mary decided to make opportunities for herself. She learned that her old friend Benny Goodman had recently formed a new septet. Mary figured that, in the worst case, Goodman wouldn't be interested in the new arrangements she had been working on. At best, he would not only purchase her arrangements but also give her a job as arranger for the group.

When she learned where Goodman was rehearsing, Mary rushed to the location with arrangements in hand. Goodman knew from the acclaim he had garnered with Mary's "Roll 'Em" and "Camel Hop" that the key to success for this group was good tunes written by Williams and other notable arrangers. Goodman had gathered some talented musicians—Wardell Gray, Billy Bauer, Mel Zelneck, Clyde Lombardi, Stan Hasselgard, and Teddy Wilson—but the ticket to longevity was an exciting debut. He offered Mary a temporary gig as arranger. Mary began sketching out charts for the group's May 10 debut at Carnegie Hall, but the concert was canceled because of poor ticket sales. Despite the setback, Mary continued writing. She produced new versions of "Bye Bye Blues," "There's a Small Hotel," and "Mary's Idea" (also known as "Just an Idea"). Goodman paid her $10 for each arrangement but promised to increase the fee as the band's success increased.

The Carnegie debacle did not deter Goodman. His group was booked into a restaurant–supper club called the Click in Philadelphia, but audiences who came to hear Goodman play his "classics" were disappointed by the smaller group playing new, unknown tunes. The septet did poorly at the Click, and the owner felt he had to renegotiate the $4,500-a-week salary he had offered to the band. Goodman decided to leave instead and hoped to resuscitate the group with a stint at the Westchester County Center in White Plains, New York. He secured the hall, paid for advertising, and booked a local big band to alternate with the septet. Goodman hoped the weekend shows, which were simultaneously broadcast on WNEW in New York, would be more successful. Shortly after the Click date, Teddy Wilson gave his notice, and immediately Goodman asked Mary to be his replacement. She hesitated at first, noting that arranging for Goodman was one thing, but playing for him was another. Mary knew of Goodman's reputation. He could be tyrannical and often suppressed the creativity of his musicians. Even worse, he never took no as the final answer. Mary accepted the offer only when Goodman announced he would record her arrangements in the fall for Capitol. Musicians in the union were hopeful that a resolution would be found before the end of the summer, despite Petrillo's unending demands.

On June 26, 1948, a revamped septet featuring Mary Lou Williams on piano and the notable bebop trumpeter Red Rodney debuted at the Westchester County Center. The result was no different from the Click experience. After three weekends, in which more money was lost than was made, Goodman canceled the remaining dates. Mary would explain that the band never played as well as it could because Goodman was too controlling. He suppressed any of the musicians' attempts to go beyond the prepared arrangements. The one occasion on which the band really played well, according to Mary, was when Goodman left the performance early. "The guys blew like mad this particular night," Mary recalled. Like many who had played with Goodman, she noted that the bandleader often made his musicians "feel uneasy by the discouraging look he gave them." [22] Goodman would later blame his policy of welcoming black patrons to the gigs as the reason ticket sales were dismal. He claimed that most white patrons were scared away by the prospect of sharing a hall with black patrons.

The septet's future was bleak, and tensions between Mary and Goodman were growing. It felt almost as if she was reliving her arguments with Andy Kirk in the 1930s. The problem lay in Goodman's rejection of modern jazz ideas, especially bop. Even when Mary tried to infuse these ideas into her compositions, Goodman would cut out those parts. Mary would recall one instance in which Goodman asked her to remove flatted fifths from an arrangement.[23] This frustrated Mary and eventually other members of the band who sought to explore the dynamics of the modern movement.[24] Mary soon rationalized that Goodman, like Kirk years earlier, only claimed to be producing music that remained true to the roots of the jazz tradition. But Mary knew that every arrangement, performance, and recording was commercially and politically motivated. Pushing past the musical boundaries through experimentation was the essence of the jazz tradition for Mary. She later said of Goodman, "I had found either a real neurotic or a monster—he was either too rich to blow or too sick."[25]

Despite the low wages and differences in musical perspectives, Mary knew that her affiliation with Goodman provided her with some stability and profile. Mary continued to endure his mood swings and demands, but being a strong-willed individual, she knew that there was a limit to what she could withstand. Throughout the summer of 1948 the band recorded several V-discs, but Goodman was unsuccessful at booking long-term engagements. The tensions between Goodman and Mary continued to brew and came to a head in September when Mary became frustrated during a recording session and left the studio. Goodman and the other musicians assumed that Mary was simply having a temper tantrum and would return soon—but she didn't. Accepting the fact that the venture would not work, Goodman decided to disband the group. Although angry initially because of Mary's behavior, Goodman forgave her in time. By 1949 he and Mary were once again corresponding, and in that year he recorded her bop fairy tale "In the Land of Oo Bla Dee" and "There's a Small Hotel." In 1950 he recorded one of Mary's new arrangements, "Walkin' Out the Door," but the record never caught on.

With the dissolution of Goodman's combo, Mary was once again faced with financial difficulties. Although she had managed, before Goodman's decision, to amass enough money to pay her monthly expenses and some outstanding debts, Mary knew it was only a matter of time before she would reenter the vicious cycle of mounting debts and low cash yield. Most would have immediately searched for new opportunities, but Mary felt physically tired and musically stunted. At thirty-eight, Mary had already experienced more than most women and musicians her age. She longed for more than the staleness of life on the road and formulaic performances. She wanted to explore the compositional aspirations that she had suppressed in favor of financial stability. So after much deliberation and financial juggling, Mary decided to take a break from full-time performing and focus on composing.

Almost four years had passed since Mary had written the *Zodiac Suite,* and she had often talked about continuing to compose, but the new works never materialized. Thinking that a change of scenery would get her juices flowing, Mary retreated to Pittsburgh, where she began working on an ambitious choral piece titled "Elijah under the Juniper Tree." Lyrics for the composition, commissioned by the director of a sixty-voice choir in the city, were taken from poetry by Ray Monty Carr. "Elijah" was more experimental than any of Mary's other compositions at this time. It was her first attempt at writing a choral work, and its biblical references foreshadowed the religious compositions that dominated her opus throughout the 1960s and early 1970s. The result was defined by harmonically complex and tightly written vocal parts juxtaposed with a sparse but often dissonant accompaniment. The Pittsburgh debut of "Elijah" in 1948 was the only performance of the work until it was resurrected in 1996 for the Lynx Jazz Festival in Florida.[26] But it had opened Mary to a new form of composition—one that extended beyond the regimented, formulaic popular songs of the time. "Elijah" rejected the AABA structure, emphasizing instead tonal colors created by voice combinations and text interpolations.

The "Elijah" commission and performance brought to life some of the musical sounds Mary was hearing in her head, but she knew that outside these special situations, there was not much interest within the mainstream jazz scene for such compositions. The reality of the time was that one-time commissions and well-attended concerts might bring in a substantial amount of money, but with the exception of Duke Ellington, one could not hope to make a living through such means. Even Ellington remained dependent on mainstream audiences who wanted to hear "Caravan," "Cottontail," and all of his other masterpieces. Mary knew she had to get booked into a club or take to the road playing one-nighters. With the competitive nature of New York and the ever-growing interest in West Coast jazz, Mary knew that neither would be easy without the right connections. Just as she began her usual routine of worrying and scrambling, Mary received a royalty check from the Disc Recording Company for the release of her last recordings, "Mary Lou" and

"Kool." The check provided temporary relief, but Mary had to make some professional decisions, and soon.

Mary contacted Joe Glaser, who mapped out a schedule of performances that would take her as far west as Iowa. The major booking on the Midwest tour was Critelli's Nightclub in Des Moines, Iowa, but Glaser planned a serious of gigs in other cities en route to Iowa and back to New York. Despite the hectic nature of touring and life on the road, Mary managed to have a good showing, but when she returned home, she found her apartment had been ransacked. Personal items such as her fur coat, records, gowns, and jewelry were missing, and she was financially unable to replace items that were important to her engagements. Although Mary treasured her records, it was the loss of her gowns and jewelry that troubled her the most. Both were essential to her live performances. She would either have to convince Glaser to loan her enough money to replace her gowns or earn enough to buy at least one or two new ones. Mary did not receive the much-needed money from Glaser, but she did receive an offer to record with an up-and-coming recording company.

Desperate to end the run of Murphy's Law that seemed to have defined the past few years of her life, Mary, without consulting Glaser or any of her friends, signed a contract to record with King Records of Cincinnati. Founded in 1944 by Sydney Nathan, King had initially focused its product on hillbilly music and the blues. However, in the late 1940s Nathan decided to expand the company's repertoire with the addition of several jazz bands. Mary was one of many jazz musicians who recorded, generally on a limited basis, with King. With two years having passed since her last recording under her name, Mary thought that a good record with the right type of marketing would resuscitate her career and bring her the type of attention that yielded extended bookings and larger salaries. Signing with King would prove to be a bad business decision. Unlike Moe Asch, Sydney Nathan and his A & R (artists and recordings) men felt it was their right to discuss with artists their song selections and performance approaches. Nathan believed he had a keen sense of what would sell and not sell, and he was willing to take the chance of angering the label's artists by making suggestions during recording sessions, if it meant the difference between a successful record and a failure. Mary would not escape this scrutiny; however, in time Mary's unhappiness with the label would go beyond such suggestions and focus on King's inability to market her recordings effectively.

Nevertheless, King and Mary were pleased with their contractual agreement, which paid Mary the standard rate of half a cent net per record. Mary's first session, on March 18, 1949, produced four bop-oriented compositions written for an octet. "Tisherome," "Knowledge," "Shorty Boo," and "In the Land of Oo Bla Dee" featured Martin Glazerbs on clarinet; Al Feldman, alto and flute; Denzil Best, drums; George Duvivier, bass; Alphonse Cimba, conga; Mundell Lowe, guitar; Idres Sulieman, trumpet; and Pancho Hagood, vocals.[27] Without immediate funds coming from the waxing of these recordings, Mary returned to performing in venues outside New York and occasionally in the few remaining clubs on Fifty-second Street.

In early April she accepted an invitation to play a concert benefiting a camp for young kids in Pittsburgh, which allowed her an opportunity to visit with family. Later that month she returned to New York to perform at the reincarnated Café Society Downtown, which was under new management and attempting to recapture the rich musical environment of its past and the accompanying crowds. Neither could be re-created, but that did not deter Mary from remaining there while waiting for other opportunities—such as the release of her King recordings.

Weeks after her opening at the new Café Society, Mary's first sessions with King were released to public acclaim. Critics applauded the first two releases, "Oo Bla Dee" and "Knowledge"; one wrote, "The recording is tubby, but it's a clever and worthwhile try, both musically and commercially."[28] Despite favorable ratings, by May 1949 King had not accelerated its promotion of the records. Troubled by the label's complacency, Mary wrote to Bob Ellis, head of the promotion department at King, that she needed help with promotion. To ensure the records received airplay, she had taken copies to all the disc jockeys in New York and sent them to two stations that requested them. She was hoping that the label would increase its participation in the recordings' "exploitation," as her touring outside the city made it difficult for her to continue her efforts.[29] Undoubtedly Mary did not receive the response she hoped for, and one week later, on May 9, she wrote to Sydney Nathan, head of King Records.

> As you probably know by this time "Oo Bla Dee" has sold out in New York and New Jersey. Believe me, they did not sell themselves. It was due to a pretty vigorous

campaign covering radio, television and newspaper plugs that I obtained myself. I'm trying so very hard to make a national hit and from the re-action up to date and with the cooperation that you promised me, I think we should have a hit record. Everybody is humming the darn thing without it being pushed down their throats. Several radio stations called last week asking for "Oo bla dee" (had many requests for it). I had to call Mr. Grogan and have him to send records to stations was surprised to find that you had not covered all radio stations. I realize that you are very busy but I really need your support. I'm really knocking myself out and not getting paid for the work.[30]

Nathan assured Mary that King would promote the record as much as possible. He explained that the lack of promotion at that point was due to a reorganization in the promotion department and that the company was arranging the delivery of records to disc jockeys. He wrote to Mary, "We are preparing streamers on 'Oo bla dee' and I last night delivered this record to three disc jockeys. I am just as anxious as you are to see this record really hit."[31] Mary, momentarily reassured of King's commitment, turned her attention to her weekly gigs throughout the Northeast, which included a booking at the Village Vanguard in August 1949 opposite J. C. Heard's trio.

During the Village Vanguard stint, Mary seemed more at peace than in previous months, and her nightly performances were well received. Although the nature of the nightclub business dictated that she perform mainly old songs like "St. Louis Blues," "Froggy Bottom," and "I Can't Get Started," Mary often spiced up these tunes with bop interpretations. On rare occasions when the audience seemed receptive, Mary would sit at the piano and compose new pieces on the spot. She sat at the piano, head erect and eyes closed. What flowed from the keys was pure Mary— music flowing from her heart. The critic for *International Musician* recalled that Mary seemed "always ahead of her playing, thinking into the next phrase, preparing, eliminating, thrusting forward."[32]

The small, intimate setting of clubs like the Vanguard suited Mary well, and she begged Glaser to search out comparable bookings. In September she was booked at the Village Barn, and on October 9, 1949, she played a recital at John Hancock Hall in Boston with Lennie Tristano. But Mary was growing more impatient and unhappy with King Records, which was still not, in her estimation, marketing her records effectively or setting new session dates for additional recordings. In her usual fashion, Mary wanted to retreat and sever her contract with the label. But freedom would come at a price. Mary was told that she owed the company over $1,000, which her royalties had not covered, and she would not be released until she produced another session.[33] Mary turned to Joe Glaser, who offered his personal attorney, Bernie Miller. But an angry exchange between the two ended the arrangement, and Mary remained obligated to King. Glaser, who often seemed more like a father and guardian angel than an agent to Mary, assured her that he would "give [her] every cooperation possible to get [her] record deal straightened out with King Records."[34]

Meanwhile, Mary continued performing throughout the Northeast. A gig at the Rendezvous Room in Philadelphia for one week was followed by an appearance on *Eddie Condon's Floor Show* on WPIX-TV in New York. The Condon appearance coupled Mary with the famed New Orleans clarinetist Sidney Bechet and the vocalists Johnny Mercer and Thelma Carpenter. Mary played several numbers with the larger group, but the highlight of the evening was her performance with a combo, which featured her interpretation of the standard "Caravan." The appearance provided Mary with some notable publicity, which Glaser wanted to capitalize on with more bookings. But Mary resisted, saying she would accept only certain bookings because she wanted to focus on making records. Her stubbornness and obsession with making a hit record eventually placed Mary in dire financial straits. She would spend the weeks preceding Christmas focused more on trying to raise rent money than on buying presents for family and friends.

Mary's obstinacy reflected her belief that she was a first-rate musician who had paid enough professional dues to deserve better working conditions and payment. But what would have been viewed as business acumen in male musicians earned Mary a reputation among booking agents and club managers of being "difficult," and Glaser found it increasingly taxing to secure comparable bookings. Mary's hopes that the 1950s would be more successful personally and professionally were dashed when she realized her mistake in turning down a lucrative booking to record a series of sessions for King. In debt and somewhat despondent over life in general, Mary returned to the King Studios on January 3 and recorded four sides with a trio consisting of Mundell Lowe on guitar, George Duvivier on bass, and Denzil Best on drums. The tracks, "Bye Bye Blues," "Moonglow," "Willow Weep for Me," and "I'm in the Mood for Love," featured Mary playing both piano and organ. What probably sounded good in theory proved to be disastrous in practice. The organ, judging by the extant recordings, sounded hampered and sluggish against the lilting piano. Nevertheless, Mary completed the sessions and immediately returned to Glaser for help. A week following the King session, Mary wrote to the agent explaining that she had not worked since the October 1949 gig in Philadelphia and was struggling financially. Glaser responded that Mary's rejection of potential bookings revealed to him that she did not really want to work or had developed an arrogant attitude that automatically eliminated certain venues. Mary's response was simple—she always appreciated a job, but there were certain places whose vibes prevented her from producing her best.[35]

Glaser may have been angered by Mary's flightiness, but his genuine love for the pianist kept him from severing his relationship with her. Instead, he would chastise her and labor behind the scenes to get her work or, in this case, to resolve her problems with King Records. He had written to Nathan early in 1949, requesting information on Mary's royalty payments and debts, and contacted Milt Gabler with Decca Records about the possibility of her recording with the company.[36] Neither result materialized quickly, and Mary worried about her mounting debts. Exacerbating the situation further was Mary's declining health. At first, she dismissed her growing tiredness as the effects of depression brought on by her financial situation; however, when the symptoms worsened, she began to fear she was seriously ill. Unable to withstand the hectic lifestyle of touring, Mary asked various friends and associates for loans. She asked Lou Levy, a jazz pianist, for $500 and Glaser for $350 but received only $100 from Levy. With no health insurance, the financial burden of her treatment, which consisted of injections for low blood pressure that cost $10 per visit, fell to Mary. Always in survival mode, something she had learned from her mother and other family members during her early years, Mary wrote to Glaser asking him to contact Leonard Feather, Barry Ulanov, and all the newspapers and magazines he had done business with and have them do a feature on her so that she could pick up an extended gig with some New York nightclub.[37] A little over a week later, she opened at Café Society Downtown at the rate of $400 a week for two weeks.

Mary's health slowly improved and she hoped that King would release her recent session soon, but the company had problems with the pressing. Mary thought that with the King release she could once again pack Café Society, which would lead to a larger tour of the United States. Once again, King and its inadequacies had slowed what Mary perceived as her forward momentum. The company continued to assure her that the records would be released as soon as the technical difficulties could be worked out, but she was not convinced that the company was treating her fairly. She struggled through her health issues and toured consistently outside New York. By May Glaser had managed to get her a two-week booking at Bop City in New York, one of the few clubs that offered patrons bop, swing, traditional jazz, and rhythm and blues. Mary formed a trio with Oscar Pettiford on bass and Kenny Clarke on drums. The combination was powerful, with each musician supporting the others. Mary, a particularly hard person to play for because of her emphasis on composing while playing and her no-nonsense attitude, was pleased with the music the group produced but soon found Pettiford's drinking a distraction. The bassist often drank excessively, which decreased his musical faculties. Despite her efforts to work around his alcohol habit, in time Mary felt she had no recourse other than to replace him with Percy Heath. Considerate of the fact that Pettiford needed to work regardless of his alcoholism, Mary placed him on cello, an unlikely instrument in jazz performances.

As it became increasingly clear that Glaser, despite all his efforts, could not resolve her conflicts with King, Mary began doubting the agent's intentions. In what could be perceived as an emotion-driven decision, Mary attempted to end her contract with Glaser and his Associated Booking Corporation. Not wanting to hold Mary back from what she perceived as better opportunities, Glaser advised her through James Petrillo, head of the American Federation of Musicians, that he would "be very happy to release her immediately upon payment of her debt to [ABC] which consists of $440 in personal loans and $80 in commissions, total $520." [38] Unable to resort to the past quick-fix solution of walking away from commitments without any thought of financial responsibility, Mary reconsidered the idea of severing the relationship with Glaser, partly because of her inability to settle her debt. But she was not so ready to give up on her fight to sever her contract with King. In the early fall she enlisted the aid of the American Federation of Musicians, hoping that the union would side with her, because of what she considered King's deliberate decision not to promote her recordings. She was right; on September 25 the union wrote her: "In compliance with the request of the American Federation of Musicians, King Records, Inc. hereby releases Mary Lou Williams from her exclusive recording contract with them. You are now free to record for any other company." [39] Mary's persistence had paid off, but the consequences would be serious. She was professionally labeled a "problem child."

But Mary had always managed to rise above the most negative situations. Before the end of 1950, she recorded several sides with Circle Records, hoping to finally achieve her goal of producing a hit record. The May 14 session consisted of a combo featuring Art Phipps, bass; Bill Clarke, drums; and the Dave Lambert Singers on vocals. Mary recorded four sides: "The Sheik of Araby" (never released by the company), "Yes, We Have No Bananas," "Walkin'," and "Cloudy" (which was never released). "Walkin'" and "Yes We Have No Bananas" did quite well and Mary hoped to capitalize on the success. She continued planning club dates in and outside New York in early 1951, including a stint at the Willows in Rochester, New York; a weeklong gig at the Comedy Club in Baltimore; and a run at the Birdland Theatre in New York. But she earned only $125 to $300 a week, which hardly covered her debts and household expenses. She once again turned her disappointment, fear, and frustration toward Joe Glaser. She accused him of being insensitive to her financial situation in his insistence that she pay her debt to ABC.[40] Glaser responded in bewilderment and reminded Mary that he was the only person who had gone out of his way to help her.[41] The heated discussion ended as most between the two had—with Mary apologizing and declaring her love for Glaser.

The tumultuous aspect of their relationship peaked in late 1951, when Mary wrote a scathing letter to the agent accusing him of being unscrupulous. "I used to worry when you told me all those nasty tales about being hard to handle but I know what people (agents) have done to me, which leaves me thinking, now that the Jewish race does not like Negroes," she wrote. As the letter progressed, Mary's anger brewed. All the disappointments and failures of the preceding thirty years spilled out onto the pages addressed to Glaser. She compiled a numerical list that chronicled the battles of a woman who wanted only to compose and perform good music and make a decent living.

> 1. I trusted you and you put me down. 2. You did not help any more than I helped you. Had you done publicity for anybody else other than me—you would not have gotten your start to work for Duke. 3. If you hadn't taken me to the Mirror, News, Telegram and Sun you would not have your contact for nothing was happening. So, I have helped you more than you have helped me. 4. I wanted you to believe I was sincere so, I let you swindle me when my record "Walking" came out. What happened? Nothing. You're under the impression that a woman should have an affair with you and also pay. 5. Andy Kirk, a Negro exploited me to one of your kind. Now if I ask for one thin dime, I'm either "Nigger Rich" or have a swell head. What kind of shit is this. I'm sick of your lies—you have insulted me and done everything conceivable. As far as Decca—you know that they owe me for a song I recorded for them 20 years ago and I haven't even received pay for the recording session. King did not give me a cent of royalty. Stinson owes me— Glaser has done his share—this you know. Now I'm supposed to kiss your—6. Do you know that there aren't any women and very few men that can do what I can musically. Women wouldn't be striving so hard to play if I hadn't started them on the road, yet I know I'm nice for I've never asked for money 'cept when I need it. You turned me down. You will have very bad-luck. Just you wait and see. I don't have to wish it on you like you wished on Thelma Carpenter. I have much patience to get what I want. If I treat everybody right, I'll get it.[42]

It is not clear if Mary actually sent the letter to Glaser or if he responded. But the intensity of the letter indicates that years of mismanagement and exploitation had taken its toll on Mary mentally and physically.

Chapter 8

THE CALM BEFORE THE STORM

In 1952 Mary continued her schedule of constant short-term gigs. In February she played the Blue Note in Philly; the Willows and Squeezers in Rochester, New York; and a stint on Peggy Lee's radio show. From May 26 until June 7 she was booked at Bill and Lou's Café in Philadelphia, and in August, along with Bruce Lawrence, Kenny Dorham, Art Blakey, and Jimmy Heath, she played Sparrows Beach in Annapolis, Maryland.

After a short stint with Woody Herman's band, Mary returned to the clubs with a revamped version of her trio. She expanded the instrumentation to include Kenny Dorham on trumpet and Kai Winding on trombone. The group was booked into the Downbeat, which had reopened at a new location, where it alternated with the pianist Billy Taylor. After three months, Kenny Clarke and Oscar Pettiford left the group to form their own trio. Mary replaced the two with Ed Shaughnessey on drums and the bassist Chubby Jackson. Although the new players were capable musicians, Mary was never able to recapture the cohesive sound she had with Clarke and Pettiford. Frustrated by her inability to jell with the musicians, Mary asked Billy Taylor to sit in with the group one night, while she collected her thoughts. "'If they don't sound any better with him,'[1] I told myself, 'I'm cutting.'" They didn't and Mary walked out, leaving the Downbeat and the band behind. Mary decided once again to hit the road and was booked into George Wein's club, Storyville, in Boston. Although the owners of the Downbeat tried to persuade Mary to return, she wouldn't and began to investigate offers to tour Europe.

There is no indication that Mary had seriously considered going to Europe before 1952. Glaser, who remained the central person handling Mary's business affairs, had discussed with her as early as 1946 the possibility of a European tour, but it never materialized. Mary had for the most part been happy, until about five years earlier, with the American scene, and jazz musicians believed their reputations and careers were established through success in New York. Acclaim from performances in other cities or countries was fine, but if you couldn't make it in New York, you were questionable. Mary had worked hard since the early 1930s building a reputation in New York, but the politics of the jazz scene and the rapid changes in the tradition had made it harder to secure prime bookings or lucrative contracts. Bebop, the controversial genre that Mary had embraced, not only had splintered the jazz community into the warring camps of the moderns and the "moldy figs" but had also opened the music to a new, unprecedented level of experimentation that led to further division into various schools of thought. By the early 1950s the focus had shifted away from Fifty-second Street and the bebop sound to a more relaxed, subtle approach defined by the West Coast movement. Mary was no long considered among the avant-garde—the forward-thinking musicians. Her age and experience had unfortunately transferred her from the category of jazz innovator to the category of jazz pioneer.

Like many other musicians, she struggled to maintain her visibility and viability in an environment that was now centered on the young and cerebral but hip white male. She was more determined than ever to remain true to her craft and not buckle under the pressure of commercialism. She could have accepted offers that capitalized on her achievements as one of the most highly recognized and celebrated women in jazz or paraded her around like a circus animal, but she would not compromise her dignity and self-respect for a dollar. Some things were more important, and she would not let her achievements be labeled as novelties, no matter what her finances. The consequences of her determination were the lack of a substantial recording contract and the disappearance of the widespread media exposure that had attended her career in the 1930s and 1940s. But Mary was steadfast in her beliefs. Her financial situation grew dimmer and she saw the very musicians whom she had mentored and assisted seemingly abandon her for their own pursuits. In all fairness, it should be stated that many of these musicians had their own professional and personal struggles, but out of them grew a mythology of the black male jazz identity that drew them more into the public eye, whether in a negative or a positive sense. After all, publicity, despite its nature, ensured that one would not be forgotten. More than ever, the exclusivity of the male jazz fraternity, in which Mary at times had earned "honorary" membership, became evident. Major and independent jazz labels ignored her, and with no stable band, such as Ellington's, which could capitalize on the public's love for past favorites, Mary was forced to take less-than-lucrative club dates when offered.

Mary faced an uncertain future that grew even dimmer when she lost her ASCAP membership in 1951 because she was unable to pay her dues. "I have not made enough royalties from my compositions to be paying an additional amount of money for dues," she wrote to the organization that year. "I have received less money in the last five years than for my entire years of writing. Have visited your office trying to obtain help. I'm sorry but publishers do not pay me. I have spent a fortune with lawyers in New York."[2] The standard fee of $500 she now received for bookings barely covered her expenses. Fifty dollars of her payment automatically went to Glaser for her debts to ABC, and $250 went to the drummer and the bassist who accompanied her. If the booking was in another city, Mary would spend $75 per week on room and board; $20 to $25 on train fare, because she refused to travel by plane; and another $25 on transportation to and from the gig. That left her with only $100, more or less, to pay her bills in New York.[3] It was hardly enough to meet the escalating cost of living in Harlem or the expenses she incurred with the frequent burglaries of her apartment. The impact of Mary's money troubles only intensified as she watched her dilemma featured in the media. She was deemed the "original hard-luck gal of jazz," and the majority of interviews and articles during this period centered on her problems. But Mary did what all the women in her family had done for many years: she went into survivor mode and began working on a way to get past her misfortunes.

She tried to convince Glaser to raise her standard fee to $1,000 a week and to advance her enough money to make another recording. Her argument was simple—she had played enough around the East Coast for "anyone to be tired" of her.[4] Glaser, in his usual fatherly mode, refused to give Mary the money needed for a recording and reassured her that he would continue to work on her behalf to get her the best bookings and salaries possible. This would prove to be the least of Mary's worries over the next few months.

In early 1951 she had received notice that Snub Mosley was suing her for $1 million in royalties from the recording "Satchel Mouth Baby." "Satchel Mouth" was one of the many tunes that Mary had written in the 1940s and recorded but failed to have copyrighted in her name. Since leaving Andy Kirk's band, Mary had been delinquent in filing for copyright protection. Many of her compositions from the 1940s, with the exception of the *Zodiac Suite,* had grown out of periods of experimentation in the studio or were ideas that Mary had randomly written down. She had not recognized the importance of registering these works, probably thinking that recording of the material under her name offered the necessary protection. Her naïveté would prove costly. Her 1944 recording of "Satchel Mouth Baby" had foreshadowed the emerging rhythm and blues sound, which combined elements of swing with the pop singing style. This style and sound became the formula used by many jazz musicians such as Louis Jordan and Amos Milburn to make the transition to the postwar popular music scene. In 1944 the song had been a moderate hit for Mary, but later a rhythm and blues group led by Bill Johnson recorded the tune, changing its name to "Pretty Eyed Baby." The number became popular in 1951 when recorded again by Jo Stafford and Frankie Laine, and Snub Mosley, who claimed he was one of the original writers, sued Mary. It was a major blow to Mary professionally, personally, and monetarily. Mosley had indeed participated on the original recording in 1944, but Mary contended that she had written the work herself without any assistance. In order to circumvent a long and costly legal battle, Mary compromised with Mosley, but at a loss. The incident left Mary cautious about the publication of her work, and from that point on, she made sure to copyright her compositions. According to Peter O'Brien, the incident with "Satchel Mouth Baby" was one of the few times when Mary was not diligent in copyrighting her work. Another involved "Swinging for the Guys," which she cowrote and recorded in 1954 with Oscar Pettiford. The tune later featured lyrics by Jon Hendricks and was retitled "Swinging till the Guys Come Home," and Pettiford alone was credited with writing the music. A third incident occurred the same year with "Chica Boom Blues," which became part of Nino Rota's score for *Nights of Cabiria,* a 1957 film by Federico Fellini.[5]

The Mosley suit brought home to Mary the necessity of a change in her professional life. She needed to start over, to reinvent herself. At forty-one, she wasn't exactly sure how she could accomplish this. She could no longer be marketed as the young, perky "lady who swings the band," and her legal battles with Sydney Nathan and King Records had tarnished her reputation within the jazz world. Mary was indeed older, and a little heavier than in her earlier years, but her face hardly revealed her real age. Nevertheless, she didn't represent the demographic that club owners and record companies were trying to capture (white college-age males). Europe, especially Paris, had ignited once again as a welcoming place for black writers and jazz musicians, but men were going there in larger numbers than women, and Mary was not sure if she wanted to leave the security of family and what little work she could get for the unknown.

One would think that when she was approached by the promoter Joe Marsolais, of Moe Gale's agency, with the opportunity to go to England and break a thirty-year ban on American and English jazz musicians' playing together, Mary would have jumped at the chance. But she declined the offer, saying she was not sure about the jazz scene in England and feared that the contract would not pay enough money to justify such a trip. Marsolais explained that the gig would bring Mary the type of exposure she had been pressing Glaser for, because the breaking of the ban would make international news. Mary remained apprehensive. She knew quite a few jazzmen and -women who had traveled to Paris and other European cities before World War II, but none had spoken about jazz in England. Was there a jazz scene there? What was the quality of the musicians? Mary argued that she had little patience when it came to finding adequate musicians who could support her. It was one thing to deal with such inadequacies in America, but to travel across the Atlantic and potentially face the same hurdles did not appeal to Mary. Her concerns were understandable; she had much to be cautious about, as she knew that she was almost powerless against the "wolves" who wanted to profit from her talents. How would English audiences react to her? Would they expect the monotony of concerts that featured only her past hits, or would they be receptive to experimentation? Marsolais pressed even harder, assuring her that the gig would be just what she needed to jump-start her career. More important, she could fulfill the contractual obligations, make some much-needed money, and be back in the States before Christmas. She wouldn't even have to forfeit or delay her booking at the Downbeat Club in mid-December. Mary thought hard about the proposition and decided that the offer might give her the type of exposure that money couldn't pay for. She signed the contract, but with the understanding that she would return immediately after fulfilling the obligation. Marsolais agreed.

Mary's fear of flying meant that she would have to leave earlier than the promoters had projected, and reservations were made for her to set sail on November 28 from New York. In preparation for the trip, Mary took some time to visit her family in Pittsburgh. In the thirty years of her career, Mary had never once left the United States, except for her short stints in Canada with the Clouds of Joy and later the Ellington band and Shorty Baker. She was now going across the ocean into a culture and world of the unknown. But she tried to ignore her fears and concentrate on her time with family. The Burley home was bustling with the excited energy of Mary's nieces and nephews, and she enjoyed the conversations, card games, and dinners of her favorite foods. The visit proved to be just what she needed to prepare emotionally for the trip. When she returned to New York, she was shocked to discover the press that was being generated around the London gig. *Melody Maker,* the English equivalent to *Down Beat,* chronicled the excitement brewing over Mary's debut at London's Albert Hall. She was deemed by the journal "one of the finest women instrumentalists that has ever been known" and advertised as the headliner for the *Big Rhythm Show* of 1952.[6] The show would feature Mary along with other notable performers who would be announced later. This was the type of assurance that Mary needed.

But unknown to Mary, another scenario was developing in England.

Harry Dawson, the promoter of the concert, had also contracted Cab Calloway and was searching for another headlining act. His plans were to make Calloway the headliner, followed by another act and then Mary. She would share headliner status and also share the stage with several British solo and ensemble groups. These changes would not be revealed to Mary until after she arrived in England. No doubt Mary would have refused to honor the contract if she had been told of them, but Dawson kept the information from Marsolais as well. Moreover, Marsolais and Dawson conspired to extend Mary's stay in England. Marsolais thought that Mary would be better off remaining in Europe beyond the contracted period, but only if Dawson could promise her steady work. "It is my personal opinion," he wrote to Dawson, "that she would like to stay over there and make money, however you will run up against her saying that she has commitments back here. She has commitments back here but I believe she can do herself a lot more good with you and I can handle the situation of any commitments for her here. Try to be completely explicit with her and definite in the amount of time of extra bookings and the amount of money. She is no fool and a very nice girl if you will be patient with her."[7] Marsolais had much more to gain than Mary if she remained in Europe. As Mary's agent of contract, he and the Gale Agency automatically received a portion of Mary's earnings. So the more Mary worked and the more money she made, the more money the Gale Agency made. It was a familiar pattern. Musicians often found themselves at the losing end of such propositions. They would sign contracts for a certain amount of money, perform, and later discover that the agent had quoted them a salary lower than the actual amount; the agent would take the difference as well as a commission. Very few musicians could say they were never victimized by unscrupulous agents. In fairness to Marsolais, however, he may have had good intentions by suggesting that Mary stay in Europe, but in time Dawson would prove to be unscrupulous. Mary would eventually see it as history repeating itself, as outsiders claimed to have her best interests in mind while manipulating situations so that they benefited from her talents.

Dawson worked to make the most of what he viewed as a lucrative opportunity. By the end of November there was already discussion of the possibility of bookings for the *Big Rhythm Show* in Spain, Portugal, Scandinavia, and America, with him serving as the major promoter. Mary's intentions of remaining in Europe for only nine days were evaporating with each day. The night before her scheduled departure from New York, Mary partied with her fellow musicians Oscar Pettiford and Erroll Garner. All wished her well as she boarded the *Queen Elizabeth* bound for England and professional uncertainty.

In negotiating Mary's contract, Marsolais had booked her an elaborate stateroom, in exchange for her providing nightly entertainment for the passengers. But this first leg of the trip proved to be more eventful than expected. After the boat got farther out to sea, Mary caught the flu, which was exacerbated by seasickness, and she remained ill for several days. The rough nature of the winter Atlantic seas left Mary despondent, ill, and regretting her decision. She would later write of the trip that she "would have parted with a hundred dollars to get off the ship, but there was no chance."[8] Finally, after six days, she managed to gain enough strength to leave her cabin and perform a concert for the crew and passengers. She began with a medley of her old standards and then, at the urging of a passenger, launched into some boogie-woogie. The next day, the ship docked in England, and Mary Lou stood at the crossroads of her past, present, and future.

*   *   *

On the pier at Southampton, waiting to be picked up, Mary realized how alone she was and had been since her divorce from John Williams and her separation from Shorty Baker. Those relationships had not been the best, nor had the momentary affairs she had had throughout the years since, but they had provided some sense of security. The hardships and uncertainties of the preceding six or seven years had so dominated her time that she had not considered her own mental and emotional needs. Now here she was standing alone on a cold, foggy pier in another country. It was a metaphor for so many areas of her life. "Forget it and work if you can," she told herself, but she could not deny her true feelings.[9] Her fears and anxieties grew as she waited for what seemed like hours in an unheated station. Finally Harry Dawson, described by Mary as a "weasel-looking chap," arrived and the two headed to London.

In London a small crowd of jazz fans and the press, who showered her with flowers, startled her with such a hospitable greeting. Later that night she was introduced to society at a reception in her honor. There she met other members of the press and the musicians Leslie Hutchinson,

Jimmy Walker, and Cab Calloway. The fears Mary had felt earlier about England were gradually disappearing as she realized that she could construct a circle of friends like those back in America. Unfortunately, her peace was soon shattered when she discovered the true nature of Marsolais and Dawson's booking. The revelation that she would not be headlining the concert but sharing the bill with Cab Calloway and Marie Bryant distressed Mary, but that was not as troubling as the disclosure that the claim that she would break the thirty-year ban on American musicians was a lie. In practice, the musicians' union considered jazz pianists to be "variety" musicians, the equivalent of vaudeville performers, and thus not affected by the ban. Mary surmised that unscrupulous individuals who intended to profit from the exploitation of her talent had once again duped her, and she planned to leave as soon as her contract was fulfilled.

England was horrible, in Mary's estimation. Her accommodations at the Airways Mansions were less than desirable and the food was not at all pleasing to her palate. These disappointments, coupled with physical exhaustion, contributed to the depression that Mary soon fell into. She wrote to Marsolais that she wanted to go home, but all she received were assurances that the situation would get better. Mary's complaints would have to take a backseat to the grueling schedule of her contracted concerts. On Saturday, December 6, she was booked on the BBC's *In Town Tonight,* and on Sunday she debuted at the Royal Albert Hall. The show, like most that had occurred up to that point, was not what Mary had intended. There was too much emphasis on entertainment and not enough on making good music. It was not at all what she desired from her performances.

To make matters worse, as was customary with London weather, a thick fog fell and paralyzed the city. More than 160 deaths were attributed to the inclement weather, and many ticket holders were unable to get to the hall. However, the show went on. The concert was deemed a success, but many, including Mary, were disappointed with the short time she was given to perform. In his December 13 review Ernest Borneman wrote, "Like a fool, I had assumed that Mary Lou Williams, having been brought all the way from America at considerable expense, would be given a correspondingly large share of the evening. Well Mr. Dawson sure had the laugh on me. And on Mary Lou, and the audience, too.

Ha-ha. For out of the nearly three and a half hours we got little more than ten minutes of Mary Lou." [10] Despite Borneman's disappointment, he praised Mary for her performance.

> And now, to wind up the inquest let me come out with an unheard-of even unqualified praise. Mary Lou on piano, Allan Ganlay on drums, Arthur Watts on bass and Donaldo on bongos were flatly the best rhythm section I have ever heard in this country, and one of the best I have ever heard anywhere. Arthur Watts hit a few wrong notes—but then, Mary Lou's harmonies make most other pianists sound like amateurs, and to follow her improvisations even within grasping range is a major achievement. . . . As for Mary Lou herself—considering the way she was treated by being given a second-rate spot after expecting a show to herself, she acquitted herself with her traditional noblesse. [11]

Regardless of the noble attitude Mary displayed publicly, privately she was unhappy and wanted to go home. She also didn't trust Dawson, who was having problems paying the contracted artists. Her intuition told her that the unscrupulous agent would attempt to get more performances from her with little pay, and she wrote to Marsolais, spelling out her concerns. He responded that he would write to Dawson and remind him that he must adhere strictly to the schedule of concerts in the contract. He also informed her that the Foster Agency in London would handle her representation in England, collect the $1,250 due her, and secure her return ticket. [12] With no immediate help from Marsolais, Mary had little choice but to honor the contract and collect her return ticket as soon as possible.

The following Saturday, December 13, Mary appeared with Peter Yorke and His Orchestra at the Royal Festival Hall, and on Sunday she made the first of many provincial appearances at the Guildhall in Southampton. It was decided that because of the bad weather the promoters would add a special performance of the *Big Rhythm Show* for patrons who had been unable to come on the initial date. The new date was January 11, 1953, a problem for Mary, who had been sure that she would be returning to the States by December 28. On December 29 Mary wrote to Dawson:

I have received a letter from Foster Agency dated the 23rd of December, wherein they state that you have me booked for two concerts—one on the 4th of January and the other the 11th of January. The fee for each performance being £45. As the two concerts alone do not represent an economical proposition, I would ask if you can either cancel these or pay me a fee of £300 per concert instead. You will of course realize that it is not possible for me to meet my expenses with only one performance a week. Producing an income of £45, less commission. I had understood that my concerts for the first period of my contract were booked before I left America—this has proved to be otherwise. I also understood that any further concerts would not be spread out over such a long period.[13]

Dawson's response reminded Mary that she was obligated to play the engagements by the contract she had signed, and he said the salary would not be increased. He closed the letter by warning that should he have any problems with Mary making future appearances or not fulfilling her obligations to him, he would take legal action against her.[14] Mary's fears of being trapped in an unhappy situation in England were materializing. How could she have trusted Marsolais, who had consistently assured her that things would work themselves out? She saw no reasonable solution; she could not simply leave for New York because Dawson had her return ticket. After performing a few more concerts in the English countryside, Mary took a short trip to Paris to visit friends. No doubt part of this time was spent with the vocalist Inez Cavanaugh, who had traveled to London to witness Mary's London debut and offered her some advice on what she should do. December 28, Mary's projected date of return, came and went, and in the New Year her series of dates began with a concert on Sunday, January 4, at the Dudley Hippodrome with Leslie Hutchinson.

Mary's success with English audiences increased when her King recordings of "Knowledge" and "Tisherome" were released abroad. Edgar Jackson, critic for *Melody Maker,* wrote that the recordings "prove that despite her metamorphosis from earlier jazz to bop, the enterprising Mary remained not only one of the best female pianists jazz ever produced, but also one of the best women jazz protagonists irrespective of instrument." [15] It was the type of "exploitation" that Mary had desired in America, but Mary's mental and emotional state prevented her from seeing anything positive about her European experience.

The second Albert Hall concert, on January 11, featured a different lineup. The jazz pianist Lil Hardin Armstrong, the woman who had opened mainstream jazz circles for later women performers like Mary, replaced Cab Calloway. History was made as two of the best pioneering women jazz instrumentalists shared the stage, with each representing different aspects of the 1950s jazz paradigm. Armstrong's style was rooted in early jazz, which had brought her fame, but Mary had evolved into a bop-influenced modernist. In its usual fashion, the press gravitated to this difference and spotlighted it. Armstrong apparently became indignant when told her style of playing was outdated and reacted with "What am I supposed to be, a bop pianist?" [16] As the media buzz continued, it became increasingly clear that Armstrong, like many pioneering jazz musicians, had taken sides against modern jazz. Although there are no indications that their views ever created personal tensions between them, it is apparent that the two women had different opinions on the merits of the modern movement.

The January 11 concert ended Mary's contracted arrangement with Dawson, but Mary now decided to stay, declaring that she "wanted to play and record with British musicians, compose, and arrange for British bands." [17] Her disappointments, though many, were overshadowed by the love affair that was blossoming between Mary and the English public. She was booked on January 25 to headline Ted Heath's *London Palladium Swing Session,* and on Sunday, February 1, she appeared at the Regal in Edmonton. Over the next two months, Mary worked consistently, recording eight sides for Britain's Vogue label with the bassist Allan Ganley and the drummer Ken Napper, and returning to the Royal Festival Hall with the Geraldo Orchestra on February 15. The sides were released in various stages. Two sides were released as singles, followed a month later by an LP consisting of all eight sides.[18] These recordings would ignite one of the most exciting critical debates in the history of *Melody Maker* and draw more attention to Mary's music.

The eight compositions of Mary's first London recording session ranged from Thelonious Monk's "Round Midnight" to Tadd Dameron's "Lady Bird," and from Gershwin's "They Can't Take That Away from

Me" to a Latin-tinged blues written by Mary called "Koolbonga." In listening to the recording, one can hear the fatigue and mental detachment that colored Mary's London experience. The compositions are well selected and well executed by Mary, but they never quite swing in the style one so readily equates with Mary. The reason for the rhythmic inconsistencies, however, may be found in a rhythm section that was less than capable of fulfilling Mary's musical needs. In fact, of the eight sides, only on "Titoros" and "Koolbonga" does it seem that the rhythm section and the lead instrument are in sync. Ironically, these are the two tunes that employ Afro-Cuban elements and are rightly served by the combination of bass, drums, and bongos.

The LP upon its release became the subject of great debate among critics and fans. This discussion began with Mark Nevard's February 7 review. Nevard opened his critical survey by asserting that Vogue had erred in its rush to release the recording. "Was it worth it?" he asked as he launched into his diatribe, which described the recording as characterized by monotony and as having traded excitement for modernity. Nevard went on, "Of course, it will go down well with the hey-hey fans and the pseudo-intellectuals with the gravel-brushed lips."

> It's 100 per cent in the modern idiom, and after all, a lot of us pay homage to the girl pianist who spans a decade, moves with the times, and all that. But when you listen to the record with the history stripped off it just adds up to a listless string of notes. There is an attempt at dynamism, but the voltage is low. There are a lot of ideas, but their conception never reaches the heights of brilliance. There is a certain uniformity about the playing; never a startling change of atmosphere. Never a feeling of warmth and sincerity. You don't need to ditch the feelings when you switch to modern. . . . The fact that Mary Lou has done much better in the past strengthens the suspicion that she was not at home on this London date.[19]

Nevard's analysis of the recordings might have faded into obscurity had it not ignited the furor of a fellow critic, Ernest Borneman. One week later, on February 14, Borneman issued his reaction to Nevard. Borneman stated that his respect for Nevard's "ear, taste and integrity" had made him uncomfortable when he read his colleague's review. To Nevard's assertion that the recordings lacked emotion or sincerity, Borneman responded that the "coldness was deliberate," and in reference to sincerity he remarked that such judgments were relative and best left to the ears of the listener.[20] No one could have predicted that Borneman's response would spark a discussion that would engage not only other critics but fans as well. The following week the debate continued in the pages of *Melody Maker*. The critic Maurice Burman wrote, "Mary Lou Williams knows it all. She has borrowed a lot from the moderns, yet still retains her old jazz feel. One track of the Vogue LP is a jewel. The rest are a mixture of delight and dullness. But on all you will find artistic taste linked with true economy of notes." Laurie Henshaw claimed that her attention "wandered long before side one had ended." Max Jones, who had befriended Mary when she arrived in England, wrote that while he was not a "believer in modern piano jazz," he did appreciate the performance of Mary on the LP. " 'Koolbonga' " he said, "excites unqualified admiration, 'Titoros' and 'They Can't Take That Away" rather less. 'Perdido' goes splendidly till near the end, while the reflective 'Round Midnight' wins favour for its mood. I am alienated by the slower pops, but respect the lyrical quality of the playing." While some of the critiques simply dismissed Mary's performance as being "cliché-ridden," others pointed to the limitations of the modern idiom as the reason behind the product. Tony Brown suggested, "It doesn't matter whether the music we've heard before came secondhand. The fact remains that Mary Lou Williams' songs are cliché-ridden and rather dull. Why? Because bop that was to have given jazz a shot in the arm has turned it into a devitalized addict." Edgar Jackson, who had reviewed Mary's King recordings of "Knowledge" and "Tisherome," wrote, "Mike Nevard stresses Mary Lou's lack of emotion but fails to point out that this is characteristic of the 'cool' trend in jazz. Also she has originality, tastefulness and general appeal, which seem to have been lost on Mike. Despite Mike's contention she does not play 100 per cent in the modern idiom. She has been greatly influenced by the modern trend, but there is the melodic and harmonic simplicity of her earlier days."[21]

Several fans also wrote in, proclaiming the merits of the recording. One claimed that Nevard's review was proof of the type of "unenlightened people [who] get to write for the musical press." This fan said he had attended three of Mary's concerts and felt that he had heard one of "the greatest modern jazz pianists of the age." The British pianist whom Nevard put forth as superior to Mary at the end of his critique also wrote to offer his opinion. Dill Jones said he had added Mary Lou's LP to his collection "so that [he could] listen and learn what a truly great artist sounds like." Despite Nevard's claims that Mary's talent paled in comparison with his, Jones wrote, he thought he could never become as proficient as she was. "Mary Lou," he said, "plays more music on one side than I could on twenty." [22]

In time, the discussion subsided, as no consensus could be reached on the merits of the recording. However, the comments revealed the true issue facing jazz critics, enthusiasts, and musicians—the debate of modern versus traditional jazz. Despite the popularity of bebop and the subsequent development of other styles, there was still a small contingent of musicians and critics who thought that jazz had moved away from its true essence and had traded away good music making for commercial viability and popularity. As one of the few musicians who musically advocated both approaches, Mary—and her London recording—became the primary evidence of what happens when "good" musicians go wrong by adopting modern approaches. Traditionalists concluded that Mary, through her experimentation with bop, had strayed from her roots in the blues, swing, boogie-woogie, and stride. Modernists and their supporters viewed Mary as an assimilator of modern approaches and not an innovator. While they respected her talent and her accomplishments of the past, many held the belief that she was of no significance to jazz modernism.

Mary seemed unaffected by the contretemps and continued to build her profile in the London jazz scene. Vogue, the record label that had released the LP, tried to capitalize on the debate by advertising the recording as the "most controversial album of the year" in London's leading publications. The campaign succeeded in garnering Mary more dates in London and the surrounding area.

Regardless of what people thought about Mary's waxed performances, it was clear that they loved her live ones. She was crowned the "Grande Dame of Jazz" in England, a title solidified by her electrifying performance with Sarah Vaughan at the singer's farewell Albert Hall concert in February 1953. But for all the success and attention Mary was receiving, she was still not earning the amount of money she felt she was due. Financially she struggled, and emotionally she tried to focus on the popularity she experienced. No doubt she assumed that the London press exposure as well as the *Melody Maker* controversy would soon bring the appropriate degree of recognition and appreciation. It is unclear why Mary chose not to return to the States in 1953. After all, her new professional and musical reputation in Europe could have brought more lucrative bookings at home. But Mary applied in March 1953 for an extension of her work permit. She was immediately contracted to star in a variety show with the comedian Jack Johnson called *To See Such Fun*. The show opened at the Finsbury Park Empire on March 14 and began a tour of the country, but three weeks into the tour, Johnson injured his leg and the troupe disbanded. Mary was unable to secure another booking right away and hoped that the Foster Agency could secure her other concert dates. Nothing substantial materialized, so Mary, tired and financially drained, decided to go to Paris to visit friends, rest, and plan her next move.

*　*　*

When Mary returned to England from Paris, she found an offer to join Louis Armstrong and his all-star band. Anyone else would have jumped at the chance to play with the legendary musician, but Mary declined the offer. Having played widely throughout the early jazz, swing, and bebop eras, arranged for some of the leading bandleaders in the 1930s and 1940s, and earned distinction as an innovative solo pianist with her performances at Café Society, Mary no longer had any desire to share the spotlight or serve as a sideman. She wanted to put together a combo of some of the most talented musicians in Europe. She wanted more than anything to produce a successful, critically acclaimed recording that would prepare the way for her return to the United States. She began preparing for a series of concert dates that would take her to Switzerland, Amsterdam, and Paris.

In July Mary left England for a one-week solo tour of Holland. The gig was supplemented by a weeklong engagement at the Dutch resort of Scheveningen. Mary was pleased with the reaction she received, but as usual the fee was less than what she wanted. She resigned herself to not complaining and looked at the stint as an escape from the monotony of the London scene and the emotional emptiness she could no longer suppress or deny. The trip proved to be just what Mary needed, and she regained her creative energies. Her gig at the Flying Dutchman in Scheveningen was so successful that Lou Van Rees, the agent who had booked the performance, wanted Mary to remain at the club for a couple of months. Although she needed the money the extended contract would provide, Mary was eager to get to Paris. The stories of the vibrant black community developing on the Left Bank and the popularity modern jazz musicians were experiencing in the city were for Mary all the reason needed to forgo any other employment opportunities.

Paris by 1952 had awakened from the devastation of Nazi occupation during World War II. It had once again become the city that drew Americans to its cafés, hotels, and nightclubs. Although jazz had been driven underground during the occupation, it continued to be popular with Parisian audiences. The city called out to American musicians to inhabit nightclubs and bring modernism to its stilted intellectual circles. Paris fully embraced blacks and in the postwar years became a haven for black writers, painters, and musicians. The center of black life in Paris shifted from Montmartre, where Josephine Baker and Bricktop had defined Parisian nightlife in the 1920s, to the Left Bank and the streets of Saint-Germain-des-Prés and the Latin Quarter.

Blacks in Paris during the postwar years reflected a new level of consciousness. Those who settled in the city during the 1940s and 1950s were viewed as political exiles and "refugees from Yankee bigotry."[23] Existentialism was the philosophic tone of the city, and Saint-Germain-des-Prés became a meeting place for Parisian intellectuals, who discussed, read, and wrote their works in the cafés. The existentialists championed jazz and regarded it as an emotional, complex symbol of modern life.[24] The city buzzed with a fascination with the African American experience, and as Tyler Stovall asserts, this interest "became the perfect expression of the love-hate attitude of the postwar Parisian avant-garde toward the United States."[25] Jazz in Paris changed from the dominant New Orleans style of the 1920s to the modern approaches of be-bop and cool jazz in the postwar years. The clubs of Montmartre now gave way to the *caves* of Saint-Germain-des-Prés. This new type of nightclub was formed in small and crowded basement rooms that featured live music and stayed open until the wee hours of the morning. The first of this type was the Tabon Club, which sparked the buzz for jazz on the Left Bank. The Rose Rouge, the Club de Vieux Colombier, and the Club

Saint-Germain followed it. The two events that solidified the place of jazz in postwar Paris were Dizzy Gillespie's 1948 tour of Europe and the inaugural Paris Jazz Festival in 1949.

According to Stovall, these events not only gave Parisians a firsthand experience with jazz but also reinspired black musicians to seek employment opportunities in the "free" environment of Europe. The migration of black musicians to France included a jazz who's who: Kenny "Klook" Clarke, Sidney Bechet, Bill Coleman, Peanut Holland, Don Byas, and others. Also changed was the role of women in the scene. Whereas Josephine Baker and Bricktop had been preeminent in the 1920s, the postwar jazz scene was dominated by men. That did not, however, dissuade aspiring women musicians and singers from coming to Paris. In the early 1950s, the pianists Lil Hardin Armstrong and Hazel Scott came to Paris hoping to reestablish their careers. Both were well received by Parisian audiences and Scott managed to secure enough work to remain in the city for extended periods. A few years earlier, the singer and dancer Eartha Kitt had wowed Parisians with sensuous performances. Although Mary knew of these success stories, the most poignant for her was that of her good friend Inez Cavanaugh. Cavanaugh had come to Paris and opened her own restaurant a block from the Sorbonne in the Latin Quarter. Every night Americans, Parisians, and other Europeans were served healthy doses of American cuisine and jazz. Chez Inez was one of the many restaurants owned by black expatriates that attracted the postwar black community in Paris. Despite her success as a restaurateur, Cavanaugh closed her establishment in 1952, shortly after Mary arrived in London, and returned to America. But her influence on postwar Parisian culture remained.

Mary figured that the depth and breadth of her talent, coupled with the fascination Parisians had with black women and black music, would lead to her success in Paris. Beyond the economic advantages that Mary thought Paris would bring, the small, intimate environment of the *caves* and the blossoming black community of the Left Bank appealed to her. London had been a very lonely place for Mary, and she often lamented the blandness of the food, the lack of a real jazz scene, and the gray, cold, and rainy weather. Paris offered Mary something she could not hope to get in London—the camaraderie of American jazz musicians and an intimate and supportive community of blacks. In November 1953, after much thought, Mary decided to move to Paris.

Like most of the postwar black community, Mary moved to the Left Bank, where there were many cheap hotels. She moved into the Crystal Hotel on the Rue Saint-Benoît, which also housed Eartha Kitt and the writers James Baldwin and Chester Himes. It was not the most plush accommodation in the city, but Mary was willing to look past the crude furnishings and lack of private baths. In her lifetime Mary had experienced worse, and the Crystal was an improvement over her London lodgings. But life in Paris was not as lucrative or successful as Mary had hoped. She lived day by day, often relying on the communal support system that had developed on the Left Bank. But this hardly affected Mary, who was fascinated and energized by the Parisian art scene.

She was contracted to play alternating sets at the Perdido Club and the Ringside. Mary's stint at the Perdido Club was so well attended that the owner decided to rename the nightclub Chez Mary Lou, to designate it the musical home of the pianist.

The hectic nature of her schedule and the move to Paris began to take a toll on Mary's health. In her younger years, she had been capable of juggling multiple jobs and an active nightlife, but at forty-three, Mary tired easily. The lack of proper rest and nutrition also wore Mary down, and after only a few weeks at the Ringside, she quit. Letting go of the Ringside gig was easy for Mary, as she had found the environment stifling to her creativity. On several occasions she had refused to play, saying she did not like the arrangement of the piano in relation to the audience and the vibes didn't feel right.

Mary rested and tried to gather her thoughts about the direction of her career. Although she had splintered the management of her career among several agents during her European tenure, Mary was now more interested in organizing her career with one person. She chose the agent Jack Higgins, who promised her he would find her the best jobs and salaries Europe had to offer. Higgins did manage to secure Mary work, but her finances and health continued to decline. On December 2 Mary entered the Parisian studios of the Vogue label to record a series of sessions with her old friend the saxophonist Don Byas. The group, which consisted of the bassist Buddy Bands and the drummer Gérard Pochonet, recorded several sides, including "Mary's Waltz," "O.W.," which would later become the introit to her first mass, and the standards "Lullaby of the Leaves" and "Moonglow."

By Christmas she was healthy enough to play for a concert sponsored by the French ministry of education and to celebrate the holiday with her friends Taps Miller, a singer and dancer, and Annie Ross. But the celebration came to an end when the three headed for London to spend time with other friends. When they arrived at the port in Dover, Mary and Miller were detained for questioning for hours. Although the two tried to assure officials that their visit was strictly for pleasure, not business, they were sent back to France. Mary was outraged and called upon her friends in the British press to investigate the matter. A clear explanation was never given and the immigration department claimed the incident never happened.[26]

Mary worked steadily in early 1954, touring Holland for three weeks and playing more gigs in the Left Bank nightclubs. Hoping to capitalize on the popularity of her live performances, Mary recorded two more LPs. The result was two sessions: one for the Barclay label Blue Star and the other for Club Français du Disque. The Blue Star session consisted of a combination of originals, standards, and French songs, and Mary honored her friend Nicole Barclay with the composition "Nicole." Critics called the Blue Star recording an example of the "total transformation of Mary Lou Williams' style" and praised the work for its uniqueness.[27] The Club Français disc was also acclaimed, and its success brought Mary the professional boost she needed to sustain her place in the fickle Parisian scene. Like many musicians who stayed in Paris for a long time, she had discovered that the longer one stayed, the less popular one became and the less money one could hope to make. In some respects, Paris had afforded Mary more opportunities for employment and interaction with talented musicians than England, but she was still short of money. Her income was low and she had accrued enormous debts by purchasing on credit the furs, dresses, shoes, and other items she thought necessary for her stage performances. With no reliable means of paying her bills, Mary was soon in trouble. In one instance creditors threatened legal action against her, but she was saved by Colonel Edward Brennan, who had developed a friendship with Mary during his regular visits to the clubs of the Left Bank. As was her nature, after a few months Mary would once again go on a carefree buying spree, then worry about the bills when they arrived. What developed was a cycle of overspending and stress over its effects that characterized much of her Parisian experience.

When Mary wasn't attempting to deal with her deepening feelings of emotional emptiness through shopping, she visited with musician friends who had come to Paris en route to other European destinations or moved to the city. Because of the popularity of bebop and other modern jazz idioms, there seemed to be a constant influx of musicians to the city. Thelonious Monk came through in 1954 while Mary was working the Salle Pleyel and met one of his later benefactors, the Baroness Pannonica de Koenigswarter. But the musician with whom Mary connected the most in Europe was the pianist Garland Wilson. Wilson, one of the many Americans who had come to Europe before the war, met Mary in 1952 when she arrived in London. The two became good friends and frequently shared the bill in some of the smaller venues. In many ways the two provided emotional stability for each other, and when Mary decided to move to Paris in late 1953, Wilson followed her. There he played at Le Boeuf sur le Toit, where he had been a regular during the 1930s. The two were not lovers, as Wilson was gay, but they maintained a very intimate relationship; he often stayed with Mary in her small hotel room. In early 1954, as Mary's debts and depression ballooned, Wilson's health began deteriorating. He clung closer to Mary as his condition grew worse, and with each passing week Mary found herself growing physically and mentally weaker. Finally, she decided to distance herself from Wilson, who by that time was clearly dying, and moved to another small hotel on the Left Bank. The distance enabled Mary to recuperate, but her friend became sicker. While working at Le Boeuf sur le Toit on May 30, he collapsed. According to Taps Miller, Wilson had complained that he was not feeling well, but he continued playing until he started coughing up blood. He lay on the floor of the club for over an hour. "He should have been taken to the hospital immediately. But incredibly, some people insisted he could not be moved without the police first being informed, and much vital time was wasted." Miller finally called a taxi and took Wilson to the American hospital, where he died from an internal hemorrhage.[28] Mary, still recovering from mental exhaustion, was devastated by the news. Wilson's death exposed how much she had counted on their friendship for security, and now more than ever she felt herself mentally unraveling.

To temper her growing anxieties and grief, Mary returned to work. Less than a week after Wilson death, Mary replaced him at Le Boeuf sur le Toit. The club had been a focus of French intellectual life in the 1920s, but by the 1950s its influence had faded. At one time it had served as the meeting place for the artists Picasso, Derain, and Picabia and the composers Ravel and Poulenc, but now it was an underground gay bar. The owners did not allow certain people to work there, especially women, but because of Garland Wilson's love for Mary, an exception was made.[29]

No matter how hard Mary tried to suppress her feelings, her worries about money and her sense of emotional emptiness grew stronger. She finally conceded that perhaps it was time for her to return home. But Mary was thousands of dollars in debt and had no return fare. She knew it would take months if not another year to straighten out her affairs. Emotionally, she was not sure if she could last another week, let alone another month. Her only hope was help from friends in the States, but there were very few people who could give Mary the $5,000 needed to settle her debts and purchase a return ticket. She could think of only one person who could help her—Joe Glaser. Although he had not been Mary's manager since she had left the States, Glaser had stayed in touch. His letters from this period testify to his undiminished love for Mary, but Glaser had been hurt by slow times in the American jazz business. Bad investments and unrecovered personal loans to other musician friends had left Glaser more cautious about the money he gave out. He wrote to Mary that he had assumed, because she had remained in Europe, that all was going well for her. "Under such conditions," he wrote, "you should have more than $5000 of your own because if you haven't, you really could do 'nothing' here as well as 'over there.'"[30]

Without Glaser's aid, Mary knew that her plans to return home would be delayed. The strain of the uncertainty of her life began to reveal itself publicly by late June. While playing a party in England for the duke and duchess of Windsor, Mary, who had never been able to tolerate much alcohol, consumed three Scotches. Anesthetizing the pain seemed a more viable solution to Mary than being honest about the emotional roller coaster she had been on during the previous two years. But instead of calming her anxieties, the alcohol magnified them. A black soldier who noticed Mary's disoriented appearance got close to her and engaged her in a very intimate conversation. "You look disturbed, upset," he said. Mary explained that she was trying to leave Europe, but had experienced some difficulties. As the two continued to talk, the young man told her that his grandmother had told him to read the Ninety-first Psalm whenever he felt threatened or in peril. Mary, who was quite inebriated, misinterpreted what he had said and started to read all the Psalms. The process took her two days, but the sacredness of the scriptures brought her some peace. Mary knew now more than ever that she had to make changes in her life. She had seen too much, experienced too much, and contributed too much to the lives of others to allow herself to compromise her emotional health any further. But those thoughts began to dissipate as she got closer to Paris. By the time she arrived at her hotel, Mary had refocused her mental energies on work and making much-needed money. She continued for a number of weeks, alternating between the Olympia Theater and Le Boeuf sur le Toit, but her performances were emotionless and empty.

Mary's anxieties reached a pinnacle during one of her nightly performances at Le Boeuf sur le Toit. In the middle of her set, Mary left the stage and did not return. It was a reprise of Washington, D.C., and the Clouds of Joy in 1942. She simply walked out, leaving her purse on the counter and her fee. "Nobody had done anything. Nothing essentially had happened," she recalled much later. "I just stopped playing." [31] Gérard Pochonet, the drummer who had played on Mary's Vogue sessions in early 1954 and expressed his unrequited love for Mary, returned to the club and retrieved her fee. He later convinced Mary, who was despondent, to leave the hectic environment of Paris and accompany him to his grandmother's house in the French countryside. There Mary began examining the past ten years of her life and reevaluating her career.

Chapter 9

THE CROSSROADS

The slow, agonizing, and lonely death of Garland Wilson was a warning to Mary that her life could end in the same manner if she did not fully address her emotional and physical problems. The two years in Europe had seen a constant series of bad business decisions, debilitating debts, and unscrupulous agents, record company executives, and suitors. She had unwillingly become caught up in the media frenzy Europeans had generated around African American culture and jazz. Instead of advancing jazz music, as she had desired since the 1920s, Mary had come to represent the "exotic other" to European audiences. This was typical of the typecasting and stereotyping that characterized the manner in which agents, promoters, and suitors viewed Mary and the other women of color who had come to Europe as performers, artists, and writers. Like Josephine Baker, Bricktop, Hazel Scott, and others who had chosen careers outside prescribed gender roles, she had become an exotic caricature of black womanhood. Most important to this stereotype was the physical beauty of these women: Mary with her Mayan features, almond-shaped eyes, high cheekbones, shapely figure, and smooth, dark skin that gave no hint of her forty-four years; Hazel Scott with her light, café au lait skin and ample bosom; and Baker with her beautiful skin and the open display of sexuality that excited and mystified her white European audiences. Europeans soaked up the energy and passion of these women each night, leaving behind emotionally depleted and lonely women. Most of the black women performers, like Mary, attempted to cover their wounds with furs, expensive gowns, jewels, and smiles. By 1954 Mary knew that material possessions, of which she had acquired many in Europe, and the constant company of dignitaries or men proclaiming their love for her were no longer filling the void she felt in her life. She had walked away from what looked to some like a successful career as a jazz musician and was seriously considering her future.

In the forty-four years Mary Lou Williams had lived, she had experienced more than most women, especially women of color, could have ever dreamed of. She had left her home at an early age to enter the field of entertainment, an occupation that generally brought to the fortunate a meteoric rise followed by short-lived success, as each new movement in popular culture gave way to another. She had distanced herself physically from the one system of support and guidance she had always known—her family. Although she maintained her familial connections as much as her schedule allowed, the separation had robbed her of a true connection to her cultural and emotional roots. She had achieved a great deal by working with notable bands and ensembles, but her experiences had left her professionally and emotionally jaded. Mary wanted badly to restart her life, but she knew she could not undergo the physical and emotional healing she needed in Europe. The key to her rehabilitation was going home. In the summer of 1954 she once again wrote to Joe Glaser, begging him to help her return. She described her declining health and her need to be near her family, but Glaser was in no position to help her. Instead, he suggested that she inquire about her return ticket with the agents who had organized the trip. Mary contacted Moe Gale, who turned the matter over to Joe Marsolais. Marsolais wrote to Mary in August 1954, confirming that according to her contract with the promoter Harry Dawson, she was to receive a round-trip ticket. But he reported that because she had decided to stay in Europe, her ticket had more than likely been cashed in by Dawson, who had since declared bankruptcy. He claimed that the Gale Agency had no responsibility to help her get home.[1] Mary did not accept Marsolais's explanation and contacted Local 802 in New York and the headquarters of the American Federation of Musicians. She cited Marsolais's push for her to remain in Europe past her contracted period as evidence that the Gale Agency had some responsibility for the situation, but the local and the federation sided with Marsolais. Mary angrily turned to the Foster Agency, which had handled her bookings in England, and was told that there was little that could be done because of Dawson's financial situation.[2] Unable to secure any money, Mary refocused her energies on the resolution of her emotional problems.

Cared for by her friend Gérard Pochonet, Mary retreated to the French countryside, where she ate, slept, prayed, and read the Psalms, which she said cooled her and made her feel protected.[3] She refused to speak with anyone and rejected offers of employment. Mary had reached a crossroads, and not even the music she loved so much could resolve the emotional conflicts that raged within her. Rejecting all the pretentious modern remedies for emotional breakdowns, Mary returned to the one thing that she knew had sustained her mother, grandmother, and family through rough times—prayer. She prayed fervently, seeking peace within her tormented soul and also direction from God as to what path she should take with her life. With the exception of a few accounts of her sudden departure from the Le Boeuf sur le Toit, Mary's departure from jazz had gone almost unnoticed. No doubt it was believed that Mary had simply taken a holiday. Most knew of the deep connection between her and Garland Wilson and assumed that his death had been more than she could handle, but no one suspected that Mary was contemplating never performing again.

During her devotional periods, Mary's intuition, which she often referred to as her "psychic" abilities, told her that the jazz scene was no longer where she was most needed. She envisioned the death of Charlie Parker, who was struggling against addiction; the further splintering of the jazz community and its separation from its musical roots; and other occurrences that would greatly affect the welfare of blacks in America. In later years she would state that she never had a conscious desire to get closer to God before 1954, but "it all seemed that night that it all came to a head. I couldn't take it any longer. So I just left—the piano—the money—all of it." [4]

Mary's visions prompted her to once again look for ways to return home. She thought if she could go back to the States, she could prevent Parker's death and counteract the displacement of the black community. She contacted her friend Inez Cavanaugh, who was then in Copenhagen. Cavanaugh and several other friends raised enough money to buy Mary a ticket, and on December 15 the two set sail for New York. Upon their arrival, Mary retreated to her home, where she attempted to exorcise her personal demons. For months Mary remained in her Hamilton Terrace apartment, cut off from the jazz scene and her friends. Cavanaugh later said she did not see Mary again for another year. [5] The weeks Mary spent locked in her apartment were torturous. She did not listen to music at all, nor did she play her old piano. Instead, she struggled to control the turbulent emotions she was experiencing. Visions of spirits, which had terrified her throughout her childhood, began to appear, and she often sat submissively in a corner of her bedroom, praying and trying to rid herself of the apparitions. As if the decline in her emotional health weren't enough, shortly after Mary returned to New York she received a letter from the Internal Revenue Service, informing her that she owed a considerable amount in back taxes on the income she had earned before leaving for Europe.

With no immediate bookings, no savings, and the daily strain of her emotional condition, Mary saw no easy resolution of the debt and wrote to the IRS explaining her situation. Furthermore, she had found her Hamilton Terrace apartment in total disarray—a humorless metaphor of her emotions and life. Although she had decided that her emotional healing required her to stay away from the jazz scene, Mary's finances dictated that she return to the one thing that had provided her with an income—her music. With the tax debt, her daily household expenses, and the assistance she was still trying to give to family members, despite the fact she received only about $300 a month from ASCAP, Mary knew she had to return to performing. As she had so often before, Mary turned to Joe Glaser, who had maintained, despite their many conflicts, a loving and amicable relationship with Mary. Although Glaser cared deeply for her and recognized her talents and abilities, he knew that the possibilities of Mary's making a comeback were uncertain. The dismal condition of the New York scene, coupled with Mary's two-year absence, meant that she would have to settle for bookings she would previously have avoided, with smaller fees. The two years in Europe had failed to generate interest in Mary among domestic jazz fans, largely because of the lack of publicity her European performances received in American publications and the lack of transatlantic distribution of her European recordings. She was now considered one of the fading pioneers, who could find her past musical contributions appreciated by older audiences and critics if she was lucky.

The jazz scene in 1950s America had become a monster, directed by commercialism, not the creation of good music. Modern jazz musicians had splintered into schools of jazz or proponents of specific styles. No longer evident were the cross-influences and cooperative experiments that had yielded some of the most exciting musical performances in the previous decades. What hurt the New York scene the most was the shift of jazz to the West Coast and other points outside the city. Central Avenue in Los Angeles, the Lighthouse in Hermosa Beach, California, and the various nightclubs and theaters of Philadelphia were the cradles of these modern jazz approaches. New York struggled to maintain a presence. Jazz clubs there closed just as quickly as they opened and promoters focused their marketing efforts on college students, their campuses, and the emerging trend of jazz festivals, which almost guaranteed the resurrection of lagging careers. The ever-popular sounds of Memphis- and Detroit-based rhythm and blues and the youth-generated rock and roll drew jazz fans away from the genre.

Cool jazz, Third Stream, West Coast, and hard bop were the styles leading modern jazz. Swing—although not completely dead, thanks in part to the big bands of Ellington, Basie, and Woody Herman—and bebop seemed somewhat out of place in jazz discussions. Mary was at a disadvantage, as she had not completely made the transition to these modern styles—or at least in the minds of audiences and other musicians, she hadn't. In early 1955 Mary was offered three bookings but, unable to get past her hatred of the nightclub environment, which had always colored her decisions about bookings, she declined the offers. In order to generate some cash, Mary recorded a series of sides for the Jazztone Society. The organization was known for its recordings highlighting varying styles of jazz. The twelve sides Mary recorded were packaged as *The History of Jazz Keyboard* and featured the drummer Osie Johnson and the bassist Wendell Marshall. It was Mary's first attempt to chronicle the varying genres of music that had contributed to her development as a pianist, composer, and arranger. The pieces included a swinging version of the spiritual "Joshua Fit the Battle of Jericho," which predated some of the exciting arrangements of similar material by hard bop and soul jazz performers. For examples of genres that preceded jazz Mary drew from her musical past. She selected "Momma Pinned a Rose on Me" as an example of the rural blues. Mary's stepfather, Fletcher Burley, had taught her the song and he often asked her to play it for him. For an example of ragtime, Mary played "Fandangle," which she credited to her mother, Virginia. Mary claimed that she played the piece in exactly the same manner in which she had heard her mother and the pianist Jack Howard play.[6] "Roll 'Em" and "Taurus" were reinterpretations of Mary's big band arrangements, performed in a combo setting. Mary's reharmonization of Monk's tune "Round Midnight," retitled "I Love Him," and "Amy," an original tune written in honor of one of Mary's numerous friends (this was a method she often used to acknowledge the benevolent efforts of friends and acquaintances), rounded out the recording with bop interpretations. The album provided audiences with documentary evidence of Mary's encyclopedic musical talent but failed to generate the type of excitement and money Mary had hoped it would.

Mary's own troubles did not stop her from trying to help others. Despite her good intentions, her efforts to help her musician friends, especially Charlie Parker, were unsuccessful. Parker's addiction was at an advanced stage. In March 1955, less than three months after her return from Europe, Mary's brother Jerry spotted Parker leaving Harlem Hospital looking disheveled and despondent. Jerry called Mary and asked if she had any money or if she could help Parker. Mary suggested that he tell Parker to come by her house. She recalled, "He told Charlie to talk with me and Charlie promised to come up the next day or so."[7] Parker never made it; he went to the apartment of the Baroness Pannonica de Koenigswarter and died several days later, on March 12. Charlie Parker was only thirty-four, but the impact he had made on the modern jazz scene was infinite. His inability to rid himself of his addiction to heroin had ended what could have been a long and profitable career.

Parker's death intensified Mary's hopelessness. She had encountered Parker in Kansas City as he maneuvered into a late-night jam session, and she had observed the mechanisms that would influence his approach to jazz; she had served as a musical and personal adviser to Parker, Gillespie, and the other beboppers at a time when most wrote them off as militant noisemakers. His death symbolized for Mary everything she thought had gone wrong with the jazz scene and the larger black community. Personal accountability and responsibility to the community had been replaced by an attitude focused on the individual and on personal advancement. Apparently no one had considered intervening with Parker; those around him simply distanced themselves when his behavior became too much to bear. Some fed his chemical demons in order to anesthetize or control him. Mary shared her sorrow over Parker's death with many, including Dizzy Gillespie. In the following days it would be the combined efforts of Gillespie, Mary, and others that would ensure that the saxophonist received a proper burial and that his estate was not mismanaged. Parker's burial was complicated by the fact that three women—his wife, Gerri, who was imprisoned in Washington, his live-in love for many years, Chan, and another wife named Doris—all claimed the right to his body. Chan wanted Parker buried in New York, but his mother wanted the body returned to Kansas City; neither woman was financially or legally able to organize the estate. Dizzy, in a final effort to help his old friend, organized a committee consisting of Mary, Hazel Scott, Maely Dufty, and the bassist Charles Mingus, who had played in Parker's last band, to determine what would happen to his remains and his compositions.[8] The committee was able to raise enough money to send Parker's body to Kansas City for burial. In April 1955, at Carnegie Hall, the Charlie Parker Memorial Concert drew luminaries from all fields of entertainment. Performers included Mary, Hazel Scott, Billy Taylor, Dinah Washington, Sammy Davis Jr., Oscar Pettiford, Pearl Bailey, Stan Getz, and Kenny Clarke. The audience was the largest ever recorded at a jazz concert, with 2,760 attendees, and the concert lasted almost four hours.[9] Norman Granz, who had provided much of the money needed to ship Parker's body to Missouri, recorded the entire concert, hoping to release it later that year. But through circumstances that are not clear, Lennie Tristano halted the release. Mary, Dizzy, and others paid homage to a musician who had done much to shape their musical and personal lives. In addition to memorializing Parker, the concert raised nearly $10,000, which was put into trust for Parker's sons, Leon and Baird.[10]

Following Parker's death, Mary went to Pittsburgh to visit with family. While there she talked very little about her experiences in Europe and simply discussed the possibility of not playing again. Mary's family was bewildered by the suddenness of her decision but respected her choice. There were other pressing matters that needed to be addressed. Grace, Mary's younger sister, seemed incapable of maintaining her household. Like so many women of color during this period, she had been a victim of limited opportunities. She had minimal job skills, and the menial labor she was qualified for often afforded her little time with her family and left her physically and emotionally depleted. Hoping to help her sister, Mary decided to move Grace and her four children to her home in New York. There, she hoped, she could aid Grace in breaking out of the monotony of her life in Pittsburgh. But years of physical neglect and the harshness of black life had taken its toll on the thirty-seven-year-old woman. Dependent upon a monthly welfare check, Grace would often take the money and squander it. Mary, recognizing the turbulence and stress in Grace's life, offered an explanation for the behavior of her beloved sister. "She couldn't sleep for weeks when she drank. What happens with most in the family is a nervous condition, which does not allow one to sleep except when doped or full of wine and whiskey." [11] The relationship between the two was colored by Grace's jealousy of Mary. According to Mary, Grace had been just as talented but had not been able to escape the traps of domestic life. She often spoke, in her drunken rages, of her resentment and lashed out at anyone within range, including her children. No matter what Mary and other family members tried to do for her, Grace never seemed able to maintain a comfortable, sober lifestyle. Tensions grew between her and Mary, and it was decided that she would find her own place. The love between Grace and Mary was not compromised, and for years Mary served as a surrogate mother to her sister's children.

Mary continued to try to straighten out the financial side of her own household, but the few royalty checks she received were hardly enough to cover the expenses. In 1956 the IRS wrote again about her outstanding debt. Mary responded as candidly as she could about her situation:

> My future in show business is very vague due to heavy competition and my ill health. I have been broke since 1947 and the few jobs I was able to obtain at indefinite intervals went toward my many mounting bills and ex-

penses. Steady employment is just about impossible for me. I am completely bankrupt and my future in show business is closed until I can have a plastic surgeon fix my face which of course is impossible as I have no income and am unemployed. If it were through some miraculous way that I was able to work again it would take me at least a year or two to pay back the personal loans and get my few last possessions out of pawn, plus get the adequate medical treatment that I need. Kindly favor me with a humane reply.[12]

There is no official response to Mary's emotional letter in her papers, but one can assume a manageable solution was found. Mary began exploring conventional religion in the hope that she could once again feel internal peace. She continued to pray daily but found her knowledge of the Bible and God limited to the Psalms. She had not shown any interest in religion before, but Mary needed more. With Islam being brought to Harlem by the Nation of Islam and with the multiplicity of Protestant churches in the area, Mary's biggest decision was which religious practices suited her the best. She and Mamie had been raised in the Baptist faith in Atlanta, but when the family moved to Pittsburgh they had begun attending the Catholic Church. Most of Mary's siblings had been raised Catholic, but she had little interest in attending church during her adolescence. "I saw so many things going down with the preacher and what was happening in the church, I felt that I shouldn't even be there," she later recalled. "So I came out; I never went to church anymore."[13] During her years with the Kirk band, however, she befriended a man who often left gifts for her behind the stage during their stint at the Apollo Theatre. He once gave her a small white Bible, telling her, "This is your wealth and your health and always keep it."[14] She had done just that, but before 1954 she had never read it.

The first church she attended in New York was the famed Abyssinian Baptist Church, where the Reverend Adam Clayton Powell Jr., the husband of Hazel Scott, was the pastor. She was drawn to the emotionalism of the church services and decided to join in late 1955. However, after a while Mary found the church too politically driven and inaccessible during the times she needed it most. During the week Mary found the building closed. So she went daily to Our Lady of Lourdes, the Catholic church on 142nd Street. Mary would go to the sanctuary to pray and meditate for hours.[15] She had almost totally closed herself off from the world. The only exceptions were her good friends Lorraine and Dizzy Gillespie, who would often take food to her.

Mary's focus gradually shifted away from her own physical welfare to her overwhelming need to devote herself to a continual state of repentance. At Our Lady of Lourdes she prayed for as many as three thousand persons whose names she catalogued on slips of paper and in a little book. Ironically, she never prayed directly for herself, assuming no doubt that through her sacrifice and devotion to others she would find forgiveness for what she deemed her past sins. Mary began living a very ascetic life that included fasting for days, during which time she would often consume only water and apples. She eliminated all her vices, including smoking, gambling, and excessive spending, and committed herself to helping others. Mary was a woman searching for inner peace, a peace that would surpass all understanding. She had experienced so many of the material pleasures the world had to offer but still had not found emotional comfort. "Everybody thought I was going crazy," she later recalled. "I gave away my Dior gowns and sold a $6500 mink for $50. I picked up seven or eight people on welfare, and I cooked for them, washed for them, and slept on the floor so they could live in my apartment in Harlem. I didn't have any money coming in—no royalties or anything."[16] A woman once known for stylish, tailored clothing now owned one pair of shoes and a single dress, which she washed by hand daily. According to her niece Helen Floyd, "Sacrifice was it for her."[17]

Those who witnessed Mary's transformation tried to adjust. Her conversations, which were once full of stories of the jazz scene or the newest musical development, were now centered on discussions of God, the fate of humanity, and the need for everyone to pray. Some musicians and friends avoided her as much as possible, unable to withstand the "sermons" she was certain to launch into or saddened by her physical deterioration. According to her niece, "She was like a bag lady—not crazy, but odd, running here and there with bags of groceries, trying to help these strung-out musicians. People laughed at her."[18] Not everyone, however, reacted to Mary in this manner. Some understood what Mary was going through because they were dealing with similar issues. Mary's turn to spirituality was emblematic of the shift toward religion that began to sweep through the jazz community in the 1940s and 1950s. Many musicians converted during this period to Islam, either the orthodox version or the alternative sects such as the Nation of Islam. Although some joined the faith for religious reasons, others saw it as a way of battling the social ills that denied black musicians equal rights. Early musician converts discovered that if they converted to the Islamic faith, they were no longer considered "colored" and thereby no longer governed by segregation laws of the South. Dizzy Gillespie described this movement to convert for social reasons:

> "You'll be white," they'd say. "You get a new name and you don't have to be a nigger no more." So everybody started joining because they considered it a big advantage not to be black during the time of segregation. When these cats found out that Idres Sulieman, who joined the Muslim faith about that time, could go into these white restaurants and bring out sandwiches to the other guys because he wasn't colored—and he looked like the inside of a chimney—they started enrolling in droves. Musicians started having it printed on their police cards where it said "race," "W" for white. Kenny Clarke had one and he showed it to me. He said, "See, nigger, I ain't no spook; I'm white, 'W.'" He changed his name to Arabic, Liaqat Ali Salaam. Another cat who had been my roommate at Laurinburg, Oliver Mesheux, got involved in an altercation about race down in Delaware. He went into this restaurant, and they said they didn't serve colored in there. So he said, "I don't blame you. But I don't have to go under the rules of colored because my name is Mustafa Dalil." Didn't ask him no more questions. Most of the Muslim guys who were sincere in the beginning went on believing and practicing the faith.[19]

Not all musicians who converted to Islam during the 1940s and 1950s did so for these reasons, as some viewed Christianity as oppressive to the black community and believed that Islam was a more suitable fit for people of color. Ironically, in the mid-1960s, when John Coltrane began infusing his conception of spirituality—one based on exploration of non-Western religions—into his compositions, he was praised for his expansion beyond the creative boundaries. However, for many, and for Mary especially, there was a fine line between religious fanaticism and strong belief. Mary had taken her beliefs to the extreme, in the estimation of many, and it was "bad for her career."[20]

Mary's musician friends, however, respected what she was attempting to do through her spirituality and began meeting her at the church for prayers. Thelonious Monk, Mary's ex-husband Harold Baker, and Bud Powell would meet Mary at 6:00 A.M. for the first mass, and she would make them stay through all three masses. Although Mary's efforts were influenced by her desire to help these musicians, she often met with surprising reactions. Monk's first visit to Our Lady of Lourdes was quite eventful. En route to the church, Monk purchased a small bottle of wine. He drank all of it, hoping it would calm his nerves, but he became so inebriated that he could not walk straight. He "fell inside on the floor," recalled Mary. She struggled to get him up. "Get up, you big ape," she yelled to no avail. Luckily the church was empty, so the hilarious scene was shared only by the two of them.[21] Monk and others continued to meet Mary and she focused her energies on trying to clean up those who were battling with chemical addiction. Not willing to see another talented musician die of an overdose or physical complications brought on by consistent drug use, Mary operated a one-woman rehabilitation center in her Hamilton Terrace apartment.[22]

* * *

The proliferation of drugs in the jazz scene in the 1940s and 1950s greatly colored the public's opinion of the music. The use of chemical substances for inspiration was nothing new, but in the years after the Great Depression the role of drugs in the world of jazz had grown considerably. New York and Chicago had built their jazz scenes around the underworld syndicate that controlled the nightclubs and speakeasies. Marijuana and alcohol had been the drugs of choice before the 1940s. Dizzy Gillespie recalled that when he arrived in New York in 1937, he was considered square because he didn't drink or smoke marijuana. Despite a federal ban on the sale and consumption of marijuana, the drug's continued popularity among jazz people was documented in various songs of the time, including "The Reefer Man," "Light Up," and "Can't Kick the Habit." It was a well-known fact that Louis Armstrong indulged in the habit daily, and Mary often smoked the drug, beginning during her years with the Kirk band. According to John Williams, two of the major dealers who serviced musicians in New York were Malcolm Little, who was later known as Malcolm X, and the future comedian Redd Foxx.

> They hung around us 'cause they were shoveling pot. They were hustlers. Redd Foxx was more of a hustler than Malcolm X. He was something! He was down trying to sell marijuana to us. A lot of us used it. Louis used it, practically all his life—Louis Armstrong. Pot wasn't all that bad. They're still arguing whether for medical use and all that. After they left, those who were weak enough to leave pot, got on stronger stuff. That's what happened, when they got on cocaine and all that stuff. That's the stuff that really messed Charlie Parker, "Yardbird," up. Charlie Parker at thirty-four overdosing—see, you can't overdose on pot. You can smoke it and just get sleepy. Sleep until it dies off.[23]

The harsh life of touring and the health problems that accompanied the strain of the lifestyle were among many reasons musicians turned to chemical stimulants. Although he did not get caught up in the drug scene, John Williams said that most musicians adopted some way of coping—alcohol, tobacco, or drugs. He chose alcohol, and he never graduated to pot or heroin. These habits were so ingrained at the time that members of jazz bands segregated themselves according to their practices. "When I was in Earl [Hines]'s band," recalled John, "we had about five who were on pot. So they sat in the back of the bus. Then we had guys who didn't drink at all, then the lushes. They called us lushes, 'cause we all drinked. Earl Hines, and all, we all drinked. We were all in the front part of the bus. And the pots, they're cool, and we'd look back and they'd be shaking their heads, calling us uncouth MFs. 'Oh, you uncouth MFs.' We'd laugh, but with them on their kick and us on ours, when we'd get to the job you're talking about some good music."[24] One of the major arguments Mary and John had during their marriage involved the use of drugs. He once caught Mary smoking pot, and the two decided to separate because he didn't approve of it. They eventually reunited for a time, but it remained one of the things John would not compromise on. He never caught her smoking again, but he would occasionally find residual evidence in the bathroom.

Although Mary continued to smoke marijuana for some time after leaving the Kirk band, her habit never grew into the life-threatening addiction that consumed musicians who graduated to cocaine or heroin. As the race record boom began to decline, as segregation limited the opportunities for black touring bands, and as black musicians found themselves excluded more and more from the mainstream commercial music scene, many musicians immersed themselves in a bohemian lifestyle. Heroin, because of its cheap price and intense physical reaction, became the drug of choice in the 1940s and 1950s. It came in capsules that cost $1 to $3 each. Taking ten of the capsules, which contained one gram of heroin each, constituted a heavy daily habit.[25] Fifty-second Street soon became the center of both bebop and drug abuse. It served the "symbolic, functional, psychological and social needs of the cool, aloof hipster jazz musician, and the whole added up to what might be called the heroin experience. Musicians became dependent on the total experience rather than the drug itself."[26] Congress moved quickly to eradicate the proliferation of drugs. The Boggs Act of 1951 established sentencing guidelines for offenders. For first, second, and third offenses, perpetrators received minimum jail sentences of two, five, and ten years, respectively. After the first offense there was no parole, probation, or suspension. Narcotics agents were armed and given the right to arrest suspects without a warrant. The New York Police Department required that each musician be photographed, fingerprinted, and charged $2 for a license to play in establishments that served alcohol. It was another way of policing musicians, as anyone with a narcotics violation was automatically denied a card, and if a musician was busted, the license would be revoked. Although jazz musicians in general were targeted, black musicians were the main objects of harassment. Fifty-second Street, which had drawn whites to jazz, was closed down. Nightclubs were bulldozed and office buildings erected. Many notable jazz musicians battled with their addictions, including Gerry Mulligan, Stan Getz, Billie Holiday, Bud Powell, and Thelonious Monk. Mary knew that the only way these musicians could survive was through around-the-clock care. She thought that she could help people more by addressing their physical needs. Mary did not discount the healing effects of her music, but decided "to help them in flesh instead of playing for them." "I understand," she would later assert, "that you can offer up every note you play to help some souls and things like that, but I was going on my own without the talent. The talent was much stronger for helping people."[27]

Mary's Hamilton Terrace apartment became the headquarters for her efforts to aid addicted and ill musicians. The flat became a halfway house where she detoxified, fed, clothed, and found work for musicians. The worst cases she housed in a room down the hall that she rented cheaply from a neighbor. They usually stayed a couple of weeks and when possible left clean, sober, and with employment. Most of Mary's "patients" were men, and she would often tell them, "'You've got to be a *man*. Stand up and go downtown and get a job. No use lying around Harlem and feeling sorry for yourself.' Sometimes they come back in worse shape and ask for money, and sometimes they get on their feet."[28] She funded the operation through royalty checks and donations from friends like Dizzy and Lorraine Gillespie. Often she would go days without food or money in her pocket, but miraculously, just before she reached dire straits, a relative of Dizzy would appear at her door with a basket full of food. Mary developed her own method for rehabilitating addicts that was centered on prayers and music. If an addict began to experience cravings for drugs, Mary would give him or her the Psalms to read or write a piece of music that would take the person's mind off the physical cravings.

> I had a drummer that was on it and his wife timed him. It took him five minutes to go home. He'd come here eight o'clock in the morning and I'd just keep him in the house. See, a dope addict, anyone on heroin, they're like a baby. So I'd keep them with me all day. If I had to go, I'd say, "Come on, we'll go to the five and ten." The first night I had him here in the house he began to want a fix, and so I said, "I just wrote a drum part." I wrote and I wrote and I said, "Dig this." He said, "Yeah." I said, "Well, play it." He had a pad and he played it and he forgot. Every time that happened I said, "Hey," and I'd write something else. That worked on him, I noticed that

night, because it took his mind off it completely or else the stuff they gave him was so weak. That whole night he didn't have anything from eight o'clock till twelve o'clock at night.[29]

Despite Mary's refusal to perform professionally, she still acknowledged the importance of music in her life. She could not divorce herself from the one thing that had defined her professional and personal identity for so many years, but she could separate herself from the lifestyle. She continued to rely on prayer and Our Lady of Lourdes as a place of grounding and meditation. Although many of Mary's former friends were put off by her fanatical spirituality, others rallied around her and aided in her full conversion and ultimate return to jazz. Two individuals had the most profound impact on Mary and her faith. Through Lorraine Gillespie, Mary met Father John Crowley, who had befriended Dizzy while serving as a missionary in Paraguay. As a goodwill ambassador of the State Department, Gillespie traveled throughout the world performing. In 1956, while on such a tour of South America, Gillespie met Crowley, who professed a love for jazz; he had once been a saxophonist. A friendship blossomed and the priest often counseled Lorraine in her desire to convert to the Catholic Church. Lorraine, sensing that a meeting between Mary and Crowley would provide the pianist with much-needed direction, introduced the two. Crowley, unlike anyone before, was able to soften Mary's fervor. His approach was stern but loving. He told Mary that she should pray for herself as well as everyone else; she should stop bringing drug addicts and mentally ill people to her home. "What you're doing is very dangerous," he said. But Mary would not concede, stating that she didn't "care as long as [she] was helping them, a poor person." [30]

The critic Barry Ulanov, who had converted to Catholicism and become a professor of theology, was concerned that Mary needed to receive religious instruction from someone with maturity, experience, and a deeper understanding of the passions of musicians. He introduced her to Father Anthony Woods, a Jesuit priest who served at St. Francis Xavier in New York. Like Crowley, he had an interest in jazz and was very active in musical circles. While serving at St. Francis, he sponsored several artistic endeavors, including The Village Light Opera Company, the Xavier Players, and the Xavier Symphony. He and Ulanov had become friends through their participation in the St. Thomas More Society for Intellectual Catholics, an organization that served as a forum for discussing the merits of contemporary theology.[31] Where others grew impatient with Mary, with her ramblings and fanaticism, Woods exercised patience and understanding. He would later describe her as "an emotional thinker, a disorganized thinker," who often needed time to sort out her own thoughts before proceeding but always reacted earnestly to the guidance given.[32] Ulanov later said, "Woods was made to order for Mary — quick, accommodating, nonjudgmental; so strong and strong-willed yet with delicate apprehensions."[33] Mary described their relationship:

> He did everything in his power to help me back to music and things that were still happening with me in a strange way, all this ESP working. He told me to call him any time and sometimes I called him at four o'clock in the morning. He and Lorraine Gillespie, they had a ball on the phone when they talked about me. It was so funny, some of the things I'd call them about. He was so very kind to me. He went along with me and finally got me back to jazz.[34]

From their first meeting in 1956 until his death in the mid-1960s, Mary and Woods maintained a very strong and personal relationship. In early 1957 Mary and Lorraine Gillespie began catechism classes with Woods at St. Ignatius Loyola Church, and they were baptized and confirmed in the Catholic Church in May of that year. Mary's baptism, which took place the day after her forty-seventh birthday, would mark her resurrection as a musician and start a new period in her life.

* * *

Dizzy, Lorraine, Woods, and Crowley continued throughout the summer of 1957 to encourage Mary to return to her music. Mary resisted, stating that she was dedicated to helping the ill and helpless. Lorraine even went as far as to entice Mary with extravagant gifts, which would once have swayed the pianist. She bought Mary a fur coat, telling her, "It will look good on you when you get back to your music." Mary sold the coat and used the money to help her boarders.[35] Dizzy would often encourage Melba Liston, a band member and arranger, to visit Mary and see what she was doing. Melba would report that Mary "played some chords and you ought to hear them. They're really great." Melba would often sit and notate the music Mary played and take the new arrangements back to Dizzy. "'Those arrangements were really good,' he said. She said, 'I didn't do them. That was Lou's arrangement.'"[36] Crowley told her, "Mary, God wants you to return to the piano. You can serve Him best there for that is what you know best."[37] Mary was not swayed and continued her work with the needy. As her debts grew and her royalty checks came less frequently, Mary pondered her future and wondered if life in a nunnery was a viable alternative. Finally, Woods went to Mary and told her that her greatest work could be accomplished through her music. "You're an artist," he told her. "You belong at the piano and writing music. It's *my* business to help people through the Church and your business to help people through music."[38] It worked, and on July 6, 1957, Mary Lou Williams appeared for the first time in five years on an American stage at the Newport Jazz Festival.

By 1957 the Newport Jazz Festival had become one of the major venues of jazz performance. It had resurrected the careers of Duke Ellington and Miles Davis and offered performers an opportunity to present to unwavering audiences their most experimental and creative compositions. Mary took the stage with the Dizzy Gillespie Orchestra, which provided accompaniment to a dance presentation by Eartha Kitt. To the disappointment of the audience, Mary performed only two of the nine numbers in the Gillespie set, and neither was new material. One was a medley of three movements, "Virgo," "Libra," and Aries," from her *Zodiac Suite* and the other was "Carioca." The performance, heralded by the press, was documented by Norman Granz, who released a recording of the performance in 1958 as *Dizzy Gillespie at Newport* (Verve 314-513-7542). *Down Beat's* review of the performance said that Mary's "inspired work indicates that her return to the active jazz scene would be a most welcome one."[39]

Mary had intended for this performance to be a one-time affair, but a lack of money soon led her back into performing full-time. Mary was booked into a modest Manhattan nightclub called the Composer. Her nightly performances, which consisted of renditions of standards and her own tunes and alternated with Billy Taylor's trio, drew audiences to the club, but Mary, who had battled with stage fright since her years at Café

Society, often avoided contact with patrons and hid in the coat checkroom at the end of each set. Mary's behavior was viewed as very peculiar, but owners didn't mind as long as she continued to draw crowds. The New York scene welcomed Mary back with open arms. The *New Yorker,* reporting on Mary's return to the club scene, remarked, "The nightclub scene has lightened up all around us in the last couple of weeks, and for the most part it is filled with very familiar touches—notably at the Composer, where the superb jazz pianist Mary Lou Williams has emerged from retirement. It is a pleasure to report that the artistry of Mary Lou Williams is undiminished. She had no new works to offer the night I listened to her (as you may recall, she is a composer of some stature, as well as a pianist), but she presented a number of old standards—'I Got a Right to Sing the Blues' and 'Willow Weep for Me' among them—elegantly and movingly, employing a fine beat, and never wasting a note." [40]

After three weeks of this alternation between playing and hiding, Mary was convinced by Cy Baron, her friend and the club's owner, to come out of the checkroom and sit with people. Although reluctant, Mary did, but she often sat in the corner, withdrawn from those around her. During the fall of 1957, Mary secured consistent bookings that took her through the remainder of the year. After her stint at the Composer, she was booked at the Comedy Club in Baltimore, followed by the Sugar Hill in Newark, New Jersey. In late November she returned to New York to play at the Cherry Lane Restaurant. Adjacent to the Cherry Lane Theater in Greenwich Village, it had attracted regular patronage through its exquisite menu. The owner, wanting to capitalize on the popularity of establishments that offered good music and good food, decided to inaugurate its music program with Mary. *Variety* reported, "With Mary Lou Williams to start things rolling, the room is off to a good start. She's only in on a two week booking, though, which may not be enough time to get the word around." Her set, which included the bassist Bill Clark and the drummer Bruce Lawrence, featured Mary playing new arrangements of her old tunes and her new interpretations of standards. But for the reviewer it didn't matter what Mary played, because "she's got a free-wheeling jazz feel out of the old school that gives each item an invigorating spark." [41] A few days after Thanksgiving, she worked at Johnny Molina's Cocktail Lounge in St. Louis, and she ended the year with two stints at the Blue Note in Chicago. Although Mary was managing financially for the first time in years, she still did not have enough money to continue helping addicted musicians.

*   *   *

In 1958 Mary decided to expand her one-woman operation. Her goal was to raise enough money to buy a home in the country and create a facility where addicts could be attended to by a medical staff and be provided with a space where they could continue to make music. It seemed a major undertaking, but few had done anything to address the problem of drugs in jazz. Mary had seen too many of her friends and too many great musicians succumb to the lure of drugs, and many had lost their lives or their careers. Parker was one of many musicians to die in the 1950s from the complications of drug abuse. The saxophonist Wardell Gray, who had sat in on many of her early sessions with Asch Records, died in the Nevada desert after being beaten for a debt he had accrued with gangsters. Tadd Dameron, who frequented Mary's apartment in the 1940s, would die in 1965 from heroin abuse. Billie Holiday, another Café Society mainstay, died at age forty-four after years of drug abuse, and Miles Davis had returned from France in 1949 addicted to heroin. Action was needed, and Mary was just one of many who knew the importance of dealing with the problem. At the 1957 Newport Jazz Festival, the critic Nat Hentoff arranged a symposium on addiction that developed into a musicians' clinic in New York. Cab Calloway, writing on the subject in *Ebony,* asserted, "If all of the most gifted musicians who have been arrested, convicted and imprisoned for being found with dope were assembled in one place, one of the greatest all-star orchestras in the history of the band business could be recognized." Calloway asserted that the specter of drugs was destroying the careers of some of the most talented performers and corrupting the morals of a new generation who would "carry the torch of our great profession's tradition when we 'old-timers' have retired from the scene." [42]

With the legal assistance of Herbert Bliss, a friend of Father Woods, the Bel Canto Foundation was incorporated. Mary immediately began planning how to raise the revenue to bring to life her vision of a facility that could offer medical care to addicted musicians. She wrote to potential donors, most of whom were agents, newspapermen, record executives, and Mary's more financially stable friends, such as Doris Duke and Barbara Hutton. Many received letters that read, "Dear wonderful populus [*sic*]—when you invest in Bel Canto Foundation, you invest in the safe hope of every creative musician performer, for his creativeness belongs to you and you belong to him."[43] Another publicity flyer sent to potential donors read:

> Helping musicians may mean many things. It may mean merely offering food and shelter. It may mean providing a congenial and creative atmosphere in which to both work and rest. It may mean giving moral support and encouragement during a period of struggle for recognition. It may mean medical aid. Perhaps, all of these things. To meet the challenge, Bel Canto Foundation has been set up especially for musical performers out of a *need*—to help them, which of course helps music. The Foundation must get started. It hopes in the future, to purchase or build a home in the country, away from the noise, pressures and stifling influences of the city, where musicians, regardless of race, color, or creed may go for a time to find peace and whatever "Help" they may require to bring *us* the music *we* require. Staffed with medical personnel, and equipped, with all home facilities, as well as work rooms with pianos and soundproofing, this country haven will stand as tangible evidence of appreciation to all musicians, who *have* and will continue to bring us the music we love.[44]

When other efforts to raise money for the foundation failed, Mary decided to hold a benefit concert that would bring publicity and revenue. With money she borrowed from Hutton and Duke, Mary rented Carnegie Hall for a September 20 concert. As early as April 1958 *Down Beat* announced that Mary had rented the hall for a September concert that would aid her newly established foundation to help musicians.[45] Mary worked feverishly to sell tickets and to secure favors from those who could offer services so that expenses would not deplete the small budget. She once again circulated flyers that spoke of the mission of Bel Canto and urged recipients to donate to the foundation. But Mary could not effectively handle both her daily operation of helping musicians and the organization of the foundation. So she established the Bel Canto Committee, which consisted of individuals who had pledged their support to the initiative. The list included such luminaries as Nat King Cole, Lena Horne, Sammy Davis Jr., Duke Ellington, Ruth Ellington, Leonard Feather, George Wein, Elaine Lorillard, John Hammond, Jackie Robins, and Joe Glaser. Performers who did not pledge monetary support volunteered to perform at the benefit concert. The program featured talent that ranged from regional groups such as the ninety-piece Xavier Symphony, which was scheduled to perform compositions arranged by Mary Lou, to big names such as the Eddie "Lockjaw" Davis Trio, featuring the organist Shirley Scott and the drummer Arthur Edgehill. Lester Young, Ben Webster, Roy Haynes, Thelonious Monk, Annie Ross, and Maxine Sullivan were also slated to perform. By the date of the concert, more than fifty performers had been confirmed.

On the night of the performance musicians and entertainers crowded the stage, but the audience was small. In the end, despite all Mary's efforts, the concert yielded no profits for the foundation; all the revenue raised went to pay expenses. The failed venture brought tension to Mary's relationships with Barbara Hutton and Doris Duke, who considered litigation against her when the money they had lent to fund the concert was not repaid. Neither woman went to court, but their friendships with Mary were never the same.

Many would have viewed the concert as a major setback, but Mary continued working to secure other means of funding for the foundation. She decided to open a series of thrift shops, which would feature items donated by musicians and her friends. Mary searched for properties and settled first on a small storefront at 308 East Twenty-ninth Street, around the corner from Bellevue Hospital. She fixed the place up, announced to her friends and supporters her newest venture on behalf of Bel Canto, and solicited donations. The store, although never well managed, accumulated many items from her supporters. A cousin of the Mellons, Peggy Hitchcock, gave Mary her trousseau and very expensive dresses valued at more than $700 each. Saks Fifth Avenue sent boxes of clothes, and Ellington and Gillespie donated shoes, ties, and other items. Mary worked twelve hours a day collecting items and running the shop. Business was slow, as most of the inhabitants of the neighborhood were working-class people who had very little money to spare or any need for the fancy, sometimes garish items Mary stocked. Occasionally, when business was bad, Mary loaded up her car and headed to Pittsburgh, where she always managed to sell the clothes. Mary also threw parties in the shop, inviting patrons to survey the merchandise while she played the piano. The shop yielded very little money, most of which went for rent and to musicians who needed help. For day-to-day expenses, Mary relied on royalty checks from reissues of recordings and uses of her arrangements, but she was barely surviving. With much hesitation she returned to performing.

On one occasion, while returning from a concert in Albany, New York, Mary and her manager Joe Glaser stopped at the Catholic community of Graymoor, fifty miles north of Manhattan. While roaming the grounds Mary spotted a young black friar. Having met only Caucasian priests, Mary was intrigued by the young man and wanted to meet him. Grady Hancock, known as Brother Mario, had been at the Franciscan community for only a short time, because of the requirements of his training, and worked in the community's gift shop. Mary entered the gift shop, walked over to Mario, and introduced herself. "I'm Mary Lou Williams," she said. But Mario had no idea who she was. The brothers were forbidden to listen to the radio, read newspapers or magazines, or watch television. She tried to explain herself to him and told him she was impressed with the community and the gift shop. Mario recalled:

> The manager came over to me, Mr. Glaser, and he said, "You know, she's a very famous jazz pianist." I said, "Oh." He said, "She writes and arranges music and we're just returning from Albany from a concert she gave." So I was impressed with that, though I wasn't too much into jazz at the time or any music. So she came over and started talking and wanted to know a bit about me and I told her some of [my] history [in the community]. And she said, "I'm going to visit you," and then she sent Mr. Glaser out to the car and he got a couple of her forty-fives, and he brought them back and he gave them to me. She said, "I want you to hear my music. And I'm impressed with this place and I've never seen a black friar—monk before." She called me a monk, but we're friars really. "I would like to come up and see you again." I said, "That would be nice, very nice. I would appreciate that." And so it was a quick visit and then they left and went back to New York. Lo and behold, she wrote me a few days later, saying that she was giving me

her address, saying that if you're in the city I want to see you. In a month she came up to see me, and that was the beginning of me really getting to know her and her getting to know me. And we shared a lot. I was impressed with her because she had such a wonderful sense of humor. She drove herself up. She came up alone without her manager, and we just sat and she had lunch with us and she stayed the full day. We walked around the property, just exchanging ideas and thoughts. This continued for months.[46]

Mary told Mario about her conversion, which, with the exception of her fanaticism and emotional breakdown, was similar to his own conversion. He too had been raised Protestant, only to be drawn to the peacefulness and holiness of the Catholic Church and its liturgy. Mary's relationship with Mario, unlike those with Father Woods and Father Crowley, was one bonded by race and the understanding of what their world experiences had meant to the development of their faith. She took Lorraine Gillespie and Lucille Armstrong, Louis's wife, to meet him, and the three women purchased several expensive rosaries the community sold. Later, Mary took Hazel Scott to meet Brother Mario, whom she talked about constantly. Eventually, Mario and Mary's conversations drifted to her music. He told her how much he had enjoyed the recordings she had given him and wondered when she would produce more. Mary explained that she hadn't written anything since her conversion. With all the work she did on behalf of the foundation and ailing musicians, she hardly had the stamina required to write. Mario was saddened by Mary's admission but reminded her that her talent was God-given and should be used to advance His people. Over the next twenty years a strong bond developed between the two, and each became critical to the spiritual and emotional survival of the other.

Virginia Burley in the 1950s. (Courtesy of Mary Lou Williams Collection.)

Fletcher Burley, Mary's stepfather (left), and an unnamed man. (Courtesy of Mary Lou Williams Collection.)

To Andy
Thanking you
for the encouragement
& the inspiration you
gave me during
our many years
of friendship
Best Wishes
always—
Mary Lou Williams
4/16/37

Mary in 1937, photo autographed to Andy Kirk. (Courtesy of Mary Lou Williams Collection.)

Mary and John Williams with the Seymour and Jeanette troupe, 1927. (Courtesy of Mary Lou Williams Collection.)

Mary and John Williams with the Hits and Bits Troupe, 1925. Mary is at far right. (Courtesy of Mary Lou Williams Collection.)

Andy Kirk and the Twelve Clouds of Joy, 1936–37 (John Williams is second from the left in the sax section; Mary is seated at the piano). (Courtesy of Mary Lou Williams Collection.)

Mary at the piano in a nightclub in 1938. (Courtesy of Mary Lou Williams Collection.)

Mary with Al Hall and Bill Coleman at her Hamilton Terrace apartment, looking through contracts, around 1944. (Courtesy of Mary Lou Williams Collection.)

Mary with Erroll Garner and Teddy Wilson at Jazz under the Stars, 1958. (Courtesy of Mary Lou Williams Collection.)

Mary with Ronnie Free, Mose Allison, Lester Young, Charlie Rouse, and Oscar Pettiford, 1958. Photographed on the street after the famous "Great Day in Harlem" portrait. (Courtesy of Mary Lou Williams Collection.)

Mary with schoolchildren after a celebration of *Mary Lou's Mass*, late 1970s. (Courtesy of Mary Lou Williams Collection, copyright Mikki Ferrill.)

Mary performing with Dizzy Gillespie at Dahlgren Chapel of Georgetown University, late 1970s. (Courtesy of Mary Lou Williams Collection.)

Mary with Ahmad Jamal, Billy Strayhorn, Duke Ellington, Dizzy Gillespie, Earl "Fatha" Hines, Billy Taylor, and Willie "the Lion" Smith after the Pittsburgh Jazz Festival, 1965.

Mary and Hazel Scott in Mary's Boutique (her second thrift shop), Amsterdam Avenue, New York City, 1965. (Courtesy of Mary Lou Williams Collection, copyright Edward Rice.)

Mary and Melba Liston at a 1957 session for Roulette Records. (Courtesy of Chuck Stewart.)

Mary with Peter O'Brien in the late 1970s. (Courtesy of Mary Lou Williams Collection, copyright Mikki Ferrill.)

Chapter 10

THE LONG JOURNEY BACK HOME

Mary continued her efforts to rehabilitate addicts well into the 1960s, but keeping her thrift shop viable became more difficult. Although she was playing the old piano that adorned her apartment more than usual, Mary was still hesitant to resume her career. She was spending most of her time alternating between her church and the thrift shop. Although she had tried to rid her life of music, new sounds filled her head, and she began sketching ideas for new compositions, but Mary feared what complete submersion in her music and the jazz scene would bring. She believed that if she returned, she would somehow be caught in the environment and be exposed to the "demons" she felt accompanied the music. She could not deny the obvious—Mary was still drawn to the music and she knew she still had much to contribute to the development of jazz, especially as the art form continued to splinter into different stylistic camps and the level of experimentation increased.

The radical social and musical environment of the late 1950s gave way to new forms of experimentation in jazz by the early 1960s. The music was deeply connected to the attitude of resistance that had evolved within the black community. The desegregation of the South and the eradication of institutions of racism and segregation became crucial to the black community. Court decisions in the case called *Brown v. Board of Education* had desegregated America's schools shortly before Mary returned from Europe, and the civil rights movement was reenergized through the Montgomery bus boycott, the Freedom Marches, and voter registration drives held throughout the South. A powerful cultural shift was under way. Jazz, like other forms of popular music, began to reflect resistance to the status quo, and "freedom" became the motif of the decade. According to Ted Gioia, "It would be hard, in fact, to find a term more explosive, more laden with depths of meaning, or proclaimed with more emotion during these tumultuous years."[1]

Within jazz, performance practices and compositional approaches advocated freedom through the rejection of harmonic and melodic structure. This rejection was an extension of the ideals of modal jazz as explored first by Miles Davis and later by John Coltrane. The progenitors of "free" jazz saw their music as being just as political as the speeches of Malcolm X, Martin Luther King Jr., and Stokley Carmichael. The leaders of the free jazz school viewed their participation in the jazz scene as a continuation of a mentality that encouraged racism against black musicians, and many rebelled against the industry. Some found community in their protest and rebellion in the Black Arts Movement, which developed as a more roots-based and all-inclusive alternative to the rhetoric and philosophical approaches of the Harlem Renaissance. It provided a means for defining the paradigm in black art and music. Mary's ideas about jazz were influenced by the new sense of racial pride that the Black Arts and civil rights movements generated. She would be one of many notable jazz musicians and composers who would voice their criticism of the industry's attempts to negate the African roots of jazz during the 1960s. The rhetoric was strong and unapologetic and called for a return to the roots of jazz, which for these advocates could be accomplished only by acknowledging the lineage of jazz and its relationship to the experiences of African Americans. In an effort to address the growing divide between black and white musicians, black musicians and white agents and club owners, and black musicians and white critics, *Down Beat* ran a two-part editorial on racial prejudice in jazz. Although the pieces highlighted the issues and opinions of those on all sides, no clear or definitive resolution could be found. Many thought the lack of a resolution could lead to the death of jazz. Such thoughts today seem extreme and reactionary, but at the time some believed the fate of jazz was tied to the splintering of the jazz scene. There is no evidence that Mary was an open proponent of the Black Arts Movement or the rhetoric of dissension developing among jazz musicians, but it is clear from Mary's own words that she believed the public needed to know more about the history of jazz and its cultural connections to the experiences of African Americans.

In the three decades she had spent in entertainment, Mary had witnessed the industry's attempts to deny the creativity of black performers and composers and the successful adaptation of black music by white performers. She knew that the tensions between artists, critics, and agents had been growing for years. Benny Goodman was deemed the "King of Swing" despite the innovative and pioneering efforts of Fletcher Henderson and Don Redman; Dizzy Gillespie and Charlie Parker were attacked by the public and the critics for their efforts to reinstill improvisation and above-average musicianship in mainstream jazz; black musicians were denied proper recognition for the advancement of modern styles. This was the social and emotional baggage that threatened to drain jazz of its vitality and legacy. Mary knew more than ever that she, as one of the living pioneers of jazz, had to rally with other musicians to reconcile the conflicts developing between jazz musicians and the American public.

It was perhaps this desire to save jazz from its own self-destructive patterns, together with a personal resolution of the conflict between her love for jazz and her spirituality, that drew Mary out of her retirement. Instead of jumping back into performance, Mary focused her efforts on educating younger generations about the legacy of the jazz tradition. In the late 1950s she accepted an offer to teach jazz history at a neighborhood public school. Previously Mary's interaction with young children had been mainly with her nieces and nephews, who by this time knew of their aunt's music only through family stories. The children of postwar Harlem knew nothing of the illustrious musical history of the area. The days of the Cotton Club and the historic performances at the Lincoln Theater and the Savoy Ballroom had now faded into a succession of doo-wop groups and rhythm and blues records. Mary vowed not to allow these forms to be the only music in these youngsters' experience. Just as she had nurtured and supported the creative efforts of the early progenitors of bebop, Mary encouraged the musical aspirations of her students. She taught them how to dance and what she called "rock" to jazz instruments. Knowing their apprehensions or prejudices about jazz, Mary introduced them to different concepts slowly. Usually she would write a new composition, combining elements of jazz with the soul and rock sounds they were familiar with, and then have the group perform it.

Mary's effort to aid youngsters in discovering jazz did not diminish her passion for helping established musicians who were struggling to navigate the limited opportunities now available to them. It was during this time that Mary was introduced, through her brother Jerry, to a young pianist named Regina Jay Allbright. Allbright's life mirrored Mary's in many ways. She had grown up in Brooklyn, in a working-class family. At nights, when her mother worked, she often sneaked into jazz clubs to listen to the latest musical explorations of New York's jazz scene and returned home before her mother could detect her absence. She loved jazz and boogie-woogie, and by age eight she was playing professionally. By age eleven she had already won the Apollo's Amateur Hour contest, which had served as the launching pad for Ella Fitzgerald and Sarah Vaughan as well as many other notable performers. She became known around New York for her talent. Allbright left the city during World War II to perform at nearby army bases and eventually joined a group of women who were forming a group out of the remnants of the International Sweethearts of Rhythm. But by the time she and Mary met in the late 1950s, she had lost her union card and was working full-time in a factory. Through her daughter's godmother, she met Jerry Burley, who introduced her to Mary. He never explained to Allbright who his sister was; he just thought the two should meet. Allbright, thinking that the two would just jam and maybe hang out, was surprised to discover that Burley's sister was Mary Lou Williams. She knew of Mary but had never seen her. During their first meeting, Mary asked the young woman to play for her. In her usual fashion, Mary sat and listened intently. Allbright was nervous and surprised to see Mary tapping her foot and enjoying the playing. "I knew I had it made," recalled Allbright, who became one of a few pianists Mary would mentor and teach over the next ten years.[2] Allbright quit her factory job and with Mary's help secured a gig at an air force base in Greenland. Mary instructed her to concentrate on her music and entertaining. "Can you imagine? In the middle of the summer, and she ships me off to an ice cap to play for the air force and practice all day long! By the time I got back, she had called the head of Local 802, and I got my union card back."[3]

Meanwhile, Mary began concentrating on getting back into the jazz scene herself. As much as she wanted to devote herself totally to the Bel Canto Foundation, she needed money. In 1961 she convinced Joe Wells, a friend and club owner, to feature her at his Wells Restaurant through one week. The gig meant that Mary, who had played only sporadically over the past three years, had to work up her repertoire and playing. It also meant that Mary had to address her reservations about reentering the jazz scene and the conflicts it presented with her faith.

* * *

As the social upheaval of the 1960s continued to affect every aspect of American life, the Catholic Church sought ways to better serve its parishioners and society as a whole. It looked not only to social programs that would serve its religious community but also to reforming the liturgy. The question of liturgical reform and renewal dominated ecclesiastical discussions in the 1960s. As early as the late 1950s the necessity of updating the liturgy and church practices to reflect the changing world had been raised within the Catholic Church. One issue would be especially difficult: How could the liturgy be reformed without breaking with Church traditions? Over time the Vatican itself addressed these concerns and attempted to bring some form of resolution. The Second Vatican Council, convened from 1962 until 1965, produced many documents, including two that were particularly significant for American Catholics: the *Declaration on Religious Freedom* and the *Constitution on the Sacred Liturgy*. Although the council did not dictate specific procedures to be carried out by the laity, it did signal the beginning of a period of significant liturgical changes within the Church and of corresponding debates. This new liturgical era would ignite a progressive musical movement that integrated various musical styles with liturgical forms and altered the performance and composition of music within the Catholic Church. The liturgical renewal provided Mary with the opportunity to create a body of work that would reflect the intersection of her faith and jazz.

Although Father Woods and Father Crowley had discussed with Mary countless times the healing effects of her music, she was not completely sold on the idea of using jazz as a means to deal with the social upheaval of the 1960s until she spoke with Brother Mario Hancock. Mario, who by this time had become a close friend of Mary, frequently stressed the importance of her music and the need for her to return to jazz. The two would often talk about St. Martin de Porres, the Afro-Peruvian human-itarian who in the early 1960s was being considered for sainthood by the Catholic Church. De Porres's life as a servant to others spoke directly to Mary's aspirations to better the lot of mankind through unselfish service; it also invigorated Mary, who sought affirmation of her place within the Church as an African American. Mario knew that Mary would not be persuaded to return to her music full-time without some assurance that her faith would not be compromised. So during a visit to Mary's Harlem apartment, he placed on her old piano a plaque of St. Martin de Porres. "You're going to play. You're going to start your music again," he said. Soon afterward Mary began working on a new composition that would commemorate the canonization of Martin de Porres and extend her skills beyond the symphonic and big band arrangements of past years.

Since Mario had been so inspirational in motivating her return to mu-sic, Mary went to him first, asking the young friar to write a poem or text regarding the life of de Porres. Mario, doubting his own ability to write anything credible or good, never made good on his promise to provide Mary with a text. Instead, she turned to Father Anthony Woods, who penned, out of an impromptu discussion with Mary, a text that described the life of de Porres, the son of a sixteenth-century Spanish nobleman and a Negro slave.

> St. Martin De Porres. His Shepherd staff a dusty broom.
> St. Martin De Porres. The poor made a shrine of his tomb.
> St. Martin De Porres. He gentled creatures tame and wild.
> St. Martin De Porres. He sheltered each unsheltered child.

> This man of love (God) born of the flesh, yet of God.
> This humble man healed the sick, raised the dead. His
>   hand is quick.

> To feed beggars and sinners. The starving homeless and
>   the stray.
>
> Oh, Black Christ of the Andes. Come feed and cure us
>   now we pray.
> Spare, oh Lord.
> Spare thy people lest you be angered with me forever.
>
> This man of love born of flesh, yet of God.
> This humble man healed the sick, raised the dead. His
>   hand is quick. St. Martin De Porres.[4]

Mary hummed the melody she had thought up and Woods worked through the rhyme scheme. The result was a composition for mixed choir entitled "A Hymn in Honor of St. Martin De Porres." The piece, which was a cappella with the exception of an eleven-measure piano solo, consisted of complex harmonies that at times coupled the voices antiphonally against one another. The melancholy, repentant mood of the piece was broken up only by Mary's piano solo, which with its Latin-tinged rhythms provided the only cultural link with de Porres's Latin American heritage.

Mary managed to complete the work in time to debut it on de Porres's feast day, November 3, 1963, at St. Francis Xavier Church. That year's celebration of the feast day was part of a concerted effort by Catholic parishes throughout the country to bring awareness about the struggle for civil rights and equality. Mary organized a small choir that presented the work to an excited and receptive audience. Less than a month later Mary reprised the work for a performance at Philharmonic Hall with Dizzy Gillespie. The concert, a benefit for the Symphony of Musical Arts, marked the first time black performers were allowed to perform at the venue, and the first time mainstream audiences heard Mary's attempts to synthesize jazz with sacred verse. Seeing the gig as an important opportunity to raise the profile of jazz, Mary decided also to perform, for the first time live, the history of jazz performance she had recorded in the 1950s for Jazztone. Mary began the program with "Fandangle" and ended with a ballad she called "The Devil." The piece was very similar in style and approach to the "Hymn in Honor of St. Martin De Porres." It was a harmonically complex work that featured a text by the vocalist Ada Moore. This text outlined the many temptations that face mankind daily and reminded listeners that in fighting off the fictional pitchfork-wielding Devil, they may discover that their own actions manifest his evil. The text no doubt reflected Mary's conviction that without complete surrender to God, everyone, despite his or her intentions, is capable of doing evil. The work was performed primarily a cappella, with a six-measure piano solo separating the piece into two sections. The composition exemplified Mary's desire to create vocal compositions that duplicated the closed harmonic style employed by jazz instrumentalists. It also recalled Mary's earliest attempt to write choral music, "Elijah under the Juniper Tree."

While critics praised Mary's innovative approach to chronicling the history of jazz, few knew what to think about "St. Martin" or "The Devil." Marshall Stearns wrote of the performance:

> A repeated rumor is making the rounds that only exper-
> imental jazz will be allowed to appear at Philharmonic
> Hall. If so, the sound of Miss Mary Lou Williams, one of
> the few seasoned performers who has kept up with the
> times, playing a rollicking set of boogie-woogie at the
> hall on November 11 in the course of her "History of
> Jazz" is quite reassuring. The line is not being drawn too
> hard and fast. All in all, the program, "New Concepts of
> Jazz," was highly pleasurable. Miss Williams was in top
> form, and her half of the program sagged only when she
> added a choral group, which got off to a good start and
> then disintegrated among vocal effects which, I imagine,
> were supposed to imitate various jazz instruments.[5]

The critic Stanley Dance said Mary's "sensitive touch, unfailing swing and skillfully developed routines were as delightful as ever, and in her hymns to the recently canonized Negro saint, Martin De Porres, she had a real surprise for the audience. Well sung by a mixed choir of fifteen voices, this was a modern spiritual which managed to commingle pride with something of the sadness that is in the blues."[6] Other critics were not as kind, one declaring that the performance was "pathetic," with a good many things wrong with it. "It is neither good liturgical music, nor good jazz, and it is certainly not a passable fusion of the two." This critic even remarked, "It's regrettable that she didn't mix politics instead of religion with jazz."[7] Mary's peers, however, praised the work for its experimentation and breadth. Marian McPartland asserted that the work had "ethereal qualities." Gérard Pochonet, who had helped Mary during her breakdown in France, said, " 'St. Martin' is a most uncommon composition moving emotionally as well as spiritually." [8]

Undeterred by the negative comments, Mary continued composing what she called "jazz for the disturbed soul." Every day she encountered the hopelessness of the lives of Harlemites. Now more than ever, Mary knew that the music needed to do more than make people dance or forget their troubles—it needed to provide emotional healing.

She needed to make the music more accessible to her targeted audience. The complexity of "St. Martin De Porres" and "The Devil" had mirrored the formality of the music of the Church before the Second Vatican Council, and Mary wanted to break out of that mold. While playing with the Dizzy Gillespie Orchestra at the 1957 Newport Jazz Festival, Mary had met the trombonist and arranger Melba Liston. Liston, like Mary, had defied the odds and established herself as a notable musician and arranger. She was the only woman ever hired by Dizzy Gillespie for his orchestra and served as a ghostwriter for many well-known composers. Mary talked with Liston about her music, and the two began collaborating on new arrangements. One of the first they produced was a gospel-tinged hymn called "Anima Christi." Where Mary's previous religious compositions only alluded to a connection between religious music and jazz, "Anima Christi" displays the strong musical and cultural connections among gospel, blues, and jazz. It uses standard hymn or strophic form, and the $6/8$ meter evokes the feeling of a swinging jazz waltz written in the blues idiom. The instrumentation is expanded beyond the traditional combo group of piano, bass, and drums to include the electric guitar and B-flat bass clarinet. The piece is scored for male soloist (tenor) and choir. Notations in the extant scores indicate that Mary had a clear sense of the style and feeling she was trying to evoke. The soloist is instructed to sing in a funky gospel style, which is periodically accompanied by the choir interjecting with sequences of call and response, a pattern used heavily in the traditional gospel style.

The text is a prayer to God for protection against the evils of the world and for a merciful response to sins. The mood of the composition is established by the clarinet, which plays a rhythmic figure that serves as the underlying ostinato heard throughout the entire performance. Unlike "The Devil" and "St. Martin De Porres," "Anima Christi" displays flexibility in the singer's rendition of the text and melody. This transition from a style of harmonic complexity and rigidity to a swinging style reminiscent of Mary's early interpretations of the blues may indicate that the pianist was growing more comfortable in her ability to combine blues and jazz elements with sacred text and with her early musical roots in the Baptist Church.

While black churches had denied for many years any connection between sacred and secular music, blues and jazz musicians openly acknowledged that they either received their early musical training within the church or adapted what they heard in the churches. Furthermore, the former bluesman Thomas A. Dorsey had become a gospel composer, and the music of the church had greatly informed the rhythm and blues styles of the 1950s and 1960s. Call and response, moaning, wailing, driving rhythms, complex harmonies, and improvisations—all the traits that had become hallmarks of jazz were also defining features of gospel music. Even as a Catholic, Mary was fully aware of gospel's growing crossover appeal and popularity outside the traditional church setting. Gospel nightclubs opened in major cities across the United States, and many whites were introduced to the art form through the television show *TV Gospel Time.*[9] Gospel was now moving into new territory, so why not jazz? If gospel could take some of its traits from the secular, why couldn't jazz model itself on the sacred? After all, they both had the same musical roots: spirituals and blues. Mary could expect one of two outcomes with her experimentations—they would be readily accepted, or they would lead to controversy and disappointment. With the belief that "jazz was the only true art and Catholicism was the only true faith,"[10] Mary gathered as much material as she could and headed to the Nola and Cue recording studios to produce what would be her first domestic album in years.

Not having the money needed to produce the recording, Mary turned to an old friend, Joe Wells. When Mary had played at his restaurant in 1961, the performances brought considerable attention to his business and Wells had made a substantial amount of money. Over the preceding several years, the two had become closer, and Wells had helped Mary with various projects, including her thrift shop. Although somewhat reluctant at first to invest in a recording, Wells eventually lent Mary the needed money. Initially she recorded eight tunes for an EP, as well as an LP titled *Mary Lou Williams Presents Black Christ of the Andes.* The album, released in 1964, was diverse in its content, including Howard Roberts and his choral group reprising their performance of "The Devil" and "St. Martin De Porres," aptly renamed "The Black Christ of the Andes"; the bassist Theodore Crommwell and the drummer George Chamble on "Miss D.D.," a composition in honor of Doris Duke; and a small combo consisting of Budd Johnson (bass clarinet and tenor sax), Grant Green (guitar), Larry Gales (bass), and Percy Brice (drums). Mary is featured on "Anima Christi" and "Praise the Lord," another collaboration with Melba Liston. "It Ain't Necessarily So," which was performed in a long-meter waltz juxtaposed against an unusual, catchy bass line, featured the bassist Ben Tucker and the drummer Percy Brice. The final selections utilizing combo included Billy Taylor's "A Grand Night for Swinging," with an Afro-Cuban flavor, the standard "My Blue Heaven," and "Dirge Blues," written to mark the assassination of President John F. Kennedy; these pieces featured Percy Heath on bass and Tim Kennedy on drums. The LP lastly featured Mary on solo piano, playing an original tune titled "A Fungus Amungus," aptly named by Lorraine Gillespie, who recounted an incident at a church where the preacher exclaimed, "There's a fungus among us." [11] In the liner notes, Gérard Pochonet wrote that the listener may initially be confused upon hearing the composition because of the impressionistic techniques Mary employed, but he concluded, "You will soon find there's more to it than meets the ear." [12]

For the marketing of the recording Mary turned to old friends. David Stone Martin, who was rumored to have been romantically involved with Mary during the 1940s, designed the cover, which consisted of praying hands. Moe Asch, former owner of Asch Records, now reborn through his new company, Folkways, pressed the records and released them. The venture was the formal reunion of Mary and Asch as musical partners after almost twenty years. As early as 1961 Mary had contacted Asch about recording a history of jazz in her own words and music. At that time she was given an advance of $200, but the project languished for many years and would not be completed until the early 1970s. [13] Both were excited about *Mary Lou Williams Presents,* but critical reactions to the recording were mixed. One reviewer called the religious works "synthetic concoctions, interesting only as curiosities." The piano solos, however, were heralded as evidence that Mary's musicianship was "unimpaired." [14] Cliff Smith, critic for the *New York Times-Union,* wrote, "For me, most of the action is on side 2, starting with the opener, Billy Taylor's 'A Grand Night for Swinging,' which Miss Williams uses for a sign-off theme for most sets on her club dates. Right here, in just about three minutes, is the whole history and exposition of swing. To understand what it's all about, you needn't go any further."[15] Mary worked hard to promote the recording, even sending it to a friend in Paris, Hugues Panasse, and hiring a publicist to place it in New York department stores. It was highly praised in Europe, earning Mary the Grand Prix du Disque Français and the Prix Mondial du Disque de Jazz from the Hot Club of France. But the recording went unnoticed in America. When sales were not being generated by record and department stores, Mary took to selling the records between her sets at the Hickory House, where she had begun performing in 1964. Enthusiastic audiences readily purchased the album for $5, in the hope of taking a little bit of Mary home. Despite Mary's efforts, the record made no profit and with the expenses incurred was registered as a loss.[16]

Mary was once again running herself ragged emotionally and physically. She spent her days praying for hours, working to get her record played on the radio, and trying to manage her thrift shop. In 1963 she faced the truth about the shop and the Bel Canto Foundation. With her recording commitments and performance obligations, Mary did not have enough time for the business, so she closed the shop. Hardly discouraged, Mary decided that the foundation needed to be restructured and that other supporters needed to take a more active role in the daily operations. She was still determined to make the thrift shop a successful venture and secured a space closer to her home on Amsterdam Avenue between 142nd and 143rd Streets in Harlem. She continued to secure items for the store but left the day-to-day operations in the hands of various friends and supporters.

Nothing mattered more to Mary than raising enough money to continue her work through Bel Canto. The dismal sales of *Mary Lou Williams Presents* and the restructuring of the foundation depressed Mary considerably, but she kept on looking for ways to raise money. Her nightly performances at the Hickory House were explosive performances of some of the most innovative piano jazz, but these shows were only temporary escapes from the despondency and confusion she felt. She prayed and fasted even more, listening and waiting intently for some divine revelation. How could her efforts to use music for positive purposes have been interpreted incorrectly by critics and the listening public? Mary concluded that she was once again being pigeonholed by the shallow, narrow-minded expectations of critics and audiences who had previously criticized her experimentations with bop and other modern idioms. She could not understand why individuals were not open to expanding perceptions about jazz beyond the norm. More important, she could not understand why individuals could not see that she was more than just "Roll 'Em," "Froggy Bottom," and the other arrangements she had produced before 1954. She had not stuck to one style or lived off monotonous performances of her past hits, like some of her colleagues; she had remained fresh, always reconceptualizing and redefining jazz.

Mary found some hope in a letter she received from a young man in South Africa. The fan wrote to Mary that he was overjoyed to discover that she had returned to music, and that her music had been a constant part of his life. After the death of a relative in a house fire, it had been Mary's music that had enabled him to recover emotionally. Recently he had heard selections from *Mary Lou Williams Presents* on a weekly radio program broadcast in his hometown, and he had asked how he could receive a copy. When the disc jockey replied that he had brought the record from America, the young man decided to write directly to Mary. "I please beg you," he wrote, "to send me an autographed copy of the album and an autographed photo of yourself."[17] Mary responded enthusiastically. The letter encouraged her and convinced her that despite low record sales and lukewarm reviews, her music was still meaningful within the shaky and unpredictable nature of the current jazz scene.

In October 1964 she wrote to Moe Asch about recording many of her compositions from the 1930s. Despite her reservations about being pigeonholed, Mary knew that people were still interested in the material she had recorded with the Andy Kirk band. Mary concluded that these records would bring the fan base she needed and provide her with a ready-made audience for her later recordings of compositions in various idioms. She would first record new arrangements of her music from the 1930s, then follow up with a biographical sketch of her life that would include musical excerpts.[18] Asch was supportive of the idea of the biography but explained to Mary that there were legal complications surrounding the Kirk recordings. Unless permission was granted and a fair settlement could be reached between him and Decca Records, rerecording those tunes was out of the question. The biggest issue with the recordings would be money, and with ownership rights belonging to Decca and not

Mary, any profit would be greatly diminished. It was risky and Asch could no longer take such chances.

Mary continued to perform nightly at the Hickory House, pitch ideas about recordings to Asch, and think up ways to make money. The Hickory House gig provided Mary with consistent work, but her outstanding debts consumed all her earnings. She thought that she could tour Catholic colleges performing and lecturing, but response to the letters she sent to several colleges was slow. Mary persisted, but she was now faced with the news that her mother, Virginia, had been diagnosed with cancer. Mary began traveling back and forth to Pittsburgh. In the past few years, the two had maintained a civil but sometimes strained relationship. Mary had not always agreed with her mother's life choices, but still respected Virginia's decisions. In subsequent years, it would be reported that Mary hated her mother and found it difficult to forgive her for past indiscretions. This may have been true, but Mary apparently forgot all this when her mother became ill. Father Woods, still important in Mary's religious and personal life, thought to introduce her to the bishop of Pittsburgh, John J. Wright, hoping to provide her with some help while she was in that city. Woods wrote to Wright, explaining Mary's importance and her deep, abiding faith. When they met, after a short conversation about her family and faith, Mary explained to the bishop the benefits of adding jazz education to the curriculum of the city's Catholic schools. He was hesitant, saying he had always associated jazz with drugs and drug addicts. She told him that drugs were more prevalent in commercial rock than in jazz, and that jazz provided a more positive means of expression. Bishop Wright, who had been involved in cleaning up the streets in the black neighborhoods, was receptive to Mary's ideas but felt that the schools were not ready to integrate jazz into their programs just yet. Instead, he proposed that the church sponsor a citywide jazz festival. Wright and his supporters provided the seed money for the venture, and George Wein, creator of the Newport Jazz Festival, was enlisted to secure top-name talent.

Mary immersed herself in the planning of the festival. It provided her with a temporary escape from the ailing health of her mother and the consuming debt she faced back in New York. Mary called upon Melba Liston, who not only aided in the coordination of the festival's activities but also served as its musical director and the conductor for the all-star big band. Mary's involvement was a historic event: the first time an African American woman had produced a jazz festival. Mary hoped that through the success of the festival, Pittsburgh's jazz scene would be revitalized and Wright would reconsider her proposal about adding jazz history to the curriculum.

The primary objective of the festival was to raise money to fund the Catholic Youth Organization (CYO), which provided educational and recreational opportunities in underprivileged areas.[19] The festival's dates were set for June 19–20, 1964, and the excitement surrounding the endeavor escalated as the date approached. The governor of the state served as honorary chairman, and the mayor of Pittsburgh, Joseph Barr, proclaimed June Jazz Month.[20] Mary viewed the concert as an opportunity not only to bring jazz to larger audiences than the nightclub environment allowed but also to celebrate the rich musical heritage of the city, which had contributed to jazz some notable musicians, including Earl Hines, Erroll Garner, and Billy Strayhorn.

Although Pittsburgh had cultivated jazz in the early twentieth century, in the years after World War II its musical activity had dissipated. Wiley Avenue, the training ground for many early jazz musicians in the city, including Mary, had become a wasteland of vacant buildings and drug addicts. Only three clubs remained in the city that offered live jazz performances—the Crawford Grill, the Attic, and the Hurricane. A major jazz festival coming to Pittsburgh not only would bring revenue but could also resurrect the jazz scene.

Shortly after the festival was announced, Mary began working on a new arrangement of "St. Martin De Porres." In its new state, the composition would be written for big band with soloist, and Mary thought the spiritual message of the text could best be conveyed through an interpretation in dance. Mary contacted Alvin Ailey to ask him to choreograph a series of dances for the composition, but he was unavailable. She then called Bernice Johnson, the wife of the saxophonist Budd Johnson and the founder of the Bernice Johnson Dancers. The two conceptualized dances not only for "St. Martin De Porres" but also for Mary's latest composition, "Praise the Lord," also featured on the recording *Mary Lou Williams Presents*. Mary wanted to include some of her early arrangements in the program being set for the all-star big band, which included Thad Jones, Snooky Young, Ben Webster, Budd Johnson, and

Wendell Marshall. Melba Liston came up with a medley of "Roll 'Em," "What's Your Story, Morning Glory?," "In the Land of Oo Bla Dee," and "A Fungus Amungus."

The festival drew a crowd of over thirteen thousand to the Civic Arena for the performances by Thelonious Monk, Dave Brubeck, Art Blakey, Jimmy Smith, and local musicians such as Walt Harper, Dakota Staton, and Harold Betters. But the star was Pittsburgh's first lady of jazz—Mary Lou Williams. It was her performances that set the pace of the festival, as the *Pittsburgh Courier* recounted. Its reviewer asserted, "Something truly beautiful and different was offered to the audience when the Bernice Johnson Dancers performed, against an orchestra background, Mary Lou's inspired jazz hymn, 'St. Martin De Porres,' dedicated to the first Negro to be canonized by the Catholic Church." Mary had provided the "evening's highest points" when she engaged in a swinging performance of "A Fungus Amungus," "Yesterdays," and "My Blue Heaven" with her sidemen, the bassist Larry Gales and the drummer Percy Brice.[21]

Stanley Dance, writing for the *Saturday Review,* remarked that what gives a jazz festival significance is "the new work it presents or inspires. In this respect," he wrote, "the chief architect was Mary Lou Williams, who happens to be an ardent Catholic and also one of the three out- standing pianists Pittsburgh has given jazz. (The other two are Earl Hines and Erroll Garner.)"[22] Although the festival did not make a profit, it was heralded as a success and planned again for the following year.[23]

The critical success of the Pittsburgh Jazz Festival and the overwhelm- ing response Mary received during her performances confirmed that the public had not forgotten her talent or her ability to compose good mu- sic. At age fifty-four and battle-worn, Mary Lou Williams was making a remarkable comeback.

Riding the high from Pittsburgh, Mary returned to the Hickory House to complete her contract. She spent her days working at the 112th Street community center. Meanwhile, her performances at the Hickory House enabled her to continue her activism and to compose. As one of New York's longest-running clubs, the Hickory House had proven to be one of the better nightclubs to play in the city. Mary inspired the audience with her ability to reconstruct standards in such a way that the well- known melodies took on new life. Mary's appearances on the *Today Show* and the *Tonight Show,* along with the publicity generated by a recent *Time* magazine profile, drew crowds to the restaurant in search of the woman called "the Prayerful One."

Mary needed her faith more than ever to strengthen her in her professional and personal difficulties. Her family problems continued into the late 1960s. With Mary's mother ill with cancer, the family's problems seemed worse than ever. Mary, still not financially stable, was unable to support her family as she had in the 1930s–1940s. Mary's sister Grace, despite her efforts to overcome her problems, still struggled to maintain her household. She was now sober, which increased her chances of employment, but competition was tough for the types of jobs she sought. She spent most of her days looking for work and her nights sulking over her failure. Whenever possible, Mary would send what little money she could gather to her mother or Grace, but mostly she traveled back and forth between Pittsburgh and New York trying to help family members caring for her ailing parent.

In the summer of 1965 she participated in the planning and implementation of the second Pittsburgh Jazz Festival. The festival managed once again to line up some of the major figures in jazz. Performers included the Count Basie Orchestra, the singer Carmen McRae, Pittsburgher Earl "Fatha" Hines, Thelonious Monk, John Coltrane, and Duke Ellington. Sunday's program featured an afternoon piano workshop with some of the most influential jazz pianists. Presented at the landmark event were Billy Taylor, Ellington, Mary, Hines, Willie "the Lion" Smith, and Charles Bell. Although the workshop was significant in its bringing together of performers from several generations, the audience was dismal, at only 495 attendees. But the festival made a moment of history when Ellington and Hines sat down to an impromptu duet.[24] The festival proved to be more financially successful than the previous year's; the crowd numbered just over seventeen thousand. The only advertised performer who did not appear was the ailing Miles Davis. The Pittsburgh Jazz Festival would continue for a number of years, but Mary's involvement would wane as she focused more on performing, composing, and her family.

She followed up her performance in Pittsburgh with a short stint at the 1965 Monterey Jazz Festival. Mary opened her set with what was deemed the "West Coast premiere" of "St. Martin De Porres." The performance featured an eight-voice choir from Los Angeles and was met with mixed reactions. One critic wrote that the performance of "St. Martin" was "bland as the Percy Faith Chorale saluting the arrival of autumn or Duke Ellington pretentiously telling some coy fable about saucy Creole elves who lived in the bells of trombones."[25] The remainder of the set included "My Blue Heaven," "Yesterdays," and "45 Degree Angle." As had happened previously, critics could not adequately interpret "St. Martin," so they dismissed it. The focus was on the three standards and her original compositions written in the traditional jazz form. These, in the critics' estimation, were evidence of Mary's musical genius. Such reviews no doubt angered Mary, who often dismissed them as the failure of "intelligent people to broaden their musical perspectives." But she viewed any opportunity to present "St. Martin" as a success, regardless of what critics thought.

Despite the new emotional high Mary was riding after the second festival and Monterey, she sensed that something devastating was looming. Little did she know it would be the death of her friend, confidant, and spiritual mentor, Father Anthony Woods. Having suffered for some time with heart disease, Woods succumbed to his illness suddenly in October 1965. Mary, still in Pittsburgh at the time, rushed back to New York. She was devastated, and she and Lorraine Gillespie fought to contain their grief. Mary would later say that she was not aware of how much she relied on Woods emotionally and spiritually until his death. Not only had he contributed to her understanding of Catholicism and the stabilization of her faith, but he was one of the influences that had led to her return to music and her experimentations with religious jazz music. In addition to losing Woods, several months later Mary saw another genius of jazz lose his fight with his addictions and personal demons. Bud Powell, who had been very shy during the early years of bebop and had also benefited from Mary's benevolence, died after years of battling drug addiction and mental problems. The loss was profound, but in contrast to past instances in which Mary was crippled emotionally by tragedy, the pianist continued her work and threw herself into the Bel Canto Foundation and composing. She prayed incessantly and sustained herself through the belief that both Woods and Powell would want her to continue trying to help others.

While her stints in Pittsburgh and at the Hickory House had dominated her time throughout 1965, Mary still managed to keep the foundation going. Joe Wells had taken over the operation of the thrift shop, but it had still not managed to earn a profit. She wrote three new compositions and returned to educating New York youth about the history of jazz. She sent her new pieces to Duke Ellington, hoping that he would purchase them. When it became apparent that Ellington was not interested, Mary decided to record and release them on 45s. The sessions yielded four sides: an ode to her hometown with lyrics by her friend and collaborator Milton Orent, called "Pittsburgh," an updated version of her composition "You Know Baby," "Chief Natoma from Tacoma," and "Joe." Folkways distributed the recordings under the Mary Records label, another of her business ventures during the 1960s and 1970s, and Mary received two thousand copies for her own use.[26] The recordings fell into obscurity almost as soon as they were released. No one was particularly interested in purchasing 45 rpm recordings of jazz performers, because the LP and EP recordings of avant-gardists such as John Coltrane were dominating sales.

Mary was at a loss. Each of her recording endeavors of the past six years had ended in failure. Yet she still managed to play to live audiences with much acclaim. No matter what Mary seemed to do, she could not transcend the marginality that had defined her career since leaving the Kirk band. Unfortunately, part of Mary's problem was her dated view of the jazz scene. Mary seemingly refused to accept the fact that what constituted success during the 1930s and 1940s no longer produced the same results in the 1960s. Mary's beliefs that a successful recording would reignite her career and that her seniority in jazz would earn her privilege in the form of higher salaries and top billing were proving to be the main source of the professional frustration she felt.

Compounding Mary's professional problems was the fact that she no longer had the personal and spiritual support of Father Woods and Brother Mario Hancock. Mario had been sent to Rome by his order. Mary and Mario had been able to visit occasionally when he was at Graymoor. But now such visits and their spiritual, laughter-filled conversations were impossible. Their only means of communication was through letters, which took a considerable time to arrive even when sent by airmail. Mary wrote feverishly to Mario during this period detailing all the "happenings" in Pittsburgh and New York and the state of her compositions. She wrote in 1966 that she was not going to write any more spirituals for the church because "the priests and nuns [were] cornying up the 'jazz world.'" Despite her reservations, these performances inspired Mary and she prepared to write new compositions. But first she would be traveling again to Pittsburgh.

Chapter 11

WHAT A DIFFERENCE A DAY MAKES

On the surface, 1967 seemed as if it was going to be a good year, but as usual Mary's luck changed for the worse. She was robbed three times and her weight ballooned to over 190 pounds. The defilement of her apartment was painful, but her weight affected Mary the most. In her early career she had maintained a svelte figure, accented by very shapely legs, but now the hormonal changes of middle age and bad eating habits had caught up. Her letters throughout the 1960s detailed the many diets and fasts she went on to eliminate the extra girth. Mary also struggled financially, as work in New York became harder to acquire and she had not received an extension of her Hickory House gig. In February 1967 Don Lass, a friend of Mary's, wrote to Moe Asch about her most recent album and about her debts. "It's a crying shame," he said, "that anyone with her great talents should have trouble finding a place to play, but that seems to be the status of the jazz scene in 1967. The trouble is that club owners are afraid to take a gamble on good music. It's ridiculous that an excellent pianist such as Mary Lou wouldn't do well in a high-class lounge or club-restaurant." [1]

Mary's fortunes began looking up when she secured a spot at an upcoming Carnegie Hall concert called *Praise the Lord in Many Voices*. The concert, sponsored by Avant Garde Records, was intended to showcase new forms of experimental sacred music. Mary wrote a composition especially for the performance, called "Thank You Jesus." In the style of a gospel hymn, "Thank You Jesus" adapted the formula of "Anima Christi," with its highly descriptive text and borrowing of gospel elements. Mary engaged a young singer named Leon Thomas to perform the solo parts. His voice appealed to Mary, who likened it to that of the jazz singer Joe Williams. "He can use his voice in a 'free' way," she said. "I've never heard anyone so versatile." [2] She arranged "The Lord's Prayer" for piano, bass, drums, chorus, French Horn, and soloist and selected Honi Gordon to sing the moving solo part. For her final selection Mary rescored the hymn "Praise the Lord," recorded on *Mary Lou Williams Presents Black Christ of the Andes*. There were thirty singers from around New York for the choir. One was the bassist and vocalist Carline Ray. Ray, a native New Yorker and occasional jazz pianist, was humbled to be in the presence of Mary. Although she had lived and worked as a musician in New York all her life, she had never seen Mary in person before. The two had a mutual friend, and Ray used that as a reason to introduce herself to Mary during a break in the rehearsal. "We hit it off right away," Ray recalled. "During the course of the conversation I found out that we were both under the same sign—Taurus. She proceeded to tell me about a recording project that she had been working on, but had quit halfway through because funds ran out." [3] Mary wanted to complete the project but needed additional singers. The two developed a friendship that continued until Mary's death in 1981.

The concert drew a large audience. Mary's fans of course came en masse. It wasn't every day that Mary Lou Williams was giving a concert in New York, especially one of her sacred music. The concert was a critical success and the recording of the event was released by Avant Garde Records.

Bishop Wright of Pittsburgh, impressed by the initiative Mary had taken in fund-raising for the Catholic Youth Organization and the positive public response the festival had received, now offered her a teaching position at the all-white Seton High School on the north side of the city. Acknowledging this as her opportunity to expand her efforts to bring youth and the larger public back to jazz, Mary accepted the offer. But she faced resistance at the school from the very beginning. The principal, steeped in the mind-set of segregation and racial prejudice, disagreed strongly with the decision. But Wright was not deterred. He fired the woman and replaced her with an administrator who was open to changing and expanding opportunities for the students. Mary sought new ways to present jazz to the eager students and decided to write a jazz mass, largely out of a need to create new compositions that combined jazz with the spiritual atmosphere of the Catholic school and with the newly reformed liturgy and music of the church.

For years the priests who had been Mary's friends had begged her to compose a jazz mass. Mary had never seriously considered it until she started working at Seton. It not only broadened her perspective on the possibilities of religious jazz music but also became a great vehicle for teaching her students. Mary protested over the large number of students she was entrusted with, and the class size was lowered to twenty-five, but Mary found the curriculum often stifling and limited. The students, often bored by Mary's instruction in theory and the fundamentals of music, reacted unhappily. "I couldn't stand it," she said.

> So finally I said, "Let's do it how it is." I wrote a bop blues and the kids went wild. After that they couldn't wait to get to class. I was teaching them to sing like Billie Holiday—teaching them the sounds the way she made them. They loved it. Several priests who were jazz fans had been urging me to write a Mass. So I began composing one during the class. I'd tell the kids to take a break and I'd write eight bars of the Mass. They'd sing it right off. Whenever the nuns came into the room, I'd shift to theory. But I wrote the Mass in a week."[4]

Mary's first attempt at writing an extended composition setting the Ordinary of the mass is called simply *Mass*. The multi-movement work indicates Mary's evolving compositional style and a sensitive liturgical approach. The work as a whole displays Mary's affinity for the blues and other jazz styles. Although Mary would later contend that her *Mass* "wasn't really jazz," she established a blues and jazz sound through her choice of instrumentation and harmonies. She would later claim to have used the distinction to save jazz.[5] Unlike Mary's previous religious compositions, this work employs unison vocal lines and decidedly less complex harmonies. This shift in approach may indicate that Mary's musical intentions had changed. The simple formula makes it possible for the average singer to perform the piece. The mass begins with a prelude entitled "O.W." It is a simple improvised blues melody based on the abbreviation "O.W." which when written in 1954 was a reference to Orlando Wright. It employs scatting, which is one of the jazz approaches that Mary had taught the students. The next movement, the "Kyrie" or "Lord, Have Mercy," is written in a "moanful" state in a steady ¾ meter. The text is an English translation of the Greek prayer "Kyrie Eleison" that separates into two prayers—one exclaiming "Lord, have mercy" and the other "Christ, have mercy." The next movement, the "Gloria," is a swinging ²⁄₄ melody, that uses a text based on the exclamation of praise at Christ's birth in Luke 2.

The "Creed," or exclamation of belief, is based on the traditional Nicene Creed. This movement is significant in that Mary's interpretation of the text governs the use of melodic material. Each passage is set to different forms of the primary melody and juxtaposed against statements regarding the life of Christ set to different versions of the melody in varying keys.

Mary's use of contrasting, totally new melodic ideas establishes, at least theoretically, a sense of difference between divinity and humanity. Of the mass's movements the "Creed" displays the most complexity compositionally and is the longest in form and scope. The "Sanctus," or "Holy, Holy, Holy," is a short movement consisting of only nine measures with the text: "Holy, holy, holy. Lord God of hosts. Heaven and Earth are filled with your Glory. Hosanna in the highest. Blessed is he who comes in the name of the Lord. Hosanna in the highest." The "Our Father" follows the same pattern, with only part of the prayer being sung, and was adapted from the 1967 Carnegie Hall concert. Following the recitation of "Forgive our debtors," the mass segues into the "Agnus Dei" or "Lamb of God." The mass as initially written ends with the "Act of Contrition"; however, in one performance of the composition in 1967,

Mary added the hymn "Thank You Jesus." The completion of Mary's *Mass* was an amazing accomplishment, considering that she had never attempted to write one before.

Bishop Wright wanted to include Mary's *Mass* in the celebration of a liturgy he was planning at St. Paul's Cathedral. The performance of the composition would bring to fruition the "new" movement of music and liturgy that the proponents of the Second Vatican Council desired. The reforms established since the council had raised questions within the church as to how far composers and church leaders would go to increase the accessibility of the liturgy. These issues would not be easily resolved. While some parishes experimented with different approaches in worship music, others continued to use traditional chants in their services. Composers of church music divided themselves into compositional "camps." Some composers used the official translations of the Roman Missal approved by the International Committee on English in the Liturgy (ICEL), others translated liturgical material into contemporary scriptural interpretations, but still others looked to musical and textual sources outside the Roman rite. The inclusion of folk, rock, and jazz elements in mass settings called for new forms of instrumentation, taking the Catholic Church beyond the traditional organist or instrumental ensemble (such as brass instruments and small and large orchestras). Although Protestant churches had long included guitars, drums, and other instruments in their worship services, these instruments had rarely, if ever, been used in Catholic worship services.[6]

The impact of the inclusion of jazz and blues elements in Catholic worship services was twofold. First, the integration of African American musical forms into the liturgy provided the church with identifying qualities that can be linked with the community of blacks within the church—an invisible church within the church. These were the black clergy and laity who, until recently, had largely been ignored by the Catholic Church but had remained loyal. Second, this act of inclusion validated, for promoters of a black liturgy, the need for such cultural rituals within the church. The inclusion of African American musical forms in worship services during the 1960s and 1970s was a continuation of the efforts of black Catholics in the late nineteenth and early twentieth centuries to create their own identifiable religious services while maintaining church order. Although Mary is often credited with being one of the first composers of jazz masses, she was preceded by Father Clarence

Joseph Rivers, best known for his efforts to revitalize American Catholic music. Rivers ignited the push for a black liturgy within the black Catholic community with his first composition, "God Is Love," and the publication of the "American Mass Program," which combined black spirituals and Gregorian chant. Mary was continuing the work of Rivers in establishing a black liturgical identity within the church. Before the decade was over, Mary had broken down many of the barriers to the idea of spiritual jazz.

This musical activism began on June 10, 1967, when Mary's *Mass*, now referred to as the *Pittsburgh Mass*, was performed at St. Paul's Cathedral in Pittsburgh. Despite the enthusiastic reception—evident in the only extant tape of the performance, made on a handheld recorder—Mary discarded the work, dismissing it as being "long, drawn out, like a symphony." [7] Mary made very little if any money from the performance. Still seeking ways to raise cash, she wrote to Duke Ellington in the summer of 1967 to see if he would consider using her arrangement "Chief Natoma from Tacoma," but she heard nothing from him. His lack of response greatly angered Mary, who wrote to Brother Mario in September, "He's begged me since 1941 to write for him, that is pleaded." [8] Ironically, Ellington had followed Mary in her composition of sacred jazz works and was gaining attention for his own Sacred Concerts. Potential help did finally come in the form of the possibility of Mary's resuming her teaching position at Seton, which she had vacated sometime after the performance of her first mass. But Mary was determined not to revisit her past mistakes with the school. During her first year she had been promised a salary of at least $200 per week, but she never received the money. There is no clear evidence whether she pursued the matter with the bishop, who had appointed her, or that the situation was corrected. She completed the year in Pittsburgh and began thinking of ways to get her spiritual jazz to larger audiences.

* * *

By 1968 Mary felt the need for another real change in her life and career. The last twenty or so years had seen a succession of personal and professional crises. And despite efforts to aid her family members, who were in constant need, Mary found her hard work to be ultimately futile. Some good times alternated with the bad, but the bad outweighed the good two to one. She was less than happy with the lack of representation she had in the jazz scene and with Moe Asch's reluctance to invest fully in her mission to bring healing to others through her sacred compositions. She was frustrated by her mounting debts and the slow but inevitable disintegration of Bel Canto. As the decade came closer to its end, it became apparent that jazz could no longer compete with the popularity of soul, rock, and funk, and clubs and employment opportunities disappeared. No one really cared about helping addicted musicians. Even New Yorkers, who had basked in the excitement of early jazz and swing, now seemed to have turned their backs on the music. Reality was hitting hard and Mary accepted the obvious: there would be no rehabilitation facility for drug addicts, there probably would not be a hit that would resurrect her career, and the thrift shop, which failed to earn much profit for Mary or the foundation, had to close. Joe Wells, who had eagerly helped Mary for a number of years, grew more frustrated with the thrift shop. He had taken over its daily management and had put a large amount of his own money into the venture. The shop was a financial sinkhole that continued to get deeper. When Wells married, he enlisted the help of his wife, who revamped the store into a boutique that featured the designer and high-end items Mary secured from Saks, other musicians, and her friends. She discarded those things she saw as lower quality, much to Mary's dismay. As the friendship became strained and Wells reached his financial limit, he decided that the store would close.

Although she was upset, Mary accepted the decision and began looking at ways to get an audience with the pope, to play and discuss her sacred music. She wrote to Brother Mario in early 1968, asking him to propose to Bishop Wright on her behalf that the bishop sponsor a concert at the Vatican featuring her. She wanted desperately to give the concert with some of her female students from Seton. She believed such a performance would bring to light the merits of her work with youth and her religious crusade through music. There is no evidence that Mario actually pursued the issue with Wright. Mary was trying throughout early 1968 to get bookings in Europe. With mounting debts and no real income, Mary convinced Moe Asch to advance her some money for a project to record her mother, her first husband, Andy Kirk, and others in an autobiographical album. In March she wrote to Asch explaining that her monthly bills were more than $210 and that she owed Gimbel's department store almost $600. She had tried to get a loan of $1,500 from the bank but was denied. She thought that Asch could help her by advancing her enough money to cover her debts.[9] Asch did advance Mary some funds—not the amount she had hoped for, but a little money was better than none.

Although nightclub bookings were few and far between, Mary kept busy composing and performing in the area's Catholic churches. Her second mass, the *Mass for Lenten Season,* was the product of a commission by the church in early 1968. Father Robert Kelly, a priest at St. Thomas the Apostle Church in Harlem, was heading a project that commissioned works by African American composers. He approached Mary about writing a mass for Lent. Mary accepted the offer and began working on a composition that would capture the quiet, reflective, and repentant spirit of the Lenten season. The result was a ten-movement work that combined revamped material from the previous mass with new compositions.

The *Mass,* which was performed for five weeks during Lent at St. Thomas, opens with "O.W.," the improvised blues that begins the *Pittsburgh Mass.* It is followed by an entrance song entitled "Clean My Heart," featuring a text based on Psalm 51: "Behold, thou desireth truth in the inward parts: and in the hidden part thou shalt make me to know wisdom" (AV). The entire text of the psalm is not used, but included is material from selected verses (6, 10, 11, 14, 15). Unlike the "Kyrie" in her previous mass, its counterpart in the new work is set to a liturgy written by Father Robert Ledogar. The text asks God for forgiveness for our lack of hope and faith and our failure to care. Intending the piece to be a celebration of the liturgy and not a concert of sacred music, Mary wrote the movement to include patterns of call and response built on the refrains "Lord, have mercy" and "Christ, have mercy." It would easily allow a soloist to sing the first section of the phrase and the congregation to respond with the unchanging refrain.

The "Offertory" is completely instrumental, with the exception of the choir singing softly on the syllable "Ooh." The remaining movements of the mass are "Amen"; "Sanctus," adapted from the *Pittsburgh Mass;* "Anamnesis," a prayer sung by soprano soloist and choir; "Agnus Dei," also taken from the previous mass; and the communion song "Martha Said to Jesus." This last movement drew its text from the biblical story of Lazarus, the brother of Mary and Martha. Lazarus became ill and Jesus was sent for. Although Jesus could have gotten to Lazarus before he died, He did not leave right away and arrived three days after Lazarus's death. As Jesus approached the mourners at the tomb, Martha ran to

Him and cried, "Lord, if You had been here my brother would still be alive." Jesus, moved by the woman's words, raised Lazarus from the dead.[10] The movement is written in strophic form with the congregation and choir singing the recurring chorus "I am the Resurrection and the Life and He who believes in me will never die." This alternates with the verses, which are sung by the soloist and convey the action of the text.

In the only recording of this mass, which is of amateur quality, the hymn "We Shall Overcome" is heard at the end. Although written by Charles Tindley in the early 1900s, it served as one of the many protest songs associated with the 1960s civil rights movement. The addition of this hymn was probably a response to the assassination on April 4, 1968, of Martin Luther King Jr. Mary recalled that the singing of Honi Gordon "brought tears to the eyes. One has to get in church before 11 am to get a seat," she continued. "Even a black nationalist has been there every Sunday."[11] The popularity of the *Mass for Lenten Season* no doubt encouraged Mary to continue her pursuit of a concert for the pope, but the excitement was curtailed with the assassination of King at the Lorraine Motel in Memphis. Harlem, more than twenty years after the last riot in the late 1940s, erupted into flames, as did many American cities. Mary watched as those around her, who had adopted King's mantra of nonviolent protest, exploded into a frenzy of anger, grief, and hopelessness. "People throw bricks at the firemen—lye at people," she wrote to Brother Mario. " 'I'm black and beautiful'. This is the new slogan and I'm not Negro, I'm African or Blackman. Hurry back and help me."[12] This eruption of racial pride expressed in slogans such as "black power" deeply troubled Mary, whose generation believed that one exercised racial pride not through hand gestures, ethnic names, hairstyles, or clothing but through personal achievement and the betterment of society.

In honor of King, Mary wrote two new compositions: "I Have a Dream," based on the leader's famous 1963 speech from the historic March on Washington, and "If You're Around When I Meet My Day," based on one of his sermons. On Palm Sunday 1968, a children's choir performed the compositions at a memorial service in Harlem. Mary was pleased with the performance and urged Moe Asch to consider the compositions and the Lenten mass for a recording project, but he was not interested, saying their appeal was too limited. Mary once again turned her attention to getting bookings in Europe and going to Rome.[13] She sent Brother Mario recordings of the mass and "I Have a Dream," hoping that he would coordinate a concert at which the compositions would be performed. In the meantime she secured a job teaching music at a summer camp for the CYO.

In May 1968 Mary prepared to leave for a European tour. But the day before she was scheduled to leave, her sister Grace attempted suicide. By July Grace was stable enough for Mary to leave. After receiving money from Copenhagen to pay her way, Mary planned her departure. God had heard her prayers; she had an invitation to open a new nightclub in Copenhagen owned by Timme Rosenkrantz and Inez Cavanaugh. Mary figured the gig would provide her with enough money to pay some of her debts in the States and travel to Rome, where she felt sure she would be in a concert at the Vatican. She left in August and arrived in Copenhagen more than a week later. Despite the advances in technology of transatlantic travel, Mary refused to fly, claiming she was morbidly afraid of airplanes. Even when she had bookings in the States, Mary would take a train or bus to West Coast and midwestern gigs. She was booked on a German steamer, which she referred to in her correspondence as the "prejudice ship." The voyage proved to be much more pleasant than her previous transatlantic trip in 1952. Mary boasted of taking advantage of the ship's steam baths, exercise rooms, and massages and eagerly awaited her arrival.[14]

When Mary got to Copenhagen, she discovered that the club's construction was not completed, despite advertisements proclaiming her appearance the following week. Complicating matters further was the fact that Rosenkrantz was ill and the conditions under which Mary was contracted were not going to be met. Copenhagen was quite expensive, but Inez managed to find Mary a reasonable apartment outside the city. Mary described the place as a "welfare deal in New York. Terrible neighborhood—community kitchen, clothes closet in the hall, toilet in the hall—just terrible. Filthy for $50 a month." [15] Mary protested and other accommodations were found, but they were only a slight improvement. Nevertheless, Mary settled in, despite her reservations. A week after her arrival, however, her mood soured and she began regretting she had come. She wrote to Brother Mario, who was preparing to return to the States for a short visit, "I stupidly took this job for what reason I don't know. It got me into $1625.32 debt—It pays $400 per week (money received in the 1940s). The advance of $800 was paid for August bills 'cept about $250 or $300. I'm now spending my loot, I should hold onto when I am stranded for rent. The rent and meals are higher than N.Y. It's the tourist season, wow!!! Thought it best to raise hell before I open— ha! By the way they haven't finished the club." [16] Mary attempted to deal with the unfortunate situation as she had handled so many of her personal setbacks in recent years. She prayed and sought instruction and solace from God. Only her faith in God could contain Mary's anger as the opening date crept further and further away. The situation was worsened by Inez's attitude. She was an aspiring singer who had, according to Mary, more personality than musical talent. Not only was she a bad singer, she was a bad singer who would not allow anyone to help her correct her problems. Although the two had known each other since the 1940s, they had never worked together. Mary wrote, "I really think I came here for a relief from my USA cross—is this possible? Doesn't seem I can get to the love I had for my sweet Jesus before now. What do you think is wrong with me—please tell me—even consulted 'Humility pamphlet' but am still getting angry and evil the way she orders me around." [17] Tension grew between the two women and Mary began reacting to Inez's duplicitous behavior by cursing her. That would contain Inez for a few days, long enough for Mary to get some peace, but sooner or later the scenario would be repeated. Mary found temporary relief from her "cross" in the fall when Dizzy and Lorraine Gillespie came to visit.

Through Lorraine's prayers and the approaching end of her contractual agreement with Rosenkrantz, Mary found happiness. But it was still not clear where she would go and what she would do. Although she had tried to push Mario into confirming a definitive concert date in Rome, nothing was settled by the end of October. Mario had returned to New York and was not answering Mary's letters or questions with the rapidity she wanted. Taking action, Mary wrote to Brother Joseph, one of Mario's fellow friars of the Franciscan Friars of the Atonement in Rome, about living arrangements and a concert date. It is not clear what Joseph's response was, but on November 2, 1968, Mary wrote to Mario that it might not have been God's plan for her to go to Rome. Mary's emotions were on edge: she had come so close, had endured so much over the past three months, and it seemed as if her dream to see Rome and play her music in the Vatican was not going to be realized. She had three options: take Rosenkrantz's offer to remain at the club for $100 a week (hardly enough to cover her expenses), go to Rome, or return to New York.

Mary decided to stay in Copenhagen and moved into the St. Lioba Kloster, a convent of religious women, which was cheaper, cleaner, and more convenient to the local church she attended. She had managed to pay off her $4,000 debt and purchase her return ticket to New York. But something about staying and playing at the club still did not sit well with her. She claimed sounds in the room "goofed" her and she received bad vibes from most of the patrons. "There too," she stated, "I'm in an almost all atheist country. My two bass men do not believe in God and I could feel this coldness in their music before they told me." [18] Mary continued to wait patiently for the possibility of a concert in Rome, operating on the faith that God had predestined her to go there and to minister through her music. During this waiting period she meditated on the past twenty years of her life. She concluded, as evidenced in her writings from this period, that the popularity of rock and roll and other forms of popular music had contributed to the dismal state of the American jazz scene and had robbed talented musicians, such as herself, of opportunities for advancement. In relation to her own experiences, Mary concluded that it had been the choices she had made out of her love for music and mankind that had stifled her career. She had openly given her money to the poor and to ailing musicians but had been unable to gain the same type of support for her thrift shop or the Bel Canto Foundation. She had, at the invitation of a priest in Pittsburgh, taken a teaching job at Seton High School but never received her promised salary. She had come to Copenhagen because of promises of high earnings and packed audiences and found neither. "[I] am accustomed," she wrote, "to the toughest of crosses (one only realizes a cross I feel, when tired or slipping or I should think nervous.)" [19] Remarkably, Mary's emotional and mental health remained stable at this time and she often recited to herself and wrote in her letters, "God is merciful." At this time Mary, inspired by the biography of the Trappist monk Thomas Merton, began writing her autobiography. Aided by the nuns at the Kloster, Mary began by revising the previous sketches she had made of her life story. Soon afterward she received word from Rome about coming to the city. She did not hesitate and prepared immediately to leave Copenhagen. When she boarded the train, she bid farewell to the nuns who had cared for her during the preceding two months and to Timme Rosenkrantz, who had facilitated her trip to Copenhagen. Little did she know that in less than a year, Rosenkrantz would die in New York at the age of fifty-eight, and Inez Cavanaugh would completely disappear after returning to the States.[20]

*   *   *

Mary arrived in Rome in January 1969, and for a time her spirits improved. But her health was deteriorating and although she simply wrote off many of her ailments as signs of old age, it was evident to those closest to her that she was not well. The ancient city, however, was good for Mary's faith. She prayed unceasingly and would often spend hours at a time meditating and praying, oblivious to all around her. Her faith was so great that the clergy recognized Mary's religious fervor and often invited her on their retreats. This seemed to have been Mary's season to be in Rome: She had reunited with her dear friend Mario, had come to a deeper understanding of her faith. Mario, once again living in community with his fellow friars of the Atonement at the Church of San Onofrio on the Gianiculum Hill, found Mary lodging nearby. The boardinghouse was clean and cheap at $7 a day, and Mary stayed in a big room overlooking the Vatican—the inspiration for her trip.

Peter O'Brien, a young seminarian the pianist had befriended during her stint at the Hickory House, had tried to help Mary stage a concert by writing to the Reverend Vincent O'Keefe, S.J. As one of four assistants to the general of the Jesuits, O'Keefe had considerable power. He met with Mary, who told him that she wanted to play for the pope. One of O'Keefe's colleagues, the Reverend Horatio de la Costa, S.J., had Mario write out Mary's biography and an application for the Templeton Foundation Prize for Progress in Religion, a humanitarian award given in Europe, hoping that the attention this award would generate would serve as the catalyst for getting a papal audience. Mary did not win the award, but O'Keefe continued to work on her behalf. He arranged for Mary to go to the Approdo Romano, a group of Roman nobility whose purpose, among other things, was to assist and help Roman Catholic seminarians from Africa who were studying theology in Rome. If Mary gained their favor, she would have a good chance of performing. They wanted to hear Mary's music, so Mario arranged for a concert. He contacted students at the North American College in Rome and the College of Propaganda

Fide, the international college in the city, which drew students from all over the world; Mary would rehearse with singers and instrumentalists from both institutions. Meanwhile, Father O'Keefe continued to press Mary's request forward. He introduced her to Marjorie Weeks, who worked for Vatican Radio, to suggest that the concert be broadcast. Weeks, who expressed an interest in Mary, attended one of the rehearsals and told Mary that she wanted to record the music for broadcast on Vatican Radio. Mary, preparing a program that would commemorate the first anniversary of King's assassination, rehearsed the two compositions she had written in honor of the leader and the *Mass for Lenten Season*.

Mary and the students from the North American College and the College of Propaganda Fide performed *Mass for Lenten Season* for the Approdo Romano in the oratory of St. Francis Xavier del' Cara Vitra. Mary had hoped that a favorable response from the group would guarantee an audience and possible concert with the pope, but the Approdo Romano did not think that the music would appeal to the pontiff.

Although Mary was not granted an opportunity to perform for the pope, she was soon offered a chance to play her mass by Abbot Rembert Weakland, the primate of the Benedictines and later the archbishop of Milwaukee. Weakland, himself a concert pianist, had learned of Mary's stay in Rome through Peter O'Brien. He was excited by the possibility of Mary Lou Williams performing in Rome and wanted to be involved in the performance of her mass. It was planned for the Pio Latino College, with Weakland participating as the celebrant. The excitement about the mass was lessened when Weakland in his enthusiasm mentioned it to Angelo Cardinal Del'Acqua, the assistant secretary of state in Vatican City, who had the ear of the pope with regard to political matters. Cardinal Del'Acqua, highly opposed to the use of drums, began campaigning against the performance of the mass as a celebration of the liturgy.

On the evening before the scheduled performance, Weakland came to Mary and told her that the music of the mass would not be combined with the celebration of the liturgy. It would be, however, presented afterward as a recital.

"Mary was so disappointed. She was so hurt," recalled Mario.[21] Unfortunately, Mary was not given the opportunity to exclude the drums, something she often did during performances. Cardinal Del'Acqua had made the final decision. There had been a great deal of publicity surrounding the event, and it was guaranteed to provide Mary with the mainstream exposure she desired. CBS had sent a crew to Rome to televise the mass worldwide, but when it was announced that the music would be performed only in concert, they packed up and left. The next day Mary performed the *Mass for Lenten Season* to a record crowd in the chapel of the Cara Vita Church. She later went to Vatican Radio, where she recorded most of the music from the concert with the choir of students from the North American College and College of Propaganda Fide.

Despite her disappointment, Mary remained in Rome through March. The stay would prove to be fruitful, as at the end of March, on the advice of O'Keefe, Mary met with Monsignor Joseph Gremillion, the secretary of the Pontifical Commission on Justice and Peace and a native of Louisiana. He suggested that Mary write another mass—a mass for peace and justice. With a renewed sense of purpose, Mary prepared to return to America. In April 1969 Mary boarded the *Michelangelo* and headed back to the tensions of the jazz scene and her family.

Shortly after arriving, Mary was offered a job by Joe Glaser, to open at a new nightclub in New York called Plaza Nine. She faced a choice between concentrating on her papal commission and making time for a regular gig. She decided to focus on composing, but soon afterward she was stunned to learn that Glaser had suffered several strokes; he was not expected to live. Although over the years the two had had a tumultuous relationship, each had respected the work of the other. When Glaser died a month later at age seventy-two, she remarked, "He has been great in the music business—will be quite tough without him." [22]

To take her mind off Glaser's sickness and death, and the pressure she felt to complete her obligations, Roland Mayfield, a longtime friend of Mary's family, took the pianist to Pittsburgh for her fifty-ninth birthday. She celebrated the day with her brother Jerry and sister Geraldine, the twins who shared her birthday, and took the time to visit with other family members. Great care and time was taken with her mother, whose health had declined further. Despite her desire to remain longer, after a couple of days Mary hurried back to New York to finish working on the new mass. She worked out the themes for each of the movements and tried to musically capture the essence of the liturgy, which had been reinterpreted by her friend Father C. J. McNaspy, S.J., an associate editor for the Jesuit weekly magazine *Opinion America*.

Mary wanted this mass, more than her previous religious works, to address the contemporary social problems of racism, war, and lack of compassion. She initially wanted to have the mass performed at St. Peter's Basilica in Rome or St. Patrick's Cathedral in New York, but she was told that there was no possibility of either. Father Harold Salmon, the vicar of Harlem and pastor of St. Charles Borromeo Church in Harlem, explained to Mary that it was a matter of church politics. It was all about whom you knew, and there was real resistance among church leaders to integrating jazz into mass celebrations in the larger churches. Mary viewed it as further resistance by the Catholic leadership to fully acknowledging black Catholics and their culture. "Who needs the Negroes in the church?" she wrote to Mario. She explained that black Catholics needed to stand up against the segregation within the church that had robbed them of their proper place. Despite Father Salmon's urgings that she perform the mass at St. Charles in Harlem, Mary refused. "It wouldn't mean a thing as far as progress," she explained. "This is what I've been doing all along. It means we've segregated ourselves but he claims that 'whitie' would have to come to us (in Harlem) for what they need in the church downtown—ha! Bullshit!"[23] Mary was so incensed by Salmon's complacency and the politics of the church that she considered for some time not finishing the work and returning to the jazz scene. But Mary wanted to see the work completed and, more important, wanted to hear the music fill the sanctuary of St. Patrick's Cathedral.

Mary's anger increased when she discovered soon after writing to Mario that Cardinal Cushing of Boston, Father Norman O'Connor, known as the Jazz Priest, and Ambassador Sargent Shriver had sponsored Duke Ellington's petition to perform at Notre-Dame Cathedral in Paris. She was furious, as all her efforts to bring sacred jazz to large and international audiences were being impeded at every turn. She ranted that Ellington had decided to write sacred music only after coming to visit her at the Hickory House and receiving from her a copy of *Mary Lou Williams Presents Black Christ of the Andes*. "This gave him," she stated, "a new insight to do the same—he was not doing too good with his orchestra. I bet you $1000 he'll play a jazz concert in St. Peters in Rome and it won't mean a thing for the survival of jazz or musicians, but more money for Duke." She deduced that "little people [could] go so far on earth but big wigs [had] to be contacted." "It amazes me," she wrote to Mario, "just to see how much politics are attached to the church. How can a small person make it or secure work without public relations or recognition for their works?"[24] Mario had no solution to Mary's dilemma but encouraged Mary to keep working.

On July 15, 1969, Mary's *Mass for Peace* debuted at the Holy Family Church on East 47th Street, at the request of Father Salmon. The composition was to serve as a memorial mass for the assassinated Kenyan leader Tom Mboya. At first, Mary had planned to stage the mass with only one singer and herself, but the day before the performance, she contacted a bass player, and the son of a friend who played flute volunteered to perform.

The mass began with the prelude "Peace Makers: Peace, O Lord," which established the mood of the complete mass with its strong social message.

> Give us peace, O, Lord. Send us peace, O, Lord.
> People in trouble, children in pain.
> Too mean to care, too weak to share.
> Work so hard trying to find a brother, became
>   impatient.
> Now we hate each other.
> O, Lord come to our aid. Make haste to help us.
> O, Lord if you will you can cure us.
>
> O, Jesus who has loved us so much have pity on us.
> For we believe, increase our faith.
> You are the resurrection and the life. Save us Jesus
>   before we perish.[25]

The mass as a whole emphasized the need for people to look at the world around them and try to make it better. It was unlike her previous works in that it employed nuances closely associated with jazz but tried not to push compositional limits. This apparent change in Mary's approach may indicate that her focus, by the time the work was completed, was on creating a mass that the Vatican and the political power structure within the American church would find acceptable.

The work was acclaimed by those in attendance but went virtually unnoticed by the church's leadership. However, Mary would not be deterred. She felt that the work's "message of hope, peace, and love was very important" and decided to revamp it into a jazz-rock idiom in hopes of drawing the attention of younger audiences and a recording contract. Not familiar with the compositional approaches of rock, Mary called on the arranger Bob Banks, who helped her reorganize the mass. Mary found a suitable benefactor for the initial recording session in Ed Flanagan. The two had met on a New York subway in 1964, and the priest had made a short film in 1968 about Mary's outreach in the Harlem community. He invested $6,000 in the recording, to be called *Music for Peace.* Mary worked feverishly to get as much done as possible. She contracted studio time and lined up musicians and vocalists. These first sessions yielded six sides: "O.W.," the prelude from the *Pittsburgh Mass* and *Mass for Lenten Season;* "Kyrie"; "In His Day"; "Holy, Holy, Holy"; the prelude "Peace Makers" from the *Mass for Peace,* revamped as the communion song "People in Trouble"; and the upbeat "Praise the Lord," first performed at the 1967 Carnegie Hall concert but also incorporated into the *Pittsburgh Mass.* Musicians featured in the first sessions included Chris White, whose bass lines established a strong jazzy funk feeling, and the flutist Roger Glenn, the guitarist Sonny Henry, David Parker on drums, and Abdul Rahman on congos. Banks, who eventually left the project because of an Off-Broadway commitment, enlisted the tenor Carl Hall and the baritone Milton Grayson to bring to Mary's music the soul and gospel sound needed to convey the music's spirituality. When the funds ran out, Mary was forced to suspend recording any more tracks. It was thought that she would just release what had been completed, but at the urging of Dizzy and Lorraine Gillespie and her brother Jerry, Mary wrote more tunes, hoping to resume recording later.

When the project was revived, Mary enlisted the help of Carline Ray, who had participated in the Carnegie Hall concert as a vocalist. Ray, an accomplished bass player, found three talented singers, Christine Spencer, Randy Peyton, and Eileen Gilbert, to sing on the date. Although Mary had hoped to end 1969 with the release of the record, she would not. She was not discouraged, however, but remained hopeful that the new year and the new decade would bring considerable change in her life, career, and music, and—most important—the release of a new album of sacred works.

Chapter 12

A SEASON OF CHANGE

"There is a time for everything and a season for every activity under Heaven."

—Ecclesiastes 3:1

In 1970, at age fifty-nine, Mary Lou Williams had no intention of slowing down or stopping. Although her body ached more than usual and her hearing in one ear was growing weaker, Mary was more determined than ever to see the fulfillment of her musical aspirations. The disappointments and successes of the late 1960s had served as assurance that her life, career, and music were undergoing a metamorphosis—a change. This change would not come overnight, but in time Mary would see her life and career unfolding in a positive manner and taking directions she had never dreamed of.

The New York scene became more competitive, and the pianist struggled to earn money. In addition, she was pushing to finish the

Music for Peace sessions. Earlier she had had reservations about marketing her sacred jazz, but this time she was sure that this project would cause a turning point in the public's perspective. She had refocused her music to include characteristics of rock, which placed her in line with the emerging style of jazz-rock fusion and jazz-funk. The "new" sound of *Music for Peace,* in the form of catchy, upbeat riffs and motives, would surely appeal to younger audiences. Mary borrowed heavily from friends and organizations to ensure the completion of the project. From the musicians' union local 802 she received $1,000, from ASCAP, $300, and from a local bank, $500. With the $6,000 invested by Ed Flanagan, who had taken a very active role in the recording sessions and final processing, the project would finally be completed. Flanagan penned Mary's biography for the liner notes of the recording but deviated from the notes Mary had provided for him. It is not clear if these deviations were accidental or deliberate, but Bob Banks was given credit for all the arrangements featured. Banks had in fact worked only on "Kyrie," "Lord Says," and "Holy, Holy, Holy," and the extent of his contribution amounted to rhythmic changes. According to Mary, Banks "put the rock rhythms to them." Mary was quite upset about the changes but decided not to address the issue with Flanagan, stating, "God works in a mysterious way from a project to make it—someone has to be hidden."

Despite the setbacks, interruptions, and oversights, *Music for Peace* was completed in February 1970. It encapsulated all of Mary's hopes and desires for bringing healing and salvation to mixed audiences. She immediately ordered a thousand copies and planned to sell them at $5.95 each. Without funds for the large-scale publicity needed to promote new projects, Mary turned to her grassroots method: calling on the connections of friends, writing letters to supporters, and selling records at live performances. It was crucial that Mary make enough money to repay Flanagan and the others who had provided financial support. So she sold records out of her car and asked friends to market the album for her. But sales were slow and Flanagan grew restless over the possibility of not being repaid. He had taken for collateral the master tapes from the session and said he would turn them over to Mary when the loan was totally paid off. This did not sit well with the pianist, but she had little choice.

In March 1970 the parish priest at St. Paul's Chapel on the campus of Columbia University in New York offered Mary the opportunity to present a concert of the music from the revamped *Mass for Peace.* Mary accepted the offer but knew that the concert would have to generate enough revenue to cover the expenses of hiring musicians and singers. The concert was planned for April 25 and 26. In the preceding weeks Mary encountered problems with the sponsoring priest. He had not done any substantial advertising and was misusing the donations that were coming in. Mary, in her usual fashion, took control and used her connections with disc jockeys and friends. She managed to draw a large crowd, which enthusiastically reacted to the music. She wrote to Brother Mario: "We did a Mass at Columbia University (hellhole—riots, etc. Black Panthers) and it was the craziest. People even applauded while Mass was on—clapped their hands on 'Praise the Lord'—kisses etc. at the end. A concert the 26 of April in the same church and the enthusiasm was the end! Sold quite a few records but not enough (6,000 involved). A priest who came out [left the priesthood] sponsored it all."[2]

John S. Wilson, writing for the *New York Times,* described the concert as an exploration of her musical experiences:

> With so much background to draw on, Miss Williams was almost too modest, for she turned a large part of her program over to several of her associates—Lisle Atkinson, who played a superb bowed bass version of "Yesterdays," David Amram who used his French horn to help Miss Williams stir up her "Timmie's Blues," and Roger Glenn, a vibraharpist whose walloping version of "Round Midnight" almost brought down the chapel. The pianist, who called her program "Music for Peace," which was also the title of her concluding selection, gave a brief sampling of her early musical surroundings before settling into her present day manner that, aside from some refinement, is still primarily the lithe, swinging, two-handed style she has always used. She is a magnificently direct performer—no frills or antic fancies—and she played with the simple power and assurance of an artist who knows precisely what she is doing and how to do it.[3]

The success of the Columbia concert brought Mary and the recording the type of attention needed to galvanize record sales. Gremillion, who had commissioned the original version of the *Mass for Peace* in 1968, requested fourteen records. Critics who had dismissed Mary's early attempts at spiritual music acclaimed the merits of the project. *Billboard* and *Record World* awarded the recording a four-star rating, and the *Saturday Review* reported, "The music is bright and positive, and the rhythm section—in which Miss Williams is a power—has a vital role." [4]

In addition to successfully completing *Music for Peace,* Mary also made the biggest decision of her late career. After contemplating the idea for several years, Mary decided in 1970 to officially make Peter O'Brien, the young seminarian she had met in 1964, her manager. Over the six years since their first meeting at the Hickory House, the two had maintained a somewhat close relationship. O'Brien, who grew up in New Jersey, had wanted to become a performer himself but had chosen instead a life in the priesthood. In 1958 he entered the Society of Jesus. He was at Loyola Seminary in New York in 1962 and was drawn to the musical world of New York City. After reading the feature on Mary in *Time* in 1964, O'Brien wrote to the pianist and followed up with a visit to the Hickory House. The first night he met Mary, she gave him her recent LP and EP. [5] After this encounter, Mary and O'Brien began cultivating a close and continuous relationship that revolved around daily telephone calls through the rest of the sixties. O'Brien's responsibilities and his pursuit of higher education would eventually lead him to the West Coast, where in 1969 he studied theology in San Francisco and then spent four months at the University of California in the Theatre Department. But the two remained in contact. O'Brien would later say, "That initial experience changed my life and pointed it in a new direction." [6] The same can be said for Mary. During the last fifteen years of her life, she experienced more happiness, stability, and appreciation than she ever had. It was an unusual pairing—a Jesuit priest and a jazz pianist—but they shared a strong affinity for jazz, black culture, and their faith. O'Brien acted informally on Mary's behalf as early as 1967, when he aided in the negotiations for the Carnegie Hall concert, but it was not until 1970 that he became her full-time manager. Following his ordination in 1971, O'Brien sought special permission to continue in the position. He split his time between Mary and his assignment as one of the associate priests at St. Ignatius Loyola Church in New York. He "was full time with her and full time with the Jesuits. The Jesuits are very flexible and [he] was authorized to travel with her and help with her career. This would have been much more difficult for [him] in any other organization within the church."[7] Over the next eleven years O'Brien worked diligently to resurrect Mary's career and aid her in educating the masses on the merits of jazz.

Following his ordination at Fordham University, Peter introduced Mary to Terence Cardinal Cooke, who headed the New York Archdiocese. Mary knew that if she could convince him of the merit of her sacred compositions, she would see her dream of performing at St. Patrick's Cathedral come to fruition. At the end of the service at Fordham, Mary followed the cardinal out the door. "I went chasing across the campus shouting 'Cardinal Cooke! Cardinal Cooke!,'" Mary recalled. When he finally stopped to acknowledge Mary's shouting, she explained to him that she had written a mass and wanted to perform it at the cathedral. "Fine," he said. Mary explained that it was not a typical mass and would probably be considered "kind of noisy."[8] The cardinal thought that would be just the thing needed to bring younger parishioners back to the cathedral. Mary was excited, but a few of Mary's friends thought he was just "fluffing [her] off."[9]

Despite the cardinal's enthusiasm, the leadership of the church was not quite ready to deal with the notion of jazz in a church setting. While Mary was waiting for a written commitment from the cardinal, the cathedral turned down Duke Ellington's proposal for his *Sacred Concert* and for a concert connected with the Newport Jazz Festival. Mary's mass, however, was not a "performance" in the traditional sense but a celebration of the liturgy. Nevertheless, Mary would have to wait. With mounting debts and slowing record sales, she turned her professional dealings over to O'Brien, who struggled to find new ways to market Mary and her music.

In early 1970 Barney Josephson resurfaced in New York, more than twenty years after the Red Scare had forced the closing of Café Society Downtown. On the northeast corner of Eighth Street and University Place, Josephson operated a restaurant called the Cookery. It featured plain, wood-top tables, murals, and reasonable prices. Unlike his previous endeavors, the Cookery did not feature live music. Instead Josephson focused on turning the restaurant into a fine eatery. Mary joined O'Brien during a visit with Josephson and suggested that he add a piano to the restaurant and hire her to perform. Although she hadn't seen Josephson during those years, Mary had occasionally called him to talk casually about some musician who was in trouble but never about her own life or career.[10] Josephson said he was not sure if he actually wanted to offer live music. Mary explained that "the happiest days of [her] life" had been during her years at Café Society Downtown.[11] It was during this period that Mary had made as much as $1,700 a week and experienced the most stability since her years with Andy Kirk's Twelve Clouds of Joy. Josephson asked for time to think about the proposition and immediately began investigating the legalities of adding live musicians to the eatery. He discovered that he did not need a cabaret license as long as there were no more than three instruments at one time. Josephson contacted Peter O'Brien and the two negotiated a deal.

In November 1970, Mary began a run at the Cookery accompanied by the bass player Michael Fleming. Five nights a week, from eight until one in the morning, Mary and Fleming played to enthusiastic crowds and critics. Critics particularly heralded Mary's return to the New York scene; one wrote, "She has lost none of the rich, swinging, subtly expressed power in her playing."[12] Mary Campbell wrote, "There's good news in jazz. Mary Lou Williams is out in the public again, in a New York restaurant, playing her superb jazz piano."[13] In the *New York Column,* Lewis K. McMillan Jr. announced after visiting the Cookery, "I heard and I was recaptured by the supreme pianistics of this grand lady of jazz. She just refused to 'fade away.' Rather, she seemed to me to just be emerging as one of the best of contemporary 88'ers [e.g., pianists]. Thank God for the likes of Barney Josephson."[14]

In time, Josephson would be just as thankful to Mary Lou. Bringing jazz to the Cookery increased the establishment's clientele. The arrangement provided Mary with the flexibility to come and go as she pleased over the next several years. Mary's shows at the Cookery exposed her to audiences who came to recapture the magic of her early years at Café Society and with the Kirk band, as well as younger audiences who were just discovering her talents. The small size of the room and the intimate atmosphere seemed just right for Mary's performance style, which generally included a bassist. The Cookery became known as the "Home of Mary Lou Williams." No matter how long Mary's absences from the room, or who replaced her, the Cookery became synonymous with good jazz and Mary Lou Williams. It was during these years and these performances that Mary created some of her best piano music and mentored a new generation of jazz musicians. But it was often the attendance of Mary's friends and jazz's elite that drew attention. On one occasion a

former Basie drummer, Jo Jones, dropped in and during Mary's set began accompanying her with brushes and a newspaper. What they created
was historic, transporting them and the audience back to the early years
of jazz when the music was governed by talent, raw expression, and
friendly competition, not record sales or cover charges. During another
performance a string broke on the bass of Milton Suggs and he was unable to replace it or borrow another instrument. Mary finished the set
and played two more solo, treating audiences to a history of jazz piano
from Fats Waller to McCoy Tyner. It was not something Mary had
planned. She simply sat at the piano and created out of her imagination.
According to O'Brien, "The results were breathtaking. Her imagination
was untrammeled and uninterfered with. She seemed to be bringing all
of her powers of invention and all of her pianistic ability to bear that
night." [15]

Critics continued to applaud Mary's return to the jazz scene throughout 1971 and she drew diverse crowds to the Cookery. She still had not
fulfilled her dream of performing her jazz mass at St. Patrick's, but Mary
held out hope that Cardinal Cooke would call with good news. Meanwhile, O'Brien worked harder to keep Mary working, but his job was
made more difficult by Mary's self-effacing and sometimes hateful attitude. She had no desire to go back into the life of performing in nightclubs, but Peter knew she had little choice. To achieve the type of success
she desired, Mary would have to return to the people—especially those
who would not be drawn to her church performances. Mary's naïveté regarding the "business" of jazz shaped her attitude of resistance. After all,
she was one of only a few living jazz musicians to have played in all the
eras of jazz and she had produced hundreds of notable compositions and
recordings. At sixty, she felt it was beneath her to hustle or work hard to
maintain a presence in the jazz scene. She refused to accept that much
had changed since her early years. Despite all her contributions and accomplishments, O'Brien could not interest any of the major jazz labels in
recording Mary, and the fees offered were often lower than what Mary
wanted. The fact was that jazz was battling more than ever for a stable
place in the popular culture. Rock, disco, and soul had eclipsed the genre
in record sales, and as modernists became more experimental in their
compositions and recordings, the once-loyal black community began
turning to other forms of music. Mary also hindered O'Brien's efforts to
push her music. "Her personality was so introverted in an extroverted

world. It was a mixture of being absolutely sure that 'I'm too fat for television' or 'No good for outdoors.' It was painful." [16] No doubt what influenced the direction of Mary's career the most was the inability of the industry to market the sixty-year-old woman. There is something to be said for aging men, but as countless female entertainers have discovered, aging women are often cast aside for younger, more nubile ones.

During Mary's early years, critics and recording executives had spotlighted her supple figure, high cheekbones, and beautiful skin, but the last twenty years had been less than kind to Mary. Though in the 1950s she seemed to be aging gracefully, by 1970 she sometimes looked haggard and worn. Her weight was now almost two hundred pounds, which led Mary into fits of depression. Throughout the 1970s she would refer to herself in derogatory ways, sometimes calling herself a "big ape" or whatever negative name she could come up with. Although such statements were always tinged with humor, they reflected the self-loathing Mary felt and served as a defense mechanism against the public's opinion. It was obvious that she could no longer be marketed by her youthful charm and svelte figure. She now stood as the Grande Dame of Jazz, the matriarch of the art form, but the narrow perspective of the industry could not easily negotiate a space for Mary in the mainstream. O'Brien directed Mary's talents toward colleges and jazz festivals, which celebrated both innovation and history, and nightclubs clamoring for the "authenticity and purity" of Mary's piano music.

The more O'Brien pushed, the harder Mary reacted. What emerged after 1970 was at times a different, harder, bitterer Mary Lou Williams. The struggles of the past years, coupled with her declining health, which she hardly addressed publicly, had taken their toll. Her moods fluctuated tremendously; she was at times a conqueror determined to overcome anything but at other times a recluse who wanted only to stay in the quiet, meditative environment of the church. She constantly blamed O'Brien for her unhappiness, claiming that he had pushed her back into performing. He continued to push her and suggested that she concentrate more on her piano works. While many have come to believe that it was O'Brien who convinced her to compose sacred works, he had advocated the opposite. He had indeed supported these aspirations, but he tried to impress upon Mary that there was more interest in her piano works than in the sacred compositions. He wanted to make piano records, but she would not be deterred from what she wanted to do. [17]

In April 1971 Mary participated in a historic jam session that brought several generations of jazz musicians together at the Overseas Press Club in New York. Featured in the concert were the two camps that had warred against each other in the 1940s after the advent of bebop. Mary, the bassist George Duvivier, and the drummer Grady Tate were the rhythm section for the trumpeters Bobby Hackett, an exponent of the early jazz styles of Armstrong and Bix Beiderbecke, and Dizzy Gillespie, one of the founding fathers of modern jazz. Although Mary played only a supporting role in the concert, she received "the strongest cheers and applause from the audience." [18] The taped concert was released as the recording *Giants* on the Perception label (LP 19; also released as *Giants of Jazz,* 53180). A short time later, O'Brien delivered to Moe Asch the tapes of Mary's interpretation of the history of jazz, which included musical performances and narration by the pianist. It had taken ten years for the project to come to fruition; it seemed the timing could not have been better, considering the excitement brewing over her live performances. Although Folkways and Asch owned the recording rights, the company agreed that if its recording went out of print for more than three years, Mary would receive full rights to the tapes and recording of the material. But the record would not appear until seven years later, in 1978, and by that time interest had waned.

In May and June Mary recorded eleven piano solos for Chiaroscuro Records, a small, independent label headed by Hank O'Neal. O'Neal had started the label in 1970 with the aim of recording primarily jazz. When he conferred with his old friend John Hammond about the best artists to record, one suggestion was Mary Lou Williams. Thirty years earlier Mary had shunned Hammond because of the control he exhibited over musicians. Her behavior had resulted in a somewhat strained relationship with Hammond, but he continued to respect her work. O'Neal was impressed by Hammond's advice and approached Mary and O'Brien one night at the Cookery. The three reached an agreement and Mary entered the label's New York studios in May. The final product was a collection of vintage piano jazz by Mary Lou Williams. The tracks included "Night Life," the composition Mary had first performed in 1930 during the Brunswick recordings in Chicago, and piano versions of her big band arrangements "Cloudy," "Little Joe from Chicago," "What's Your Story, Morning Glory?," and "Scratchin' in the Gravel." Also on the album were three of Mary's modern compositions: "Blues for John," written in honor of Hammond, "The Chief," which was a reworking of "Chief Natoma from Tacoma," and the blues-tinged prayer "Anima Christi." The record, consisting of eleven of the eighteen tracks recorded, was called *From the Heart* (CR 103). It was Mary's first solo LP in a career of more than forty years. *Down Beat* awarded the LP five stars, its highest rating, stating, "Under the star system of rating records, critics sometimes succumb to momentary enthusiasms and elevate to the highest rating albums that deserve less. There are five star albums, in other words, and there are five star albums. After two months of hearing 'From the Heart' regularly, my momentary enthusiasm has become permanent admiration. This indispensable recording is a FIVE STAR album."[19]

* * *

While Mary was in the studio, O'Brien got the idea of a collaboration with the famed dancer and choreographer Alvin Ailey on the *Mass for Peace.* Mary dismissed the notion at first, but when O'Brien learned that Katherine Dunham had set dances to some of Mary's compositions, he pushed the issue. It is not clear what Mary's reservations were. No doubt she was still hoping to gain the approval of the church and perform *Music for Peace,* the revamped *Mass for Peace,* at St. Patrick's, but it was only an aspiration, as little had changed in the cathedral's position on jazz. Mary was well aware of Ailey's work and his elevation of black culture through his dance company. In 1965, for the second Pittsburgh Jazz Festival, Mary had approached the choreographer about "St. Martin De Porres," but Ailey was unavailable at the time. He was very much aware of Mary's music and was said to have attended the memorial service for Mboya, where the *Mass for Peace* debuted. After hearing *Music for Peace,* Ailey agreed to choreograph several dances to Mary's music.

In the fall of 1971 Ailey took over the choreography of Leonard Bernstein's *Mass,* commissioned for the opening of the John F. Kennedy Center for Performing Arts in Washington, D.C., after Jerome Robbins quit. Thus, Ailey's prestigious black dance company was the first to perform in the newly constructed theater. But the experience was less than rewarding. The dancers were, in Ailey's estimation, reduced to second-class performers by Bernstein's preoccupation with the orchestra and the singers. According to Judith Jamison, a principal dancer with the company, "the dancing was gradually reduced to minimal movement, as far back on stage as possible, and a little in the corners."[20] As soon as the production was over, Ailey began working on a new piece that would feature the music of Mary Lou Williams. The composition would be known as *Mary's Lou Mass,* which became the title used for the *Mass for Peace* after 1971. For the production Mary composed a new "Agnus Dei." The remainder of the music came from *Music for Peace.* The result was a thirteen-section work that displayed the same overtly religious aspect of the black aesthetic that was represented in Ailey's famous *Revelations.* He called the mass "a soul dance—a series of ecstatic dances, I call them. What is wonderful about this music is that it is a sum total of black music, a retrospective."[21]

In 1971 Alvin Ailey's American Dance Theater opened its short pre-Christmas season (December 7–19) at the New York City Center with *Mary Lou's Mass.* Reactions to the composition were mixed. During the rehearsals Mary had become frustrated with Howard Roberts's conducting style and decided to direct the choir and play the piano for the performance. But Mary was not experienced in theater productions and could not adjust to the small mishaps that plagued the early performances. During the first show the scenery fell, and in another, Sara Yarborough's toe became caught in the hem of her dress. When Mary was distracted by the bassist Milton Suggs and missed a whole chorus, causing confusion onstage, Ailey stormed out of the theater and later declared that Howard Roberts would conduct from then on.

Regardless of the mishaps, the performance and Mary's music were highly praised. *Newsweek* reported that Mary's "spirit and rhythms were made for the Alvin Ailey American Dance Theater." The combination of music, dance, and religion had indeed created a new form of praise and worship unlike anything ever witnessed before.[22] The reviewer for *Hi/Fi America* wrote, "Despite the genuineness of its emotion and devotion, the piece—scored for singers, French horn, drums, conga, bass, and reeds—lacks character, particularly melodic character."[23] *Dance Magazine* declared, "These dances of supplication, repentance, fellowship, and exultation reveal the spirit, if not the essence, of the liturgical celebration."[24] Apart from the individual opinions of the critics, most agreed that the climactic point of the ballet was the interpretation of the parable of Lazarus. Performed by the dancers John Parks (the rich man), Dudley Williams (Lazarus), and Kelvin Rotardier (the priest-narrator), the parable describes Lazarus's interaction with a rich man. Lazarus, a poor man, begs for the crumbs off the rich man's table, but is refused. That night, when they both die, Lazarus goes to heaven and the rich man to hell. After the inaugural performance, Mary happily wrote to Mario that the performances were sold out. "People are crying (touched) and are happy. My opening night there was a six minute standing ovation." [25] The Ailey company included *Mary Lou's Mass* in its repertory until 1973, but Ailey and Mary never collaborated again. Since then other companies, including Cleo Parker Robinson Dance, and the Nanette Bearden company, have performed selections from the work.

In January 1972 Mary recorded (at Ailey's expense) the additional movements of *Mary Lou's Mass* that had been written specifically for the Ailey production: "Act of Contrition"; "Medi I/Medi II," "Old Time Spiritual," "Lamb of God," and "(Come Holy Spirit) Praise the Lord." The master tapes were made available to Ailey, which allowed him to take the work on the road without the added expense of live musicians. Ailey would in turn allow Mary to include the material in 1975 for the album *Mary Lou's Mass* (Mary 102).

* * *

Invigorated by the overwhelming response to *Mary Lou's Mass*, Mary worked even harder to book performances of the work. She was driven by the hope that enough attention might convince church officials to program it at St. Patrick's Cathedral. She and O'Brien battled over Mary's determination to work solely on promoting the mass. He still wanted to focus on Mary's piano works, but the two eventually compromised. In addition to her regular stints at the Cookery and other clubs outside the city, O'Brien set up performances of the mass in schools, churches, and recreation centers. Wherever Mary was booked throughout the country, Peter had to ensure that there was at least one performance of *Mary Lou's Mass* as well. When she was not concentrating on the mass, her history of jazz dominated her performances. During a two-week run in Washington, Mary performed her history of jazz at one of the area's colleges. During that same trip Mary, along with Dizzy Gillespie, six singers, and the bassist Larry Gales, performed *Mary Lou's Mass* at the Dahlgren Chapel at Georgetown University. But Mary's standout engagement of 1972 was perhaps her appearance at the Newport Jazz Festival.

The mother of all jazz festivals in America, the Newport had provided, since its inception in 1954, a venue where performers and composers could showcase talents and music that would not be readily marketed by recording executives. Despite all that Mary had accomplished, her appearance in 1972 was only her second showing at the festival. She had been slated to perform the previous year, but a riot broke out shortly before she took the stage, closing the festival down. The 1972 festival would show those who doubted the freshness of her playing how Mary was continually developing as an artist. George Wein, the founder of the festival and Mary's former collaborator on the Pittsburgh Jazz Festival, had decided to move the event to New York, in part because of the events of the previous year. The concerts would be staged in different venues throughout the city over a weekend and would range from jam sessions and panel discussions to historic concert performances. Mary performed in the first of two jam sessions held at Radio City Music Hall and in the festival's Connoisseur Concerts, which featured a mixture of new and old jazz.

Mary's Connoisseur Concert, the first of four, was held at Carnegie Hall on July 2 with the JPJ Quartet, a group featuring the tenor saxophonist Budd Johnson as leader and the avant-gardists Cecil Taylor and Rashaan Roland Kirk. The following day, July 3, she shared the stage with many notable "old school" musicians, including Gene Krupa, Benny Carter, Teddy Wilson, and Roy Eldridge. The all-star roster was divided into three jam groups; Mary was placed with Benny Green, Max Roach, Percy Heath, Big Black, Milt Jackson, Kenny Burrell, Stan Getz, and Dizzy Gillespie. Despite some technical difficulties, the band finally got itself together and performed Jackson's "Bag's Groove" and Gillespie's "A Night in Tunisia." Mary, in her usual fashion, subtly rose above the highly touted male performers with whom she shared the stage. She returned to the stage to perform with the next group, which provided a heavy dose of saxophones in the form of James Moody, Zoot Sims, Dexter Gordon, and Rashaan Roland Kirk. Also onstage were the pianist Herbie Hancock, Tony Williams, Chuck Wayne, and Kai Winding. Unlike the previous jam group, this aggregation suffered from ego problems as each player tried to dominate the others. But the concert as a whole was successful; it was recorded on *Newport in New York '72: The Jam Sessions, volumes 1 and 2,* released on the Cobblestone label in 1973.

Mary had much to be happy about, given the progression of her career and the reception she was receiving during her community-based concerts. Noting the popularity of *Mary Lou's Mass* with community- and college-based choirs, she recorded some new material. Mary recorded three new compositions: "Jesus Is Best," "Willis," and "Let's Do the Froggy Bottom," which featured lyrics by Juanita Fleming and bore no relation to the tunes of 1929 or 1936. Released on Mary Records, the singles went virtually unrecognized, and Mary lost a considerable amount of money trying to get them played on mainstream radio. Much to Mary's chagrin, black radio and mainstream radio were radically altering their play rotations. Jazz had lost favor with much of the black community, with the exception of the funk, soul, and rock-tinged varieties. Moreover, Mary Records did not have the type of working capital that labels such as Blue Note, Impulse!, Prestige, and Fantasy had. It remained a grassroots label that operated by mail order.

But Mary's inability to catch the attention of the media was not simply an issue of the independent versus the major label. Jazz as a whole was suffering from a communal backlash within the black community that was rooted in the eccentric and often complex nature of the avant-garde movement. Although the Black Arts Movement, the artistic and spiritual sister to the Black Power Movement, had adopted the avant-garde approaches of John Coltrane, Archie Shepp, Ornette Coleman, and others as the "true" articulation of blackness and cultural consciousness, the public had rejected such notions and turned to the sounds of Motown, Stax, Atlantic, and other labels manufacturing soul music. Within certain intellectual circles there was a call for the "Black Revolutionary Artist" who would completely reject white critical standards and assumptions in the quest for a "pure" expression of blackness.[26] Mary understood the need to elevate the cultural consciousness of the race but disagreed with the model the movement had erected in the form of the avant-gardist. She believed that a true understanding of the race and its culture lay in the exploration of its roots, the history of the music, and experiences, not the radical intellectual hyperbole of the musicians, activists, and writers who were constructing their own sense of cultural reality. Mary became more determined than ever to bring clarity to the historical and cultural merits of jazz. She would often begin her discussions of jazz with the assertion, "Jazz and the spirituals are the only American born art. From suffering came the spirituals. Songs of joy and songs of sorrow. The main origin of American jazz is a spiritual. Because of the deeply religious background of the Black American he was able to mix this strong influence with rhythms that reach deep enough into the inner self to give expression to outcries of sincere joy, which became known as

Jazz." Mary generally explained, in her lectures, that she and many other musicians objected to the use of a single word to describe the diverse approaches within the tradition. Although musicians and scholars have attempted to use numerous terms to describe the music, she explained, "The title Jazz has survived it all." [27] So, even though Mary and other musicians opposed this terminology, they had come to accept that it would not die easily.

Second in strength only to her faith was Mary's view of the history of jazz. She wrote to Mario in 1971, after completing her *History of Jazz* recording:

> After the era of bop, the Negro began losing his heritage, in jazz. Dizzy is the most copied musician in the world. He's modern yet stuck to the heritage. In other words one does not have to play cornball to retain his heritage. It grows. You see the things Aretha [Franklin] is singing, if they were made modern, the beat would not be as strong. Her tunes would become artistic, yet some musicians that are artistic, has some of the blues strain left in their music. The musicians of today are playing the upsetment of the world. These young cats had gotten a hold of Coltrane before he died. You'll faint when you hear what they are playing. And most of it is evil to listen to. Real jazz soothes the soul, makes one happy. [28]

Ironically, thirty years later, Wynton Marsalis would assert the cultural connection between jazz, spirituals, and slavery and draw acclaim from critics and audiences. But it should be noted that the public articulation of such ideas began with Mary Lou Williams in the 1970s. Among her jazz peers, Mary's perspective seemed dated and old-fashioned. To them, crossover appeal, not historical rhetoric, was going to bring audiences back to jazz.

Mary's efforts to advance jazz composition and the heritage of jazz intensified in the summer of 1972 when she received a Guggenheim Fellowship for Music Composition. The prestigious award, given to scholars, scientists, and artists on the bases of demonstrated accomplishment and strong promise for the future, would provide Mary with much-needed money and support for her composing. That year's awards were historic in that of the 372 grants given, 5 were awarded to jazz musicians.

It was the boost Mary needed to finish projects she had in the pipeline and, she hoped, draw the attention and approval of the governing body of St. Patrick's Cathedral. She continued to alternate between her local gig at the Cookery and out-of-town ventures. In February she returned to Pittsburgh, where she visited with family and performed a concert at Chatham College. In addition to the Chatham concert, Mary also performed *Mary Lou's Mass* at several local churches. She returned to New York in time to be honored as a part of the city's monthlong celebration of jazz. Mayor John V. Lindsay declared April Jazz Month in the city and planned a special ceremony to honor musicians who had contributed to the development of the local jazz scene. On the steps of City Hall, Mary, Teddy Wilson, Jo Jones, Willie "the Lion" Smith, and Maxine Sullivan, led by the pianist Billy Taylor, were honored for their contributions. Mary followed the celebration with two eagerly awaited concerts, one at Fordham University, during which she received an honorary doctorate of humane letters, and one at St. Ignatius Loyola Church.

The success and attention she had clamored for before were now coming her way. In May she was invited to participate in a benefit concert for the Charlie Parker Memorial Foundation in Kansas City, Missouri. It had been years since Mary had walked the streets of Kansas City and jammed in the nightclubs of the Vine Street district, but the sounds and smells were still vibrant. In recent years the area had fallen into disrepair. It remained only a shadow of its grand days, but the city had renewed interest in restoring the area as well as erecting a memorial to one of its favorite sons—Charlie Parker. Mary relished her time there and the visit was highlighted by the naming after her of a residential street near what would become the Eighteenth and Vine Historical District. Mary performed in a concert celebrating the naming of various streets after jazz musicians and in her mass at St. Francis Xavier Church in the city. The concert was received warmly, but the mass was caught up in the growing controversy over the use of secular music in churches. This was in Mary's mind the same debate that was holding up any performance of the mass at St. Patrick's in New York. Church leaders were still having difficulty bringing new forms of music and worship into the more established and hard-line churches. Officials of St. Patrick's, one of the largest churches in New York, supported the reforms of the Second Vatican Council and were prepared to move forward slowly, but they did not want to alienate or offend certain segments of the congregation.

O'Brien explained the delay in performing *Mary Lou's Mass* at St. Patrick's differently. At least a year after his ordination in 1971, he had managed to schedule an appointment with Monsignor James Rigney, the pastor of the cathedral, and John Grady, the director of music at the cathedral. He said that in his enthusiasm he went to the meeting "brandishing" Cardinal Cooke's excitement over Mary's music. He "all but [told] them they had to do this," he recalled. However, Grady and Rigney had no idea what he was talking about and they responded adamantly that the mass would not be performed.[29] Church officials perhaps did not want the type of protests that were taking place nationwide to take place at St. Patrick's. In the hours before the celebration of the 11:00 A.M. mass, the Kansas City church was picketed, but the celebration of *Mary Lou's Mass* went ahead. According to Mary, the church was packed, and "afterwards, people screamed and ran up to the stand and hugged and kissed me. They almost tore me apart. I never knew people to act like that after a Mass."[30] The successful performance, however, could not calm the escalating debate, within Protestant and Catholic churches, regarding "sacred jazz" and its appropriateness in worship services.

As early as 1972, a writer-scholar, William Banks, had openly scorned the performance of not only Mary's religious compositions but also Duke Ellington's in church settings. He insisted that churches and preachers took interest in the "new" music only because it was financially profitable—a notion seen in Mary's own letters of the late 1960s and early 1970s. Although the composers, he asserted, claimed that their music had its roots in the spiritual, this did not overcome the fact that the music was sinful. Regardless of rhetorically sound arguments trumpeting its merits, Banks concluded that there was no justification for the use of jazz in sacred settings. The idea of jazz being performed in churches was sacrilegious. Although Banks believed that artistic and musical abilities were gifts from God, he alleged that the jazz musician misused his or hers by willingly choosing a form of music that incited people to act immorally. "The exaggerated self-pity of the blues, the double entendres, and the suggestive words carelessly tread upon human emotions," he wrote. "Some contend that there is therapeutic value in the release of such emotional energy. However, in the long run, misdirected energy has a detrimental effect. Only when our energies are superintended by God's Holy Spirit and channeled into activities which honor Jesus Christ is there any lasting value for all concerned." [31] "Naturally," he stated, "the jazz musicians justify their actions."

> The jazz pianist–composer, Mary Lou Williams, said, "The ability to play good jazz is a gift from God. This music is based on the spirituals—it's our only original American art form—and should be played everywhere, including church. Those who say it shouldn't be played in church do not understand they are blocking the manifestation of God's will." The famous Duke Ellington justifies his "sacred jazz" concerts this way: "Every man prays in his own language, and there is no language that God does not understand." On another occasion he said, "When a man prays, he prays in his own language. I've been praying with saxophones, trumpets, and a rhythm section for 40 years. This is my language. It's my way of praying." [32]

Banks did not completely blame Mary and Ellington for the misconceptions that had developed, but he contended that many churchgoers mistakenly believed that because something occurred in the church, it must be holy. He asserted that even those who were staunch opponents of jazz would soften their views because of the popularity of the composer. He argued, however, that performance in a church did not mean that the nature of the object had been changed. True praise could be achieved only when God was worshiped as *He* liked. Jazz in whatever form could not achieve this. Thus the "sacred jazz concerts" were a "devil" and had "no business in the Christian church. The Black Christian must resist the incursion of jazz into our churches, whether it be the 'sacred jazz' of Duke or the jumping gospel or a choir or chorus." [33]

It is clear that Banks and other detractors were not totally aware of the nature of Mary's religious compositions. He had simply lashed out against the music because it used the moniker jazz. His concept of edification, or the uplifting of a moral and spiritual being, kept him from a true understanding of *Mary Lou's Mass*. He stated that religious music was useful only if the message was biblical; that most jazz and gospel was used for entertainment, not for the uplift of spirituality; and that performers of such music were exalting only themselves with their theatrics and showmanship. Performances of all Mary's sacred works refute his views, in that the texts of the majority of these compositions are based on biblical scriptures. The only exceptions are the hymn "The Devil" and some movements of *Mary Lou's Mass* (such as "People in Trouble" and "The World"). Mary was so meticulous about the composition of these pieces that she specified in the scores from which book, chapter, and verses the texts were taken. Furthermore, the performance of her masses did not depend on theatrics or showmanship; in local performances she often used choirs and singers from the larger community. Mary only reluctantly accepted the notion of her masses being performed as concert pieces; she had envisioned them as celebrations of the liturgy to be used within the church. However biased Banks's opinions were, they were very important in that they indicated the resistance and the negative perspectives that blacks and whites had toward jazz. Many blacks, particularly middle-class and affluent blacks, were still crippled in their thinking about jazz by images of juke joints and sexual deviance. No one could deny that the jazz world had seen drug abuse, promiscuity, violence, and premature death, but these phenomena were the catalyst for Mary's compositions. These negative perceptions did not prevent Mary from performing *Mary Lou's Mass,* which she continued to do until her death.

Having survived the firestorm of criticism of her religious compositions, Mary once again turned back to arranging new material for a possible recording. She traveled and worked even harder throughout 1973 and 1974 than she had in the previous twenty years. Although she badgered O'Brien and argued with him, she could not deny that since he had become her manager, she had been able to get the type of media attention she wanted and had earned good money.

In early 1974 Mary began recording material for a new album. Assisted by the bassist Bob Cranshaw and the drummer Mickey Roker, Mary conceived of an album that would capture all the dimensions of her musical personality. Entitled *Zoning,* the work represented the modern maturity of Mary's musical style beyond bebop. It offered listeners Mary's interpretations of the avant-garde in a variation of her 1965 composition "A Fungus Amungus," now titled "Zoning Fungus II"; the modern approaches of Ahmad Jamal in "Olinga," a Gillespie composition; and an exploration of unusual meters, in the Dave Brubeck style, in "Intermission," "Zoning Fungus II," and "Medi II." The pieces were performed in a variety of settings—trio, duet for piano and bass, duo pianos and rhythm section, and solo piano. The combination of Cranshaw, Roker, and Williams proved exceptional. Cranshaw's careful articulation of funk and blues-tinged bass lines (he used electric bass during their session because of an injury) and Roker's easy but swinging drumming provided the rhythmic "pocket" that allowed Mary to produce some cleanly articulated improvisations. The inclusion of a second piano, played by the classical pianist Zita Corno, added depth to two of the compositions, "Zoning Fungus II" and "Intermission."

During "Zoning" the pianos worked in opposition to each other—one presenting a sweet and lyrical melody and the other offering dissonant commentary that threatened to overshadow the other. The unaccompanied duet, which encompasses only the first few minutes of the track, is a study in consonance and dissonance that is resolved with the entrance of the bass and drums and the overlaying of structure in the form of a 7/4 rhythm pattern. The significant melodic interplay between the two pianos is no doubt a musical metaphor for Mary's perceived "war" between the consonance of previous jazz styles and the dissonances of the avant-garde era.

Mary's modernization of the blues is heard on four tracks, "Medi I," "Medi II," "Rosa Mae," and "Play It Momma." "Medi II," an up-tempo blues in 8/8 time, is centered on a rhythmic and melodic figure played by the bass. It maintains this rhythmic pulse until the release of the chorus, or the contrasting section when considering the classic AAB structure of blues form, when it switches to 12/8. What results is a fast-paced groove that complements the fluid melodic lines punctuated by chordal responses that Mary plays. The four-chorus composition slowly begins to resolve when Mary plays a short interlude of chords as the rhythm section, still emphasizing the opening rhythmic and melodic pattern, gets softer. It is a complementary opposite to "Medi I," which is a medium-tempo blues focused on motivic material presented by the bass.

Overall, the final product, a mixture of instrumental versions of her sacred works ("Gloria," "Praise the Lord"), statements of the avant-garde, and modern interpretations of the blues, left little doubt about whether, at sixty-four, Mary could easily synthesize post-bop modern approaches. It was a communion of McCoy Tyner, Ahmad Jamal, and Mary Lou Williams, and the critics acclaimed its merit. Phyl Garland, a record critic for *Ebony*, wrote:

How anyone could sound this fresh after 50 years at the keyboard is almost beyond comprehension. Unlike some of her earlier albums that emphasized message and compositional components, this album focuses on the way she plays—which she does consummately. Her adventuresome spirit is most obvious on "Zoning Fungus II," which harkens back to her experimental "A Fungus Amungus" of many years ago. Again, she employs atonal harmonies before settling down to a steady funky base. This is music by a woman for all seasons, from the pensive Ellingtonian drift of "Ghost of Love," through the sophisticated instrumental shouts of "Praise the Lord" and the contemporary soulful insistence of "Play It Momma." Long live Mary Lou Williams.[34]

Billboard declared it "a very welcome album to any listener's collection," and the *Sunday News* asserted, "It contains a great deal of music, over 50 minutes worth and it's all well worth listening to."[35] The album, her most successful solo venture since her early Asch recordings, was nominated for a Grammy in 1975. While it did not win, it was the one project that Peter O'Brien was most proud of during his ten years as Mary's manager.[36] In May 1974 Mary received honorary degrees from Loyola University in New Orleans and Manhattan College. For the former she composed "Ode to St. Cecilia," and for the latter, "Manhattan Degree."[37]

*   *   *

With the death of Duke Ellington in 1974, Mary felt an added responsibility to continue the advancement of jazz, especially in the form of large-scale compositions. Together the two had done much to expand jazz beyond its traditional boundaries and had raised the expectations of composers. Despite the disagreements of the past few years, and what Mary perceived as Ellington's unabashed replication of her compositional ideals, there was still a feeling of closeness and camaraderie between the two. Ellington, one year before his death, devoted a section in his autobiography, *Music Is My Mistress,* to Mary. So it was only natural that his sister Ruth would ask Mary to perform at his funeral. Unlike the other performers, Mary and Ella Fitzgerald chose not to perform an Ellington composition. Mary played the ballad "Holy Ghost" from *Zoning,* and Ella sang "Just a Closer Walk with Thee." Many in attendance were put off by Mary's decision, but she firmly stated that she had offered it up as a prayer. Over the next few years she would experience the deaths of other friends and family, and each only reminded her of how fortunate she was, despite all the problems she thought she had.

In 1975 Mary finally received word from St. Patrick's Cathedral that her mass would be performed there. Although Cardinal Cooke had apparently not been able to convince the governing body of the church to present the mass, Monsignor Rigney was successful. His apparent change of heart was born of the excitement that was brewing about the mass at other performances and the fact that all other efforts to attract younger parishioners to the cathedral had failed. He wrote to all the principals of the New York Catholic high schools, stating that he wanted the schoolchildren to feel they had a claim on the cathedral. Thomas Murphy, S.J., president of Regis High School, was familiar with the work Mary had done with the community through her music and suggested that *Mary Lou's Mass* be given for the students. Mary decided not only to perform the mass but also to include the students in the performance. As she had done so many times before, she rescored the vocal lines and trained a choir of forty students from the grammar school of Our Lady of Lourdes, Fordham Prep in the Bronx, and the Cathedral High School for Girls in Manhattan. She divided the students into two groups so that the choir could engage in call and response. Accompanying Mary were the bassist Buster Williams and Jerry Griffin on drums.

On February 18, St. Patrick's Cathedral became the site of a historic event that has yet to be replicated—the performance of a jazz liturgy. At 2:10 P.M. the concelebrants of the mass filed in and *Mary Lou's Mass* began. Over three thousand people filled the church, leaving little room for latecomers. Despite the overflow crowd, the sanctity and decorum of the church were maintained throughout the service. The readings, taken from Psalms and Isaiah, were set for the Tuesday of the first week of Lent and performed by Mabel Mercer, a friend of Mary's and a legendary singer. Monsignor Rigney offered a welcome and Peter O'Brien gave the homily, which drew on the theme of jazz as a music of great power and spiritual effect. "The saint and the artist do not belong to different realms," he stated. "Artists suffer far more than the rest of us. They are wide open to their own experience far more profoundly than the rest of us. It's customary in the Church to recite a litany of saints. In terms of this art form, I suggest we form our own litany of artists—Louis Armstrong, Duke Ellington, John Coltrane, Thelonious Monk, Dizzy Gillespie, Charlie Parker, Mary Lou Williams, Max Roach, Art Blakey, Oscar Pettiford, Billie Holiday, and Bessie Smith. These great creators of our American music will some day be seen for who they are and what they have given us." [38] Mary conducted the group from the piano, leading the singers with short introductory passages that established the mood of the mass's movements. Mary supported "the singing with light, flowing lines that danced under the voices. Occasionally Mr. Williams or Mr. Griffin played a brief subdued solo; Mr. Williams plucking somberly on his bass and Mr. Griffin employing his brushes lightly and deftly." [39] According to John W. Donohue, S.J., who covered the event for *America,* "The combined choirs nobly confirmed Mary Lou Williams' wisdom in choosing them. They may not have projected the music as impressively as professionals would have done, but they brought a freshness to it that was wonderfully appropriate for a true liturgy." [40] The mass ended with Mary's setting of Psalm 150, "Praise the Lord," and was greeted with "waves of applause and a general air of exhilaration that animates a crowd when people know they've shared a momentous and uplifting experience." [41] Rigney called the event "an inspiring, lovely, religious experience," and Mary was "happy it happened for the sake of jazz. Americans don't realize how important jazz is. It's healing for the soul. It should be played *everywhere*—in churches, nightclubs, everywhere. We have to use every place we can." [42]

But the success of the performance at St. Patrick's was not simply a question of the acceptability of jazz. It represented the culmination of Mary's efforts to alter the traditional attitudes of the Catholic Church toward its black parishioners. Although the history of black Catholics in America can be traced back to before the Civil War, the church leadership had not sought to fully integrate black parishioners into the priesthood and church leadership. Mary knew that getting this work performed in the stronghold of New York Catholicism meant not only the acceptance of jazz as a viable art form but the acknowledgment of the cultural and spiritual contributions of black Catholics such as herself.

The mass was performed again shortly after the St. Patrick's performance at the Composers' Showcase at the Whitney Museum. For this performance Mary used Tony Waters on congas and Carline Ray with a small choir. Once again, the audience proclaimed the vitality and spiritual purity of the music, but Mary still was not happy. In her mind she had not yet escaped the marginality that had defined most of her late career. For her, true success was measured by the industry's opinion. So when the recording industry largely ignored the performance at St. Patrick's Cathedral and no lucrative recording contract with a major label materialized, Mary thought that she had failed once again. But O'Brien would not allow her to slip into the depression that had sometimes plagued her. He pushed her to work even harder and persuaded her to turn her attention to other projects.

In the summer of 1975 Mary received an offer to record an album with the Danish label Steeplechase. It paid very little but allowed her to exercise complete creative control. She entered the studios on July 8, 1975, accompanied by Buster Williams and Mickey Roker. For one critic, the album, called *Free Spirits,* indicated that Mary had "heard and understood all the modal things that have happened in the interim. She is still instantly identifiable as Mary Lou Williams, as somehow she seems to be saying that there is an unbroken thread running from spirituals and blues through McCoy Tyner." [43]

Although Mary was unhappy with what she viewed as a lack of real support or publicity from the recording industry, she had somehow become a spokesperson for jazz. She was often featured on television and radio, and the mainstream press took great interest in her. In September 1976 she appeared on the CBS program *Look Up and Live.* The half-hour program showcased Mary's jazz crusade. Mary's friend the Reverend C. J. McNaspy filmed the show in front of the altar of Our Lady of Lourdes Church and included his commentary. The segment featured live performances of parts of *Mary Lou's Mass* and "Ode to St. Cecilia." [44]

By 1976, Mary had indeed entered the season of change and blessings that she had feverishly prayed for and written about to friends. Mounting debts and low wages had ruled her life in the early years of her return to jazz, but now through renewed interest in her music and the efforts of Peter O'Brien, Mary was earning some of the largest fees she had ever received. Cognizant of the mistakes of the past, when she spent without discipline and loaned money without discernment, Mary lived frugally, saving what she could to ensure that her dry periods would not be as horrendous as before. She would often take the subway to work dressed in a thin coat, despite owning a full-length fur, and on the occasions when she did drive the Cadillac she owned, she would often sleep on the front seat until she could legally park the car across from her building. She and O'Brien developed her presentation on the history of jazz into a well-oiled machine, with his reading the lecture and Mary providing musical examples that ranged from spirituals to bebop. Mary did not entirely stop her community-based performances of *Mary Lou's Mass,* but she was focused more on spreading her message about the history and development of jazz. She centered her discussions on the "Americanness" of jazz, a perspective that mirrored that of emerging black scholars, activists, and writers. Amiri Baraka, known previously as LeRoi Jones and one of the leaders of the Black Arts Movement, published in 1963 the landmark text *Blues People,* in which he discussed the development of jazz out of the slave experience. He, like Mary, believed that jazz was a derivative of the African's transmutation into the American. But Baraka's assertions did not seem to breed the type of venom that Mary attracted when she said the same thing. To illustrate her view of the development of jazz, Mary enlisted David Stone Martin, who created Mary's "Tree of Jazz." The illustration has three major parts: the trunk, which represents the inspirations of jazz (such as the suffering of slaves and the blues) and the evolution of the genre, from spirituals to ragtime to Kansas City swing to bebop; the leaves of the tree, which contain the names of musicians and composers who have contributed to the genre; and the barren limbs, which bear the names "commercial rock," "black magic," "cults," "avant-garde," "exercises," and "classical books." Perhaps the most tangible representation of Mary's rhetorical perspective on jazz in the 1970s, the "Tree of Jazz" closely matched her mantra, which appeared in almost every interview dating from this period: "Jazz is Black Heritage and a true American art form, which is spiritual and healing to the soul."

While many seasoned jazz musicians shared Mary's thoughts, few had spoken publicly. As was the case in the 1940s when bebop emerged, dissension was brewing within the jazz community. As the scene grew more competitive and audiences became smaller, many of the early figures of modern jazz began to speak up. In 1979 the singer Betty Carter broke her silence during an interview with *Down Beat.* She spoke against what she called "intellectual shit," that is, what most referred to as avant-garde. She thought that the jazz tradition, which she and others had fought hard to legitimize and develop, was "lying in ruin." She blamed the leaders of the free jazz movement for the dulled senses of the "uneducated" younger generation. "You're gonna sit in a loft and say, 'I'm a genius'? You don't say that. We tell you that—after you have done your groundwork and you're on the job training on stage. In front of us you make mistakes; you do your thing and you grow. It's okay for you to make mistakes, but you can't do it unless you work."

> Charlie Parker didn't complain; he worked. He worked until he died. Anywhere for anybody. And he did his thing. He didn't sit back and say, I'm the greatest so I don't need to do this and I don't need to do that and when you come and catch me I'll show you I'm the greatest. And most of your listeners go there and don't accept it, but you say, "I'm supposed to accept it." Be honest. If you don't like it, you don't like it. I'm being honest because I think they cheated you by not giving you everything they had to give. You're getting intellectual shit and you're suppose to dig it because you're in-tell-ec-tu-al. . . . They have a reasonable excuse for . . . what they're doing, but the only excuse is money. In order for you to get with a top notch record company you're going to have to do what they want you to do.[45]

Carter repeated Mary's view that the black community had turned away from jazz because of the complexity of the avant-garde movement. "Nobody admits [it], but free jazz and the late years of Coltrane turned black people away from the music. They did not absorb it. They cannot relate to free non-rhythmic music. Black people are used to rhythm, African rhythm. Rhythms. Tempo. Beat. The moment the music got free you gathered more whites and lost blacks."[46] Mary and Carter both took criticism for their views but were unapologetic. Chuck Berg, a critic for *Down Beat,* accused Mary of being arrogant and charged her with making "narrow, misguided and incomprehensible pronouncements."[47] But she remained devoted to her efforts to reeducate Americans about jazz and took her "gospel of jazz" lecture across the country, presenting it at recreation centers, public schools, and colleges.

During the fall of 1975 Mary had returned to the Cookery, but with a new bassist. Twenty-one-year-old Brian Torff had earned the spot as

Mary's accompanist after several others auditioned unsuccessfully. He was young, naïve, and overwhelmed by being in Mary's presence, but under her loving and stern tutelage he developed into a fine jazz bassist. His three-month stint with Mary at the club developed into a live recording for Chiaroscuro. Called *Live at the Cookery*, the recording, a project of Hank O'Neal, captured the ambience of the live setting, especially the spontaneity and creativity that live performances generate. It was the last project Mary produced for O'Neal's label and the first of four produced in the last six years of her life. In 1977 Peter O'Brien collaborated with Moe Asch to release a collection of the recordings Mary had produced for his label in the 1940s. Made from the original 78-rpm discs, the two-record set chronicled Mary's transition from band member to soloist, from swing pianist to convert of bebop, and from big band arranger to jazz composer. The limitations of technology meant that some of the sides were slightly distorted, but these technical blemishes did not prevent the final product from being heralded as "one of the finest reissues of 1977."[48]

*　*　*

The debate between the modernists and traditionalists took a surprising turn in the 1970s. Mirroring the musical debates of the 1940s over the emergence of bebop, this schism sought definitive answers to the question "What is jazz?" Of course, this question was not easily answered, especially as fusion, in all its manifestations, began to dominate the scene. This conflict pitted the traditionalists, largely represented by the purveyors of bebop and earlier jazz styles, against the modernists, the subscribers to the avant-garde, free jazz, and fusion movements. Just as it seemed no real resolution would be found, two unlikely people extended musical olive branches to each other and decided to create a musical fusion of both sides for one night. The jazz world took note in early 1977 when Mary Lou Williams announced she and avant-gardist Cecil Taylor would present a collaborative concert at Carnegie Hall on April 17.

For forty years, Carnegie Hall had served as the setting for many historic performances in jazz: Benny Goodman's 1938 concert, Duke Ellington's 1943 debut of *Black, Brown, and Beige,* and the 1945 performance of portions of Mary's *Zodiac Suite.* But this event carried particular importance. It marked the coming together of the musical factions. Most were unaware that Cecil Taylor and Mary Lou Williams had much in common musically, philosophically, and personally. The two had performed at the 1957 Newport Jazz Festival. Taylor was a young, introverted pianist who was exploring the various dimensions of rhythm and combining his conservatory training with the tenets of jazz. Mary was not particularly drawn to him at the time, but she became better acquainted with him in 1969 when she stopped in at Ronnie Scott's in London after performing at the Jazz Expo. Mary's opinion of Taylor's playing changed. She wrote, "I felt great warmth from him. Being a creative and searching kind of musician, such as I am, Cecil thrilled me with his integrity and originality." She referred to him as "My Giant of the Avant-Garde." [49] When Mary began playing at the Cookery, Taylor would come in and listen. He often said to her, "No one's playing anything but you." Mary thought he was just putting her on, but he came back every night. In 1975 they performed opposite each other at the Composers' Showcase at the Whitney Museum. Finally, during one of Taylor's visits to the Cookery, Mary asked if he would consider their doing a concert together. He agreed and suggested the performance be called Embraced, because it was the joining of varying generations of music.

The public and the media viewed the concert as a declaration of solidarity between the mainstream and the avant-garde; it would be the first time "so vivid a confrontation between generations—and stylistic conventions—[had] taken place. It [was] undeniably a seventies event." [50] Mary attempted to raise funds for the event in her usual manner of soliciting friends, but the majority of the funding came from her own savings. Although each musician insisted that the concert was a musical collaboration and not a competition, tensions began brewing during the rehearsals. Mary wanted to use a rhythm section, but she did not consult Taylor as to his preference. He was overpowering her and not conforming to the idea of collaboration. She wanted Taylor to play an arrangement of the spirituals she had written, but he refused to use a written score.

By the day of the concert, Taylor was angry. Nevertheless, the concert went on, but not without problems. During the first half the sound was not balanced, so each piano dominated on its own side. Taylor seemed unresponsive to Mary's give-and-take approach to each composition and attempted to overpower her. The program began with Mary's composition "The Lord Is Heavy," followed by the rag composition "Fandangle," a blues called "The Blues Never Left Me," the Kansas

City–style swing number "K.C. 12th Street," some boogie-woogie, and a bop-inspired composition called "Basic Chords (Bop Changes on the Blues)." According to Gary Giddins,

> The first set was continuous. It began with a rocking, spiritual-like piece started by Williams and amplified by Taylor, followed by a quite charming rag. Taylor soon shot off into the upper register with a characteristic flurry, while Williams cool-handedly searched for propitious moments to jump in. The predetermined format tended to fragment his solos, with the not unattractive effect of making them highlight passages: He was never given more than a few minutes to flex his muscles before getting strong-armed into the next movement. Some transitional back building ensued, leading to an apparently serendipitous Taylor train rhythm, with colorful comments from the second piano. [Mickey] Roker and [Bob] Cranshaw entered, precipitating an assertive boogie-break and solo by Williams, whose strength of touch was much in evidence."[51]

Another critic wrote, "It often seemed as if the two pianists were simply playing at the same time on the same stage, nothing more."[52]

The second set was much more effective. With the amplification problems corrected and the pianists settling into a more cohesive performance, the concert seemed salvageable. But the tide changed again. "Taylor bounded into his own world, entranced and intractable, and Williams was back on the outside looking in. Retaliation came quickly as Roker and Cranshaw rejoined them, initiating a straight four. This was the chance for the lady to strut her stuff, and she did so jubilantly, with Taylor laying out. Her cohorts were rewarded with solos, after which all three turned silently to Taylor, the stranger in a strange land, who responded lustily for (a mere) ten minutes. All four united for a finish that Taylor seemed to regard as premature. They bowed and walked off."[53] Everyone but Taylor returned to the stage for an encore. Mary played "A Night in Tunisia" and "Bag's Groove" with Cranshaw and Roker, and followed it up with an unaccompanied version of "I Can't Get Started." Taylor later explained that he had always planned to leave the stage, to allow Mary to play alone.[54] But it was clear that

Taylor was very angry. In a rare interview, he said, "I rehearsed everything, but she didn't rehearse none of my music." Mary's response was "I didn't have to rehearse it—all I do is pretend I'm crazy!" [55]

The concert was deemed a "noble failure" and broke even with the house. Less than a year later, Norman Granz's recording of the concert would appear on his Pablo label, one of two projects involving Mary on that label, and it received the same mixed response as the concert had. Brother Mario Hancock, who had returned to the United States in 1976, recalled that following the concert he, O'Brien, and Mary went out to dinner, and she said, "He couldn't beat me. He tried. He tried [but] I gave him a hard way to go. He wanted to really make a fool of me, but I told him who I was." She knew she was the greatest woman in jazz. [56]

Chapter 13

THE FRUIT OF ONE'S LABOR

I have fought the good fight, I have finished the race, I have kept the faith. Now there is in store for me the crown of righteousness, which the Lord, the righteous Judge, will award to me on that day.

—2 Timothy 4:7–8

As the 1970s progressed and perceptions of jazz continued to change, Mary found herself the beneficiary of a new and expanding appreciation of her craft. After decades of fighting for the legitimacy of jazz, it seemed as if Americans were finally ready to accept the cultural connections they had with the music. No longer limited to the recorded performances, festivals, and nightclub runs that had been the most vital forms of dissemination, jazz in the 1970s could once again be heard on radio.

National Public Radio had contributed to this renewal with its live jazz programming and expanded formatting on college radio stations. It provided an alternative to mainstream programming and chipped away at the dominance of both commercial radio and network television. The

Smithsonian Institution's interest in jazz also inspired new programming initiatives. In 1975 it began its Jazz Heritage Series of performances and lectures. The program was later expanded to include an oral history project, which consisted of interviews of jazz performers chronicling their experiences and the evolution of jazz, an anthology of classic jazz, and other specialty recordings. But it was the integration of jazz into the curricula of public schools and colleges that affected Mary's life most directly.

In 1976 Duke University in Durham, North Carolina, offered Mary the opportunity to teach jazz history and direct the school's jazz ensemble. Under the direction of President Terry Sanford, a former state governor, a series of faculty positions had been created to increase staff diversity. Because the number of faculty positions was limited, departments were chosen for the program on the basis of their ability to recruit and retain top faculty. The department of music, chaired by the jazz scholar and saxophonist Frank Tirro, was awarded one of these positions. Tirro thought the department could best be served by the acquisition of a notable jazz performer. He put together a list of possible candidates and conferred with his administrative assistant, Marian Turner. Turner shared Tirro's love for jazz and often played the music on the radio near her desk. Her appreciation was rooted in her family's experiences at Alabama Agricultural and Mechanical University, where her father had served as the band director and was a notable member of the college's faculty. When she enrolled in college at Virginia State University in Petersburg, Virginia, two of her classmates were Camilla Williams and Billy Taylor. Both had gone on to great heights, in opera and jazz, respectively. So, naturally, when Tirro asked Turner for suggestions, she recommended Billy Taylor. Since Turner and her husband had maintained a relationship with the pianist, Tirro asked if she would make the call. She called Taylor, who thought it was an excellent opportunity but worried that the structured schedule of the university would adversely affect his ability to travel and perform. He suggested that Turner call Mary Lou Williams, explaining that her work with community-based choirs and college choirs and jazz bands had made her a perfect candidate. With Tirro's agreement, Turner called Mary. She was surprised to find herself speaking directly to Mary, who then steered her to Peter O'Brien. O'Brien said he wanted to discuss the matter thoroughly with Mary.

When Mary had not agreed to the offer after a few weeks, Tirro invited Mary and O'Brien to visit the campus. The two boarded a bus for

Durham. The small southern city was rapidly growing, as it was at the apex of the "Research Triangle," which was attracting industry and people to the area. The city was much different from what Mary remembered from playing there in the 1930s. The Kirk band had been booked there during an East Coast tour and had found its activities dictated by segregation laws. Mary and the other members of the band had been forced to stay in the black area of Durham, then called Haiti. It was a self-sustaining neighborhood with the same entrepreneurship and communal spirit as the Eighteenth and Vine district in Kansas City, the Mount Vernon area in Columbus, Ohio, Beale Street in Memphis, and Auburn Avenue in Atlanta. The growth, expansion, and desegregation of Durham had robbed the area of its vitality, and only weeds remained where black hotels, restaurants, and residences once lined the streets. Durham now boasted a growing, active black middle class, whose lifestyle mirrored that of their white counterparts. The natural beauty of the Duke campus and the slow pace and eclectic nature of Durham appealed to Mary, who, despite her attempts to ignore the signs, was feeling the effects of her age. The pain she suffered in her joints, especially her wrists, and her chronic backaches, which dated back to the 1960s, had worsened.

Mary returned to New York undecided. In one last effort to woo Mary to the school, Tirro came to New York, where he discussed the offer and the benefits of the position. According to Peter, Mary listened to Tirro's proposition, cooked for him, and played for him. But she did not take the offer seriously, and although Tirro thought he had won Mary over, she still refused to consider the offer. Tirro asked her what type of salary she would like. Her response was $100,000. According to Brother Mario, Tirro explained that some of the faculty with Ph.D.'s didn't get that much, even with tenure. She responded, "I have an MLW." He said, "What's that?" "A Mary Lou Williams." Mario recalled, "That's what she said at Duke University and she got the job. I guess she got the money too. But she knew she was a powerful person, although she was very shy in many ways."[1]

Mary finally decided to accept the offer, but the closer she came to signing the contract and preparing to move, the more apprehensive she grew. When the letter arrived confirming the offer, "I didn't even look [at it]. When the letters came and the contracts—I just left it in the envelope. Didn't even think about it because it meant a big uprooting. You're in

New York doing one thing. Concert after concert, work after work, traveling and this. And all of a sudden you have to rearrange. You drop everything. I had a job I had to leave, move, find a house. It meant a big change."[2] Mary finally signed the contract in the spring of 1977 and prepared to enter the next phase of her life.

O'Brien was on the phone with a real estate agent in Durham throughout the summer. He returned to Durham alone shortly before the start of school to finalize the purchase of a home pending Mary's approval, a nine-room house on Shepherd Street. Until the closing took place, Mary stayed at a hotel called the Downtowner. She was given the position of artist-in-residence, which superseded past affiliations between the department and musicians that were only temporary. Her responsibilities included teaching an introductory jazz history course and jazz improvisation. She would also direct the university's jazz ensemble, which provided an outlet for compositions. It was a good period in her life and the only time in her sixty-seven years that she owned her own home and had a regular salary with the benefit of health insurance.[3] Mary found it hard to believe that the arrangement was legitimate and that the university would honor the contract. Past experience had taught her that contracts didn't mean anything, and you could be penniless and jobless without notice. But Marian Turner assured her that Tirro and the university would stand by the deal.

Mary's first contract was for only two years, 1977–79, but during the second semester of the first year she signed on for three more years. Here was Mary, a black woman who had not graduated from high school and never taken a college course, teaching as a college professor. She could hardly believe it. After years of struggle—fighting against the racism that said she was inferior because of her color, against the sexism that said her place was not on stage or on record but in the kitchen, serving as someone's maid or providing for her husband, against the professional jealousy that had robbed her of her proper place in jazz history and had stunted her professional advancement—Mary had entered a period of happiness, stability, and security. Despite her teaching load, the contract allowed her to continue performing. At first she had problems adjusting to life in North Carolina. She wasn't much of a party person, even when she lived in New York or visited family in Pittsburgh, and she had often isolated herself in her apartment. But her life now required her to socialize. She was quite reluctant, but Marian Turner kept pushing her.

Turner understood Mary's hesitation but assured her that there was nothing to fear. In time the two became the best of friends; other than O'Brien and a graduate student named Marsha Vick, Marian was the only person Mary trusted fully during this period. At first Mary limited her social appearances to functions at the university, but in time, through the efforts of Turner and her decision to worship at Holy Cross Church, an African-American parish that had existed since the 1930s, she came to know and befriend townspeople. Marsha Vick and Marian Turner spent much time with Mary; the women would often sit around and talk and laugh about Mary's experiences.

While Mary's professional life was improving, her personal relationship with O'Brien suffered. When Mary accepted Duke's offer, O'Brien naturally decided to move with her in order to continue as her manager and assist her in teaching the jazz history course. He was granted a one-year leave from his job at St. Ignatius Loyola and joined Mary in Durham, but he had no steady income, because Duke had hired only Mary, not him. He had no financial support, no medical insurance, and no place for himself outside Mary's life. He recalled, "When I went to Duke with Mary I was told, 'Yeah, you can go, but you're on your own.' So everything—insurance, everything—I had to earn." [4] He lived with Mary for just a few days before he decided their relationship could be salvaged only if he moved to the rectory of Holy Cross Church. For the next year, Peter survived on his 10 percent commission from Mary's concerts and a salary of $135 a week. His financial struggles increased his tensions with Mary. He could barely afford his rent and food, but Mary bought expensive things for her home and herself and saved the rest. His anger brewed and he decided to seek help. "I went into analysis in Durham; I got so angry, I can't remember what it was, but the rage was so great. It must have built up over a period of time that was a rough period down there. The first year in Durham—'77 to '78, the rage was so great that I finally got a shrink." [5] The therapy eased O'Brien's anger, and by the second semester of the first year the two had reconciled. What has been previously reported as a tense and strained relationship during the Duke years was actually a very happy time for them both. O'Brien emerged out of the shadow of his role as Mary's manager and established his own life in Durham. In fact, he would often return to the city following Mary's out-of-town gigs and trips to New York and Pittsburgh.

The climate of Duke was surprising to Mary when she arrived. She found the black students distant, while the white students packed her office and classroom, hoping for an opportunity to talk with her. In the months preceding her arrival, the white students had stirred with excitement. The black students, who constituted only a small percentage of the school's total enrollment, had very little knowledge of who she was and what the hype was all about. Their reaction confirmed what Mary had been saying for the past ten years—that blacks no longer had a cultural link to jazz and that black youth for the most part had no knowledge of jazz or its purveyors.

On the first day of class, Mary had about thirty students. She opened the course with a discussion of the history of jazz, and O'Brien played recorded musical examples. Mary captured their attention with her free method of discussing and integrating them into the course's material. "Usually you have kids squirming and leaving, but mine sit with their hands crossed and *listen,*" she recalled. "There's so much love when they leave, they go out laughing." [6] Word about the course spread, and the next day the enrollment had doubled to over sixty students. By the second semester of class, the enrollment had increased so much that the course had to be moved to an auditorium. More than seven hundred students had requested the class, but the enrollment was limited to 150 for two sections (morning and afternoon). Her classes became the most popular on campus, and sales of jazz albums in the area increased by 40 percent. Mary's pedagogical approach differed from the manner in which most mainstream jazz instructors taught. She operated on the premise that jazz could not be learned from a book, so she encouraged her students to listen carefully to her playing, then join in with their own vocal improvisation. This would open them up to the music in a way that books could not. She would take a similar approach in the rehearsals of the jazz ensemble, urging them to sing their arrangements first, before playing a note.

After her first semester Mary returned to New York, where she recorded a series of sessions for Pablo Records. Norman Granz, a longtime fan of Mary's work, gave her complete creative control. The result was a sixteen-track retrospective of Mary's experimentations with the blues. *My Mama Pinned a Rose on Me* (Pablo 2310–819) featured the vocalist Cynthia Tyson, whom Mary had met in Durham, on various tracks and Buster Williams on bass. Included on the LP were "Dirge Blues," written in 1963 to commemorate the assassination of President Kennedy;

"Blues for Peter," written for O'Brien; and "N.G. Blues," written for Norman Granz.

Upon its release, the LP received five stars from *Down Beat* and was called a "welcome relief."[7] Just before *My Mama* came the release of *The History of Jazz,* recorded for Moe Asch eight years earlier. But the highlights of Mary's career in 1978 were her appearances at various nightclubs and jazz festivals throughout Europe. By summer's end Mary had performed at the Montreux Jazz Festival in Switzerland; the Grand Parade du Jazz in Nice; the North Sea Jazz Festival at the Hague in the Netherlands; and Ronnie Scott's in London.

By the beginning of the 1978–79 school year Mary had strengthened her place in jazz history with her string of recordings and highly acclaimed live performances. But she was beginning to feel more pain in her joints, stomach, and back than usual. Although she was slow to admit it, she was also tiring more easily, and her hearing loss greatly disturbed her. She was never one to complain, however, and just continued to work at a feverish pace. She began to worry only when her urine consistently showed blood. Not wishing to discuss such personal matters with O'Brien, Mary went to Marian Turner, who suggested she see a doctor. The doctor told her to check into the hospital immediately; her condition was not simply a kidney or urinary tract infection but bladder cancer. Because the disease rarely responded to conventional treatment in advanced stages, the doctor stressed to Mary the importance of having a biopsy to determine the progression of the disease. But Mary wanted some time to think over the situation. Keeping the doctor's revelation to herself, Mary boarded a bus and headed for a gig in Washington, D.C. While there she spent a couple of days with Mario Hancock, who had been transferred to Howard University. The two talked about the diagnosis and Mary decided to undergo the biopsy.

The test revealed stage III bladder cancer, meaning that Mary would have to begin treatment as soon as possible. The doctors were not sure if they could totally eradicate the cancer; they would concentrate on preventing its spread. The diagnosis and subsequent treatments did nothing to slow Mary down. At sixty-nine she was more determined than ever, with or without cancer, to continue performing and teaching. She taught twice a day, two days a week, and spent most of her weekends traveling from city to city performing. O'Brien believed that Mary would overcome the disease and continued to secure bookings for her. More of a personal blow to Mary than her own diagnosis was the revelation that her sister Mamie was dying. Mary immediately left for Pittsburgh and arrived in time to see and talk with Mamie during the last days of her life. Mamie's death, more than her mother's in 1974, affected Mary deeply. She had maintained a strong and loving relationship with the one sibling who had endured the harsh poverty and loneliness of her early years in Atlanta and Pittsburgh. When Mary left Pittsburgh in 1979, she never returned. It was as if the city was a painful reminder and an empty place without her beloved sister.

In spite of the urgings of physicians and friends, Mary continued to perform frequently throughout 1979. Even on her worst days she would remark, in martyr-like fashion, "God loves me," reminding those around her that the disease was just one of the many crosses she had to bear. In the summer of 1979, she returned to New York and informed Barney Josephson that she was leaving the Cookery for its rival the Knickerbocker. Josephson was upset, of course, but he could not persuade Mary to stay. She wowed audiences as usual and set a new standard for her performances when, on one particularly noisy night, she made the audience sing her tune "Rosa Mae." "Wait a minute," she shouted at the audience. "I'm trying to bring some love or something to you. But you aren't paying any attention. You know I have only one good ear. I can't hear my chords." She informed the onlookers that she wanted them to sing with her. She would sing one stanza and have the audience repeat it. It was a hit, and from that point on, no one made excessive noise during Mary's stints at the Knickerbocker.[8] She also performed at the Spoleto Festival in Charleston, South Carolina, and the Atlanta Free Jazz Festival, where the Clark College Jazz Orchestra (now Clark Atlanta University) performed excerpts from *Mary Lou's Mass*.

Mary returned to Duke energized in spirit but weak in body. Despite her diminishing health, she traveled to Richmond, Virginia, for the first of three visits sponsored by the Special Arts Project of the Emergency School Aid Act. During the trip, orchestrated by D. Antoinette Handy, Mary gave a public concert, a master class to public school teachers, and two youth concerts. The schedule was grueling, but Mary enjoyed the interaction she had, particularly with the young people. Five months later, in April 1980, she would return to the area, this time as Virginia State University's resident eminent scholar. Mary spent three days there lecturing and working with the students at the predominantly black university. The culminating event of her stay was supposed to be her final public concert, but miscommunication between the maintenance crew and the music department resulted in the piano's not being tuned. According to members of the audience, Mary sat at the piano, played through a few songs, then got up and asked one of the faculty members where she could get some good fish. It was hilarious but indicative of Mary's attitude. (Her visit made such an impact on students and faculty at Virginia State that when I matriculated there several years later, the infamous concert incident was still being discussed.)

Mary's physical condition continued to decline in 1980, but she remained hopeful that God was going to perform a miracle. She was determined not to stop living or playing just because she had some disease. But in early 1980, doctors discovered that her cancer had spread to her uterus. They immediately scheduled Mary for major surgery that would remove her bladder and uterus. As those around her braced themselves for what they thought was going to be a painful period in Mary's life, she remained optimistic. During her recuperation in the hospital, she asked that a piano be brought in so that she could keep working on the arrangements she had written for the jazz ensemble. The hospital obliged her and soon she was entertaining patients and staff with her playing. She seemed to recover quickly from the surgery, no doubt because she had been allowed to continue playing her music, but she felt more pain in her back. The cancer was steadily spreading and was now in her spine. In addition to the excruciating pain she experienced daily, Mary was now forced to wear an ostomy bag. Sooner or later she would have to face the fact that her condition was deteriorating and that the treatments were not working.

Mary faced her mortality and began working to start another foundation that would revive the dream that had been deferred by the dissolution of the Bel Canto Foundation. Where Bel Canto had been therapeutic, this new foundation would be educational—catering to children ages six to twelve. The purpose of the Mary Lou Williams Foundation would be to provide scholarships to gifted children for instruction with established jazz musicians. With the foundation established, Mary began setting her personal affairs in order.

Despite Mary's attempts to work through the pain of the cancer, the symptoms and treatments were taking their toll. By early 1981 she was no longer able to teach her classes. She focused instead on completing a new composition chronicling the history of jazz. A grant from the National Endowment for the Arts and her salary from Duke enabled her to concentrate totally on the work without worrying about household and medical expenses. She worked diligently on the piece, often referring to it as her "wind symphony." But her strength was waning and she could not work for long periods of time.

On Valentine's Day O'Brien held a party at Mary's house that included more than sixty guests. The filmmaker Joanne Burke, who was creating a documentary on Mary's life and career, recorded the event, showing the pianist playing, surrounded by her family and friends—for what would be the last time.

O'Brien, no longer in denial about Mary's condition, contacted Brother Mario, informing him that if he wanted to see Mary, he needed to come soon. Mario came but found Mary in a semiconscious, drugged state. When she was lucid enough to talk with him, she simply said, "I'm tired." O'Brien and Mary's younger sister Geraldine worked to make Mary as comfortable as possible. Her treatment progressed to hospice care and she spent a great deal of the time sleeping.

However, on May 10, two days after her seventy-first birthday, Mary was recognized with a special award at Duke. (Unable to walk, Mary did not attend the graduation ceremonies. President Sanford presented her with the award later at her home.) She became the first person to receive the Trinity Award, created to recognize service from a faculty member to the university.[9] It seemed a fitting tribute to a woman who had given so much of herself for the advancement of her people and their culture. She celebrated the moment, but she knew she did not have much more time.

On May 28, 1981, Mary Lou Williams, jazz pianist, composer, lover, wife, and friend, made her transition at home in the presence of the nurses who had worked tirelessly to treat her. O'Brien and Marsha Vick wrote her obituary, and her body was prepared for the trip back to New York. Her body lay in state for two days at the Campbell Funeral Home at Eighty-first Street and Madison. On June 1 friends and family filled St. Ignatius Loyola Church to pay their last respects to Mary. The critic Gary Giddins delivered a eulogy that highlighted Mary's contributions in the face of the sexism of the jazz world. Dizzy Gillespie, who had been Mary's close friend since their early years in New York during the 1940s, played a stirring solo version of his composition "Con Alma." Mary's protégé Hilton Ruiz played "Medi II," and Buster Williams, who had worked often with Mary during the previous five years, performed "I Love You." Marian McPartland, who had counted Mary as one of her early musical role models, played "What's Your Story, Morning Glory?," and the choir that had participated in the original recording of *Music for Peace* sang selections from her religious opus. It was a deeply moving service, filled with loving musical tributes to a woman who had brought so much to the lives of others through her music. After the funeral, Mary's body was transported to Pittsburgh for another funeral and final burial. On June 3, at Saints Peter and Paul Catholic Church in East Liberty, Mary's friends and family gathered for a final tribute. She was interred in Calvary Cemetery, close to other family members who had passed on. But death did not silence the musical voice of Mary Lou Williams.

On June 20, 1981, a concert celebrating the life of Mary Lou Williams was held. Called *A Song of Love for Mary Lou Williams,* the event served as a memorial to the pianist, with the proceeds going to the Mary Lou Williams Foundation. It was produced by Cobi Narita of the Universal Jazz Coalition and featured many of Mary's close friends performing her music. Carline Ray and Honi Gordon sang excerpts from *Mary Lou's Mass,* and the pianists Barbara Carroll, Rose Murphy, and Hazel Scott performed some of Mary's compositions. An eighteen-minute segment of Joanne Burke's documentary *Mary Lou Williams: Music on My Mind* was shown. An ensemble that included Buddy Tate, Budd Johnson, Charlie Rouse, Al Grey, Britt Woodman, Jack Jeffers, Ernie Royal, Jon Faddis, Jaki Byard, Buster Williams, and Mickey Roker played some of Mary's big band arrangements. It was a fitting final tribute to a woman who had defied the odds and endured many hardships and struggles just to make good music.

NOTES

CHAPTER I

1. Mary Lou Williams, interview by John Wilson, July 26, 1977, transcript, National Endowment for the Arts/Institute of Jazz Studies. Referred to hereafter as the Mary Lou Williams Oral History Project.
2. Geraldine Garnett, interview by author, July 15, 2001. Many sources have mistakenly assumed that Virginia married Winn after the birth of Mary, but the family insists that it was before.
3. Mary Lou Williams Oral History Project.
4. Geraldine Garnett and Bobbie Ferguson, interview by author, August 31, 2002.
5. Linda Dahl, *Morning Glory: A Biography of Mary Lou Williams* (New York: Pantheon Books, 1999), 13.
6. LeRoi Jones (Amiri Baraka), *Blues People: Negro Music in White America* (New York: William Morrow, 1963), 52.

7. Angela Davis, *Women, Race, and Class* (New York: Vintage Books, 1983), 87–88. For more information on the working conditions of black women, see Paula Giddings, *When and Where I Enter: The Impact of Black Women on Race and Sex in America* (New York: William Morrow, 1984), and Tera Hunter, *To 'Joy My Freedom: Southern Black Women's Lives and Labors after the Civil War* (Cambridge: Harvard University Press, 1997).

8. Mary Lou Williams, "Mary Lou Williams: Musician as Healer," interview by Melinda Mousouris, *Village Voice,* July 23, 1979, 82.

9. For more information about the Sanctified Church and worship within the churches of the movement, see Cheryl J. Sanders, *Saints in Exile: The Holiness-Pentecostal Experience in African American Religion and Culture* (New York: Oxford University Press, 1996).

10. This story is recounted in various interviews. Among them are Mary Lou Williams, "The Mary Lou Williams Story," interview by Les Tomkins, *Crescendo International* 9 (July 1971): 6–7; Joan Kufrin, *Uncommon Women* (Piscataway, N.J.: New Century Publishers, 1981), 155–73; Mary Unterbrink, *Jazz Women at the Keyboard* (Jefferson, N.C.: McFarland, 1983), 31–51.

11. D. Antoinette Handy, "Conversation with Mary Lou Williams: First Lady of the Jazz Keyboard," *Black Perspective in Music* 8, no. 2 (fall 1980): 198.

12. Williams, "Mary Lou Williams: Musician as Healer," 82.

13. The exact date of Virginia's marriage to Burley is not known, as family members were unable to document it, but it is known that the two were married before moving to Pittsburgh.

14. Peter Gottlieb, "Reaching Pittsburgh," in *Making Their Own Way: Southern Blacks' Migration to Pittsburgh, 1916–1930* (Urbana: University of Illinois Press, 1987), 42.

15. Ibid., 39–62.

16. P. Gottlieb, "Places in the City," in *Making Their Own Way,* 66.

17. Mary Lou Williams Oral History Project.

18. Mary Lou Williams, as quoted in Kufrin, *Uncommon Women,* 159.

19. Mary Lou Williams Oral History Project.

20. Garnett and Ferguson, interview.

CHAPTER 2

1. For more information on the experience of migrants in Pittsburgh, see Abraham Epstein, *The Negro Migrant in Pittsburgh* (New York: Arno Press and the New York Times, 1969).

2. Ibid., 13.

3. Jervis Anderson, *This Was Harlem: A Cultural Portrait, 1900–1950* (New York: Farrar, Straus and Giroux, 1982), 152.

4. Ibid.

5. Ira De A. Reid, "Mrs. Bailey Pays Her Rent," in *The New Negro Renaissance*, ed. Arthur P. Davis and Michael W. Peplow (New York: Holt, Rinehart, and Winston, 1975), 164–72. Also quoted in Anderson, *This Was Harlem*, 153.

6. Garnett and Ferguson, interview.

7. Mary Lou Williams Oral History Project.

8. Ibid.

9. Ibid.

10. Ibid.

11. Ibid.

12. Robert Gottlieb, "Mary Lou Williams," in *Reading Jazz: A Gathering of Autobiography, Reportage, and Criticism from 1919 to Now,* ed. Robert Gottlieb (New York: Pantheon Books, 1996), 88.

13. Mary Lou Williams Oral History Project.

14. For discussion on women and attitudes about public performance, see Judith Tick, "Passed Away Is the Piano Girl: Changes in American Musical Life, 1870–1900," in *Women Making Music: The Western Art Tradition, 1150–1950,* ed. Jane Bowers and Judith Tick (Urbana and Chicago: University of Illinois, 1986), 325–48.

15. John Chilton, "McKinney's Cotton Pickers," in *The New Grove Dictionary of Jazz,* ed. Barry Kernfeld (New York: St. Martin's Press, 1995), 736. Also see Gunther Schuller, *The History of Jazz,* vol. 1, *Early Jazz: Its Roots and Musical Development* (New York: Oxford University Press, 1968).

16. Mel Watkins, *On the Real Side: Laughing, Lying, and Signifying: The Underground Tradition of African-American Humor That Transformed American Culture, from Slavery to Richard Pryor* (New York: Simon and Schuster, 1994), 155–56.

17. There are many conflicting accounts of the genesis of the TOBA. Some attribute the founding to F. A. Barrasso, a Memphis-based Italian businessman who owned several theaters in the South. It is believed he started the TOBA in 1907. Other sources attribute it to Sherman Dudley. Dudley was connected with the administration of the circuit and may have been a manager or booking agent but was not the creator of the TOBA. For information on the TOBA, see Watkins, *On the Real Side;* Daphne Duval Harrison, *Black Pearls: Blues Queens of the 1920s* (New Brunswick, N.J.: Rutgers University Press, 1998); Athelia Knight, "In Retrospect: Sherman Dudley: He Paved the Way for TOBA," *Black Perspective in Music* 15, no. 2 (fall

1987): 153–81; Marshall Stearns and Jean Stearns, *Jazz Dance: The Story of American Vernacular Dance* (New York: Schirmer Books, 1968), 75–84; Langston Hughes and Milton Meltzer, *Black Magic* (Englewood Cliffs, N.J: Prentice-Hall, 1967), 67–72.

18. Watkins, *On the Real Side,* 367.

19. Unterbrink, *Jazz Women,* 34–35.

20. Williams, "Mary Lou Williams Story," 6. Also in R. Gottlieb, "Mary Lou Williams."

21. Mary Lou Williams Oral History Project.

22. Earl Hines (1903–1983) was born and raised in Pittsburgh. He later went to Chicago, where he played with numerous groups, including one led by Louis Armstrong. He was most notable as a bandleader and featured many important jazz musicians, including Dizzy Gillespie, Charlie Parker, and Sarah Vaughan. Erskine Tate (1895–1978) led the resident orchestra at the Vendome Theatre in Chicago from 1919 to 1928. His orchestra served as the training ground for many notable musicians, including Louis Armstrong, Earl Hines, Milt Hinton, and Freddie Keppard. For more information, see *New Grove Dictionary of Jazz.*

23. Mary Lou Williams, "Mary Lou Williams: A Diamond Mouthful," *Melody Maker,* April 10, 1954.

24. Ibid.

25. For additional information, see Albert McCarthy, *Big Band Jazz* (New York: G. P. Putnam's Sons, 1974), 242–46. The quotations from John Williams are from a taped interview by the author in Columbus, Ohio, February 4, 1995.

26. John Williams, interview.

27. Watkins, *On the Real Side,* 365–66. See also Garnett Warrington, "Big Protest: Conditions at Atlanta and Pensacola Cause Righteous Indignation," *Chicago Defender,* October 8, 1921.

28. John Williams, interview.

29. Ibid.

30. Ibid.

31. Perry Bradford (1893–1970) was a singer, musician, bandleader, and writer who was active mainly in the 1920s. He is sometimes called the "King of the Blues" or "Mule" and is credited with the first recording of an African American singer. Bernard L. Peterson Jr., *Profiles of African American Stage Performers and Theatre People, 1816–1960* (Westport, Conn.: Greenwood Press, 2001), 29–30, 299.

32. Williams, "Mary Lou Williams: A Diamond Mouthful."

33. Ibid.

34. Ibid.

35. John Williams, interview.

36. Williams, "Mary Lou Williams: A Diamond Mouthful."
37. Information on Harlem is from Anderson, *This Was Harlem,* and Roi Ottley, *New World A-Coming* (Boston: Houghton Mifflin, 1943).
38. Mary Lou Williams Oral History Project.
39. For more information on Fats Waller, see Alyn Shipton and Bill Dobbins, "Fats Waller," in *New Grove Dictionary, of Jazz,* 1257–60. Connie's Inn moved downtown to West 48th Street in 1933 and continued in operation until 1936. For more information on Connie's Inn and other venues in New York, see "Nightclubs and Other Venues: U.S.A., New York," *New Grove Dictionary of Jazz,* 892.
40. Quoted in Unterbrink, *Jazz Women,* 35.
41. Clarence Williams was a composer and pianist who traveled as a singer and dancer with minstrel shows. Later he founded a music publishing company and several music stores. Jelly Roll Morton was best known as an itinerant pianist whose compositions aided in the standardization of the New Orleans style of jazz. He was the composer of "Grandpa's Spells," "Black Bottom Stomp," and "King Porter Stomp," which are jazz standards.

CHAPTER 3

1. For more information on segregation, see C. Vann Woodward, *The Strange Career of Jim Crow,* 2d rev. ed. (New York: Oxford University Press, 1966).
2. Larry Nager, *Memphis Beat: The Lives and Times of America's Musical Crossroads* (New York: St. Martin's Press, 1998), 47.
3. Nager, *Memphis Beat,* 51–52.
4. Giles Oakley, *The Devil's Music: A History of the Blues* (New York: Taplinger, 1977), 145.
5. Ibid., 146.
6. Ibid.
7. Ibid.
8. Mary Lou Williams, "Mary Lou on the Clouds of Joy," *Melody Maker,* April 17, 1954, 5.
9. Mary Lou Williams Oral History Project.
10. Ibid.
11. This contradicts most accounts of how Williams became a part of the band. John stated that he was contacted by telegram and that, contrary to popular belief, he was not stranded in Oklahoma with the Seymour and Jeanette tour.
12. Andy Kirk and Amy Lee, *Twenty Years on Wheels* (Ann Arbor: University of Michigan Press, 1989).
13. Nathan W. Pearson Jr., *Goin' to Kansas City* (Urbana and Chicago: University of Illinois Press, 1987), 56.

14. Williams, "Clouds of Joy," 5.
15. Kufrin, *Uncommon Women,* 161.
16. Mary Lou Williams Oral History Project.
17. Ibid.
18. Williams, "Clouds of Joy," 5.
19. Ibid. For additional information on the history of Andy Kirk and the Clouds, see Gene Fernett, "Andy Kirk and His Clouds of Joy," in *Swing Out: Great Negro Dance Bands* (Midland, Mich.: Pendell, 1970), 77–82.
20. John Williams in his recounting of the years of the TOBA talked about how he was called upon once to don blackface, big shoes, and big lips when the regular comic did not show up. Although he did not indicate that at the time the act was degrading, history has taught us that such images were later used to degrade and dehumanize the African American's existence in America.
21. Kirk and Lee, *Twenty Years on Wheels,* 62.
22. John Williams, interview.
23. Kirk also doubled on alto and baritone saxes with the Clouds.
24. Williams, "Clouds of Joy," 5.
25. The Negro Baseball League was founded in Kansas City, Missouri, and the games played in the city were held at Muehlebach Park. The Monarchs were the home team for Kansas City and boasted a roster that included some of the most talented black players at the time, including Satchel Paige.
26. Eric Hobsbawm, *The Jazz Scene,* rev. ed. (New York: Pantheon Books, 1993), 78.
27. Pearson, *Goin' to Kansas City,* 98.
28. Ibid., 99.
29. Anderson, *This Was Harlem,* 235–46.
30. Lewis A. Erenberg, *Swingin' the Dream: Big Band Jazz and the Rebirth of American Culture* (Chicago: University of Chicago Press, 1998).
31. Mary Lou Williams, "The Battle of the Tenor Kings," *Melody Maker,* May 1, 1954, 11.
32. Mary Lou Williams Oral History Project.
33. Mary Lou Williams, "Mary Lou Williams: Musician as Healer," 81. Later Mary would increase her knowledge of music theory with the help of Don Redman, Edgar Sampson, Milton Orent, and Will Bradley.
34. The years 1921 to 1942 were the peak period for the blues race record strategy. Jazz titles, however, were generally circulated on lists that did not distinguish between black and white performers. For more information on race records, see *New Grove Dictionary of Jazz.*
35. For more information, see R. C. Freeman, "Jazz and Race Records, 1920–32" (Ph.D. diss., University of Illinois at Urbana-Champaign, 1968), 136–38.
36. Kirk and Lee, *Twenty Years,* 70–71.

37. Andy Kirk, "My Story by Andy Kirk as Told to Frank Driggs," *Jazz Review* 2 (1959): 14.
38. Brunswick acquired Vocalion in 1924 but released recordings under both labels, often exchanging material. It did not officially have a race record series until 1927, when one was directed by Jack Kapp.
39. Erenberg, *Swingin' the Dream,* 17.

CHAPTER 4

1. Ted Gioia, *The History of Jazz* (New York: Oxford University Press, 1997), 125.
2. Mary Lou Williams, "Battle of the Tenor Kings," 11. During this stint in Philadelphia, the Clouds accompanied many artists, including Blanche Calloway (Cab's sister), Bill Bailey, and Ethel Waters.
3. Gunther Schuller discusses the contributions of Morrison in great detail in *Early Jazz.*
4. Ross Russell, *Jazz Style in Kansas City and the Southwest* (Berkeley: University of California Press, 1971), 165.
5. Erenberg discusses how race affected the careers of black swing bands in *Swingin' the Dream,* chapters 4, 5, and 6.
6. Mousouris, "Musician as Healer," 82.
7. Ibid.
8. Erenberg, *Swingin' the Dream,* 99.
9. Ibid., 173.
10. Kirk and Lee, *Twenty Years,* 85. Parts of Kirk's quote are taken from Kirk, "My Story," 15.
11. Kirk and Lee, *Twenty Years,* 85.
12. Two versions of this song were recorded in 1936. The first featured the drummer Ben Thigpen on vocals and was made on March 11, 1936; the second featured Pha Terrell on vocals and dates from April 2, 1936. The Pha Terrell version is often cited as the popular recording, which is why its date is given in the text. See the recording *The Chronological Andy Kirk and His Twelve Clouds of Joy 1936–1937* (Classics 573).
13. "Andy Kirk Is Apollo's Big Noise," undated, unsourced article in Williams File.
14. Dempsey Travis, *An Autobiography of Black Jazz* (Chicago: Urban Research Institute, 1983), 100–105.
15. Contractual agreements between Decca Records and Mary Lou Williams indicate that the two parties agreed she would be paid a royalty of 1.2 cents net per record for the recordings made with the company between 1936 and 1940. Duplicates of these documents are in the Williams Collection.

16. Unterbrink, *Jazz Women,* 37–38.
17. Erenberg, *Swingin' the Dream,* 175.
18. Ibid.
19. Kirk and Lee, *Twenty Years,* 89.
20. Mary Lou Williams, "My Friends the Kings of Jazz: Charlie Christian." *Melody Maker,* May 15, 1954, 11.
21. Ibid.
22. For more information on the relationship between Goodman and Mary, see James Lincoln Collier, *Benny Goodman and the Swing Era* (New York: Oxford University Press, 1989), and Ross Firestone, *Swing, Swing, Swing: The Life and Times of Benny Goodman* (New York: W. W. Norton, 1993).
23. "Twinklin'" and "Little Joe from Chicago" were recorded on February 8, 1938.
24. John Williams, interview.
25. Mary Lou Williams Oral History Project.
26. John Williams, interview.
27. John Williams would stay in New York after the stint there in the late 1930s and go into the barbecue business with Mary Kirk, Andy's wife. Williams was not the only member to leave that year. Don Byas and Edward Inge also parted ways with the Clouds.
28. Williams, "Charlie Christian."
29. Mousouris, "Musician as Healer," 82.
30. Andy Kirk offered a different slant on Mary Lou Williams's leaving in *Twenty Years on Wheels,* 110–11, 168. He claimed that the addition of June Richmond (vocalist) and Floyd Smith (guitar) led to personality clashes. The evident conflict between Mary's and Kirk's accounts shows their varying interpretations of the environment of the band. Kirk, more concerned about the widespread fame that the band was experiencing, was probably less concerned about the personality clashes.

CHAPTER 5

1. Williams, "Mary Lou Williams Story," 7.
2. Mary Lou Williams Oral History Project.
3. Ibid.
4. Ibid.
5. Joe Glaser to Mary Lou Williams, November 10, 1942, Williams Collection.
6. Mary Lou Williams Oral History Project.
7. Stan Britt, "The First Lady of Jazz: Mary Lou Williams," interview by Stan Britt, *Jazz Journal International* 34 (September 1981): 10–11.

8. "Carnegie Revisited," in *The Duke Ellington Reader,* ed. Mark Tucker (New York: Oxford University Press, 1993), 211.

9. Stanley Dance, *The World of Duke Ellington* (New York: Da Capo Press, 1970), 152–153.

10. Phyl Garland, "The Lady Lives Jazz: Mary Lou Williams Remains as a Leading Interpreter of the Art," *Ebony,* October 1979, 60.

11. Mary Lou Williams Oral History Project.

12. Dizzy Gillespie and Al Fraser, *To Be, or Not—to Bop: Memoirs* (Garden City, N.Y.: Doubleday, 1979), 148–49.

13. For more information on Café Society, see Elijah Wald, *Josh White: Society Blues* (Amherst: University of Massachusetts Press, 2000), 103.

14. Mary Lou Williams Oral History Project.

15. Garland, "Lady Lives Jazz," 62.

16. "No Kitten on the Keys," *Time,* July 26, 1943, 76.

17. Mary Lou Williams Oral History Project.

18. Sally Placksin, *American Women in Jazz: 1900 to the Present: Their Words, Lives, and Music* (New York: Seaview Books, 1982), 88.

CHAPTER 6

1. Benjamin J. Davis, *Communist Councilman from Harlem: Autobiographical Notes Written in a Federal Penitentiary* (New York: International Publishers, 1969), 111.

2. Hazel Scott Powell, Testimony, *Hearing before the Committee on Un-American Activities,* 81st Congress, 2d sess., September 22, 1950, 3621.

3. Ted Yates, "I've Been Around," *New York Age,* November 18, 1944.

4. Mary Lou Williams Oral History Project.

5. Mary Lou Williams, *The Mary Lou Williams Trio—1944: Roll 'Em.* Solo Art SACD-43.

6. Peter O'Brien, liner notes for *Mary Lou Williams—The Asch Recordings, 1944–47,* Folkways Records FA 2966.

7. Stanley Dance, "Review of *Mary Lou Williams: The Asch Recordings, 1944–47,*" *Radio Free Jazz,* June 1978, 23.

8. Peter D. Goldsmith, *Making People's Music: Moe Asch and Folkways Records* (Washington, D.C.: Smithsonian Institution Press, 1998), 133.

9. Mary Lou Williams Oral History Project.

10. "Broadway Chatter," *New York Age,* June 23, 1945, 11.

11. Dan Morgenstern, "The Origin of the Zodiac Suite," liner notes for *The Zodiac Suite,* Smithsonian Folkways SF CD 40810.

12. Ibid.

13. Mary Lou Williams, "Why I Wrote the Zodiac Suite," liner notes for *The Zodiac Suite,* Smithsonian Folkways SF CD 40810.
14. "Broadway Chatter," *New York Age,* May 12, 1945.
15. "Ethel Waters and Josh White Star in 'Blue Holiday' at the Belasco," *New York Age,* May 19, 1945, 12.
16. Dahl, *Morning Glory,* 155.
17. Ibid., 156.
18. "Ethel Waters and Josh White Open in 'Blue Holiday.'" *New York Age,* May 26, 1945, 11.
19. Kufrin, *Uncommon Women,* 166.
20. This quote is a combination of two different discussions by Williams about these years. The first half is taken from Placksin, *American Women,* 128, and the second is from Williams, "Mary Lou Williams: The Mad Monk," *Melody Maker,* May 22, 1954, 11.
21. Mary Lou Williams Oral History Project.
22. Ibid.
23. Ibid.
24. Leslie Gourse, *Straight, No Chaser: The Life and Genius of Thelonious Monk* (New York: Prentice-Hall, 1997), 95.
25. Mary Lou Williams Oral History Project.
26. Mousouris, "Musician as Healer," 83.
27. Mary Lou Williams Oral History Project.
28. Ibid.
29. Ibid.
30. Williams, "Mad Monk."
31. Jimmy Butts and Pitt Smith, "Places and Personalities," *New York Age,* September 1, 1945.
32. "Record Reviews: Mary Lou Williams," *Down Beat,* March 15, 1945.
33. Leonard Feather, *The Jazz Years: Earwitness to an Era* (New York: Da Capo Press, 1987), 131.
34. "Mary Lou's Opening at Uptown a Big One," *Down Beat,* November 1, 1945.

CHAPTER 7

1. Mary Lou Williams, "When Those Paper Men Dug Jazz at Carnegie," *Melody Maker,* June 5, 1954, 11.
2. "Mary Lou Williams Plays 'Zodiac Suite,'" *New York Times,* December 31, 1945, 15.
3. Barry Ulanov, "Mary Lou Williams," *Metronome,* February 1946, 18.
4. Goldsmith, *Making People's Music,* 169.

5. Ibid., 170.
6. "Record Reviews:" Mary Lou Williams, *Down Beat,* July 15, 1946.
7. "Album Reviews," *Billboard,* June 29, 1946, 34.
8. Williams, "When Those Paper Men Dug Jazz" 11. Although Mary also scored "Libra," the composition was not used for the concert.
9. Ibid.
10. Mary Lou Williams Oral History Project.
11. Ibid.
12. Williams, "When Those Paper Men Dug Jazz," 11.
13. Mary Lou Williams Oral History Project.
14. Williams, "When Those Paper Men Dug Jazz," 11.
15. Ibid.
16. Ibid.
17. Feather, *Jazz Years,* 131.
18. Michael Levin, "Fair Sex Cops Honors at Concert," *Down Beat,* April 23, 1947, 2.
19. Ibid.
20. "Diggin' the Discs: Mary Lou Williams," *Down Beat,* January 14, 1948, 34.
21. Leonard Feather, "The Street Is Dead: A Jazz Obituary," *Metronome,* April 1948.
22. Williams, "When Those Paper Men Dug Jazz," 11.
23. "Benny Blows Bop," *Metronome,* August 1948.
24. Leonard Feather, "The Changing of the Hasselgard: Sweden's Stan Moves Out of the Goodman Groove into Bop Playing with Benny," *Metronome,* September 1948.
25. Collier, *Benny Goodman,* 200.
26. Ibid.
27. "King Goes Modern with Mary Lou 9," *Down Beat,* May 6, 1949, 7.
28. Record Reviews: Mary Lou Williams," *Down Beat,* June 17, 1949, 15.
29. Mary Lou Williams to Bob Ellis, May 3, 1949, Williams Collection.
30. Mary Lou Williams to Sydney Nathan, May 9, 1949, Williams Collection.
31. Sydney Nathan to Mary Lou Williams, May 11, 1949, Williams Collection.
32. "Mary Lou Williams Plays," *International Musician,* October 1949, 10.
33. Joe Glaser to Mary Lou Williams, November 7, 1949, Williams Collection.
34. Joe Glaser to Mary Lou Williams, October 29, 1949, Williams Collection.
35. Mary Lou Williams to Joe Glaser, January 10, 1950, Williams Collection.
36. Joe Glaser to Mary Lou Williams, February 3, 1950, Williams Collection.
37. Mary Lou Williams to Joe Glaser, March 19, 1950, Williams Collection.
38. Frances Church to James Petrillo, July 14, 1950, Williams Collection.
39. James Petrillo to Mary Lou Williams, September 25, 1950, Williams Collection.

40. Mary Lou Williams to Joe Glaser, May 12, 1951, Williams Collection.
41. Joe Glaser to Mary Lou Williams, May 14, 1951, Williams Collection.
42. Mary Lou Williams to Joe Glaser, November 11, 1951, Williams Collection.

CHAPTER 8

1. Mary Lou Williams, "When Those Paper Men Dug Jazz," 16.
2. Dahl, *Morning Glory,* 218.
3. Mary Lou Williams to Joe Glaser, July 15, 1951, Williams Collection.
4. Mary Lou Williams to Joe Glaser, July 11, 1951, Williams Collection.
5. Peter O'Brien to author, July 28, 2003.
6. "Mary Lou Williams Booked for British Tour," *Melody Maker,* October 18, 1952, 16.
7. Joe Marsolais to Harry Dawson, December 1, 1952, Williams Collection.
8. Mary Lou Williams, "Mary Lou Williams: Britain Has Some of the Best Jazz in Europe," *Melody Maker,* June 12, 1954, 11.
9. Dahl, *Morning Glory,* 224. Portions also quoted in "Mary Lou Williams Says," 11.
10. Ernest Borneman, "Ernest Borneman Writes of Chocolate Ice Cream and Pickled Herring: The Big Show," *Melody Maker,* December 13, 1952, 13.
11. Ibid., 19.
12. Joe Marsolais to Mary Lou Williams, December 8, 1952, Williams Collection.
13. Mary Lou Williams to Harry Dawson, December 29, 1952, Williams Collection.
14. Harry Dawson to Mary Lou Williams, December 30, 1952, Williams Collection.
15. Edgar Jackson, "Mary Lou Williams and Her Orchestra," review, *Melody Maker,* January 3, 1953, 9.
16. Lil Armstrong, "Max Jones Interviews Lil Armstrong," *Melody Maker,* January 17, 1953, 8.
17. Dahl, *Morning Glory,* 227.
18. "Mary Lou Cuts 8 Sides with Britain's Two 'Star Hopes,'" *Melody Maker,* January 24, 1953, 12.
19. Mark Nevard, "And Mary Lou on LP," *Melody Maker,* February 7, 1953, 5.
20. Ernest Borneman, "That Mary Lou LP," *Melody Maker,* February 14, 1953, 3.
21. "More Melody Maker Critics Enter the Fray: Mary Lou," *Melody Maker,* February 21, 1953, 8.

22. Dill Jones, letter to "Melody Mailbag," *Melody Maker,* February 14, 1953, 5.

23. Tyler Stovall, *Paris Noir: African Americans in the City of Light* (Boston: Houghton Mifflin, 1996), 132.

24. Ibid., 134.

25. Ibid., 136.

26. "Dover Turns Back Mary Lou and Taps as Christmas Party Waits," *Melody Maker,* January 2, 1954.

27. "Record Review: Mary Lou Williams and Her Rhythm," *Jazz Hot,* June 1954, 35.

28. Henry Kahn, "Death of Garland Wilson Casts Shadow over Paris Fair," *Melody Maker,* June 5, 1954.

29. Mary Lou Williams Oral History Project.

30. Joe Glaser to Mary Lou Williams, May 6, 1954, Williams Collection.

31. The quote combines material from two sources: Kufrin, *Uncommon Women,* 169, and R. Gottlieb, "Mary Lou Williams," 88.

CHAPTER 9

1. Joe Marsolais to Mary Lou Williams, August 2, 1954, Williams Collection.

2. Gladys Toyme to Mary Lou Williams, September 1, 1954, Williams Collection.

3. Whitney Balliett, *American Musicians: Fifty-six Portraits in Jazz* (New York: Oxford University Press, 1986), 107.

4. John Wilson, "Mary Lou Williams," *International Musician,* January 1973, 22.

5. Max Jones, "Mary Lou Feels the Spirit," *Melody Maker,* December 6, 1969, and Inez Cavanaugh," Mary Lou—The Boss Piano," *Melody Maker,* February 15, 1964, 15.

6. Program notes for performance of the *History of Jazz Keyboard* at Lincoln Center, Philharmonic Hall, New York, in 1963. Williams Collection.

7. Mary Lou Williams Oral History Project.

8. For more information regarding the death of Charlie Parker and the controversy regarding his burial, see Gillespie and Fraser, *To Be,* 391–402; Ira Gitler, "Charlie Parker and the Alto Saxophonist," in *The Charlie Parker Companion,* ed. Carl Woideck (New York: Schirmer Books, 1998), 23–58.

9. "Bird Memorial Jams Carnegie," *Down Beat,* May 4, 1955, 4.

10. The actual amount that went into trust for Parker's sons was a little over $5,000, which was what was left after expenses related to the concert and taxes were paid. "Parker Concert Raised $10,000," *Down Beat,* August 10, 1955, 6.

11. Mary Lou Williams to Robbie Mickles, quoted in Dahl, *Morning Glory*, 253.
12. Mary Lou Williams to Internal Revenue Service, Williams Collection. Also quoted in Dahl, *Morning Glory*, 253.
13. Mary Lou Williams Oral History Project.
14. Ibid.
15. Unterbrink, *Jazz Women*, 42.
16. Barbara Rowes, "From Duke Ellington to Duke University, Mary Lou Williams Tells the World: 'Jazz Is Love,'" *People*, May 12, 1980, 73–77.
17. Dahl, *Morning Glory*, 257.
18. Ibid., 255.
19. Gillespie and Fraser, *To Be*, 291.
20. Dahl, *Morning Glory*, 256.
21. Mary Lou Williams Oral History Project.
22. Mary Lou Williams Oral History Project.
23. John Williams, interview.
24. Ibid.
25. Harry Shapiro, *Waiting for the Man: The Story of Drugs and Popular Music* (New York: William Morrow, 1988), 64.
26. Ibid., 64–65.
27. Mary Lou Williams Oral History Project.
28. Balliett, "Out Here Again," *New Yorker*, May 2, 1964, 78–80.
29. Mary Lou Williams Oral History Project.
30. Ibid.
31. Brian Q. Torff, "Mary Lou Williams: A Woman's Life in Jazz," in *Perspectives on American Music since 1950,* ed. James R. Heintze (New York: Garland, 1999).
32. Marian McPartland, "Into the Sun: An Affectionate Sketch of Mary Lou Williams," in *All in Good Time* (New York: Oxford University Press, 1987)," 73.
33. Dahl, *Morning Glory*, 260.
34. Mary Lou Williams Oral History Project.
35. Mousouris, "Musician as Healer," 84.
36. Mary Lou Williams Oral History Project.
37. Lewis K. McMillan Jr., "Grand Lady of Jazz," *Musical Journal* (September 1974): 51.
38. Balliett, *American Musicians*, 107.
39. "Newport Jazz Festival," *Down Beat*, August 8, 1957, 16.
40. "Tables for Two," *New Yorker*, October 5, 1957, 125–26.
41. "Night Club Review," *Variety*, November 27, 1957, 77.

42. Cab Calloway, "Is Dope Killing Our Musicians? Famed Orchestra Leader Sees Use of Narcotics as Dire Menace to Future of Band Business," *Ebony,* February 1951, 22.
43. Correspondence regarding Bel Canto Foundation sent to Moe Asch, Folkways Archives and Collections, Smithsonian Institution, Washington, D.C.
44. Ibid.
45. "One for the Money," *Down Beat,* May 29, 1958, 9.
46. Mario Hancock, interview with author, January 2001.

CHAPTER 10

1. Gioia, *History of Jazz,* 337.
2. Cheryl Miller and Toni Armstrong Jr., "The Life and Musical Times of Jay Allbright," *Hot Wire,* May 1994, 41.
3. Ibid.
4. Mary Lou Williams, notes for "St. Martin De Porres," Williams Collection.
5. Marshall Stearns, "Jazz in New York: In Search of Swing," *Musical America* 83 (February 1963): 35.
6. Stanley Dance, "Jazz," *Music Journal* 21 (1963): 109–10.
7. Fran Goulart, "For It Was Mary, Mary," *Sounds and Fury,* December 1965, 41.
8. Ibid.
9. Horace Clarence Boyer, *How Sweet the Sound: The Golden Age of Gospel* (Washington, D.C.: Elliott and Clark, 1995), 190.
10. Dave Dexter Jr., "Crusade by Mary Lou Williams," *Billboard,* April 30, 1977, 34.
11. Gérard Pochonet, liner notes for *Mary Lou Williams Presents Black Christ of the Andes,* Folkways Records FJ 2843.
12. Ibid.
13. Contract between Mary Lou Williams and Folkways Records, September 15, 1961, Folkways Archives and Collections.
14. Undated review from *Audio,* Folkways Archives and Collections.
15. Cliff Smith, "Mary Lou Williams—'Mary Lou Williams Presents,'" *New York Times-Union,* March 9, 1973.
16. Les Tomkins, "It's Going to Be Much Cooler," *Crescendo International* 10 (August 1971): 26.
17. Tsehla Phahlane to Mary Lou Williams, December 20, 1964, Folkways Archives and Collections.
18. Mary Lou Williams to Moe Asch, October 7, 1964, Folkways Archives and Collections.

19. Hazel Garland, "Mary Lou Williams Spearheads Drive to Bring Jazz Festival to Pittsburgh," *Pittsburgh Courier,* April 18, 1964, 13.

20. Hazel Garland, "Interest Mounts in First Pittsburgh Jazz Festival," *Pittsburgh Courier,* May 20, 1964, 23.

21. Phyl Garland, "Mary Lou Williams Conceived Idea: Pittsburgh Jazz Festival Began as a Dream," *Pittsburgh Courier,* July 4, 1964, 2: 1.

22. Stanley Dance, "Jazz in Pittsburgh," *Saturday Review,* July 11, 1964, 43.

23. Roy Kohler, "Caught in the Act: First Annual Pittsburgh Jazz Festival," *Down Beat,* July 30, 1964, 13.

24. "Jazz Greats Jam Steel City for Festival," *Pittsburgh Courier,* July 9, 1965; Kohler, "Caught in the Act."

25. Fran Goulart, "For It Was Mary."

26. Contract between Folkways Records and Mary Lou Williams, August 24, 1966, Folkways Archives and Collections.

CHAPTER 11

1. Don Lass to Moe Asch, February 13, 1967, Folkways Archives and Collections.

2. Tomkins, "Much Cooler," 25.

3. Carline Ray, "My Reflections of Mary Lou Williams," in *Mary Lou Williams: Her Life and Artistry* (Washington, D.C.: Kennedy Center Publications, 1999).

4. John S. Wilson, "Mary Lou Takes Her Jazz Mass to Church," *New York Times,* February 9, 1975.

5. Tomkins, "Much Cooler," 25.

6. J. Michael Joncas, "Reforming and Renewing the Music of the Roman Rite," *Pastoral Music* (August–September 1994): 30–32.

7. J. Wilson, "Mary Lou Takes Her Jazz Mass to Church."

8. Mary Lou Williams to Mario Hancock, September 28, 1967, author's collection.

9. Mary Lou Williams to Moe Asch, March 23, 1968, Folkways Archives and Collections.

10. The story is recounted in detail in Luke 2:1–44.

11. Mary Lou Williams to Mario Hancock, April 3, 1968, author's collection.

12. Mary Lou Williams to Mario Hancock, August 8, 1968, author's collection.

13. Morris Goldberger to Moe Asch, June 10, 1968, Folkways Archives and Collections.

14. Mary Lou Williams to Mario Hancock, August 16, 1968, author's collection.

15. Mary Lou Williams to Mario Hancock, August 21, 1968, author's collection.
16. Ibid.
17. Mary Lou Williams to Mario Hancock, August 23, 1968, author's collection.
18. Mary Lou Williams to Mario Hancock, November 17, 1968, author's collection.
19. Mary Lou Williams to Mario Hancock, November 24, 1968, author's collection.
20. Dahl, *Morning Glory,* 303.
21. Mario Hancock, interview by author, January 2001. The story is also reported in "Roman Cardinal Okays Jazz Masses Minus Drums," *Jet,* April 3, 1969, 47.
22. Mary Lou Williams to Mario Hancock, April 21, 1969, author's collection.
23. Mary Lou Williams to Mario Hancock, June 25, 1969, author's collection.
24. Mary Lou Williams to Mario Hancock, June 29, 1969, author's collection.
25. *Mass for Peace,* Mary Lou Williams Collection.

CHAPTER 12

1. Mary Lou Williams to Mario Hancock, May 2, 1970, author's collection.
2. Ibid.
3. John S. Wilson, "Mary Lou Williams Plays Jazz Piano," *New York Times,* April 27, 1970, 44.
4. Stanley Dance, "Recordings Report: Jazz LPs," *Saturday Review,* June 13, 1970.
5. Torff, "Mary Lou Williams," 190–91.
6. Unterbrink, *Jazz Women,* 43.
7. Dahl, *Morning Glory,* 314.
8. J. Wilson, "Jazz Mass."
9. Mary Lou Williams to Mario Hancock, June 13, 1970 [1971]. O'Brien states that Mary must have mistakenly written the wrong date, as his ordination took place in 1971.
10. "Nightclubs," *New Yorker,* October 9, 1971, 73–74.
11. Ibid., 74.
12. "Jazz Finds Home at The Cookery," *New York Times,* November 27, 1970, 50.
13. Mary Campbell, "Pianist Mary Lou Williams Is Back Again, Jazz Fans," *New Brunswick Sunday Home News,* December 13, 1970, C15.
14. Lewis K. McMillan, Jr., "Swingin' With," *New York Column,* February 5–11, 1971.

15. Kufrin, *Uncommon Women,* 172.

16. Peter O'Brien, interview with author, May 16, 2003.

17. Dahl, *Morning Glory,* 319.

18. John S. Wilson, "Jazz Club Gets Bobby Hackett and Dizzy Gillespie Together," *New York Times,* February 2, 1971.

19. "Record Review," *Down Beat,* April 26, 1973.

20. Olga Maynard, *Judith Jamison: Aspects of a Dancer* (Garden City, N.Y.: Doubleday, 1982), 145.

21. Anna Kisselgoff, "Ailey Dancers to Give 'Mary Lou's Mass,'" *New York Times,* December 9, 1971, 62.

22. Hubert Saal, "The Spirit of Mary Lou," *Newsweek,* December 20, 1971, 67.

23. "Review: Mary Lou's Mass,'" review of performance, Alvin Ailey American Dance Theater, *Hi/Fi America,* March 1972, MA 15.

24. "Review of 'Mary Lou's Mass,'" review of performance, Alvin Ailey American Dance Theater, *Dance Magazine,* February 1972, 26.

25. Mary Lou Williams to Mario Hancock, December 16, 1971, author's collection.

26. Brian Ward, *Just My Soul Responding: Rhythm and Blues, Black Consciousness, and Race Relations* (Berkeley: University of California Press, 1998), 410.

27. Mary Lou Williams, liner notes for *The History of Jazz,* Folkways FJ 2860.

28. Mary Lou Williams to Mario Hancock, [1970], author's collection.

29. Peter O'Brien to author, July 28, 2003.

30. Wilson, "Jazz Mass."

31. William Banks, *The Black Church in the U.S.: Its Origin, Growth, Contributions, and Outlook* (Chicago: Moody Press, 1972), 113.

32. Ibid.

33. Ibid., 116.

34. Phyl Garland, "The Lady Lives Jazz: Mary Lou Williams Remains as a Leading Interpreter of the Art," *Ebony,* October 1979.

35. "Jazz: Mary Lou Williams—Zoning," *Billboard,* October 12, 1974; Douglass Watt, "True Blue Lou," *Sunday News,* November 3, 1974.

36. Torff, "Mary Lou Williams," 190.

37. "Manhattan College Graduates 800; Mary Lou Williams Honored," *New York Times,* May 19, 1975, 33.

38. Quotes of Father O'Brien's homily are from John S. Wilson, "Mary Lou Williams, at Piano, Leads Her Jazz Mass at St. Patrick's," *New York Times,* February 19, 1975, 37, and Peter Keepnews, "Liturgy of Jazz at St. Patrick's," *New York Post,* February 19, 1975.

39. J. Wilson, "Mary Lou Williams, at Piano."
40. John W. Donohue, "'Mary Lou's Mass': Music for Peace," *America*, March 8, 1975.
41. Ibid.
42. Keepnews, "Liturgy of Jazz."
43. Tom Piazza, "Review of 'Mary Lou Williams: The Asch Recordings, 1944– 47' and 'Free Spirits,'" *Jazz* 2, no. 2 (1978): 64.
44. Gilbert M. Erskine, "TV Review: 'Look Up and Live,'" *Second Line*, Winter 1976, 15.
45. Linda Prince, "Betty Carter: Bebopper Breathes Fire," *Down Beat*, May 3, 1979, 14.
46. Ibid., 43.
47. "Review of Mary Lou Williams/Cecil Taylor: Embraced," *Down Beat*, December 7, 1978, 29.
48. Bob Rusch, "Review of Mary Lou Williams, The Asch Recordings, 1944– 47," *Cadence* 3, no. 6 (November 1977): 43.
49. Mary Lou Williams, liner notes for *Embraced*, Pablo 2620108.
50. Gary Giddins, "Search for a Common Language," *New York*, April 18, 1977, 110.
51. Gary Giddins, *Riding on a Blue Note: Jazz and American Pop* (New York: Oxford University Press, 1981), 286.
52. "Doggin' Around: A Noble Failure," *Jazz Journal International* 30 (August 1977): 15.
53. Giddins, *Riding on a Blue Note*, 287.
54. Ibid.
55. The quotes of Cecil Taylor and Mary are taken from Williams, "First Lady."
56. Peter O'Brien, interview with author, January 2000.

CHAPTER 13

1. Hancock interview.
2. Mary Lou Williams, interview by Mary Oneppo, 1981, Yale Oral History American Music Series, 77c.
3. John Williams interview.
4. Torff, "Mary Lou Williams," 192.
5. Ibid., 195.
6. Kufrin, *Uncommon Women*, 158.
7. "Record Reviews," *Down Beat*, May 3, 1979, 30.
8. Handy, "Conversation," 208.
9. John S. Wilson, "Mary Lou Williams: A Jazz Great Dies," *New York Times*, May 30, 1981.

BIBLIOGRAPHY

The material used for this text came from a number of different sources. In addition to print materials, a great deal of the personal and firsthand information was extracted from interviews conducted by the author; interviews conducted through oral history projects such as the National Endowment for the Arts/Institute of Jazz Studies (the 1977 John Wilson interview of Mary Lou Williams) and the Yale Oral History American Music Series (the 1981 Martha Oneppo interview of Mary Lou Williams); documentaries such as "Music on My Mind" (Joanne Burke, 1981); and the personal correspondence, business papers, scores, photos, and recordings in the Mary Lou Williams Collection at the Institute of Jazz Studies at Rutgers University. The following is a selected listing of articles and books used in the writing of this book.

ARTICLES

"Album Reviews." *Billboard,* June 29, 1946, 34.

Anderson, Jack. "New York Newsletter [December 1971 events]." *Dancing Times,* February 1972, 244–45.

"And Mary Lou on LP." *Melody Maker,* February 7, 1953, 5.

"Andy Kirk Is Apollo's Big Noise." Undated, unsourced news clipping in the Mary Lou Williams Collection, Institute of Jazz Studies, Rutgers University, Newark, N.J.

"Annie Ross in London: Talks to the MM." *Melody Maker,* October 10, 1953.

Armstrong, Lil. "Max Jones Interviews Lil Armstrong." *Melody Maker,* January 17, 1953, 8.

Balliett, Whitney. "Nightclubs." *New Yorker,* October 9, 1971, 50–92.

———. "Out Here Again." In *American Musicians: Fifty-six Portraits in Jazz,* ed. Whitney Balliett. New York: Oxford University Press, 1986, 96–107.

Barnes, Clive. "Ailey Dancers in 'Mary Lou's Mass.'" *New York Times,* December 12, 1971.

"Benny Blows Bop." *Metronome,* August 1948, 12–22.

Berger, Monroe. "Jazz Resistance to the Diffusion of Culture-Pattern." *Journal of Negro History* (October 1947): 461–94.

"B.G. and Bebop." *Newsweek,* December 27, 1948, 66–67.

"BG Cries 'Nuff' as Costs Climb, Crowds Fall Off." *Down Beat,* July 28, 1948.

"Bird Memorial Jams Carnegie." *Down Beat,* May 4, 1955, 4.

"Bop-Styled BG Septet Stars All but Goodman." *Down Beat,* July 14, 1948, 6.

Borneman, Ernest. "Ernest Borneman Writes of Chocolate Ice Cream and Pickled Herring: The Big Show." *Melody Maker,* June 12, 1954.

———. "Long Night Stand." *Melody Maker,* February 7, 1953, 4.

———. "That Mary Lou LP," *Melody Maker,* February 14, 1953, 3.

Bowman, Sister Thea. "The Gift of African American Sacred Song." In *Lead Me, Guide Me: The African American Catholic Hymnal.* Chicago: G.I.A. Publications, 1987.

"Brit Nix Work Permit for Mary Lou Williams." *Variety,* February 17, 1954, 46.

Britt, Stan. "The First Lady of Jazz: Mary Lou Williams." *Jazz Journal International,* September 1981, 10–11.

———. "Obituary." *Jazz Journal International,* August 1981, 18–19.

"Broadway Chatter." *New York Age,* May 12, 1945.

"Broadway Chatter." *New York Age,* June 23, 1945.

"Broadway Chatter." *New York Age,* August 18, 1945.

"Broadway Chatter." *New York Age,* January 26, 1946.

Burley, Dan. "Miss Mary Lou Swings for You." *New York Amsterdam News,* October 8, 1938, 20.

Butts, Jimmy. "Places and Personalities." *New York Age,* August 11, 1945.

Butts, Jimmy, and Pitt Smith. "Places and Personalities." *New York Age,* September 1, 1945.

Calloway, Cab. "Is Dope Killing Our Musicians? Famed Orchestra Leader Sees Use of Narcotics as Dire Menace to Future of Band Business." *Ebony,* February 1951, 22–28.

"Calloway, Mary Lou in Big Rhythm Show." *Melody Maker,* November 1, 1952.

Campbell, Mary. "Pianist Mary Lou Williams Is Back Again, Jazz Fans." *New Brunswick Sunday Home News,* December 13, 1970, C15.

"Carnegie Revisited." In *The Duke Ellington Reader,* ed. Mark Tucker. New York: Oxford University Press, 1993.

"Caught in the Act." *Down Beat,* April 12, 1962, 37–38.

"Caught in the Act." *Down Beat,* February 4, 1971, 30–31.

"Caught in the Act." *Melody Maker,* July 29, 1978, 14–45.

"Caught in the Act." *Variety,* January 25, 1978, 72.

"Caught in the Act: The First Annual Pittsburgh Jazz Festival." *Down Beat,* July 30, 1964, 13.

"Caught in the Act: Pittsburgh Jazz Festival." *Down Beat,* July 29, 1965.

Cavanaugh, Inez. "Mary Lou—The Boss Piano." *Melody Maker,* February 15, 1964, 15.

"Cherry Lane Rest." *Variety,* November 27, 1957, 77.

"Christmas in Paris." *Melody Maker,* December 19, 1953.

"La Chronique des Disques Black Christ." *Jazz Hot,* October 1971, 34.

Close, Al. "Fashion and Jazz." *Jazz Monthly,* May 1959, 28.

———. "Mary, Mary, Quite Contrary." *Wrightstown Leader,* February 26, 1959.

———. "Music Is Love." *Wrightstown Leader,* February 12, 1959.

"Concert Reviews." *Variety,* January 25, 1978, 72.

"Cookery N.Y." *Variety,* August 30, 1972, 53.

Coyle, Owen. "Mary Lou Williams and Her Jazz Crusade." *Mississippi Rag* (Minneapolis), April 1976, 5–6.

Cusana, Michael. "Mary Lou Williams Presents 'St. Martin de Porres.'" *Record World,* August 28, 1971.

Dance, Helen, and Stanley Dance. "Here's a Girl Who Plumps for Them All." *Melody Maker,* January 10, 1953, 4.

Dance, Stanley. "An Afternoon with Mary Lou Williams" (1964 interview). *Jazz Journal International,* October 1989, 8–10.

———. "Jazz." *Music Journal* 21 (January 1963): 109–10.

———. "Jazz in Pittsburgh." *Saturday Review,* July 11, 1964, 43–47.

———. "Recordings Report: Jazz LPs." *Saturday Review,* June 13, 1970.

"Decries 'Jazz Thinking.'" *New York Times,* February 15, 1925, 17.

"Deeps and Six Bands plus Cab and Mary Lou." *Melody Maker,* November 8, 1952.

Degange, Stephen. "Oo–Oo, Mary Lou! A Remembrance of Mary Lou Williams, May 8, 1910–May 28, 1981," *Freedomways* (Fourth Quarter 1981), 231–33.

Delaunay, Charles. "Interview de Mary Lou Williams." *Jazz Hot,* February 1953, 10–12.

Dexter, Dave, Jr. "Crusade by Mary Lou Williams." *Billboard,* April 30, 1977, 15.

"Diggin' the Discs: Mary Lou Williams." *Down Beat,* May 15, 1945.

"Diggin' the Discs: Mary Lou Williams." *Down Beat,* July 15, 1946.

"Doggin' Around: A Noble Failure." *Jazz Journal International,* August 1977, 15.

Donohue, John W. "'Mary Lou's Mass': Music for Peace." *America,* March 8, 1975.

"Dover Turns Back Mary Lou and Taps as Christmas Party Waits." *Melody Maker,* January 2, 1954, 7.

Driggs, Franklin S. "Kansas City and the Southwest." In *Jazz: New Perspectives on the History of Jazz by Twelve of the World's Foremost Jazz Critics and Scholars,* ed. Nat Hentoff and Albert McCarthy. New York and Toronto: Rinehart and Company, 1959, 179–230.

"The Duchess of Oo-bla-Dee." *Our World,* January 1950, 3–35.

Erskine, Gilbert M. "TV Review, 'Look Up and Live.'" *Second Line,* Winter 1976, 17–18.

"Ethel Waters and Josh White Open in 'Blue Holiday.'" *New York Age,* May 26, 1945.

"Ethel Waters and Josh White Star in 'Blue Holiday' at the Belasco." *New York Age,* May 19, 1945.

"Fast-Moving Mary." *Melody Maker,* February 21, 1953.

Feather, Leonard. "The Changing of the Hasselgard: Sweden's Stan Moves Out of the Goodman Groove into Bop Playing with Benny." *Metronome,* September 1948, 20–21.

———. "Feather's Nest." *Down Beat,* May 6, 1953, 21.

———. "Jazz: Mary Lou: Soul upon Soul." *Melody Maker,* June 20, 1981, 27.

———. "Mary Lou." *Melody Maker,* December 6, 1952, 16.

———. "The Street Is Dead: A Jazz Obituary." *Metronome,* April 1948, 16–33.

"Five Guggenheims to Artist." *Down Beat,* June 8, 1972, 9.

Frances, H. "Obituary." *Crescendo International,* July 1981.

Garland, Hazel. "Interest Mounts in First Pittsburgh Jazz Festival." *Pittsburgh Courier,* May 30, 1964, 23.

———. "Mary Lou Williams Spearheads Drive to Bring Jazz Festival to Pittsburgh." *Pittsburgh Courier,* April 18, 1964, 13.

Garland, Phyl. "The Lady Lives Jazz: Mary Lou Williams Remains as a Leading Interpreter of the Art." *Ebony,* October 1979, 56–64.

———. "Mary Lou Williams Conceived Idea: Pittsburgh Jazz Festival Began as a Dream." *Pittsburgh Courier,* July 4, 1964, 2: 1.

"Garland Wilson N'est Plus." *Jazz Hot,* July 1954, 21.

"Garvin Bushell and New York Jazz in the 1920s." *Jazz Review,* January 1959, 12.

Giddins, Gary. "Search for a Common Language." *New York,* April 18, 1977, 110.

———. "Weatherbird: Mary Lou Williams 1910–1981." *Village Voice,* June 10, 1981, 80.

Gitler, Ira. "Charlie Parker and the Alto Saxophonist." In *The Charlie Parker Companion: Six Decades of Commentary,* ed. Carl Woideck. New York: Schirmer Books, 1998.

Gottlieb, Robert. "Mary Lou Williams." In *Reading Jazz: A Gathering of Autobiography, Reportage, and Criticism from 1919 to Now,* ed. Robert Gottlieb. New York: Pantheon Books, 1996, 87–116.

Goulart, Fran. "For It Was Mary, Mary." *Sounds and Fury,* December 1965, 40–64.

Handy, D. Antoinette "Conversation with Mary Lou Williams: First Lady of Jazz Keyboard." *Black Perspectives in Music* 8, no. 2 (Fall 1980): 194–214.

Harman, Carter. "'Got to Move On,' Says Mary Lou." *New York Times,* August 28, 1949, 2: 5.

Harris, Michael. "Conflict and Resolution in the Life of Thomas Andrew Dorsey." In *We'll Understand It Better By and By: Pioneering African American Composers,* ed. Bernice Johnson Reagon. Washington: Smithsonian Institution Press, 1992, 165–82.

Heckman, Don. "Jazz for the Few Is Heard by Many." *New York Times,* July 3, 1972, 7.

———. "Midnight Jam Session at Music Hall." *New York Times,* July 5, 1972, 31.

Henry, Jacques. "Disques" *Jazz Hot,* June 1954, 35.

Holmes, L. D. "The Jazz Clock: A Look at Aging and Creativity in Jazz." *Jazz Times,* April 1983, 122–213.

Jackson, David. "Jazz Is Her Religion: Mary Lou Williams." *Black Creation Annual* (1974–75), 50–52.

Jackson, Edgar. "Mary Lou Williams and Her Orchestra." *Melody Maker,* January 17, 1953.

"Jazz Greats Jam Steel City for Festival." *Pittsburgh Courier,* July 9, 1965, 2: 1.

"Jazz Jive by Jax." *Down Beat,* July 15, 1945, 9.

"Jazz: Mary Lou Williams—Zoning." *Billboard,* October 12, 1974.

"Jazz Resistance to the Diffusion of a Culture-Pattern." *Journal of Negro History* (October 1947): 461–94.

Jolles, Naomi. "Music Is Her Passion." *New York Post,* December 11, 1944.

Joncas, Michael J. "Reforming and Renewing the Music of the Roman Rite." *Pastoral Music* (August–September 1994): 30–32.

Jones, Max. "Mary Lou Feels the Spirit." *Melody Maker,* December 6, 1969, 10.

Kahn, Henry. "Death of Garland Wilson Casts Shadow over Paris Fair." *Melody Maker,* June 5, 1954.

Kaplan, E. "The Lady Who Swings the Band: The Legacy of American Pianist, Composer Mary Lou Williams." *NAJE Research* 9 (1989): 129–39.

Keepnews, Peter. "Liturgy of Jazz at St. Patrick's." *New York Post,* 19 February 1975.

Kenney, William Howland, III. "The Influence of Black Vaudeville on Early Jazz." *Black Perspective in Music* 14, no. 3 (Fall 1986): 233–48.

"King Goes Modern with Mary Lou 9." *Down Beat,* May 6, 1949, 7.

Kirk, Andy. "My Story by Andy Kirk as Told to Frank Driggs." *Jazz Review,* February 1959.

Kisselgoff, Anna. "Ailey Dancers to Give 'Mary Lou's Mass.'" *New York Times,* December 9, 1971, 62.

Knight, Athelia. "In Retrospect: Sherman Dudley: He Paved the Way for TOBA." *Black Perspective in Music* 15, no. 2 (fall 1987): 153–81.

Knight, Bob. "Mary Lou Williams Dies at 71; Had Major Influence on Jazz." *Variety,* June 3, 1981, 69.

Kohler, Roy. "Caught in the Act: First Annual Pittsburgh Jazz Festival." *Down Beat,* July 30, 1964, 13.

Kreisberg, Louisa. "Music Flows Easily from Mary Lou. [White Plains] *Reporter Dispatch,* January 18, 1974, 14.

"Land of Oo-bla-dee." *Time,* September 12, 1949, 77–79.

Levin, Michael. "Fair Sex Cops Honors at Concert." *Down Beat,* April 23, 1947, 2.

"Manhattan College Graduates 800; Mary Lou Williams Honored." *New York Times,* May 19, 1975, 33.

"Marian McPartland Discusses Jazz Great Mary Lou Williams." *Morning Edition* (NPR), August 25, 1994. Transcript no. 1419, segment 14.

"Mary Lou." *Down Beat,* October 17, 1954, 12.

"Mary Lou and the Duke and Duchess." *Melody Maker,* June 26, 1954.

"Mary Lou Breaks British Barriers." *Down Beat,* December 3, 1952.

"Mary Lou Cuts 8 Sides with Britain's Two 'Star Hopes.'" *Melody Maker,* January 24, 1953, 12.

"Mary Lou Declines Armstrong Offer." *Melody Maker,* May 30, 1953.

"Mary Lou Due Next Week for Rhythm Show." *Melody Maker,* November 29, 1952.

"Mary Lou Gets Doctorate." *Variety,* June 16, 1976, 76.

"Mary Lou Gets Good Break." *Down Beat,* November 5, 1947.

"Mary Lou Goes into Variety." *Melody Maker,* March 7, 1953, 7.

"Mary Lou Joins Duke Faculty." *Instrument* 32 (September 1977): 87.

"Mary Lou Leaves Kirk after Twelve Years." *Metronome,* July 1942.

"Mary Lou Leaves the Ringside." *Melody Maker,* December 19, 1953.

"Mary Lou Plans to Form Own British Group." *Melody Maker,* June 13, 1953.

"Mary Lou Plays." *International Musician,* October 1952, xi.

"Mary Lou Plays the Melody." *Melody Maker,* March 21, 1953, 12.

"Mary Lou Rolls 'Em." *Down Beat,* October 2, 1958, 12.

"Mary Lou Still Learning, Teaching, and Progressing." *Down Beat,* December 17, 1952, 7.

"Mary Lou's Opening at Uptown a Big One." *Down Beat,* November 1, 1945.

"Mary Lou to Star at Heath Concerts." *Melody Maker,* January 17, 1953, 7.

"Mary Lou Williams" *Down Beat,* May 27, 1971, 16–17.

"Mary Lou Williams." *Ebony,* November 1950.

"Mary Lou Williams." *Kansas City Times Star,* June 1, 1981.

"Mary Lou Williams." *Musical Jazz,* November 1962, 44.

"Mary Lou Williams." (Portrait). *Village Voice,* May 10, 1983, 68–69.

"Mary Lou Williams au 'Boeuf sur le Toit.'" *Jazz Hot,* July 1954, 21.

"Mary Lou Williams aux Galeries." *Jazz Hot,* January 1954, 35.

"Mary Lou Williams Back at Cookery." *New York Times,* March 22, 1973, 53.

"Mary Lou Williams Booked for British Tour." *Melody Maker,* October 18, 1952, 16.

"Mary Lou Williams Dies." *Variety,* June 3, 1981, 69.

"Mary Lou Williams, Jonah Jones et Peanut Holland en France." *Jazz Hot,* September 1953, 20.

"Mary Lou Williams' $1,000,000 Suit Claims." *Variety,* February 24, 1965, 2.

"Mary Lou Williams Plays." *International Musician,* October 1949, 10.

"Mary Lou Williams Plays 'Zodiac Suite.'" *New York Times,* December 31, 1945, 15.

"Mary Lou Williams: The Musician's Musician." *Jazz Journal* 6, no. 2 (February 1953): 18–19.

"Mass Meetings." *New Yorker,* May 14, 1979, 29–31.

Maultsby, Portia. "The Impact of Gospel Music on the Secular Music Industry." In *We'll Understand It Better By and By: Pioneering African American Gospel Composers,* ed. Bernice Johnson Reagon. Washington: Smithsonian Institution Press, 1992: 19–33.

McDonough, J. "Mary Lou Williams." *Down Beat,* September 1990, 21.

"McKenzie for Mary Lou in Jazz Wagon Show." *Melody Maker,* February 13, 1954.

McMillan, Lewis K., Jr. "Grand Lady of Jazz." *Musical Journal* 32 (September 1974): 50–60.

———. "Mary Lou Williams." *New York Column,* February 12–18, 1971.

———. "Mary Lou Williams: First Lady of Jazz." *Down Beat,* May 27, 1971, 16–17.

———. "Mary Lou Williams—Jazz Pianist." *Tablet Magazine,* January 14, 1971.

McPartland, Marian. "Into the Sun: The Sketch of Mary Lou Williams." In *All in Good Time.* New York: Oxford University Press, 1987, 69–80.

———. "Personality." *New York Column,* February 19–25, 1971, 1–4.

———. "Swingin' With." *New York Column,* February 5–11, 1971.

———. "Mary Lou: Marian McPartland Salutes One Pianist Who Remains Modern and Communicative." *Down Beat,* October 17, 1957, 12–41.

———. "Mary Lou Williams: The Cookery." *Down Beat,* February 4, 1971, 30–31.

"Melody Mailbag." *Melody Maker,* February 14, 1953, 5.

Miller, Cheryl, and Toni Armstrong Jr. "The Life and Musical Times of Jay Allbright." *Hot Wire,* May 1994, 40–43.

Miller, Edwin. "Take Me to Froggy Bottom." *Negro Digest,* December 1946, 82–85.

Miller, Paul Eduard. "Best Solos of the Year." *Down Beat,* January 1939.

———. "Critic Deplores Recording of the 'Jazzed-Up' Classic." *Down Beat,* June 1937, 14.

———. "Few Bands Ever Get in Real 'Jungle Jazz' Groove." *Down Beat,* July 1937, 34.

Mitchell, James R. "The Legacy of Mary Lou Williams." *Jazz Listeners/Musicians Newsletter,* March 1991.

Moore, Bill. "Pianist Mary L. Williams Appears at Bluett Theatre." *Philadelphia Tribune,* May 14, 1976.

"More Melody Maker Critics Enter the Fray: Mary Lou." *Melody Maker,* February 21, 1953, 8.

Mousouris, Melissa. "Mary Lou Williams: Musician as Healer." *Village Voice,* July 23, 1979, 81–84.

"Music in Catholic Worship and Liturgical Music Today." In *The Liturgy Document: A Parish Resource,* ed. Mary Ann Simcoe. Rev. ed. Chicago: Liturgy Training Publications, 1985.

"Musicians in the News." *International Musician,* October 1952, xi.

Myers-Spencer, D. "Bobo and Doodles by Mary Lou Williams: A Rare Display of Contemporary Elements." *NAJE Research* 9 (1989): 166–68.

Nevard, Mark. "And Mary Lou on LP." *Melody Maker,* February 7, 1953.

"Newport Jazz Festival." *Down Beat,* August 8, 1957.

"Night Club Review." *Variety,* November 27, 1957.

"Nightclubs." *New Yorker,* October 9, 1971.

"No Kitten on the Keys." *Time,* July 26, 1943, 76.

"Nobody's Playing Anything but You." *Melody Maker,* August 26, 1978.

"N.Y. Gets 3 New Jazz Dens." *Down Beat,* September 9, 1949, 13.

"NYC Café Society Is Sold." *Down Beat,* April 8, 1949.

"Obituary." *Black Perspective in Music* 9, no. 2 (1981): 241–42.

"Obituary." *Down Beat,* September 1981, 12.

"Obituary." *International Musician* 80 (July 11, 1981): 11.

Oliver, Paul. "Race Records." In *The New Grove Dictionary of Jazz,* ed. Barry Kernfield. New York: St. Martin's Press, 1995, 1011.

"One for the Money." *Down Beat,* May 29, 1958, 9.

O'Neill, Catherine. "Swinger with a Mission." *Books and Arts,* December 7, 1979, 30–31.

"Operation on Jack Jackson Ousts Mary." *Melody Maker,* April 11, 1953, 6.

Palmer, R. "Mary Lou Williams 1910–1981." *Rolling Stone,* July 9, 1981, 52.

"Parker Concert Raised $10,000." *Down Beat,* August 10, 1955, 6.

"Passing of a Legend: Agent Joe Glaser, 72." *Down Beat,* July 24, 1969, 7–8.

"Paul Robeson to Head Cast at Victory Show for Benjamin Davis." *New York Age,* October 23, 1943, 10.

Pease, Sharon A. "Andy Kirk's Pianist Also Brilliant Arranger." *Down Beat,* October 1937, 30.

———. "Mary Lou Williams Still Top Rated Femme Pianist." *Down Beat,* November 2, 1951, 16.

Peck, Marshall. "Jazz Hymn to Honor Negro Saint." *New York Herald-Tribune,* October 30, 1962.

"Pianist's Return." *Time,* September 16, 1957, 76–78.

Piazza, Tom. "Review of 'Mary Lou Williams: The Asch Recordings, 1944–47' and 'Free Spirits.'" *Jazz* 2, no. 2 (1978): 64.

———. "Riffs: Mary Lou Williams Keeps the Faith." *Village Voice,* November 19, 1979, 75–76.

Porter, Lewis. "Jazz Women." *Music Educators Journal* 71 (September 1984): 47.

———. "Jazz Women: You Can't Get up There Timidly." *Music Educators Journal* 71 (October 1984): 46–50.

"The Prayerful One." *Time,* February 21, 1964, 58–59.

Prince, Linda. "Betty Carter: Bebopper Breathes Fire." *Down Beat,* May 3, 1979, 12–43

"Profiles." *New Yorker,* May 2, 1964, 52–85.

"Racial Prejudice in Jazz, Part 1." *Down Beat,* March 15, 1962, 20–26.

"Racial Prejudice in Jazz, Part 2." *Down Beat,* March 29, 1962, 22–25.

Ray, Carline. "My Reflections of Mary Lou Williams. In *Mary Lou Williams: Her Life and Artistry* (Washington, D.C.: Kennedy Center Publications, 1999): 17.

"Record Review." *Down Beat,* April 26, 1973.

"Record Reviews." *Down Beat,* May 3, 1979.

"Record Reviews: Mary Lou Williams." *Down Beat,* March 15, 1945.

"Record Reviews: Mary Lou Williams." *Down Beat,* July 15, 1946.

"Record Reviews: Mary Lou Williams." *Down Beat,* January 14, 1948.

"Record Reviews: Mary Lou Williams." *Down Beat,* June 17, 1949, 15.

"Record Reviews: Mary Lou Williams." *Metronome,* July 1946.

"Record Reviews: Mary Lou Williams." *Metronome,* October 1946.

"Record Reviews: Mary Lou Williams." *Metronome,* January 1947.

"Record Reviews: Mary Lou Williams." *Metronome,* May 1947.

Reda, J. "Bye Bye Mary Lou." *Jazz Magazine,* July–August 1981, 30–33.

Reid, Ira De Augustine. "Mrs. Bailey Pays Her Rent." In *The New Negro Renaissance,* ed. Arthur P. Davis and Michael W. Peplow. New York: Holt, Rinehart, and Winston, 1975, 164–72.

"Review: 'Mary Lou's Mass.'" *Hi/Fi America* (March 1972): MA 15.

"Review of 'Mary Lou's Mass.'" *Dance Magazine,* February 1972, 26–31.

"Review of Mary Lou Williams/Cecil Taylor: Embraced." *Down Beat,* December 7, 1978.

"Revue de Presse." *Jazz Hot,* January 1953, 23.

Riis, Thomas. "Pink Morton's Theater, Black Vaudeville, and the TOBA: Recovering the History, 1910–1930." In *New Perspectives on Music: Essays in Honor of Eileen Southern.* Warren, Mich.: Harmonie Park, 1992, 229–43.

Rockwell, John. "It's Rollins to Jarrett to Right On!" *New York Times,* July 2, 1973, 23.

"Roman Cardinal Okays Jazz Masses Minus Drums." *Jet,* April 3, 1969.

Rosenthal, David. "Conversation with Art Blakey." *Black Perspective in Music* 14, no. 3 (Fall 1986): 267–89.

"Round the Clubs with Mary Lou Williams." *Jazz Journal* 6, no. 2 (September 1953): 18–19.

Rowes, Barbara. "From Duke Ellington to Duke University, Mary Lou Williams Tells the World: 'Jazz Is Love.'" *People,* May 12, 1980, 73–77.

Saal, Hubert. "The Spirit of Mary Lou." *Newsweek,* December 20, 1971, 67.

Savicky, Randy. "Mary Lou Williams, Paul Motian Trio, Newman Theatre." *Good Times,* June 6–19, 1978, 45–46.

"Shearing 5, Mary Lou Go into Café Society." *Down Beat,* May 6, 1949, 15.

Simon, Jeff. "A Jazz Treasure Is Rediscovered." *Buffalo Evening News,* February 17, 1977.

Smith, Arnold Jay. "Jazz at St. Pat's." *Down Beat,* April 10, 1975, 8.

Smith, Charles Edward. Liner notes to *Mary Lou Williams with an All Star Combination.* Asch 450, 1944.

Smith, Cliff. "Mary Lou Williams—'Mary Lou Williams Presents.'" *New York Times-Union,* March 9, 1973.

Solomons, Gus, Jr. "Hail Mary Lou." *Village Voice,* June 14, 1988.

Stearns, Marshall. "Jazz in New York: In Search of Swing." *Musical America,* February 1963, 35.

St. Julien, Mtumishi. "From the Heart: A Reflection on the Essence of Jazz." *Black Sacred Music: A Journal of Theomusicology* no. 1 (1992): 162–69.

Stowe, David W. "The Politics of Café Society." *Journal of American History* (March 1998): 1384–1406.

"Straton Says Jazz Is 'Agency of Devil.'" *New York Times,* May 7, 1926, 10.

"Strictly Ad Lib." *Down Beat,* March 1, 1943.

"Strictly Ad Lib." *Down Beat,* May 15, 1945.

"Strictly Ad Lib." *Down Beat,* December 20, 1962, 10.

Sudhalter, Richard. "Remembering Mary Lou," *New York Post,* June 4, 1981, R41.

"Tables for Two." *New Yorker,* October 5, 1957, 125–26.

Taylor, J. R. "Andy Kirk." In *The New Grove Dictionary of Jazz,* ed. Barry Kernfield. New York: St. Martin Press, 1995, 654–55.

"Theatrical Notes." *New York Age,* May 16, 1942.

Tick, Judith. "Passed Away Is the Piano Girl: Changes in American Musical Life, 1870–1900." In *Women Making Music: The Western Art Tradition 1150–1950,* ed. Jane Bowers and Judith Tick. Urbana and Chicago: University of Illinois, 1986, 325–48.

Tomkins, Les. "It's Going to Be Much Cooler." *Crescendo International,* August 1971, 25–26.

———. "The Mary Lou Williams Story." *Crescendo International,* July 1971, 6–7.

Torff, Brian. "Mary Lou Williams: A Woman's Life in Jazz." In *Perspectives on American Music since 1950,* ed. James R. Heintze. New York: Garland, 1999, 153–201.

Ulanov, Barry. "Mary Lou Williams." *Metronome,* February 1946, 18–35.
———. "Newport Jazz Festival." *Down Beat,* August 8, 1957, 14.

"War Gives Women Their Chance in Jazz Says Connie Berry." *New York Age,* January 24, 1942, 10.
Warrington, Garnett. "Big Protest: Conditions at Atlanta and Pensacola Cause Righteous Indignation." *Chicago Defender,* October 8, 1921.
Watt, Douglass. "True Blue Lou." *Sunday News,* November 3, 1974.
Weinreich, Regina. "Play It Momma." *Village Voice,* July 3, 1978, 64+.
"Whatever Happened to Mary Lou Williams?" *Ebony,* October 1971, 202.
"Williams Joins Duke Staff." *Down Beat,* October 6, 1977, 11.
Williams, Mary Lou. "The Battle of the Tenor Kings." *Melody Maker,* May 1, 1954, 11.
———. "Mary Lou on the Clouds of Joy." *Melody Maker,* April 17, 1954, 5.
———. "Mary Lou Williams: A Diamond Mouthful." *Melody Maker,* April 10, 1954, 5.
———. "Mary Lou Williams: Britain Has Some of the Best Jazz in Europe." *Melody Maker,* 30 June 12, 1954, 11.
———. "Mary Lou Williams: The Mad Monk." *Melody Maker,* May 22, 1954, 11.
———. "Mili and Martin." *Melody Maker,* May 29, 1954, 11.
———. "Mr. 5×5 Had a Ten Block Voice." *Melody Maker,* April 24, 1954, 5.
———. "My Friends the Kings of Jazz." *Melody Maker,* May 8, 1954, 11.
———. "Then Came Zombie Music." *Melody Maker,* May 8, 1954, 11.
———. "When Those Paper Men Dug Jazz at Carnegie Hall." *Melody Maker,* June 5, 1954, 11.
Wilson, Garland. "Self-Portrait of a Jazz Pianist." *Melody Maker,* June 5, 1954, 13.
Wilson, John S. "The Ageless Jazz of Mary Lou Williams," *New York Times,* February 18, 1979, D-10.
———. "Jazz Club Gets Bobby Hackett and Dizzy Gillespie Together." *New York Times,* February 2, 1971, 31.
———. "Jazz Finds Home at The Cookery." *New York Times,* November 27, 1970, 50.
———. "Jazz Women Off to Kansas City." *New York Times,* March 16, 1978, C17.
———. "Jazzwomen Jam First Festival." *New York Times,* March 20, 1978, C20.

———. "Mary Lou Williams." *International Musician,* January 1973, 8.

———. "Mary Lou Williams Adapts Piano Style to Outdoor Setting." *New York Times,* July 19, 1974, 24.

———. "Mary Lou Williams: A Jazz Great Dies," *New York Times,* May 30, 1981.

———. "Mary Lou Williams, at Piano, Leads Her Jazz Mass at St. Patrick's." *New York Times,* February 19, 1975, 37.

———. "Mary Lou Williams, on Piano, Tailors Style to Jazz History." *New York Times,* January 7, 1974, 39.

———. "Mary Lou Williams Plays Jazz Piano." *New York Times,* April 27, 1970, 44.

———. "Mary Lou Williams Uses Musical Past in Her New Pieces." *New York Times,* December 11, 1974, 53.

———. "Mary Lou Takes Her Jazz Mass to Church." *New York Times,* February 9, 1975, 2: 20.

"Winners Named by Guggenheim." *New York Times,* April 7, 1972, 25.

Yates, Ted. "I've Been Around." *New York Age,* September 4, 1943, 10.

———. "I've Been Around." *New York Age,* September 18, 1943, 10.

———. "I've Been Around." *New York Age,* November 18, 1944, 10.

BOOKS AND MISCELLANEOUS WORKS

Anderson, Jervis, *This Was Harlem: A Cultural Portrait 1900–1950.* New York: Farrar, Straus and Giroux, 1982.

Balliett, Whitney. *American Musicians: Fifty-six Portraits in Jazz.* New York: Oxford University Press, 1986.

Banks, William. *The Black Church in the U.S.: Its Origin, Growth, Contributions, and Outlook.* Chicago: Moody Press, 1972.

Boyer, Horace Clarence. *How Sweet the Sound: The Golden Age of Gospel.* Washington, D.C.: Elliott and Clark, 1995.

Cell, John W. *The Highest Stage of White Supremacy: The Origins of Segregation in South Africa and the American South.* New York: Cambridge University Press, 1982.

Charters, Samuel B., and Leonard Kunstadt. *Jazz: A History of the New York Scene.* New York: Da Capo Press, 1962.

Clark, John Henrik. *Harlem U.S.A.* Berlin: Seven Seas Publishers, 1964.

Collier, James Lincoln. *Benny Goodman and the Swing Era.* New York: Oxford University Press, 1989.

Cone, James H. *The Spirituals and the Blues: An Interpretation.* New York: Seabury Press, 1972.

Dahl, Linda. *Morning Glory: A Biography of Mary Lou Williams*. New York: Pantheon Books, 1999.

Dance, Stanley. *The World of Duke Ellington*. New York: Da Capo Press, 1970.

Davis, Allison, Burleigh B. Gardner, and Mary R. Gardner. *Deep South: A Social Anthropological Study of Caste and Class*. Chicago: University of Chicago Press, 1941.

Davis, Angela Y. *Women, Race, and Class*. New York: Vintage Books, 1983.

Davis, Benjamin J. *Communist Councilman from Harlem: Autobiographical Notes Written in a Federal Penitentiary*. New York: International Publishers, 1969.

Davis, Miles, and Quincy Troupe. *Miles: The Autobiography*. New York: Simon and Schuster, 1989.

Du Bois, W. E. B. *The Souls of Black Folk*. Chicago: A. C. McClurg, 1953.

Epstein, Abraham. *The Negro Migrant in Pittsburgh*. New York: Arno Press and the New York Times, 1969.

Erenberg, Lewis A. *Swingin' the Dream: Big Band Jazz and the Rebirth of American Culture*. Chicago: University of Chicago Press, 1998.

Feather, Leonard. *The Jazz Years: Earwitness to an Era*. New York: Da Capo Press, 1987.

Fernett, Gene. *Swing Out: Great Negro Dance Bands*. Midland, Mich.: Pendell, 1970.

Firestone, Ross. *Swing, Swing, Swing: The Life and Times of Benny Goodman*. New York: W. W. Norton, 1993.

Frazier, E. Franklin. *The Negro Church in America*. New York: Schocken Books, 1974.

Freeman, R. C. "Jazz and Race Records, 1920–32." Ph.D. dissertation, University of Illinois at Urbana-Champaign, 1968.

Giddings, Paula. *When and Where I Enter: The Impact of Black Women on Race and Sex in America*. New York: Bantam Books, 1984.

Giddins, Gary. *Riding on a Blue Note: Jazz and American Pop*. New York: Oxford University Press, 1981.

Gillespie, Dizzy, and Al Fraser. *To Be, or Not—to Bop: Memoirs*. Garden City, N.Y.: Doubleday, 1979.

Gioia, Ted. *The History of Jazz*. New York: Oxford University Press, 1997.

Gitler, Ira. *Swing to Bop: An Oral History of the Transition in Jazz in the 1940s*. New York: Oxford University Press, 1985.

Goldsmith, Peter D. *Making People's Music: Moe Asch and Folkways Records*. Washington, D.C.: Smithsonian Institution Press, 1998.

Gottlieb, Peter. *Making Their Own Way: Southern Blacks' Migration to Pittsburgh, 1916–1930*. Urbana: University of Illinois Press, 1987.

Gourse, Leslie. *Straight, No Chaser: The Life and Genius of Thelonious Monk*. New York: Prentice-Hall, 1997.

Harrison, Daphne Duval. *Black Pearls: Blues Queens of the 1920s*. New Brunswick, N.J.: Rutgers University Press, 1988.

Hobsbawm, Eric. *The Jazz Scene*. Rev. ed. New York: Pantheon Books, 1993.

Holmes, Lowell D., and John W. Thomson. *Jazz Greats: Getting Better with Age*. New York: Holmes and Meier, 1986.

Huggins, Nathan Irvin. *Harlem Renaissance*. New York: Oxford University Press, 1971.

Hughes, Langston, and Milton Meltzer. *Black Magic: A Pictorial History of the Negro in American Entertainment*. Englewood Cliffs, N.J.: Prentice-Hall, 1967.

Hunter, Tera. *To 'Joy My Freedom: Southern Black Women's Lives and Labors after the Civil War*. Cambridge: Harvard University Press, 1997.

Hurston, Zora Neale. *The Sanctified Church*. Berkeley, Calif.: Turtle Island, 1991.

Jones, LeRoi. *Blues People: Negro Music in White America*. New York: William Morrow, 1963.

Kirk, Andy, and Amy Lee. *Twenty Years on Wheels*. Ann Arbor: University of Michigan Press, 1989.

Kufrin, Joan, and George Kufrin. *Uncommon Women*. Piscataway, N.J.: New Century Publishers, 1981.

Leonard, Neil. *Jazz: Myth and Religion*. New York: Oxford University Press, 1987.

Lewis, David Levering. *When Harlem Was in Vogue*. New York: Alfred A. Knopf, 1981.

Lincoln, C. Eric. *The Black Church since Frazier*. New York: Schocken Books, 1974.

Maynard, Olga. *Judith Jamison: Aspects of a Dancer*. New York: Doubleday, 1982.

McCarthy, Albert J. *Big Band Jazz*. New York: G. P. Putnam's and Sons, 1974.

Nager, Larry. *Memphis Beat: The Lives and Times of America's Musical Crossroads*. New York: St. Martin's Press, 1998.

Nelsen, Hart M., Raytha L. Yokley, and Anne K. Nelsen. *The Black Church in America*. New York: Basic Books, 1971.

The New Grove Dictionary of Jazz, ed. Barry Kernfield. New York: St. Martin's Press, 1995.

Oakley, Giles. *The Devil's Music: A History of the Blues.* New York: Taplinger, 1977.

Ogren, Kathy J. *The Jazz Revolution: Twenties America and the Meaning of Jazz.* New York: Oxford University Press, 1989.

Ottley, Roi. *New World A-Coming.* Boston: Houghton Mifflin, 1943.

Pearson, Nathan W., Jr. *Goin' to Kansas City.* Urbana and Chicago: University of Illinois Press, 1987.

Peretti, Burton W. *The Creation of Jazz: Music, Race, and Culture in Urban America.* Urbana and Chicago: University of Illinois Press, 1992.

Peterson, Bernard L., Jr. *Profiles of African American Stage Performers and Theatre People, 1816–1960.* Westport, Conn.: Greenwood Press, 2001.

Placksin, Sally. *American Women in Jazz: 1900 to the Present: Their Words, Lives, and Music.* New York: Seaview Books, 1982.

Powell, Hazel Scott. Testimony. Hearing before the Committee on Un-American Activities, House of Representatives, 81st Congress, 2d sess., September 22, 1950.

Russell, Ross. *Jazz Style in Kansas City and the Southwest.* Berkeley: University of California Press, 1971.

Sanders, Cheryl J. *Saints in Exile: The Holiness-Pentecostal Experience in African American Religion and Culture.* New York: Oxford University Press, 1996.

Schuller, Gunther. *Early Jazz: Its Roots and Musical Development.* Vol. 1 of *The History of Jazz.* New York: Oxford University Press, 1968.

———. *The Swing Era: The Development of Jazz 1930–1945.* Vol. 2 of *The History of Jazz.* New York: Oxford University Press, 1989.

Shapiro, Harry. *Waiting for the Man: The Story of Drugs and Popular Music.* New York: William Morrow, 1988.

Spencer, Jon Michael. *Black Hymnody: A Hymnological History of the African-American Church.* Knoxville: University of Tennessee Press, 1992.

Stearns, Marshall, and Jean Stearns. *Jazz Dance: The Story of American Vernacular Dance.* New York: Schirmer Books, 1968.

Stovall, Tyler. *Paris Noir: African Americans in the City of Light.* Boston: Houghton Mifflin, 1996.

Travis, Dempsey. *An Autobiography of Black Jazz.* Chicago: Urban Research Institute, 1983.

Trotter, Joe William, Jr. *The Great Migration in Historical Perspective: New Dimensions of Race, Class, and Gender.* Bloomington: Indiana University Press, 1990.

Unterbrink, Mary. *Jazz Women at the Keyboard.* Jefferson, N.C.: McFarland, 1983.

Wald, Elijah. *Josh White: Society Blues.* Amherst: University of Massachusetts Press, 2000.

Ward, Brian. *Just My Soul Responding: Rhythm and Blues, Black Consciousness, and Race Relations.* Berkeley: University of California Press, 1998.

Washington, Joseph R., Jr. *Black Religion: The Negro and Christianity in the United States.* Boston: Beacon Press, 1964.

Watkins, Mel. *On the Real Side: Laughing, Lying, and Signifying: The Underground Tradition of African-American Humor That Transformed American Culture, from Slavery to Richard Pryor.* New York: Simon and Schuster, 1994.

Weiss, Nancy J. *The National Urban League, 1910–1940.* New York: Oxford University Press, 1974.

Winter, Nina. *Interview with the Muse: Remarkable Women Speak on Creativity and Power.* Berkeley, Calif.: Moon Books, 1978.

Woodward, C. Vann. *The Strange Career of Jim Crow.* 2d rev. ed. New York: Oxford University Press, 1966.

SELECTED DISCOGRAPHY

The recordings made for Asch Records from 1944 to 1947 were released in a complete collection in the 1970s (marked*). The recordings are listed here under the title of this collection and not as individual records. Many of Mary Lou Williams's recordings with Andy Kirk and the Twelve Clouds of Joy are listed under various collections from that period as well.

COMPILATIONS FEATURING SOLO AND ENSEMBLE WORKS
OF MARY LOU WILLIAMS

A Keyboard History. Concert Hall 1007.
Barrel House Piano. Brunswick 58022.
Black Legends of Jazz. Decca 641.
Bluebird Sampler 1990 Bluebird 2192.
Blue Boogie and Bop 1940's Mercury Sessions. Mercury 525609.
Boogie Blues—Women Sing and Play Boogie Woogie. Rosetta 109.
Classic Jazz Piano. Bluebird 6754.

Classic Jazz Piano 1927–1957. Bluebird 6754.
First Ladies of Jazz. Savoy 1202.
Forty Years of Women in Jazz. Jass 9.
Forty Years of Women in Jazz. Jass 10.
Golden Era of Jazz Vol. 5. Savoy 8957.
Jazz Greats. Allegro 737.
Jazz Greats—Piano Players. Emarcy 36049.
Jazz Piano. Smithsonian 39.
Jazz Piano Anthology. Columbia 32355.
Jazz Piano Greats. Folkways 2852.
Jazz Women—A Feminist Retrospective. Stash 109.
Kansas City Jazz. Decca 8044.
Kansas City Piano 1936–1941. Decca 9226.
Ladies of Jazz. Atlantic 1271.
Lady Piano. Blackbird O.
Modern Jazz Piano. RCA LPT 31.
Newport in New York '72. Cobblestone 9032.
Piano. Atlantic 81707.
Piano Anthology. Decca 693.
RCA Victor Encyclopedia of Recorded Jazz 12. RCA LEJ 12.
RCA Victor Jazz: The 20's–60's. Bluebird 66084.
Upright and Lowdown—Boogie Woogie Barrelhouse and Blues. Columbia 685.
Women: Classic Female Jazz Artists 1939–1952. Bluebird 6755.
Women in Jazz. Stash III.
Women in Jazz—Pianists. Stash 112.

MARY LOU WILLIAMS AS LEADER AND/OR ARRANGER OR PIANIST

The Chronological Andy Kirk and His Twelve Clouds of Joy 1936–1937. Classics 573.
The Chronological Andy Kirk and His Twelve Clouds of Joy 1937–1938. Classics 581.
The Chronological Mary Lou Williams 1927–1940. Classics 630.
The Chronological Mary Lou Williams 1944. Classics 1944.
The Chronological Mary Lou Williams 1945–1957. Classics 1050.
Embraced. Pablo 2620108.
Free Spirits. SteepleChase SCCD 31043.
From the Heart. Chiaroscuro 103.
Her Progressive Piano Stylings. King 85.
History of Jazz. Folkways FJ 2860.
Jazz for the Soul. Mary 6362 [3626 on jacket].

Mary Lou. Emarcy 26033.

Mary Lou's Mass. Mary 102.

Mary Lou's Mass. Smithsonian Folkway SFW CD 40815.

Mary Lou Williams. Contemporary 2507.

Mary Lou Williams and Orchestra/Meade Lux Lewis. Collectables COL 5612.

Mary Lou Williams—I Made You Love Paris. Gitanes 013 141-2.

Mary Lou Williams—Key Moments. Topaz LC 7234.

Mary Lou Williams Live at the Cookery. Chiaroscuro 146.

Mary Lou Williams—Live at the Keystone Korner. Highnote HCD 7097.

Mary Lou Williams: Nite Life. Chiaroscuro CR 103.

Mary Lou Williams Presents Black Christ of the Andes. MPS 15020.

Mary Lou Williams Presents Black Christ of the Andes. Smithsonian Folkway SFW CD 40816.

Mary Lou Williams Story 1930/1941. Jazz Archives 116.

Mary Lou Williams—The Asch Recordings, 1944–1947. Folkways Records FA 2966.*

Mary Lou Williams: The London Sessions. Vogue 74321409312.

The Mary Lou Williams Trio—1944: Roll 'Em. Solo Art SACD-43.

Mary Lou Williams Trio at Rick's Café Americain. Storyville STCD 8285.

Music for Peace. Mary 0.

My Mama Pinned a Rose on Me. Pablo 2310819.

Norman Granz Presents Pablo Jazz Sampler Vol. 11. Pablo 2310179.

Praise the Lord in Many Voices. Avant Garde 103.

Rehearsal Vol. 1. Folkways 32.

Roll 'Em 1944. Audiophile 8.

Solo Recital—Montreux Jazz Festival 1978. Pablo 2308218.

Zodiac Suite. Smithsonian SF CD 40810.

Zodiac Suite. The Mary Lou Williams Collective (Geri Allen, Andrew Cyrille, Billy Hart, Buster Williams). Mary M104.

Zodiac Suite—Town Hall Concert December 12–31–1945. VJC 1035.

Zoning. Smithsonian 40811 [also listed as Mary 103].

INDEX

Abyssinian Baptist Church (New York), 179
Ailey, Alvin, 209, 242–44
Allbright, Regina Jay, 198–99
American Communist Party, 100, 102
American Creolians, 96
American Dance Theater, 243
American Federation of Musicians, 91, 133, 135, 143–44, 173
"American Mass Program," 220
Amram, David, 245
Andy Kirk and the Twelve Clouds of Joy: artists accompanying, 281n2; and black vernacular forms, 71; in Chicago, 74–75; Dark Clouds of Joy transformed into, 49; decline of, 79–80; John Williams joins, 72, 279n11; in Kansas City, 53, 66, 68–69; members of, 45, 69, 70, 72, 78; MLW as arranger for, 55–56, 74–75; MLW leaves, 80, 83, 282n30; MLW officially joins, 65; MLW's disenchantment with, 76–77, 78; in New York, 61, 66–67, 71, 75; popularity of, 60, 74; and race records, 68, 69–70; radio broadcasts of, 69,

74–75, 76; recordings of, 57–59, 61, 71–74, 77–78, 104, 281n12; and segregation, 76, 265; as sweet band, 66, 70, 73, 76; swing sound of, 56; tours of, 6, 62, 68, 70, 76, 152, 265; wages paid in, 76–77, 78
Annapolis (Md.), 147
Apollo Theatre (New York), 71, 74, 179, 198
Approdo Romano, 227–28
Arkansas, 32–33
Armstrong, Lil Hardin, 26, 65, 158, 164
Armstrong, Louis: in black elite, 129; Glaser as manager of, 70; Hines and, 278n22; marijuana use of, 182–83; MLW as arranger for, 74–75, 77; MLW declines job offer from, 162; MLW meets, 30; northward migration of, 50; and racism, 68; and woman instrumentalists, 65
Armstrong, Lucille, 194
Arnheim, Gus, 77
ASCAP, 149, 174, 234
Asch, Moe: and Disc, 125; leftist political involvement of, 102, 107; MLW meets, 103–4;

TAMMY L. KERNODLE is a professor of musicology at Miami University of Ohio. She served as associate editor of the three volume *Encyclopedia of African American Music* and as a senior editor for the revision of *New Grove Dictionary of American Music.*

Dewey and Elvis: The Life and Times of a Rock 'n' Roll Deejay   *Louis Cantor*
Come Hither to Go Yonder: Playing Bluegrass with Bill Monroe   *Bob Black*
Chicago Blues: Portraits and Stories   *David Whiteis*
The Incredible Band of John Philip Sousa   *Paul E. Bierley*
"Maximum Clarity" and Other Writings on Music   *Ben Johnston, edited by Bob Gilmore*
Staging Tradition: John Lair and Sarah Gertrude Knott   *Michael Ann Williams*
Homegrown Music: Discovering Bluegrass   *Stephanie P. Ledgin*
Tales of a Theatrical Guru   *Danny Newman*
The Music of Bill Monroe   *Neil V. Rosenberg and Charles K. Wolfe*
Pressing On: The Roni Stoneman Story   *Roni Stoneman, as told to Ellen Wright*
Together Let Us Sweetly Live   *Jonathan C. David, with photographs by Richard Holloway*
Live Fast, Love Hard: The Faron Young Story   *Diane Diekman*
Air Castle of the South: WSM Radio and the Making of Music City   *Craig P. Havighurst*
Traveling Home: Sacred Harp Singing and American Pluralism   *Kiri Miller*
Where Did Our Love Go? The Rise and Fall of the Motown Sound   *Nelson George*
Lonesome Cowgirls and Honky-Tonk Angels: The Women of Barn Dance Radio   *Kristine M. McCusker*
California Polyphony: Ethnic Voices, Musical Crossroads   *Mina Yang*
The Never-Ending Revival: Rounder Records and the Folk Alliance   *Michael F. Scully*
Sing It Pretty: A Memoir   *Bess Lomax Hawes*
Working Girl Blues: The Life and Music of Hazel Dickens   *Hazel Dickens and Bill C. Malone*
Charles Ives Reconsidered   *Gayle Sherwood Magee*
The Hayloft Gang: The Story of the National Barn Dance   *Edited by Chad Berry*
Country Music Humorists and Comedians   *Loyal Jones*
Record Makers and Breakers: Voices of the Independent Rock 'n' Roll Pioneers   *John Broven*
Music of the First Nations: Tradition and Innovation in Native North America   *Edited by Tara Browner*
Cafe Society: The Wrong Place for the Right People   *Barney Josephson, with Terry Trilling-Josephson*
George Gershwin: An Intimate Portrait   *Walter Rimler*
Life Flows On in Endless Song: Folk Songs and American History   *Robert V. Wells*
I Feel a Song Coming On: The Life of Jimmy McHugh   *Alyn Shipton*
King of the Queen City: The Story of King Records   *Jon Hartley Fox*
Long Lost Blues: Popular Blues in America, 1850–1920   *Peter C. Muir*